The Conquest of
NORTH [illegible]ICA
194[illegible]

BY ALEXANDER G. CLIFFO[illegible]

Map Sketches in Text by Author

LITTLE, BROWN AND COMPANY · BOSTON
1943

FIRST EDITION

Published September 1943

PRINTED IN THE UNITED STATES OF AMERICA

Author's Note

THIS is the story of two years and eleven months of fighting along the North Coast of Africa — from the day Italy declared war to the day organized Axis resistance in the continent ceased.

I have told the story as I saw and experienced and understood it. It is a story that most people know only from the disjointed, spasmodic, often unwittingly distorted accounts in the daily newspaper. I have tried to write it as a coherent, integrated whole. The plot, perhaps, suffers from a certain repetition, a certain poverty of background. But at the same time it has an admirable simplicity and completeness — a clear-cut beginning and development and end.

I have included a good many of my own personal experiences, not because I think that they are in any way remarkable, but for precisely the opposite reason — because they are typical and representative; and because I believe that a first-hand account of experience must ring more true than a second-hand account.

It is a very big, rich story and I have had to omit many things. I have deliberately omitted a great many proper names and dates and figures which seem to me irrelevant to the story as a whole. I have tried to tell the truth and nothing but the truth, but the whole truth I do not claim. Some day, I suppose, someone will write that. But even if I knew it, I could not write it now.

I have used the Commanders-in-Chief of the Middle East to personify the Army in the Desert. Wavell had the first, tiny, embryonic army, the seed from which it all grew. Auchinleck handled the period of growth and development. Alexander won with the complete and final Eighth Army. But the real hero of it all, of course, is the Eighth Army itself.

A.C.

Tunis
May 1943

Contents

THE CONQUEST OF NORTH AFRICA
1940–1943

CHAPTER 1

The Opening Gambit

SEEN from the flying-boat window, the sea was turquoise-blue and sparkling and faintly patterned like morocco leather. But the curious thing about it was that, all the way from Crete to Alexandria, it was empty; emptier, probably, than it had been since Homer's days.

Way up in Northern France, in those early days of June 1940, empires were falling — tremendous tragedy and tremendous triumph on a scale and at a speed that found no parallel in history. But down here in the Mediterranean the lesser danger near at hand outweighed the greater peril in France. And ships were staying in their ports in the expectation that Mussolini would declare war.

Alexandria's harbour, when we dropped down into it, was full enough. The flying boat sizzled across the felucca-dotted waters between two great rows of spick-and-span British warships. It was an inspiring gateway, then, to the glamour and the squalor that are Egypt. Alexandria's smart sun-filled streets sparkled with the white-duck uniforms of naval officers. If Mussolini did declare war, it seemed, Britain was ready.

In Cairo I just had time to introduce myself into an embryonic, chaotic Public Relations unit, buy myself the necessary uniforms, and learn where the numerous military, naval, R.A.F., political and Egyptian censors would be at given hours of the day. Then on June 10, much as everyone had expected, Mussolini made a bombastic speech from his balcony in Rome and declared war.

It was timed with a shameless opportunism that excited our jeers rather than our fears. Indignantly we railed against this barefaced Italian bid to go scavenging among the ruins of the French and

British empires. We were furiously angry at that moment, but I don't think many people in the Middle East felt very apprehensive.

It was still, you must remember, the era of blind confidence. In view of what was happening in France it had to be blind; otherwise it couldn't have remained confidence. But the tragedy of France was too big, too new, too remote to be digested immediately. It could not at one fell swoop efface that long propaganda era when all German tanks were made of cardboard, when the German people had been half-starving for six years and their clothes were made of ersatz fabrics which melted in the rain, when Hitler was an incompetent nincompoop who had no following in Germany. The Middle East in June 1940 shared the same absurd, illogical inability to recognize probable defeat which carried Britain through that perilous summer and the terrible winter which followed.

In our more sober moments we did, I think, consider that Italy was a serious military power. We recalled that within living memory she had beaten the Turks, fought victoriously with us in World War One, been on the winning side in Spain, conquered Ethiopia and Albania. True, the last three exploits were not very glorious or creditable. But they had been carried out with very considerable technical efficiency and they did seem to show that Italy was a warlike nation. For years Mussolini had been talking about his seven million bayonets, and he had not hesitated to flout the whole of Europe in the shape of the League of Nations. His armed forces must certainly be treated with respect.

But against that we told ourselves that Egypt was surrounded on three sides by impassable deserts and on the fourth by the sea. No conqueror in history had successfully attacked her from the west. Certainly Italy had a fleet, but the British had a bigger one. And so during those stifling first days in Cairo the gossip was mostly about the Italian ship which had been caught napping in the Suez Canal fully laden with Chianti, and the adroit machinations of Signor Mazzolini, the Italian Minister to Egypt. The military aspect was left in the background.

But in the converted luxury hotel which was British G.H.Q. there was a man who knew the truth. A man with a straight firm mouth and eyes which crinkled at the corners when he smiled and, these days, a rather worried frown. General Sir Archibald Wavell, Commander-in-Chief of the British Forces in the Middle East, sat at his desk doing sums which never came out right. They couldn't come out right because he simply hadn't got the right figures. And by the time Mussolini declared war, Wavell knew that if he was going to get anywhere near the correct answer, he would have to cheat.

He knew, with devastating certainty, that he had just about 36,000 troops in the whole of the Middle East; that his batteries of field guns could be counted on the fingers of one hand; that his tanks were not fit to be called tanks; that he had no proper anti-tank guns; that his tiny air force was completely out of date. And he knew that Italy had a fully equipped army at least a quarter of a million strong in Libya and another army equally numerous in Ethiopia.

Wavell had pleaded desperately for more men and better arms. Earlier in the year they had sent him, in a somewhat flamboyant blaze of publicity, the Australian Seventh Division: a full division of tough, rough men, magnificent human material but sadly in need of training and experience, who were sent off to the fly-blown dreariness of Gaza in Southern Palestine. More than that Britain could not send. She was going through her own terrible hour of trial. A fabulous amount of her best war material was being lost in France. Invasion might come at any moment. The Middle East would just have to make do with what it had got until times were better.

So Wavell knew that he was beaten — on paper — before he started. There were just two factors that might save him. The first was the inefficiency of the Italian Intelligence Service. It was just possible that the General Staff in Rome might be unaware how weak the Middle East was. The second was the possibility that Mussolini might not be prepared to fight at once. There was a chance, even a likelihood, that the Duce was gambling on the immediate collapse of the British Empire. Evidence trickled in to show that Italy, while eager to reap the fruits of victory, had made no plans to fight for them. It proved nothing that Marshal Balbo had rushed his Libyan army up to the borders of Egypt. He was bound to do that anyway. The point was that he showed no signs of coming any farther.

Either of these two possibilities — Italian ignorance and Italian unpreparedness — would at least give Wavell time. Boldly he began to work on the assumption that both were in his favour. And while the gay, rich, easy life of Cairo flowed on by its own momentum — while they still played cricket at the Gezira Club because no one had thought to stop it, while the lowered lights of the semi-blackout only gave additional glamour to open-air restaurants and cabarets — Wavell acted.

ii

Within a few hours of Mussolini's war declaration, the pitifully thin khaki line along Egypt's western border had struck into Libya. That great pendulum of warfare that was to swing in ever-widening arcs for three more years quivered faintly and made its first little move — a move westwards. From an essentially defensive situation Wavell made a sharply offensive gesture.

British sappers crept forward and made gaps in the great wire fence — an elaborate entanglement six feet high and nine feet wide — which the Italians had built to keep the Libyans in Libya. Then in small but brisk skirmishes British troops stormed and occupied Forts Maddalena and Capuzzo, two theatrical desert strongholds of the Beau Geste type which were supposed to guard the frontier.

The Italians recoiled sharply. Then they gathered their forces, counterattacked and retook Capuzzo. There the situation stabilized as the choking heat of June settled down over the battlefield. But Wavell was pleased, for much had been done. The principle was established that on this frontier the British were, if anything, superior, for they had taken the initiative and captured some territory. Consciousness of this heartened the British troops, who could hardly help being aware of their own inadequacy in arms and numbers.

And the Italian High Command were forced to the conclusion that Wavell's army must be taken seriously.

Back in Cairo the handful of war correspondents accredited to the Middle East clamoured to be allowed up to this desert front. But things moved slowly and painfully in those early days and nearly a week passed before I was able to set out, eager and excited, on that horrible journey I have made so many times since.

You leave Cairo by the dead-straight double-tracked motor road which leads to Mena. And there, where the great pyramid of Cheops squats in its monstrous geometrical uselessness, you quit the green luxuriance of the Nile Valley and swing out abruptly into the desert. Between Mena and the coast there is precisely one house—a restaurant called the Half-way House, where it became fashionable to stop off for drinks. When you reach the coast you turn due west, and immediately you are in the desert proper.

I don't quite remember what I expected. I suppose I inevitably had vague thoughts of rolling golden sand dunes, sheikhs on pure-blooded Arab steeds, romantic green oases. But the desert I found was a beige-coloured, slightly undulating landscape spotted with stringy greyish clumps of scrub which camels, incredibly, seem to enjoy eating. Sometimes the scrub faded away and there was nothing but hard bare sand. Sometimes there were great ridges of stone. Always there was dust—dust as fine as snuff or flour which can seep through closed lips and eyelids, through any clothing, which gets into food and bedding and gun barrels and aeroplane engines; which, when it blows, makes men pray for deliverance.

And this desert was empty—uncannily, almost frighteningly empty. For mile after mile the road was a shining black-satin ribbon bisecting an utterly monotonous landscape. It was all so unchanging that one had little or no sense of progression. The road might have been a continuous band going round and round. At the end of that first trip my memory of it was telescoped into one static picture of a dun-coloured countryside slashed by a black strip of sand-proof tarmac.

Yet, surprisingly, there was life in the desert. Little by little I discovered about the gazelle, the hares, the horned vipers, the desert rats, the scorpions and double-beaked spiders, and the snails which turn themselves upside-down to catch the dew and which, the Fighting French subsequently claimed, are eatable. Most surprising of all, there was human life. Just occasionally, hurrying purposefully from one patch of wilderness to another precisely similar, one met grave-faced Bedouins, heavily wrapped in camel-hair rugs however hot the weather, driving their little flocks of goats and camels, and overdressed women. It was always incongruous in this landscape to come upon some girl apparently in full evening dress, heavily made up, with massive ear-rings and ropes of coins round her neck, tending a couple of goats.

And yet neither then nor later did I ever find any mystery or fascination in this desert. It is thoroughly bewildering until you know it. You find your sense of direction completely fuddled and you can't tell whether the horizon is one mile away or five. You need to get your stomach and your mind and your eyes and your habits thoroughly acclimatized to it before you can be happy living and fighting in it. That is why it invariably proved unwise to send men into action in it before they had spent some time learning its ways. But fundamentally this desert is just a flat empty space where you can have battles without doing the least damage to civilian life and property.

Nevertheless this first time it was new and absorbingly interesting. We bumped and jolted our way forward over the thirty terrible miles known to thousands of drivers as the "Humpty Dumpty," where the tarmac has been laid straight onto the desert surface, without foundations, and faithfully follows every bump (the contractor who built it, we learned, was still in prison). We passed the Red Cross camp at Daba and the air field at Fuqa. We passed Marten Bagush where there was a real big camp with tents, and men were bathing naked from the silver beaches.

At Mersa Matruh, two hundred miles from Alexandria, we breasted a shallow rise and for the first time saw trees. They were poor things — a few dusty tamarisks and a clump of sagging palms

—but they were green. And among them were little white houses arranged in broad, straight intersecting streets, a mosque, and two hotels. Matruh, on the strength of its superb bathing, had become a mildly popular seaside resort for Egyptians until war drove all its inhabitants away. Centuries earlier Cleopatra had dallied and bathed with Antony there. In those days we never wrote of Matruh without referring to this fact—we were pathetically grateful for any shred of glamour or interest to colour this monotonous background.

Already the Italians had been sending their triple-engined Savoia bombers over by day and by night. The little white houses were split open and scarred and empty and there were bomb craters alongside the road. But British Headquarters had laughed and gone underground, establishing themselves in deep-dug catacombs where by artificial light staff officers worked over maps and documents, while fine brown dust sifted endlessly in through the ventilators. The Italians were doing no good with their bombing, but what else was there for them to bomb? And in any case Mersa Matruh looked good in their communiqués—it was the one place in the desert whose name was in the least familiar to the outside world.

Matruh was the terminus of the single-track railway which ran from Alexandria, a railway whose existence was justified solely, but amply, by strategical considerations. The tarmac road, equally unjustified by any but military reasons, ran on another eighty miles to Sidi Barrani. And here too the Italian Air Force had been busy. The rough white cottages lay scorched and riven, with gaping windows. The sand had already covered all footprints in the now untrodden streets. There was not a tree, not a blade of grass, to be seen. Swarms of flies, rising in obscene clouds from the garbage, were the only life. It was a place of unspeakable desolation.

Beyond Barrani there was no road, only a waste of deep, choking dust. Each individual vehicle moved along in an inverted yellow pyramid thicker than any London fog. The dust clouded windscreens, streamed through the cracks of doors and windows, rose in waves through the floor boards. Cars ploughed along infinitely slowly despite their broad desert tyres, and the dust made a soft swishing sound as it continuously rose from the wheels and fell back with gentle impotence against the windows, like fine yellow rain.

The taste of the dust was acrid and strangely familiar. It carried me abruptly back to those cold bright winter days round Teruel during the Spanish Civil War; that too had been a dusty land, with dust that tasted just the same, but it had been so infinitely richer in colour and interest than this. Quickly disgust drowned the pleasure of my reminiscences.

At Buqbuq — a name without a place, for it simply doesn't exist except as a map reference — we turned diagonally inland. And finally, shaken and bruised and with our belongings scattered topsy-turvy all over us, we reached the plateau above Halfaya Pass where the desert army was fighting.

For a week I stayed and watched them. I saw one troop of twenty-five-pounder guns shell Fort Capuzzo, and was in my turn shelled by much heavier Italian artillery. I visited the burning desolation of Fort Maddalena with its tall wooden lookout tower. I looked down on empty Sollum in its wonderful amphitheatrical setting beside the amaranthine sea. I drove far into Libya with a patrol and saw the show battle-field — a gruesome little knot of sun-dried bodies and twisted two-man tanks and shattered lorries where an Italian supply column had been caught.

I saw, gradually, what was happening. Subtly and systematically Wavell was doing his sums and faking his figures. These tiny British patrols were staging big demonstrations. Continually they were making nuisances of themselves, moving rapidly from place to place, shooting up convoys, flinging ambushes across roads, attacking forts and positions, always pretending they were much bigger than they were. Dummy tanks were toted about to give the idea that we had strong armoured units. Biplane Gloster Gladiator fighters — the only type we had — and old Bombay transport planes — our only bombers — worked day and night to build up in the enemy's mind the idea that we had all the squadrons we wanted. In every way that tiny army set itself to gain time by frightening the enemy.

The desert in those days was a fresh, exhilarating place. There was an atmosphere of intimacy, because we were so few; a spirit of adventure, because it was all so novel and individual. It was a pioneering phase, a period of wild experimentation. Very little was known of the technique of desert warfare by either side, but we at least were desperately anxious to learn. The desert then was full of fallacies, of theories which have since been disproved. It was assumed that it was too hot to fight at all in the summer, that supply problems on a large scale were insoluble. The difficulties of water supply, in particular, were enormously exaggerated. It was thought that health would probably be bad in the desert. Both sides believed the best form of defence lay in heavily defended bases on the coast, so that concentric rings of barbed wire and trenches were flung round Tobruk, Bardia and Mersa Matruh.

There was in those days a rule that in camps there should be a distance of two hundred yards, not only between vehicles, but between camp-beds. We used to sleep dotted about all over the landscape, each with a grave-like slit trench beside him. We war correspondents made a point of being completely self-contained. Every drop of water we used we had to bring with us from Cairo, and we almost never accepted the hospitality that was offered us for no one had anything to give away. In those early days a whole method and standard of living was being worked out empirically, and at the same time an entire specialized technique of fighting was evolving.

While I was up in the desert this first time, something else happened which may have helped Wavell's plans. Marshal Italo Balbo, Governor-General and Commander-in-Chief of Libya, was killed at Tobruk during a British air raid. His big transport plane, it seems, was just coming in to land at the time, and he may have been shot down by Italian ack-ack. But it is more likely that his machine was hit by a British bomb — at any rate I have seen a somewhat blurred photograph which strongly supports this view. Inevitably rumours started that Balbo had been deliberately bumped off by Mussolini's orders; but it seems very improbable. It was a little too early in the game for the Duce to start eliminating competent men, especially by such melodramatic methods.

The British, with possibly misplaced chivalry, went over Tobruk and dropped a note of condolence about Balbo. There had been no time, and so far no occasion, to arouse great hatred or bitterness against the Italians. Until a couple of weeks previous, we had been repeatedly told that Britain had no quarrel with Italy, and in these early stages they were still merely opponents rather than enemies. Indeed it was becoming clearer every day that we had never prepared to fight Italy and had never really expected to do so.

CHAPTER 2

Mediterranean Warfare

So THE desert army settled down to its routine of bluff. And soon we were able to stand away from it and take a wide view and realize that this was not an isolated front. It was an integral part in a much more comprehensive scheme of things. We were not, after all, fighting for possession of an uninhabitable desert, but for mastery of the Mediterranean. And there were half a dozen other vital factors playing their parts in addition to Libya.

Malta was important because it was our single stepping-stone between Gibraltar and Alexandria, our only half-way house in the Mediterranean, precious beyond computation as an air and submarine base. Italian East Africa was important because it dangerously threatened our alternative Red Sea route to the Middle East. Syria was important because General Weygand had a powerful French army there. Greece was important, because if the Axis took it, Britain's routes to the Balkans and the Black Sea would be blocked and Italy would have safe access to her Dodecanese possessions.

In the summer of 1940 and the autumn that followed there were more or less major developments in all these spheres. But in the intervals of covering them for my paper I found time to get a first-hand view of the Mediterranean itself.

It started when I went to Squadron-Leader Bray who controlled R.A.F. Public Relations and asked for an operational flight. No war correspondent had ever yet had one, but I hoped that the smallness and informality of the Middle East Command might work in my favour. I waited a few days and then Bray told me that there was no room for me in any aircraft carrying out actual operations; but if I cared to go out submarine hunting with the Sunderland flying boats, I was to report to Alexandria immediately.

When I got there, I found I was luckier even than I thought. For the Sunderlands could take me to Malta for a week's patrolling from there. It was exactly what I wanted. No correspondent up till then had visited Malta. It was the only part of the British Empire which had been and was being heavily bombed. And I should be able to view the Mediterranean from its focal point.

With the utmost secrecy, for fear someone should find out and stop me from going, I made my arrangements and embarked at Alexandria. For ten hours we flew steadily across the blue waste of seas. Once we glimpsed the faint-purple snow-tipped screen of Crete's mountains, but otherwise we saw nothing. I sat up in the cockpit and wondered whether we should ever be able to find Malta. But we hit it fair and square and in the evening we dropped down gently into Calafrana Bay.

ii

Malta then was by no means the fortress it later became. It had been decided that if Italy did go to war against us (which was unlikely) then Malta could not be held anyway. So the island had only the merest handful of troops to resist an invasion. It had very few ack-ack batteries. On its unprotected air fields were a tiny group of out-of-date fighters which valiantly, and not always effectively, took off to do combat with the clouds of Italian planes that came over. The best plane was a crazy thing called a Hurriglad — a Gladiator with a Hurricane engine. Pilots who flew it claimed that the engine would shake off the fuselage in fifteen minutes if they did not land to screw it all up again.

But the Italians had missed their opportunity here as elsewhere. So far they had contented themselves with large-scale, spectacular, and not very efficient bombing raids. No effort had been made to invade the island.

This was before the Battle of Britain. Hardly a bomb had yet fallen on any other corner of the British Empire. But that morning in Valetta the sirens howled to announce Malta's hundredth raid.

I took shelter in one of those great tunnels which the Knights of Malta burrowed centuries ago to store their gunpowder and their grain and their captives. To my sun-filled eyes it was pitch-black inside and after two steps I stumbled over a great brass bedstead. When I could see better, I made out two great rows of beds stretching away into the darkness — a fantastic collection of beds, most of them double, but of all shapes and sizes and none of them in very good condition. It looked like the worst sort of junk shop. But it was in fact one of those great ready-made day-and-night shelters which later enabled Malta to endure consecutive months of concentrated blitz. The Maltese simply lived here.

When the sirens sounded, mothers called their children in from the streets and went back to their cooking or sewing or gossiping. When the All Clear went, they set forth with their shopping bags to the market. Old men set up mobile stalls of fresh fruit and cooked meats at the entrances to the shelters and pushed their wares in to safety when the bombs began to fall. In the evenings the menfolk came back from work and whole families went to bed in the dungeons and tunnels.

The Maltese, an excitable people, were taking it all much better than the British had dared hope. The main effect of the raids was to arouse a venomous hatred of the Italians. Those first bombs undid the work of years of careful underground and overt propaganda paid for by Rome. I drove round the town, talked to the people shopping, admired the lovely sun-soaked façades of the old *auberges* of the Knights, and I wrote a rather emotional despatch urging that Malta should be given the Victoria Cross. Two years later the island got its cross — the George, not the Victoria. But by that time it had been earned a hundred times over.

iii

Back in Egypt, I began to pester the naval authorities. The "silent service" was won round slowly and reluctantly to the idea of publicity. But the moment came when I received vague and mysterious orders to present myself at Alexandria with clothing sufficient for several days.

We steamed out of Alexandria next morning, a proud imposing fleet of three battleships, half a dozen cruisers, and a great screen of destroyers. I was aboard *H.M.S. Ramillies,* an old-fashioned, inconvenient and uncomfortable battleship, but impressive enough to the non-naval eye. This, I thought, is really something. Here at least Britain is well-equipped and strong. There is no need for any bluff on sea as there is on land.

But even as we left harbour I got a hint that the navy, like the army, was going through an experimental stage. All around me officers were gazing back towards Alexandria, looking to see whether the aircraft carrier *Eagle* was coming with us. And when she did not move, they said with a note of bitterness, "Oh God, another trip without air protection."

As a matter of fact they were wrong. But they couldn't be expected to know it, for the object of this trip had not yet been announced. All morning we steamed along the Egyptian coast in the sunshine, while I clambered about exploring the ship, picking out possible vantage points in case anything happened, helping Ted Genock, the Paramount photographer who came with me, to take a few documentary shots. With the stately discipline of a minuet, the ships zigzagged, turned and manœuvred. Once we stopped and rehearsed an intricate series of evolutions, which experts diagnosed as referring to a bombardment. And this was confirmed at lunch-time when Admiral Sir Andrew Cunningham sent round a signal from his flagship, *H.M. Battleship Warspite,* saying "We are going to have some fun this trip. All guns will probably be in action."

We kept west all the afternoon and sailed through a gaudy, vulgar sunset into the night. And by that time we knew what it was all about. We were to be off the Libyan seaport of Bardia at dawn and give it a pasting it would never forget.

All that evening men were busy taking down pictures from the walls, packing away glass and chinaware, removing anything loose or breakable. In their cabins officers cleared away the litter of photographs, bottles, books and knick-knacks which covered their tables and bookshelves. I began dimly to understand what the tremendous force of this bombardment was going to be like.

In the sweltering heat of a blacked-out cabin I lay naked with a fan trained on my stomach, while the ship strained and creaked and pulsed rhythmically all round me. Towards dawn I slept fitfully. Then someone was shaking me and shouting "Get up, get up, bombardment starts in half an hour."

I dressed, and groped my way hastily along the dim corridors, stumbling up companion-ways, tripping over coamings, fumbling with unfamiliar doors. I passed the six-inch guns, where the men were already fusing the shells. At last I came out into the open and reached the gun-control turret — a little round armoured pill-box just below the bridge — which I had selected as the best view-point.

There were ten minutes of cold, rather apprehensive waiting. We talked tensely and jocularly, and drank gratefully the mugs of hot cocoa that were thrust through the entrance to us. Then the world began to lighten and framed in a slit-like aperture I could see the battleship *Malaya* bouncing gently on the sea ahead of us.

There was no colour in the world yet, and the great ship swung there like a black-and-white film on a cinema screen. I saw her catapult away her aeroplane to do spotting for her guns. There was another interval. Then without warning *Malaya* burst into flame all along one side and heeled over sharply as she took the recoil of her mighty guns.

The sound came over the water to us in a rolling boom. There was another silence. Then a trivial little tinkling bell rang somewhere near us. Then, a few feet away from me, our own fifteen-inch guns went off — eight of them all together — with a concentrated roar so loud that it filled one's head to the exclusion of consciousness or thought. Instinctively we had ducked our heads to avoid the blast which whistled in through the slits, but for just one fraction of a second we were stunned by the sound waves themselves.

Then the six-inches chimed in with their sharper crack and for half an hour they all fired away in a hellish chorus. Through the slits I could see Bardia's puny white buildings on the cliffs a few miles away, and the sudden spasms of flame and smoke as the shells landed among them. The spotter in his plane was broadcasting a running commentary on the marksmanship, guiding the shells nearer and nearer to the ordained targets. Behind us *Warspite* was firing in a different direction and at greater range, aiming for Fort Capuzzo down inland.

Then abruptly it all stopped and the silence came as a benediction to our battered ears. Something was splashing feebly into the sea a mile away and the officer next me laughed contemptuously and said, "Look, they've got their little shore batteries going at last." A butterfly flew in through one of the slits, fooled around for a little while, and flew out again.

We trooped away to breakfast. The muzzles of the fifteen-inch guns were blackened and the grey paint was blistered. The passages and ward-rooms were littered with debris and dirt and broken glass despite all the precautions of the night before. Innumerable cockroaches had been shaken down from cracks and crevices, and the ship's cats were chasing them enthusiastically.

"I calculate the bombing will start about ten o'clock," someone said calmly as we sat down to breakfast; and I realized gradually that this was by no means the end. The Italians would put every bomber they could into the air and come and bomb us. I wondered why *Eagle* was not with us.

I went to a sheltered spot and began typing the despatch I hoped to send when we got back to Alexandria. I was on the third page when the ship seemed to blow up. Something exploded with a hideous metallic crack that stabbed agonizingly through the brain. My typewriter flew from my knee to the deck.

Then I saw that a four-inch ack-ack gun had gone off just beside me. The bombers had come.

And when they came it was a pitiful anticlimax. They were flying too high to be seen properly and they were dropping their bombs in long sticks way out beyond the destroyer screen, raising avenues of mighty waterspouts on the horizon.

Then the fleet's barrage stopped abruptly and something started to happen in the sky which we couldn't make out. A big three-engined bomber floated down slowly with a swelling wake of smoke, and erupted in flames on the sea. Another followed, already blazing in the air. Bombs were being jettisoned with hysterical abandon. The attacking force was melting away.

This, then, was the reason why *Eagle* had been left behind. The Italian bombing squadrons had been lured into an ambush. British fighters were waiting on the air fields along the Egyptian coast for precisely this opportunity. And the Italians, seeing no aircraft carrier and expecting no opposition, had been pounced on from above and sent scurrying home.

This little expedition was in itself an unimportant one. But it showed up clearly two distinct ingredients that were later to become more and more intricately mixed: a naval force doing a purely naval job, and an air force attacking the naval force. In those days the British Mediterranean Fleet was behaving as fleets had behaved down history. Admiral Cunningham was in the piratical tradition of Drake and Nelson and any other British naval hero you like to think of. His ships moved freely about the Mediterranean, and we jeered a lot at Mussolini who had called this sea "Mare Nostrum" and whose navy hardly ever left port. It was daring and exhilarating, it was picturesque, useful and romantic. But only the inefficiency of the Italian Air Force saved it from being old-fashioned and appallingly costly.

I had one other chance to see this Mediterranean fleet at the most brilliant moment of its career, before it had been whittled away in doing jobs that were not purely naval, before the Germans had come to the Mediterranean and introduced dive bombers, torpedo-carrying planes, scientific submarine attacks, and all the factors which have influenced the evolution of modern naval technique.

In November I went out again, this time in the destroyer *Janus*. We knew we were in for something big the moment we left port, for Admiral Cunningham sent round one of his characteristic signals: "It is my intention to act offensively in the Ionian Sea and seek an engagement with the enemy."

For the first week we made the Eastern Mediterranean look like a busy railroad junction. Our programme covered pages of official paper with its complicated details. There were convoys to be escorted in every direction, and others to be fetched and brought home. Important stores had to be taken to the British forces in Greece. Individual warships were constantly being detached on some special mission. There were punctually kept rendezvous all over the Mediterranean. At odd moments submarines were attacked and aircraft shot down. Foodstuffs were run in to Malta.

When we were all together we were the biggest British fleet that had put to sea in the Mediterranean this war. We had five battleships, two aircraft carriers, and innumerable cruisers and destroyers, which lay strewn across the blue waters in a vast formation that overlapped the horizon in both directions.

There was little interference. On one of the first days our fighters caught a Cant flying boat spying on us and shot it down. A day later a fighter came home doing a double "victory roll" and reported he had destroyed two S79's. I enjoyed the compactness and intimacy of life in the destroyer, the friendliness of the ward-room, the functional precision of the whole routine. We stood on the bridge watching flying fishes skim from wave to wave and one-thousand-foot-tall water-spouts joining the sea to the dark clouds. One dawn was so black we had to use navigation lights and huge flares of lightning slashed the inky sky. We went in to Malta to oil and for a couple of hours I went ashore and talked to my Sunderland friends in their air-raid shelter while fifty Italian fighters flew above. Every evening we stood at action stations waiting for the bombers to swoop down on us out of the flamingo-coloured sky but none came. We got through our long list of jobs with no trouble at all.

Then came the big night. We steamed up dead north all one afternoon towards the heel of Italy. And in the evening we got our orders. There were to be two attacks. *H.M. Aircraft Carrier Illustrious* was to fly off her planes for a night torpedo attack on the Italian fleet in Taranto. And simultaneously a tiny force, including my destroyer, was detailed to take part in an audacious raid up the Adriatic.

Excitement mounted as we made our preparations. And it was a bitter disappointment when a message came cancelling our orders and telling us that other destroyers had been given the job. The destroyer next us, which had been similarly disappointed, flashed us a message: "Isn't it a damned shame?" With fierce envy we watched the raiding force steam off into the dusk, leaving us behind to screen the aircraft carrier.

When darkness came we knew no more, for there was wireless silence in force. And for hours we stood on the moonlit bridge imagining what was going on away up in Italy.

We never really sorted out the details until we returned to port. But this is what had happened. Swordfishes, the oldest, slowest operational aircraft still in service, had made the raid on Taranto in two waves. Coming down so low that they skimmed the water, nine pilots had launched their huge torpedoes at three of Italy's crack battleships as they lay scattered in the outer harbour. Bombers had dropped their sticks along the quay where enemy cruisers and destroyers lay in a serried row like sardines side-by-side. Two planes dropped flares to illuminate the whole fantastic scene, and two took a seaplane base and a petrol dump as their targets.

The most spectacular exploit was that of a young pilot who fouled his wing-tip before starting and could not take off with the others. Almost with tears in his eyes he begged his commanding officer to let him make a quick repair and catch up. He got his permission, did his patching up, and blazed off into the night in the hope of cutting off corners and being in time for the bombardment.

He arrived a quarter of an hour later. "Taranto Harbour," he told me, "was a bowl of flame. The ack-ack guns were firing vertically and all sorts of guns horizontally until the whole area round the warships was criss-crossed with a blazing mesh of fire. Some guns were patriotically firing red, white and green tracers, and there were things like flaming onions coming up.

"Everyone else had finished so we had to dive down alone into this fiery furnace. For about ten seconds I seemed to be holding my breath while bullets and shells cracked all around. It looked as though all the guns were firing astern of us, which was comforting. Then we dropped our stuff and flew up out of it all, astounded to find that we were still alive and the plane in one piece."

It turned out that by this action Italy's naval strength had been reduced—at least temporarily—by just about one third. Reconnaissance planes found two of the battleships down with their bows under water. The third was clearly severely damaged. And at least two cruisers were put out of action. It was a magnificent result that had cost practically nothing.

Next morning the Adriatic raiding party arrived back simultaneously with another squadron of cruisers, and the whole fleet broke into excited conversation, exchanging news with lamps and flags. As a modest destroyer, we could not ask many questions. But we sidled up to a destroyer which had taken part in the raid and asked what had happened. It told us crisply: "We put up a regular fireworks display. We got in among a convoy running from Brindisi to Valona and we sank three of the four ships and probably hit the fourth. The escorting torpedo boats fired two shots and bolted."

Then we sailed on along the Greek coast, gazing at the mountains behind which the Greeks were fighting so superbly for their freedom, and waited for Mussolini's answer to our challenge.

But still none came. Three times in one day shadowing aircraft were reported. Three times fighters peeled off casually from the aircraft carrier and within a few minutes the shadower was spinning down in flames, leaving a great plume of mauve smoke marking the spot where he hit the sea. Once I watched fascinated while two of our fighters sneaked up on the Italian flying boat from behind a cloud and then pounced.

Occasionally there were alarms and our bearded captain, who had won a reputation for dodging bombs in Norway, sent his Scotch terrier down off the bridge. But nothing materialized.

And so we sailed home. For all that had been so brilliantly achieved, Admiral Cunningham had failed to do what he had set out to do. He had hoped to precipitate a second Jutland. He had tried to lure or sting the Italian fleet into giving battle. But the Italians would not play. We jeered and scoffed at them a lot, and we boasted again that we could do what we liked in the sea that Mussolini had called an Italian lake. But the Italians were perfectly right.

They had no interest in risking their fleet in a huge naval battle with ours. They needed their ships for other things. They never regarded their navy as an instrument for destroying other navies, but as an integral part of the war machine as a whole. In consequence they sedulously avoided purely naval engagements. Again and again in those early months Italian battleships and cruisers and destroyers turned and fled rather than give battle. In their construction the emphasis was always on speed, so that they could easily get away. The Italian navy did its job by staying in harbour as a potential menace, by convoying material to North Africa, by saving itself up for the day when it might be called on to do a really vital job. It was true enough that the Regia Marina did not seem to be very good. It sadly lacked experience and competent leadership. But these considerations only strengthened the force of the arguments in favour of keeping the fleet in being rather than risking it in a large-scale engagement.

So Cunningham sailed into Alexandria proud but disappointed. It had been a glorious ten days. Skill and judgement and daring and a certain amount of luck had achieved brilliant results. But that was very nearly the end of the golden age of classical naval warfare. Soon the full compass of modern aerial warfare would come into play over the Mediterranean. And then things would be different.

CHAPTER 3

The Great Decision

ALL THROUGH the summer and autumn of 1940, while this sparring was taking place in the Mediterranean itself, the countries of the Middle East were simmering with activity. Events followed one another with a confusing, bewildering lack of cohesion. It was only towards the winter that it became possible to trace any pattern in them at all.

After Wavell's forces had taken the initiative in Libya in June, Syria provided the next development. Following a week of ambiguous pronouncements, political shilly-shallying and Axis intrigue, Syria, with Weygand's fine army, sidled shamefacedly across to Vichy's side of the line. And so we lost what we had regarded as the backbone of the Allied land forces in the Middle East. There was just one small but inspiring consolation, big with promise for the future. The first battalion of the French Infantérie de Marine had been stationed in Cyprus. And when Syria went over to Vichy a Colonel came from Beirut to talk to this battalion. He reminded them of their duty to their fatherland and asked them to return to their base. There was a moment's silence. And then with a unanimity born of a deep common emotion, the men stepped forward and broke into the "Marseillaise."

So Free France was born in the Middle East. A couple of months later I saw these same men parade at Ismailia, fully armed and equipped with British arms. A couple of years later I saw them at Bir Hacheim.

On July 4 the Duke of Aosta's great army in Ethiopia invaded the Sudan and, in a bright blaze of propaganda, occupied the towns of Kassala and Gallabat.

To defend the whole vast territory of the Sudan, an area nearly as large as Europe, Wavell had exactly 2500 British troops; the Sudan Defence Force was 4500 strong. They had no tanks and no guns. Their best artillery was some old cannons used for firing ceremonial salutes. Their seven aeroplanes were hopelessly obsolete.

The two Sudanese motor machine-gun companies defending Kassala retired in good order before 6000 infantry, 2000 cavalry, camel-corps units, 18 tanks, plentiful artillery, and a strong air force. The one British platoon at Gallabat even put up a fight when 2000 men with guns and aircraft came against them. But serious resistance was clearly out of the question. The British frontier screen retired and prayed that the Italians would be content with these victories.

On August 4 the Italians launched an extravagantly over-elaborate invasion of British Somaliland. They sent 25,000 men in a three-pronged advance against a British force rather less than one twelfth the size of their own. The British put into action the plan they had decided on — the only possible plan in the circumstances. The defending forces did what damage they could to the attackers and then withdrew. In twelve days Somaliland had become Italian.

In one way that looked bad. Apart from the Channel Islands this was the first slice of British territory to be lost to the enemy this war. What was left of British prestige fell a few pegs lower. But Wavell smiled. British Somaliland is the least attractive, least useful jewel in the British Imperial crown. Of all the places they might attack, this was the least profitable to the Italians. But it was far and away the easiest place they could attack. With a dozen possibilities open to them, they picked this cheap, easy victory. It was one proof more that Italy was not sure of herself or of British strength, that she had planned no blitzkrieg in the Middle East.

On August 13 Marshal ("Butcher") Graziani, the successor of Italo Balbo, brought his army ponderously into Egypt. It came accompanied by grandiloquent orders of the day, spectacular artillery barrages, flamboyant communiqués. Once again the British could not hope to resist. They fell back cleanly and nimbly, inflicting what damage they could. They mined every house in empty Sollum, and the gunners found that if they fired when they saw a windscreen flash at one turn of Halfaya Pass, the shell would hit the vehicle accurately on the next turn. But they did not attempt to give battle.

Three days of cautious advance brought Graziani to Sidi Barrani. And there he stayed while Rome Radio magnified his petty successes into historic triumphs and gave Sidi Barrani a fictitious tramway system in order to increase the importance of its capture. Doubtless Graziani was over-impressed, as we were, with the difficulties of food, water, petrol and ammunition supplies. It was true enough that he was operating with a very considerable army, and that much of his war material had to come hundreds of miles by road from Bengasi, and some even from Tripoli. So he flung out a semicircular arc of camps and fortified positions round Sidi Barrani and then started to build a modern tarmac road linking the Egyptian road head at Barrani with the Libyan road head above Sollum.

While alarm flared up in Cairo, Wavell's army was preparing to fight for the Middle East at Mersa Matruh. The defence plan was based on the fortress area of Matruh itself, a string of mine fields stretching inland, and a mobile armoured force somewhere down south. It was all pitifully small in numbers of men and tanks and planes. But as summer merged into autumn it became clear that Graziani had shot his bolt for the time being. We could rely on his staying where he was until his road was finished.

On October 28 Italian forces attacked Greece from Albania. The whole world was prepared to call the Greeks heroic if they attempted to resist at all. No one expected them to succeed. I had spent three weeks in Athens the previous May, and I had written an article weighing the various factors and finally coming to the conclusion that the Greeks would not even pretend to fight. I did not think that their small out-of-date army was capable of taking part in a modern war at all.

The miracle of that autumn is too well-known to need repetition. Again the Italians' Intelligence had been wrong, their appreciation of the situation had been wrong, their methods had been wrong, their equipment had been wrong. And the Greeks, with an efficiency and courage which surprised the world, came back on the rebound and entered Albania.

Those were the main events of 1940 in the Middle East. This is the pattern which emerged from them.

The Italian armies had advanced into Egypt, into the Sudan, into Kenya and into Greece. The lines of their grand strategy were therefore clear. They intended to use their numerically superior forces to keep the British Middle East armies split into small isolated fragments, and to annihilate these fragments one by one.

But nothing had gone quite right. The advance into Egypt had bogged down at Sidi Barrani. The Duke of Aosta had taken his armies no farther than Gallabat and Kassala. The advance into Kenya had petered out in a big area of desert. The attack on Greece had recoiled into Italian territory. Malta was battered but still incontestably British. Only in irrelevant British Somaliland had an attack been carried through to its conclusion.

Wavell could afford to smile. His judgment had been right. The Italian High Command had clearly not been prepared to act with any speed or vigour. The timidity, slowness and elaboration of their offensives showed that they still greatly overestimated British strength. Partly by guile, partly by courage, partly by luck, Wavell had taken the first round.

But that did not mean the danger was past. On the contrary, it was if anything greater than ever. Having taken successful first steps, the Italians would be encouraged to continue further. Sooner or later they were bound to find out about Wavell's bluff and call it. Already Graziani was quite obviously mounting a serious offensive against the Egyptian Delta.

So, with an audacity that takes the breath away, Wavell prepared to attack on every front. His decision was the only logical alternative to complete defeat or surrender. But the decision itself was so illogical that only a genius or a fool could have taken it.

Italian superiority in numbers of men, tanks, guns, planes — in everything — was still enormous. There were only two things that Wavell could possibly have on his side: quality of men, and quality of leadership. Confidently he gambled on having them both.

He had not been idle during the summer. In August I had gone to Suez and Port Said to watch the unloading of the first great convoy of armaments and reinforcements from England. The Fourth Indian Division arrived and went up to the desert. The Fifth Indian Division was sent to East Africa. Fast convoys were whipped through the Mediterranean itself with urgent stores. Troops came from New Zealand and more from Australia. Blenheims and Wellingtons and Hurricanes superseded the original Bombays and Gladiators.

With staggering confidence in the future, the Emperor Haile Selassie had been flown out from England, ready to regain his Abyssinian throne. He had come right over Occupied France by night in a flying boat. At Alexandria a riot was deliberately provoked on the quayside to divert the attention of bystanders when he came ashore. In the former Italian yacht club an R.A.F. squadron gave a party for the King of Kings. He donned his gorgeous uniform as Commander-in-Chief of the Ethiopian Army, presented a gold watch to the pilot who had brought him out, invited everyone to visit him in Addis Ababa, and flew off south to Khartoum.

In November two sharp attacks were made against the Italian positions in the Sudan, designed not so much to gain a military success as to keep the enemy quiet and prove that the British were strong enough to take the initiative. And under cover of this Wavell planned a full-scale offensive for the winter.

Even to Greece the diminutive Middle East Forces were able to send help. It came in the form of R.A.F. units, for the Greeks were hopelessly outclassed in the air. Bomber and fighter squadrons went to air fields on the mainland; and in Crete there were reconnaissance squadrons and naval authorities and a small army garrison.

At the end of November I flew across to Crete to visit my friends of the Sunderlands, who had moved from Malta to Suda Bay. For a week I flew with them on patrol over the isle-encrusted Ægean and far up the Ionian Sea to the limits of Albania. We camped in an olive grove and lived idyllically on the island's wine and honey and oranges and delicious bread; we climbed the mountains and talked to the Greek conscripts — friendly, shabby little men who deeply enjoyed English cigarettes and whose exuberant *feu de joie* was a constant peril: one morning as I was shaving beneath an olive tree some marksman picked off the mirror eighteen inches from my face. For two days I drove trucks to help the men who were building the new air field at Maleme. Then I flew back to Egypt, in time for the greatest of all Wavell's offensive moves.

CHAPTER 4

The Rout of Graziani

IT CAME with almost theatrical secrecy and suddenness.

At breakfast time on December 9, all the war correspondents in Cairo received an urgent summons by telephone. They were to go to General Wavell's office at G.H.Q. immediately. There were not more than seven or eight of us in those days and we exchanged excited speculation as we mounted the stairs of the big block of flats where Headquarters were now housed. This summons was quite unprecedented. We could not guess what it meant.

Wavell was standing in his shirt sleeves in front of a wall covered completely with maps. There was no litter or piles of papers on his desk. His voice was level and unhurried. Without any excitement or introductory explanation he told us the desert army had attacked that morning.

He called it a big raid, not an offensive. He left himself this loophole in case no big results should be achieved. On paper the attack was so ridiculous that ordinary military experience gave no clue as to how it would turn out. But clearly enough Wavell had big hopes of it — otherwise he would not have taken the unusual step of summoning the war correspondents to hear about it. He told us that already the first Italian camp had fallen, but he still did not dare predict how far it would go. "Much depends," he said, "on the quantity of supplies and provisions we capture and how much petrol we find." Meantime it was to be described as an important raid, not an offensive.

Then, when he had made his little speech, he relaxed for the first time. He smiled quietly and his eyes crinkled at the corners as they always did when he smiled. And he said, "Now I should like you to tell me honestly whether any of you knew anything about this attack beforehand."

Not one of us did. And there can be no higher tribute to Wavell's security than this, for Cairo is a place where no secret is a secret for longer than a few hours, and it is a war correspondent's job to know them all.

There were, of course, contributing reasons. For one thing an ingenious method had been invented that autumn of keeping the war correspondents out of the desert. An edict came forth forbidding us to sleep west of Fuqa. No specific reason was given; but it meant that our visits to the front were limited to short sharp dashes lasting at best a couple of hours and very soon we stopped going to the desert at all—much more interesting things were usually happening elsewhere. Then again, in those days traffic between Cairo and the desert was small, and the chances of secret information leaking back was reduced. The forces involved were small, so the preparations for the attack were comparatively limited and not likely to attract undue attention. Finally the very idea that we might attack was in itself so wildly improbable that it simply entered no one's head to try and find out. And if we in Cairo knew so little, it was a safe bet that the Italians knew nothing at all.

We left Wavell's office in a mad rush to get to the front. And there began for us then as arduous, heart-breaking, exciting a sequence of days as I have lived in my career as a foreign correspondent. The Public Relations Unit had never envisaged a successful British attack, and arrangements had to be improvised on the spot. We forced our way into the desert through a fearful concatenation of mishaps and discomforts, always desperately trying to catch up the front line. Again and again our vehicles broke down. Once we had to draw lots to decide who should stay behind to rescue our truck and the lot fell on me and I wasted half a day trying to find my companions again. We hitchhiked desperately. Bit by bit we shed our baggage until we had jettisoned our beds and all our luxury tinned food and all our clean clothes. We travelled with just enough blankets to keep alive as we lay on the hard cold desert at night, a basic iron ration of food, and our typewriters. We wrote in primitive mess tents by the light of a single guttering candle, or in the cabs of trucks during sand-storms. We broadcast our despatches all over the desert, sending them by air, by road or by rail, giving copies to anyone who would take them in the hope that something would get back to Cairo. But all the time we were getting more and more details of this astounding attack, the first British land success of the war.

The situation when the British attacked on December 9 was this:—

Graziani had disposed his forces in a series of fortified semi-permanent camps, starting on the sea-coast a dozen miles east of Sidi Barrani, and swinging down south and west in a big arc. There were seven of them and their names, starting from the coast, were Maktila, Point Ninety, Tummar East, Tummar West, Nibeiwa, and the two Sofafis. They were linked by a system of dusty tracks but they did not in any sense of the word form a continuous front line. The Italians, convinced partly by the heroical exuberance of their own propaganda, partly by sheer common sense, had long ago given up anticipating that the British would attack. They therefore did not consider a front line necessary. These camps were built merely to live in and as bases for the forthcoming invasion of Egypt. Ramparts were dug and mine fields were laid down as a mere matter of the most elementary military discipline. But no one expected to use these fortifications, except perhaps to beat off some over-confident British patrol.

Holding this ring of forts were three complete divisions. Up on the coast, from his headquarters in Sidi Barrani, General Gallina commanded one Libyan and one Metropolitan division. Down in the desert was a special semi-armoured unit known, after its commander, as the Ragruppamento Maletti. Farther back, based on Bardia, were two more divisions under Generals Berti and Bergonzoli. And General Amico's Catanzaro Division was actually on its way forward to relieve the front-line units when the battle began.

Opposite all this General Sir Henry Maitland Wilson — Wavell's commander in the field — had precisely two divisions. They were the Fourth Indian Division up near the coast under Major-General Beresford-Pierce, and the Seventh Armoured Division down inland under Major-General O'More Creagh. They were banded together in a single corps under General O'Connor.

The Seventh Armoured Division were veterans of the desert. Attached to them was a new type of formation called a "support group," consisting of the Third Coldstream Guards, the First King's Royal Rifles, the Second Rifle Brigade, the Eleventh Hussars, one squadron of the Sixth Royal Tank Regiment, and two batteries of the Royal Horse Artillery. All these names were to become famous in the annals of desert fighting; and nothing was more fitting than that two years later the Eleventh Hussars should be the first troops into Tripoli.

All through the late summer and autumn months, the support group had been pushing its patrols through the interstices between Graziani's fortified encampments. They went to get information, to cause trouble, to keep their own hands in. And it was entirely on the basis of their information that Wavell's plan was built.

As the patrol reports were collated over a period of weeks, one curious fact began to emerge more and more clearly. There were of course gaps between all the Italian camps. But between Nibeiwa and the Sofafi camps there seemed to be an enormous, glaring gap, and it was apparently entirely undefended.

A major on General Creagh's staff pondered over this deeply. Finally he went out alone to investigate himself. He made several expeditions, each time pushing farther and farther through the gap. He encountered nothing whatever.

So the plan became obvious. And as it was made, so it was carried out.

Deep down in the desert, the Seventh Armoured Division moved on the night of December 7. They had a tough march of over sixty miles to do before they reached the enemy lines, and they could not be asked to march all night and attack immediately the next morning. So they would have to lie for a day out in the open while they rested and serviced their vehicles. And that was the most doubtful part of the whole plan.

But it worked. Of course they had luck. But they also had the crass blindness of the Italians. As they lay there all that Sunday watching the shadows shrink to nothing at midday and stretch out again towards evening, covering themselves with scraps of camel-thorn as camouflage, mending cracked springs and filling their tanks from the secret dumps of petrol made in advance by the patrols, an Italian reconnaissance plane flew over them, circled lazily round, and drifted away again. What happened to that pilot no one ever knew. Perhaps he crashed on the way home. Perhaps he turned in his report and someone overlooked it. Perhaps he never even saw the British troops lying there, simply because he never expected to see them there. At any rate no bombers came, and by nightfall the Seventh knew they were undiscovered.

That night the navy bombarded Sidi Barrani and Maktila with fifteen-inch shells. The R.A.F. turned on all the bombers it could muster to attack the Italian landing grounds. And before dawn the Seventh moved.

Swiftly and unobserved they streamed through the gap, turned right, and stormed into the Nibeiwa camp from the one direction the Italians had presumed impossible — from behind.

General Maletti and his staff were at breakfast. Some men were still in bed. No organized resistance was possible. For one thing all the guns were mounted facing the wrong way; for another, no one was manning them anyway. Maletti himself, a brave, resourceful man, grabbed a machine-gun and fired it from his tent mouth until he was wounded and finally killed. What defence there was crumbled into chaos. In half an hour it was finished.

The British troops scarcely paused to examine what they had won. There came to them that sure instinct of success which sometimes comes to men on battle-fields, a purely intuitive knowledge that everything was all right, that they were winning, that they could take risks, break rules, forge fearlessly ahead. They split into two columns. One party drove north and cleaned up the two Tummar camps in the same cyclonic way as they had taken Nibeiwa. The others cut dead across country north-west, aiming at Buqbuq.

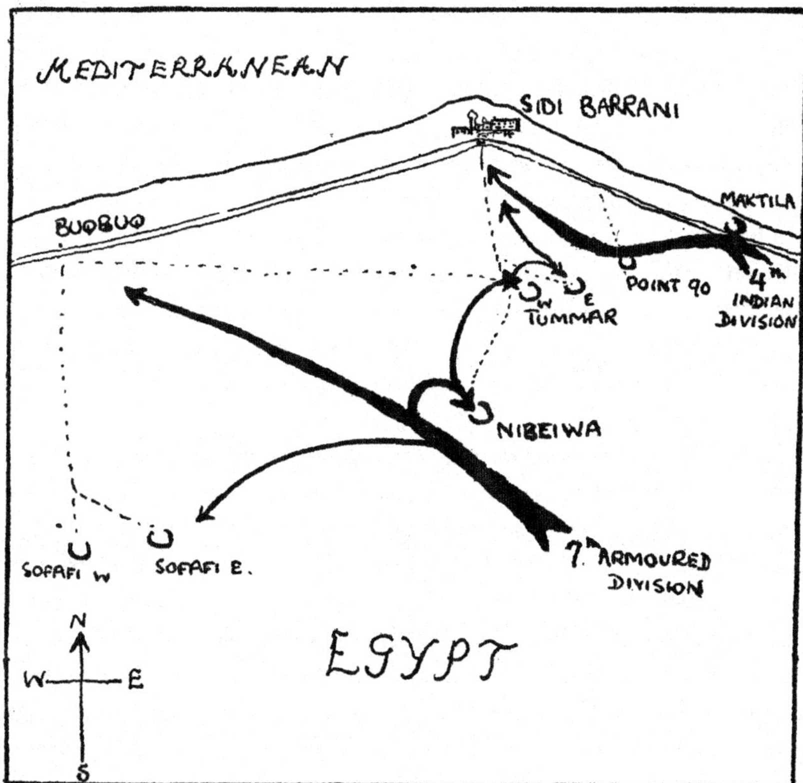

Wavell's attack on December 9th 1940

Meantime the Indian Division had advanced along the coast and swept the defenders out of Maktila. Point Ninety sent a high-flown, defiant message of refusal in answer to the first demand for surrender, then surrendered incontinently when the attack started. Down in the south a British force so small that it could not possibly take the offensive was watching the Sofafi camps fester into flight.

At Sidi Barrani next day there was the first regular battle. The Italian positions were undoubtedly of some strength and their gun positions numerous and well-placed. The nucleus of the defenders consisted of a Blackshirt Division, convinced Fascists who might be expected to show some fight. But the British commanding officers, filled with the excitement of the moment, were all for an immediate attack. It would have been more orthodox to have waited, for they had not nearly enough artillery support on the spot. But this was no orthodox campaign, and on the morning of the tenth the infantry went forward.

They moved in three battalions — the Second Queen's on the left, the First Argyll and Sutherland Highlanders in the centre, the Second Leicesters on the right. They had to advance up towards a rise, where a clever trench system had been worked in among the sand dunes, and then down over the other side to Sidi Barrani.

In the early afternoon the Italian artillery barrage was very heavy and the attackers were pinned down. Their advance so far had been not without casualties and the resistance was strong. But two things finally decided the issue. One was a great charge by the Highlanders, who got to close quarters and reduced the battle to hand-to-hand fighting. The other was the intervention of the twenty-eight–ton infantry tanks, which were another of Wavell's surprises for the Italians. The "I" tanks worked their way right round east and west until they had got down to the seashore beyond Barrani. The Italians had no sort of anti-tank weapons to cope with such thickness of armour. And at five o'clock in the evening resistance collapsed.

General Gallina, an operatic figure with a forked beard, made a farewell speech to his men while tears flowed down his cheeks. To his British captors he said dramatically, "We have fired all our ammunition down to the last cartridge." One of the first things the victors found was an ammunition dump so enormous that it took the sappers weeks to clean it up.

So Graziani's front line crumbled. The defenders of Sofafi began to speed back towards the frontier in a swelling stream while the R.A.F. bombed and bombed them. The Catanzaro Division, which no one had thought to warn, marched complete into our hands. Buqbuq fell, if you can talk about the fall of a place that has no existence. The forces set in motion by Wavell went raging on by their own impetus in a mad, piratical race, knowing with utter certainty that everything had been delivered into their hand, that this was their hour of unbelievable opportunity and they had better make the most of it.

ii

I and the other war correspondents, fighting against mounting transport difficulties, began to catch up with all this at Nibeiwa. We arrived there simultaneously with the sappers who had come to examine the captured war material, and we drove carefully into the camp in the tracks of those who had gone before us so as to avoid land mines.

Nibeiwa as we found it that day might have been a museum arranged to demonstrate just why the Italians had failed. It started by taking our breath away with astonishment at its luxury and elaboration. And it left us filled with equally great astonishment at the evident wrongness of the enemy's methods.

To begin with, the very existence of such a camp in the front line was wrong. There is no more sense in permanently occupying a patch of desert than there is in permanently occupying a patch of sea. Mobility and fluidity are what the desert demands in defence and attack. Graziani's system of clotting his army into a string of immovable fortresses was liable to the precise treatment we applied to it: encirclement, isolation and attack from its weakest point.

But the Italians, it seemed, were psychologically and temperamentally incapable of playing things the desert's way. They were filled with an unconquerable urge to alter the desert, improve it, turn it into a home-from-home. They needed, it seemed, an exceedingly elaborate mode of life in the desert. And the maintenance of such a mode of life was only possible with permanent establishments like Nibeiwa.

So we found there stores of foodstuffs infinitely more varied and succulent than our own: great tins of ham, huge Parmesan cheeses, long blue packets of spaghetti, seven-pound pots of tomato extract, green vegetables and delicious fruits in tins, jams and quince jelly, tongues and tunny fish in olive oil. There were great vats of exceedingly good wines. There were barrels of brandy. Oil and vinegar stood on mess-tent tables in artistic porcelain vases. Crockery and cutlery were of the finest.

There were sheets on the beds in the private tents of the officers. On their dressing tables were bottles of scent and pomade. Their ceremonial uniforms depended from coat-hangers, carefully shrouded against the blowing sand. Maletti's own tunic, smothered with ribbons and gold braid, hung over the back of a chair outside the tent in which he lay dead.

For an hour or more I wandered round tent after tent, looking in trunks or suitcases, brushing the already drifting sand from one unexpected object after another. The tiny individual coffee percolators, the ingenious mackintosh ground sheets which buttoned together to make a tent, the swords and the cloaks and nutmeg graters and wireless sets all excited our admiration. It was like picking through the wreckage of some popular department store after an earthquake. The sudden discovery of a handsome young officer stretched stiff as a poker across the roof of his own tent struck me as oddly incongruous in these surroundings.

Blowing everywhere, chased by the wreathing yellow whorls of an incipient dust-storm, were letters and postcards, notepaper and newspaper, official reports and orders of the day. This army's consumption of paper was incredible. Some of it must have been absorbingly interesting, but my interest faltered in the presence of so much of it.

I picked up a few letters. Most were in the baroque peasant style, filled with invocations to the Virgin and the Saints, petty news about friends and relatives, and ardent desires for the return of the loved one. Many revealed a love life of astonishing complication, which in the absence of physical contact had been reduced to an extreme refinement of psychological nuances. Almost none mentioned the war and those that did showed not the faintest interest in it.

A big fat black notebook blew against my legs and I picked it up and glanced inside. It was the frank personal diary of a colonel —an extremely intelligent colonel. He freely criticized his superior officers. And he hit the nail neatly on the head when he wrote, "The High Command is trying to fight this campaign out here as a colonial war. Can the fools not see that this is a modern European war and must be fought by modern European methods? They think that just because it is taking place in Africa they must necessarily use the methods suitable for fighting savages."

I browsed on among the debris, fascinated by what I found. In an ambulance tent I ran across an Italian Medical Officer I had known in the Spanish War, and he invited me to join his meal of ham, bread and wine. It seemed to me that I should be the host now, not he. But with that astonishing national resiliency which seemed so peculiar then, but which later became sickeningly familiar, he was not one whit abashed at being defeated.

At that first view of how the Italians lived, it seemed to us that their desert existence was marvellously well-equipped compared with the bare austerity of our own. But we were mistaking luxury of equipment for appropriateness of equipment. Everything that they had above the level of bare necessity was an anchor to pin them down to a fixed spot in the desert, a drag on their essential mobility. Their already difficult supply problem must have been vastly complicated by these great crates of mineral water, this wealth of furniture and comforts. Their only excuse was that they had underrated their opponents hopelessly and therefore felt they could well afford what luxury they could get.

And in the things that really mattered the Italian shortcomings were obvious. Their thinly armoured two-man baby tanks were useless death-traps. Their good-looking M13's were mechanically weak and made of inferior steel, and the turret had an excessively small traverse. The staff cars they had brought to this desert were ordinary Fiats built for Italian *autostradas*. They even included the diminutive six-horsepower model called the "Balilla." Many of their field-guns were shockingly old-fashioned. So was their ordinary infantryman's rifle. Their huge ten-ton Diesel lorries were useful on roads, but too heavy and rigid for desert surfaces.

In the late afternoon we reluctantly left Nibeiwa and drove up north to Sidi Barrani. We passed the fringes of the two Tummar camps where, it was said, the booty had been richer still. And for the last three miles of our road, we drove through a strip of countryside that was literally checkered with big regular dumps of ammunition. There were thousands and thousands of tons of it, all destined for the invasion of Egypt.

Sidi Barrani was an even bleaker, more shattered edition of the dreary ruins I had seen on my first visit to the desert. Systematic bombings had helped to do this, but most of all the fifteen-inch shells of the navy. Yet during the Italian occupation Barrani had been a place of gaiety and song. We found the grave of a cabaret artiste who had been killed while working there. Barrani had been the headquarters of the Italian army's mobile brothels. General Gallina had had his luxurious headquarters near by. But now, one day after the battle, it had sunk back to its sand-strewn, fly-blown desolation. Its miserable houses could not boast a roof among the lot of them. In some curious way all the window apertures had been blown in and instead of neat rectangles they were mere shapeless gaps. Strewn about the desert near by were lines of guns with drooping muzzles, broken lop-sided tanks, and as far as the eye could see the chunky black shapes of ten-ton trucks.

We slept down by the sea, away from the flies and the garbage, alongside a hospital where the Italian doctors had abandoned on the operating table a patient already cut open for an appendicitis operation.

Next day we drove to where the old Egyptian road had ended and deciphered the florid, over-optimistic inscription on the monument which Graziani had erected to celebrate the completion of his new road. As a matter of fact it was not really completed. It still needed a surface on it. But everything else was ready. And we drove on westwards along it, admiring the solidity of its foundations, the well-banked sweeps of its curves, the breadth and firmness of its embankments. Every few miles or so we passed abandoned steam-rollers. And even more frequently we saw pompous little memorials bearing a profile of the Duce, or some quotation from one of his speeches, or simply a statement that this bit of road had been finished in record time by such and such a labour company.

As we neared Buqbuq the setting sun was striking down obliquely through the haze of golden dust ahead of us. And suddenly over the brow of a rise, tramping steadily through this cloud of glory, came the entire Catanzaro Division. They marched complete in their units, each officer in his place — one whole untouched Italian division. They might almost have been on parade. But not quite. For they had no rifles. And on either side of them, distributed at fifty-yard intervals, walked a handful of British soldiers — stalwart, harassed-looking youths dressed in khaki shorts, with tin hats set rakishly on their heads and rifles slung over their shoulders, their faces wearing the slightly dumbfounded look of men called on to deal with a situation outside all normal human experience.

The Italians were short, scruffy, shabby little men and they trudged by, company after company, carrying their bulging cardboard suitcases and leading their pet dogs on strings. When I shouted to them asking what their division was, they shouted back without resentment, almost without interest, just giving information out of ordinary politeness. There was not — there never had been — any fight in them. Even now, on this lonely road which Graziani had unhappily named the Via della Vittoria, they could easily have overwhelmed their tiny guard and got away. But it was obvious that no such thought had entered the minds of any of them. It was stupid to despise them because they were bad soldiers. They had all the virtues and qualities appropriate to peacetime, and peace is a better thing than war. One despised them because, being bad soldiers, they had deliberately entered a war and made themselves ridiculous.

So they faded away into the evening, marching towards Alexandria as Mussolini had promised them, but to captivity instead of victory. And we went on and slept more comfortably than we had done for many nights in the soft sand-hills beyond Buqbuq.

Now the impetus of that first mad rush was slowing down. Generals Berti and Bergonzoli had had time to impose some sort of organization on the chaos that had filled the desert for four days. The mighty escarpment which leaves the coast at Sollum and swings down inland had obvious defensive value and here the British spearhead paused. In a sticky salt marsh a little short of Sollum, it had tried to fight a tank battle and for once it had not won. The tanks bogged immovably in the paste-like mud and the Italian guns picked them off one after another. The hero of that engagement was a doctor who ran from tank to blazing tank, pulling the wounded and trapped and dying to safety, until there was no one left to save.

Of their own volition the Italians went back a little farther. They left Sollum and retired to the top of the escarpment by way of the two serpentine roads, breaching them with dynamite as they went. Then they surrendered Fort Capuzzo and Musaid and Sidi Azeiz and any other point up there which was sufficiently noticeable to have a name. And a week before Christmas they shut themselves up in the fortress area of Bardia.

It was now that I began to feel sick — sicker than I could ever remember feeling in my life. One morning I couldn't drag myself from my sleeping-bag and the others had to leave me, rolled up there in the sand-hills. During the morning a group of Italian soldiers drifted by, armed to the teeth, and asked me if I knew anywhere where they could surrender. Feebly I directed them. At midday I crawled out into the chilly winter sunshine and cooked some *spaghetti alla Milanese* for my companions when they came back to lunch. Then I returned to my blankets.

But we had to go on. We had to look at the ruins of shell-shocked Sollum and climb the winding road of Halfaya Pass on to the escarpment. Up there a wind as coldly knife-edged as I have ever felt blew tiny stinging grains of grit icily against our raw skin. When we had to get out of the car we walked sideways or even backwards rather than face into it. It was not to be borne. We had no food and little petrol and there was no looting to be done up here. I tried hard not to let my sickness influence me into persuading the others to turn back eastwards, but I felt I should die if I had to stay there. So we went back painfully and slowly through the sand-storm to Fuqa where we had left the rest of our luggage and stores. I hadn't been able to eat anything for three days and all the way back I felt that the only thing I wanted in the world was a drink of orange juice. I knew I had a tin waiting for me at Fuqa. But when I opened it it tasted in my mouth like liquid sawdust.

Then suddenly we were all panicked. What if Bardia should suddenly surrender? Our place was obviously back on the bleak escarpment. Four of us decided to make one more trip up to Sollum. We set off in two cars, and a little beyond Matruh one of them broke down. We drew lots to see who should go on and with stupid obstinacy I insisted on drawing with the others. Alan Moorehead of the London *Daily Express* and I won. We reached Sollum that night and camped in what looked like a sheltered *wadi* (Arabic for gulley). But we hadn't noticed that it lay next to Halfaya Pass, and all that night Italian planes bombed the Pass. I lay for hours and watched the blue exhaust flame of each bomber slash through the sky above me as it climbed after dropping its bombs.

In the morning we met someone who told us authoritatively that Bardia would not be attacked for days, probably weeks. So we turned again back to Fuqa, and that same evening we caught a goods train to Cairo.

I spent Christmas in bed with jaundice and sand-fly fever.

CHAPTER 5

Bardia, Tobruk, Derna

THE FANTASTIC, swift-moving first stage was over. It had succeeded beyond anything that Wavell can possibly have hoped. In a week we had taken nearly forty thousand prisoners and incredible quantities of tanks, guns, lorries and stores. Not an Italian soldier remained east of the frontier. The army destined for the invasion of Egypt had been smashed beyond repair. And it had all cost us just over seventy killed and just over seven hundred wounded.

But now Wavell was faced with a very different proposition. And it is characteristic of him that he was not carried away by the ease and excitement of his initial success. He might have tried to rush Bardia and taken it at once, regardless of losses. But he desperately needed to regard losses. For all the vast total of prisoners taken, the British desert army was still inferior in numbers. It was vitally important that every success should be a cheap success, for a costly success would leave us with no army to exploit it.

The attack on Bardia was going to be a totally different type of warfare from that of the past weeks. Mobile fighting was being replaced by static fighting. The theory of fortress areas as a method of defending deserts was about to be put to the test.

We ourselves believed in the theory, in the absence of evidence to the contrary. We had fortified Mersa Matruh in this way and we had planned to make it the pivot of our defence of Egypt. Clearly enough the Italians believed in it, for they had fortified Bardia and Tobruk and now they had shut up a considerable army inside Bardia and were preparing to hold it. True or false, the theory had sufficient backing to be treated with respect.

Other considerations too obliged Wavell to pause. In the first place the disposal of this unexpected horde of prisoners raised a very urgent problem. Second, the forward troops had long ago outrun their supplies, and food, water, ammunition and petrol were pressingly needed up on that wind-scoured plateau. Third, it was decided to withdraw the tired Indian Division from the battle and replace it with the Sixth Australian Division from Gaza. So while Bergonzoli in Bardia and Mussolini in Rome exchanged flowery messages referring to Bardia as the "bastion of Fascism" and promising resistance to the last drop of Italian blood, Wavell planned his attack.

Bardia was a street of modern white-stucco cottages set bleakly on a cliff 350 feet above a small heart-shaped harbour. At a radius of about ten miles round the town concentric rings of fortifications had been built. Behind mine fields, barbed-wire fences and anti-tank ditches, the Italians had laid down a series of concreted strong-points holding machine-guns and anti-tank guns, with low stone breastworks and galleries leading to ammunition stores. Immediately round the strong-points were special tank traps built on the elephant-trap principle—holes camouflaged with thin, sand-covered planking that would bear a man but not a vehicle.

Some forty thousand men were holding these positions. They had little aerial support, but plenty of artillery including one heavy gun which quickly became known as "Bardia Bill." The place was commanded by General Bergonzoli, nicknamed Barba Elettrica or Electric Whiskers, a dashing and picturesque soldier. I had once seen him at the village of Andorra, in the Pyrenees, melodramatically continuing to direct a small battle after he had been wounded.

In the biting sand-storms that blew between Christmas and the New Year, Wavell established an ever-thickening ring round Bardia. More and more Australians arrived, superbly healthy, desperately bored with Gaza, almost irrestrainably anxious to get into action. Many came in Italian trucks, for that was how the British had been obliged to solve their transport problem. Supplies came in by small steamers to Sollum. New batteries of guns arrived and went straight into action. The main road west from Bardia to Tobruk was cut and the armoured division was astride it. By New Year's all was ready.

The Italians showed every sign of playing a purely passive role. The British had at least extended the fortress-area theory to include a mobile armoured force operating outside. But there was no movement at all from Tobruk. Bardia was to get no assistance.

Wavell's plan involved the closely knit co-operation of all forces. His resources were so barely sufficient that he must use everything available to him. His intention was to soften Bardia with all the shells and bombs he could put into it, and then stab it with a sharp armoured spearhead as one might puncture a balloon or an egg.

The softening process lasted all of January 1 and 2. Four shallow-draft gunboats and a monitor (a sort of floating fortress designed to be practically unsinkable) bombarded from the sea. Twenty-five-pounders and a battery of sixty-pounders shelled from the land. The R.A.F. bombed incessantly from the air.

In pale moonlight just before dawn on January 3, the sharp spearhead went in. Australian sappers and infantry cut gaps in the wire of the western perimeter and filled in the anti-tank ditches with pick and shovel. Then the tanks crashed through. Behind them came Australian infantry with fixed bayonets. And that morning, though it was a long time before the fact was recognized, the fortress-area theory as such collapsed.

The Italian defences, all pointing outwards, were hopelessly disorientated by this wedge that drove right past them and on behind them. By evening the wedge was stuck two miles inside Bardia and the Australians had turned right and left and widened the gap to something like nine miles. Already around 10,000 prisoners were in our hands.

From then on resistance was not organized. It could not be. Many Italian strong-points fought their individual battles with unexpected bravery, but there was no hope of saving Bardia. Prisoners poured from caves with white handkerchiefs tied to their wrists in surrender, clamouring for food, water and cigarettes. A big blue-green column of Italian captives was accurately shelled by Italian batteries. Wadi Gefani, a canyon-like ravine that slashes the fortress area in two, was passed by Australian infantry assaulting on foot. By the afternoon of January 4 it was as good as all over.

So we got another 40,000 prisoners. We now had 80,000 in all, including nine Generals and 3250 officers. We had captured 200 tanks, some 800 guns and over 1300 machine-guns, all for a total of under 1500 battle casualties.

But Bardia brought one disappointment. Old Electric Whiskers got mysteriously away. We heard rumours that a submarine had picked him up, that a fast plane had flown him out at the last minute, even that he had never been there at all. I did not discover the truth until I heard it much later from his own lips. But from that moment he became just about the most famous person in the desert.

ii

Tobruk came next.

The swift fall of Bardia demonstrated to Graziani the fallacy of his fortress-area theory. It was scarcely to be hoped that he would try the same experiment again. But he did. With a staggering lack of originality and initiative he shut up another army in Tobruk, in precisely similar circumstances, and waited for the British to attack it.

Had he known accurately how small was the force against him he must have seen that his best chance lay in a counterattack from Tobruk while Wavell was still only half-prepared. But the Rome newspapers were saying that the British were several hundred thousand strong, that there were six Australian divisions alone, and countless tanks. And Tobruk was left sealed up in helpless isolation, just as Bardia had been.

If Graziani had wanted to change his mind, we gave him time enough. Our maintenance and supply problems had suddenly become very pressing. The lengthening lines of communication, the growing mass of prisoners, the increasing demands for petrol and ammunition and the decreasing serviceability of guns, tanks and vehicles, all told. But as fast as we could we moved the whole paraphernalia of the Bardia attack sixty miles farther on and put it into position again round Tobruk. Zero hour was planned for first light on January 21.

I was still in bed at the time of Bardia, and the doctor forbade me to go to Tobruk. But I thought I could do something else. I applied for another operational flight with the R.A.F. and I was even luckier than before. They said I could go on a bombing raid over Tobruk on the morning of January 21 — zero hour.

The night before it happened I went with the pilots of a Wellington squadron to a sandy fly-haunted shack beside a remote desert air field to get the Squadron-Leader's instructions.

"Blitz on Tobruk to-night," he told us. "Take-off after midnight at ten-minute intervals. There are five targets — you can take your choice."

I looked on rather diffidently while they clustered round maps and photographs and filled in the details, discussing the weather, debating the relative merits of the targets. For them it was pretty nearly routine, but not for me. I felt the sensation I always feel before going on one of those giant racers at fun fairs — excitement more or less strongly tempered with alarm. I looked through the dirty windows and watched the crews loading up with bombs and petrol, and checking over the guns. I wished strongly that I could do something to help.

As darkness fell everyone trooped in for a noisy, boisterous meal of stew, potatoes and onions. The atmosphere was less routine now — there was a mood of suppressed exhilaration. The conversation was nearly all shop, most of it over my head, but I felt pleased when I could contribute some bit of gossip I had picked up at another squadron.

Afterwards, for the few intervening hours, we dozed on straw mattresses. Then booted, helmeted and very warmly overalled we walked out to the dimly silhouetted plane.

A moon which looked to my over-excited eye like a luminous slice of melon was just topping the horizon. In a matter of minutes we had climbed aboard, roared down the winking flare path and lifted gently into the night. I stood with my head in the little glass bubble which stuck out above the top of the machine, and watched the desert sink away into a misty blur. Little white clouds drenched with moonlight sailed past. A dim white streak was the coast-line and the sea beyond it looked like another desert.

There was nothing to see. I crouched down, trying to keep warm and watching spangles of stars slide past the little glass bubble above my head. Vaguely in my earphones I heard the crew chatting on the "intercomm" about height, courses, clouds and navigation signals. As the plane droned on into Libya I fell asleep.

Then someone was shaking me awake and yelling "Tobruk." I fumbled my way forward and peered out of the plane's transparent nose to see earth and sky slashed with flame.

Groups of big yellow flashes were bombs landing. Clusters of incendiaries wove crazy patterns of dazzling white flame athwart the landscape. A parachute flare hung like a great orange star burning steadily above Tobruk Bay.

To my unaccustomed eyes the ack-ack barrage seemed stupendous. String after string of red tracer shells spurted up like ruby necklaces. Ack-ack shells bursting splashed the sky with sudden stars and left little balls of smoke hanging aimlessly about.

It was our turn to go in. Just for one second there was icy panic inside me and I wished I hadn't come. I wondered whether I was trembling from cold or fear. Then I grew far too excited to be afraid.

I clambered back through the plane's darkened belly, past the bomb aimer lying flat on his stomach, and over the racks of sleek yellow bombs waiting to be released. Clumsily I eased myself into the rear gunner's turret—another bigger bubble, half-filled with intricate gun mechanism. That was my grand-stand seat.

Through my earphones I heard the bomb aimer's steady monologue:—

"Bomb doors open . . . left . . . left . . . steady . . . right . . . steady . . ." Then a pause, and then sharply: "Bombs gone."

I swivelled my turret round, manœuvring to see the bombs land. I had almost given them up when the earth below erupted into five flaming volcanoes.

"Plumb in the target area," came the bomb aimer's voice.

Stuff was coming up all around us. The sky seemed filled with coloured tracers and the heavy ack-ack guns were firing for all they were worth. By now the whole Tobruk area was picked out in dazzling lights as cluster after cluster of incendiaries sprang into flame.

The pilot called me up on the intercomm.

"We're going in again," he said. "Tell me if anything bursts close behind us."

"O.K.," I said. It was icy-cold and my hands were numb as they manipulated the levers to swing my turret.

Back we turned and plunged again into the fantastic blaze of bursting shells. Another flare was burning and Tobruk's bay and promontory showed up like a gigantic thumb sticking out into the dark sea.

We made straight for the target, but showers of tracers met us and barred the way. The pilot swerved aside and tried from another angle. Again I heard "Bombs gone" and this time I saw flame belch up straight across the road junction at which we were aiming.

Two blinding flashes on my left made me rock in my seat. "Ack-ack shells close behind," I reported to the pilot, and for a couple of seconds we swerved and twisted, eluding the gunners. Then we jockeyed into position for the third run.

This took us slap through the thickest barrage. The cruiser *San Giorgio,* half-sunk in the harbour, was pumping up stream after stream of tracers. I saw a white one coming straight at me — diamond necklace this time — then it veered off slowly and missed.

Right in the middle of the barrage our bombs fell, and a flare with them. This time the result was spectacular. A large barn-like building flashed into orange flame and its roof soared gently upwards, then fell back in fragments. Swirls of white smoke spiralled up, and as we swung away out to sea I saw two more explosions shatter the flaming walls.

Those were our last bombs. But we still had some leaflets to drop — why I don't know, for the Italians were going to be given no time to read them. We dropped down to a couple of thousand feet well west of Tobruk and shovelled the packets of pamphlets out through a hatchway. Then we made for home, and Tobruk dwindled to a faint firework display behind us. My first wild exhilaration at having got out of it alive gave way to the flat feeling which follows a moment of high adventure. While dawn was just glimmering in the east, we met a squadron of Blenheims on their way to continue the raid. Then we circled down to our air fields again, to a good hot breakfast of fried bread and bacon.

Even while we were eating it, the attack had started on land. Tobruk differed from Bardia only in minor details. Its outer perimeter was a little longer. Its defenders were fresher, but less numerous, and lacking in seasoning and experience. It was commanded by an Admiral instead of a General. The town was considerably bigger. And it was certainly much more important for it had a fine natural harbour, the best between Alexandria and Bengasi.

The problem was the same as at Bardia and the same treatment was applied. By the evening of the first day the Australians were eight miles inside the south-eastern sector, where the initial stab had been made. Before noon next day they battled their way into the town itself. English and Free French units cleaned up the western end where there was still some resistance. It had all taken just thirty-six hours.

An Admiral, a Corps Commander, a Divisional Commander and two other Generals, all immaculate in dazzling uniforms, offered the surrender of the town and its fifteen thousand defenders. Impatiently the Australian Brigadier waved aside this untimely ceremony. He outlined tersely the reprisals he would take if any of his men were blown up on mines or booby traps. The bemedalled

Italian commanders scattered smartly, issuing a flurry of orders to their sappers to clean the place up at once.

The ill, dazed, famished, thirsty prisoners were marshalled on beaches and open patches of desert, fed and watered, and sent marching off to captivity in harmless docility. And the army forged unappeasably ahead.

iii

I had returned from my raid to Cairo and I had seen none of this. In those days correspondents were so few that we had a pooling arrangement—two or three newspapers agreed to share the services of their several correspondents. Since there was a representative of my "pool" already in the desert I had no business to be there. But I could not bear the tranquillity of Cairo with all this going on. Alan Moorehead was in a like situation. And we talked one another into a state of rebellion, took our skeleton baggage out to the air field, argued our way onto a couple of planes, and flew up to Sollum.

At the battered house in Bardia where the journalists were living we had a chilly reception. We were told: "You have no business to be here at all. You are nothing but supernumeraries. We have no accommodation for you—there are not enough vehicles to go round as it is." Feeling unpopular and abashed Alan and I slept one night on a decrepit billiard table. Next morning we made an arrangement with Captain Geoffrey Keating, the War Office photographer, and he took us both and our kit in his fifteen-hundredweight truck.

I had met Geoffrey in the first month of the war at Le Mans, when that was British G.H.Q. in France. He had been the first photographer and I the first war correspondent, and we had shared a table at the Hôtel du Pélican and driven round the Normandy countryside and watched the troops lounging in haystacks, picking apples for farmers, doing arms drill in fields with the front line still five hundred miles away. He had seen all there was to see in France, done the full Norwegian campaign, then come out to the

Middle East. His own regiment was out here and he knew everyone. It seemed he might be a good person to go along with.

We slept one night in Tobruk. A huge black column of smoke was still rising from the harbour, beside where the half-sunken Italian cruiser *San Giorgio* lay surrounded by its anti-torpedo net. An impressive number of freight and passenger steamers were sunk or beached in the bay, victims of the R.A.F. The streets were littered gaudily with ribbons and crockery, cheap pictures and children's toys, the discarded loot from a dozen little second-rate shops. Furniture lay cracked and smouldering in the gutter, and men with tin helmets and slung rifles picked perfunctorily through the rubbish as they passed, on the off-chance of finding something interesting. But there was plenty of food in the warehouses down by the harbour and good stuff in the naval store-rooms. I picked myself out a pair of good warm trousers, for I had not been able to bring any spare clothing with me from Cairo.

Next day we drove out west from Tobruk along the great metalled coast road which runs from end to end of Libya and on which all its town and villages are strung like beads on a black thread. We passed the twin air fields of Gazala, the seaplane base of Bomba, the palm grove of Umm er-Rzem — the first trees since Mersa Matruh — and sped on towards Derna. It was not thought that Derna would give any trouble. It was not a fortress like Bardia and Tobruk, and anyway Graziani had probably learned his lesson about fortresses. A couple of Australian brigades had gone on ahead, expecting to take Derna in their stride.

But, surprisingly, Derna held. In a series of minor actions up and down the valleys and ravines, the Italians offered a more determined resistance than they had shown yet. In particular their artillery was good and for three days no real progress could be made. I spent half a morning and an afternoon with an Australian infantry platoon and a British machine-gun platoon in the front line on the great red expanse of the Derna air field and I was more severely shelled there than I have ever been before or since.

This field, fringed with the wrecks of Italian bombers and fighters, had been taken the afternoon before. The Australians had advanced straight across it in the open while the Italians fired at them furiously from the shelter of the aerodrome buildings. In the grey dusk the Australians had charged and the Italians had disappeared into the night. Next morning the Australians were awakened by voices. They peeped round the corner of the hangar where they had camped and saw Italian tanks not a stone's throw away. Hardly daring to breathe they sent for an anti-tank gun. And the tanks were knocked out before their crews knew what was happening.

That had finished just before we arrived. Now the Australians were cooking tea behind the shelter of the hangar's huge metal door while a couple of sullen, frightened prisoners looked on. Soon the shelling started. The enemy batteries had clearly got the place pin-pointed in squares, and they ranged over the area blasting now one section, now another. But mostly they blasted our hangar. When a shell landed inside the hangar it made a noise like an express train blowing up in a tunnel, and it was better not to lean against the metal doors because of the concussion. The shells weren't very big shells but they were diabolically accurate. It didn't seem sensible to go anywhere and it didn't seem sensible to stay. In the end we stayed. But that shelling was a good thing in its way — a salutary cold douche to the superiority complex we were all developing with victories coming so easy to us.

In the afternoon another company of Australian infantry advanced across the air field through the shelling, strung out evenly in sections. Their faces were serious and intent as they passed us, not excited or afraid. In another couple of minutes they would be in action and the machine-gunners were going forward to support them.

We went up to the next ridge with them and saw them move steadily down into the valley and up the other side. Their objective was a fort and meantime a troop of twenty-five–pounders was shelling it, firing at point-blank range over open sights. It was almost too dark to see when the fort was captured, but the Italian shelling hadn't stopped. So we drove back a few miles to camp near Brigade Headquarters and write our despatches.

Maybe we were a little nervous that night. At any rate when we saw a brightly glowing cigarette moving along the *wadi* near us we all three burst out into abuse. "For Christ's sake put out that damned fire," we shouted. "Don't you know the Brigadier is particularly strict about that sort of thing?"

The cigarette was thrown to the ground and trodden underfoot. And an Australian voice replied, "Oh, sorry . . . As a matter of fact, I am the Brigadier."

It was, of course, a very good introduction. The Brigadier's name was Robertson and he was nicknamed "Red Robby" in tribute to his flaming-red hair. And as the result of our rudeness Alan and I were offered a special quick way of sending our despatches back so that we were able to return to the air field next day.

We lived there almost till Derna fell. We built ourselves a blacked-out hut of empty mineral-water crates inside a garage and there we entertained people at little dinners of Italian rations. Only fleas and shells disturbed our comfort. So accurate was the Italian system of sectional shelling that one evening we just stood and laughed when the guns began to bombard a near-by house where an Australian platoon was camped. Men were running out of doors and being chased back in again, they were pursued in and out of windows and all around the block and finally up the hillside and out of sight. But we were perfectly safe and we stood and laughed. It sounds silly but it was the sort of thing we laughed at then.

Every day we went out and got a bit nearer Derna. One day we went with a platoon to assault Fort Rudero. It seemed to be empty and Geoffrey made the men do a couple of trial assaults so that he could photograph them. When we got inside we found eighty Italians lined up there with all their baggage packed, waiting only to surrender. Yet they could have killed us fifty times over as we stood there outside posing for photographs.

There were three Italian officers in Rudero, and we offered to escort them back to headquarters. We had not gone fifty yards before we were all in among a thick-sown mine field.

"What courage, what organization!" cried the Italian major.

"What do you mean?" I asked.

"What brave engineers you must have, to plant mines so near to our fort."

"They aren't our mines — they're yours," I said, and showed him the official stamp on them. He was apparently dumbfounded — he swore he did not know they were there.

Three minutes later very heavy machine-gun fire sent us racing for a little dip beside the road. The dark young Italian lieutenant beside me kept breathing "*Mamma mia, Mamma mia,*" as any Italian will in serious trouble. Then the other lieutenant made a suggestion. He claimed that this was British machine-gun fire. One of us would stand up and try and stop it. If it did not stop, then it must be Italian fire and he would stand up and stop it. We told him not to be idiotic, and we all started a discussion about Fascism. No one present seemed to believe in it and the argument flagged. The young lieutenant showed me a photo of his wife and burst into tears. Finally we made a run for it and got away.

This sort of thing went on for three days. Then Geoffrey had a hunch that something much more interesting was happening down inland. The Armoured Division was massing at a dusty desert outpost thirty miles away called Fort Mechili. It seemed likely that they were planning a spectacular run clean through the desert to the sea south of Bengasi, short-circuiting the coast road. Derna, it seemed, was no nearer falling than it had been the day before. We set off for Mechili.

The track the Italians had marked on their map did not exist, but we took a bold compass course and found our way. We called on Brigadier Gott, commander of the Support Group, who was later tragically killed at the moment when he was about to take over command of the whole Eighth Army. Already he was collecting that wealth of experience which made him such a superb desert leader, and in his spare time he was already mapping out a text-

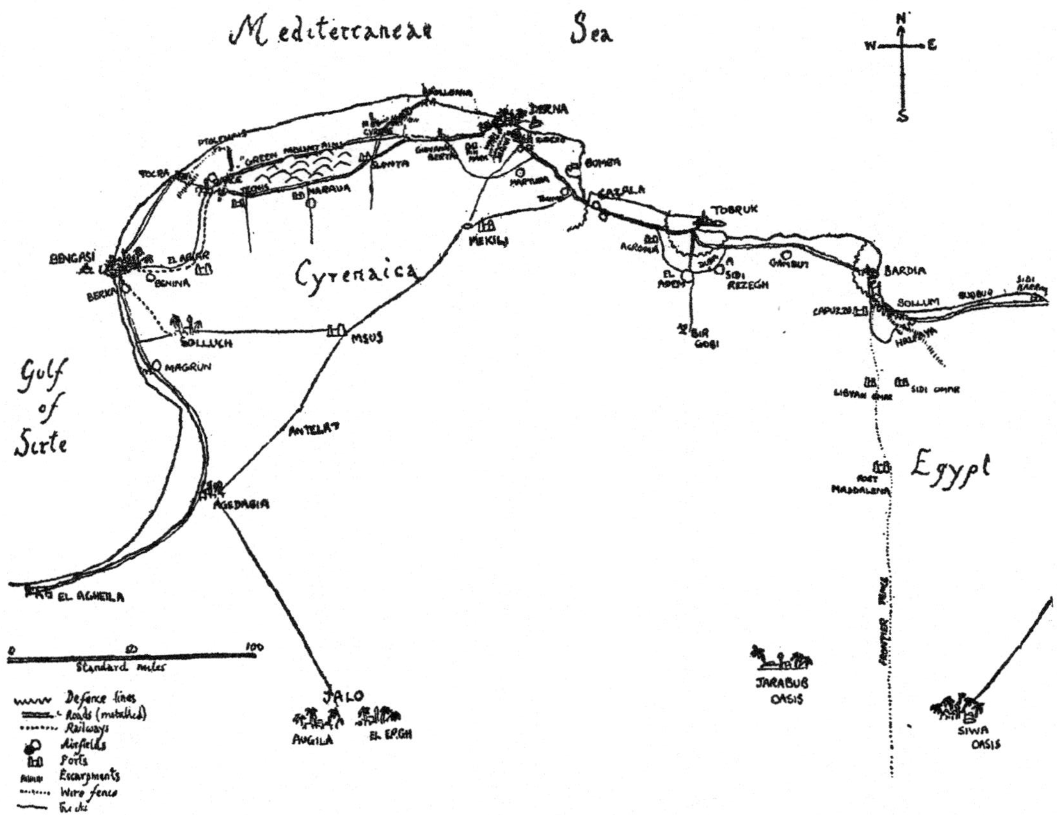

Mediterranean Sea
N
W
E
S
Cyrenaica
Gulf of Sirte
Egypt
BENGASI
BERKA
BENINA
EL ABIAR
TOCRA
PTOLEMAIS
GREEN MOUNTAINS
BARCE
TECNIS
EL MARAUA
SLONTA
APOLLONIA
CYRENE
GIOVANNI BERTA
DERNA
BOMBA
MARTUBA
TMIMI
GAZALA
MEKILI
MSUS
SOLLUCH
MAGRUN
ANTELAT
AGEDABIA
EL AGHEILA
JALO
AUGILA
EL ERGH
TOBRUK
ACROMA
EL ADEM
SIDI REZEGH
BIR GOBI
GAMBUT
BARDIA
CAPUZZO
SOLLUM
HALFAYA
BUQBUQ
SIDI BARRANI
LIBYAN OMAR
SIDI OMAR
FORT MADDALENA
FRONTIER FENCE
JARABUB OASIS
SIWA OASIS
0
50
100
Standard miles
Defence lines
Roads (metalled)
Railways
Airfields
Ports
Escarpments
Wire fence
Tracks

book on the technique of desert warfare. His mess was said to be the most uncomfortable in the desert, for he simply paid no attention to it. But on this occasion we bartered a case of Italian mineral water with him in exchange for a tin of army biscuits.

He told us of the tank battle they had had here the day before — a battle about which Headquarters were apparently not very pleased. The Seventh had been a little too precipitate. They had waded straight in, beaten the Italians hands down and chased them from the field with heavy losses. But Headquarters had hoped for a better result. They had been planning to cut this entire Italian tank force off and capture it intact. We gathered from Gott that the Seventh was indeed planning to go straight across to the sea, though it was all very hush-hush. We went off to sleep on the proposition that we go along with them.

In the morning a signaller strolled over to where we lay in our sleeping-bags and remarked casually, "They've entered Derna. Just heard it on the wireless."

With desperate fury we packed our truck and got under way without bothering about breakfast. I had missed Bardia and Tobruk — and now Derna. All that time we had spent waiting under shell-fire was wasted and our competitors would be in ahead of us. Geoffrey drove furiously while he and I wrangled about the compass course. We strained our springs and our bedding was soused in petrol from tins which had burst in the back of the truck. But we got back by lunchtime, and drove down the winding escarpment road into the miracle that was Derna.

It lay there with a wall round it, a little kidney-shaped green-and-white promontory, jutting into the sea, and it just did not seem possible after so many hundred miles of desert. Derna had streets and sidewalks and bright-green hedges along the roadside, and trails of flaming purple bougainvillea splashed down the walls of the white villas and often flung across the street itself. There was a market-place with thick trees and shops with people in them and gardens and palm groves and fresh vegetables and eggs. All, you must understand, on a very small scale, all crammed into an area not much larger than Central Park, but for that very reason all the more enchanting. It was as though some tiny fragment of the Garden of Eden had got marooned in the desert, and the desert had been fought off with walls and with water and had never been able to reclaim this exquisite little clot of fertility.

For the secret of Derna was water — the freshest, purest, most abundant water in all Cyrenaica. It came from springs way up in the Jebel Achdar — the Green Mountains — and flowed down the Wadi Derna, a mighty ravine which slashes the desert in two right down to the sea, and of which Derna itself is the mouth. There were taps in Derna, taps which you could turn on and leave running. You could draw as much water as you liked instead of just a couple of pints of salty, muddy liquid a day. That in itself was sufficient to constitute a paradise in this desert.

There had been little drama about Derna's capture. Day after day the Australians had been edging farther and farther west, across the Wadi Derna and up into the hills the other side, until the Italians saw they were in danger of being surrounded. So during one night they slipped silently away. They blew up the high road where it winds down the cliff face into Derna, and they blew it again where it winds up the other side. All the Australians had to do was to mend the road.

Alan and Geoffrey and I found a little villa and installed ourselves in it. According to the name-plate on the telephone it had belonged to Marshal Graziani himself, and we bathed luxuriously in his bath and cooked on his stove and ate from his dining table. Exploring a *wadi* one day we found a huge enemy food dump, and we came home with a forty-pound Parmesan cheese in the back of our truck and a small barrel of brandy and enough stores to keep us going for days. We kept open house and friends dropped in casually for a bath and a meal. One afternoon while we were out someone even left cards on us.

CHAPTER 6

Barce, Bengasi, Beda Fomm

But this luxurious pause could not last. Quickly the Australians gathered momentum, and as soon as the roads were mended we were off again on a wild, unorthodox chase. Try as we would, it was impossible to keep the campaign within the bounds of normal military procedure. Patrols were sent out and they simply captured the objectives instead of reporting on them. Time and again Alan and I drove forward to a front line which merely consisted of men sleeping off their tiredness in the sun, waiting to get the order to go on. The Italians had abandoned even a pretence of resistance.

Once Alan and Geoffrey and I casually captured the day's objective. We knew what it was and we asked a passing Arab the way to it. He took us to the top of a hill and pointed it out to us and said, "Just follow this track." So we followed it. The place was built round two forts on a hillcrest. It was uncannily deserted when we got there and we realized uneasily that we had never inquired whether it had been captured. And then, just as we were approaching the larger of the two fortresses, the doors burst open and the Arab population, with their head-man leading them, charged towards us with white flags.

We listened politely to their speeches of welcome and gave them a chit saying they had surrendered peaceably and were to be well treated. Then we briefly inspected their castles. The place was called Ain Mara, and it had a startling green fertility, for it possessed some of the best springs in Cyrenaica. There was a power station already built there, and the Italians had started on the construction of a pipe-line to Bengasi.

We drove off by another road while the women at the well waggled their tongues at us in a shrill trilling yodel which we hoped was complimentary. At a demolished bridge on the main road we once more met the army, which had been making some pretence at capturing Ain Mara in proper military manner. Sappers were working round the bridge and they stopped us just in time — just ten inches in front of a thick band of land mines. We got out and ran across on foot to report to the Brigadier, and the sappers began to pull mines out of the path along which we had run. Again we were jerked back sharply to the realization that this was, after all, a real war.

Then we drove on up into the hills, through a countryside of chocolate mud and bright-green grass and stunted evergreens and white standardized stucco farmhouses which Mussolini had built for his peasant colonists. We passed Giovanni Berta, the first of the colonists' model village centres and in the market-place two Australian Brigadiers were arguing hotly, each hinting that the other was poaching. When they parted, it was obvious that there was going to be a race for Bengasi, so we hurried on.

We passed a freshly dug anti-tank ditch which no one had ever manned and flashed on through a landscape of bare fields and stone walls which might have been England's Yorkshire dales. Where the great coastal highway splits in two to cross the Green Mountains — which are only hills really, though they look like mountains after the desert — we forked right. We had no information about which was the better way; we just took our choice.

Now we began to pass little villages and colonists' settlements and grizzled Italian peasants and their families were running into the road to greet us. In the hysterical enthusiasm of their welcome we did not at first understand why they were so pleased to see us. But it soon came out. As soon as the Italian army had gone, the Arabs had attacked their farmhouses, looted their goods, raped their women. Desperately they begged us not to leave them alone. One man, old enough to be my grandfather, literally wept on his knees to me, pleading with me to stay the night.

We couldn't stop. For us the stupendous background of the advance dwarfed these personal problems which meant all the world to them. And yet as they stood there weeping and offering us handkerchiefs filled with eggs, I realized that there had come into the campaign a new element, more real and fundamental than any before. So far the fighting had been as free and unencumbered as a boxing match in a ring. Now it was intruding into private lives.

But in any case, what was the solution to this problem? The Italians were the enemy. This land belonged originally to the Libyan Arabs and they were supposed to be our friends. They had been maltreated by the Italians and they very naturally looked on us as deliverers. To them it was the most natural thing in the world to loot the Italian peasants at their first opportunity, and they fully expected our approval.

No one had warned us of this problem; no one had told us whether we were on the Italians' side or the Arabs'. We could only shrug our shoulders, ask the Arabs to behave, and drive on.

We turned off the road to glance briefly at the astounding ruins of Cyrene and eat a picnic lunch in the vast hotel there. Then we heard that the northern branch of the main road was blocked while the southern branch was open, so we packed up our lunch hastily and set off again to catch up the army.

That evening the Italians fought just one more action — their last before Bengasi. It was in itself a very small affair. But I happened to be one of the principal victims.

All afternoon we bowled ahead along the fine main road as it twisted through the hills, and Geoffrey, who was driving, gradually wormed his way through to the head of the column. At odd moments the leading patrols were capturing prisoners and Alan and I, who seemed to be the only people there who could speak Italian, were called on to interrogate them. The advance was going forward at a vertiginous speed, and it began to be urgently necessary for us to know what was ahead.

We talked to a dapper Italian lieutenant who had driven from Barce that afternoon, and he swore the road was clear. So we told him: "You will get into your truck and drive two hundred yards ahead of the British column." We watched him closely but he did not blench or try to talk himself out of it. He climbed quietly into his truck and started off. So we assumed he had been telling the truth and did not bother about him any more.

A handful of armoured cars began to race on ahead and Geoffrey and Alan and I went with them. "Am I responsible for your lives?" the Major in charge asked us. "Of course not," we answered, so he told us to come along.

The kilometre stones said twelve to Barce when we ran into trouble. We were travelling third in the procession, and as we rounded a corner we saw that the two armoured cars ahead of us had stopped and men in blue-green uniforms were running up the road and away into the bushes. The road had been hacked up ahead and the long blue-black cases of Italian mines lay stacked in the gutter, ready to be buried.

It didn't seem important. We had merely caught up with the Italian rear-guard laying a mine field. Men jumped from the armoured cars and began grubbing up the mines, tossing them carelessly away into the bushes. No one gave a thought to the Italians—it was tacitly assumed they had fled.

Then we saw a bunch of them in the bushes higher up the road. They were not fleeing. They were just standing there looking at us.

"Give 'em a burst," someone shouted, and at that moment it all started.

My legs had carried me automatically across the road, up the bank to the left and into the woods before my mind had worked it all out. We were being ambushed. Italian bullets and shells were screaming down the road, bursting violently on the metal of the armoured cars, ripping through the windscreens and bonnets of the trucks, sizzling through the trees above us. First one, then another armoured car burst explosively into flame. A man was moaning bestially in the gutter near me. The Italians were firing at almost point-blank range.

Then I saw Geoffrey hurrying up and down the line of cars, apparently looking for something inside them. And a second later I saw that our driver, who had been riding on the baggage in the back of the truck, was lying helpless in the road.

Alan and I reached him and dragged him to the side while Geoffrey continued his search for a first-aid kit. The skin of the man's arm was slit open and his raw flesh was bulging horribly out. We cut off the sleeves of his greatcoat and his sweater and his shirt and Alan took off a bandage he had on his own sore knee and roughly bound up the wound. The firing had died down, but now it started again. And it was quickly clear enough that we were the sole target.

Geoffrey raced back with a first-aid kit and threw himself down beside us. We were lying, all four of us, side by side just off the road. The ground sloped up for, I suppose, six inches ahead of us and then there were some thin, straggly bushes. That was all the cover we had. Alongside of us our truck was being blown to bits piecemeal. They were putting anti-tank gun shells into it and the crack of their explosions made us wince spasmodically. Another armoured car burst into flames. The Italians were so near that we could hear their voices, and feel the blast of their guns on our faces.

Twice Geoffrey jerked convulsively but he said nothing. Then some Arabs who had somehow got mixed up in it all went screaming away over the hillside. Then something struck me hard on the back of the thigh and I knew I was hit and I lay and waited for the wave of pain to sweep over me. But I felt nothing but a little dull ache and some wetness and I knew it couldn't be bad. So I began to worry about how I had now twice been hit this war and each time in the behind, which was not a very creditable place to have wounds.

I held my field glasses in front of my head in an absurd effort to protect myself. But it was soon evident that it was madness to stay here at all. Our only hope was to run for it. Alan and I took the wounded man by the ankles and dragged him a few yards through the bushes to where the cover was better. Then we all got to our feet and bolted.

The Italians fired wildly at us as we went, but it was getting towards dusk and the visibility was poor. Then we found a deep-dug trench and we dropped into it. Geoffrey was hit through the wrist and in the leg, but he was still holding the first-aid kit so I broke an ampule of iodine and poured it into the holes the bullets had made. We clamped a wound dressing on the driver's arm. Then we started off again.

The Italians got in one more harmless burst at us before we rounded the bend and were safe. But the driver was weak and in pain and we had to make haste for it seemed likely that we should be pursued. There was danger, too, from British patrols for we were well in front of our own front lines. We stumbled on in the gathering darkness, I supporting the driver and Alan helping Geoffrey, not daring to speak above a whisper or light a cigarette or pause a moment to rest.

We had been going a good two miles when we heard voices. We hid for a little and listened. We couldn't distinguish the words but the intonation was calm and level and unmistakably English. We shouted to them and they shouted back reassuringly. So we limped to the road and climbed into their Bren-gun carrier and rode back to an Advanced Dressing Station.

They dressed our wounds and took Geoffrey and the driver away in an ambulance. But my wound was nothing at all, and after it had been bandaged, Alan and I were given a tin of Italian tunny fish for our supper and a couple of stretchers to sleep on. We lay there and argued foolishly about why we had not run up a white flag and surrendered. It was so much the obvious thing to do, for we were entirely unarmed, and yet the idea had occurred to neither of us. We couldn't decide why not.

At dawn we went back to the scene of the ambush and stared forlornly at the ruins of our truck. It was hardly recognizable as a truck and everything we possessed was riddled through and through with bullets. With genuine sadness I gathered from the road the little heap of intricate mechanism that had been my typewriter. It had accompanied me round most of Europe and I remembered how it had been rescued from the Sunderland, blown to the deck of a battleship by a gun blast, dropped in a slit trench in Crete, suffered a hundred mishaps, and still gone on working. My tin hat — which had fortunately not been on my head — was torn into shapeless strips of metal. Only my pair of Italian naval trousers was untouched. They had been packed behind the forty-pound Parmesan cheese and though the cheese was as full of holes as a Gruyère, nothing had gone right through. I put on the trousers at once, for my own were torn and bloodstained.

Alan and I sat there miserably till some of our colleagues came along and rescued us. We were beggars now, for we had no bedding, no typewriters, no clothes, no food, nothing. But Bengasi was less than a hundred miles away, and they charitably took us aboard their trucks for the last stage.

ii

We could not get down into Barce, for the Italian engineers had dynamited the cliff road too well. For a little while we stood above it watching an ammunition train blowing up in the station. Then someone found an alternative route and we slithered down a steep muddy track onto the plain below.

We spent that night in a deserted railway station and next morning we were off again early. Cold bitter rain was slashing down across the bare countryside and the thick red mud of the fields was turning quickly to a slimy bog. Again and again whole columns would get stuck and no one could move until the first truck had been dug out. Often a vehicle would suddenly spin round, the driver wrenching helplessly at the wheel, and start going the other way. The rain changed to a stinging hail which beat our faces into a cold numb misery. Frenziedly men filled in dynamite craters and collected rocks to build impromptu causeways for their wheels. Again and again the speed of the huge column slowed down to walking pace and it seemed impossible to go on. But nothing was going to beat the Australians that day. They were filled with a burning determination to get through to Bengasi before nightfall, and often it seemed that the sheer urgency of their desire carried them through rather than any physical means.

On we slithered all morning through this desolate land which, with its long rows of lean poplars, looked curiously like Flanders. At lunchtime we reached El Abiar, and the regiment which had been stationed in its fortified barracks had clearly only just gone. We rebuilt the fire in a kitchen stove that was still warm and made ourselves tea while the Brigadier paced up and down gnawing a piece of cheese impatiently. Then we went on again.

A little before evening, in another icy downpour, we reached the cliff above Benina and looked across to Bengasi itself. It was a screen of white buildings framed in green down by the sea, with the twin domes of its cathedral half-obscured by soaring columns of smoke. We gazed at it almost incredulously while the sappers struggled to repair the road down the cliff. Then we jolted down to Benina's great air-port.

A score or more of wrecked machines lay scattered round it and two of them had swastikas painted on them — a sinister foretaste of the future. The giant hangars were twisted and roofless from bombing. But there were rooms with beds in them in the little pink bungalows where the airmen had lived, and here we camped for the night.

For the Brigadier would not let us enter Bengasi immediately. Having got so far, he wanted to do this thing with due ceremony. It was, after all, easily the biggest town captured by British arms this war, and it must be properly and formally surrendered. So he sent in a major who returned with the Mayor, the Bishop and the Chief of Police, and all the details were arranged that evening. The date was February 6.

We drove in next morning through sunny rain-washed streets. Yesterday's downpour had cleaned the façades of the white villas and blocks of flats, and washed the dust off the leaves of the trees. There were men and women in European dress on the sidewalks and they smiled at us and pointed us out to their children and some of them clapped. I was bubbling with excitement. We swished over the wet roadways through the Opera Square, along the arcaded main shopping street, and drew up in front of the Municipio. Mayor, Bishop and Chief of Police were duly waiting there in full regalia, to hand over the keys of the city.

It was only a short ceremony. The Brigadier simply told the local authorities what buildings he proposed to occupy, and asked that the normal police arrangements should continue. There was in fact nothing else he could do. He had not come prepared for the occupation of cities, and he could not spare any troops for garrison work. There was still a big Italian army at large somewhere, and all British troops must be fighting troops. Bengasi must be got back to normal as quickly as possible, and as far as possible it must run itself.

Then a company of Australian infantry marched into the square, halted, turned left and stood at ease. They were muddy and dusty and tired and unshaven, stained with the toil and the sweat of days of desert fighting. I don't know what the Bengasi populace had expected to see, but they were probably prepared for a few gala uniforms, a band playing martial music, some attempt at pomp and showmanship. At first they just stared. Then the drama of it reached them. As conquerors these mud-stained men were a brilliant understatement. And the people, as though in spite of themselves, lifted up their hands and clapped.

Then the parade dispersed and that amazing national resilience of the Italians came into play. They were conquered. So what? They still had shops to open, hotels to manage, profits to make. Five minutes after the city had been handed over, barbers had taken down their shutters and were shaving Australian soldiers. At the Hotel d'Italia we simply signed our names in the register and had our tattered kit carried up to our rooms. It all seemed wrong that conquerors should have to pay for their breakfast and give a tip to a vanquished waiter. But what could you do? The

Australians, who had picked up thousands and thousands of Italian lire in the earlier parts of the campaign, meekly paid.

So with an acute sense of bathos we occupied Bengasi. There was nothing left to do but see the sights. We looked at the wrecked ships in the harbour and admired the fine appointments of the Hotel Berenice, which had been Italian G.H.Q. We gathered details about the panic-stricken last days of the city when, as the tiny Australian force approached, Graziani had gathered the remnants of his huge army and fled southwards. We penetrated to the Arab quarter and haggled for eggs and yellow-leather slippers and cheap tinware. It was more like tourism than war.

iii

But there was an epilogue, an epilogue so brilliant that it went far toward eclipsing anything else in the whole campaign. The Seventh Armoured Division had indeed made its trip straight through the desert from Mechili to the sea. And it had cut off all the remaining Italian forces in Cyrenaica and smashed them utterly.

The Seventh set out from Mechili on February 4 to do nearly two hundred miles across completely unmapped country. An advance patrol had gone forward the day before and returned to report that the country was "impossible." But this advice was swept aside. It just had to be possible. General Creagh said, "Give us enough petrol and ammunition and I and my men will starve if necessary."

The maps were just blanks, so the only thing to do was to set a compass course and stick to it. The advance patrol had not lied: in all ordinary circumstances the going would have been considered impossible. But just as the Australians had been irresistibly determined to get to Bengasi, so nothing was going to stop the Seventh now. For mile after mile they juddered over great slabs of sharp uneven rock. Then they crossed belts of soft fine sand which engulfed vehicles up to their axles. Sand-storms blew up and the trucks had to keep almost touching if they were not to lose one another. Whole convoys lurched off into the gloom and only re-established contact hours later. It was freezingly cold and the latter half of the division had to contend with fierce, icy showers. All kit had been cut to the bone and there were no extra blankets or greatcoats and scarcely more than a glass of water per man per day.

The main column reached Fort Msus at one o'clock next morning, and there they rested a little. But by dawn they were on their way again, this time split into two sections: one went south-west towards Beda Fomm and the other north-west towards Solluch.

Thus it was that early on the afternoon of February 5 the Seventh Armoured Division cut the road in two places some fifty miles south of Bengasi. And they found they had straddled the entire remaining Italian army, sandwiching it between their two prongs.

The battle that began then was long and bewildering, fought by the British with unquenchable courage and an audacity that sometimes blossomed into impudence; by the Italians with some bravery but never with any organized coherence. The British had the luck they deserved. Even the first shot was lucky for the columns met head on and the leading Italian truck was knocked sideways across the road. So the Italians started the battle in a traffic jam.

But they were enormously superior in numbers. In that column there were 216 guns of all descriptions, 112 tanks, over 1500 lorries. The 20,000 men included the commanding officer General Tellera (Graziani was back in Tripoli), seven other generals, and even a number of women and children who were being evacuated from Bengasi. Tellera had known something of the British Armoured Column at Mechili, but he could not believe that it was dangerous. "They can't do it," he had said, "and even if they do do it, we still have two days to spare." As a matter of fact, he had not even two hours to spare. For if he had been there two hours earlier, he would have arrived before the British and the result might have been very different.

The battle raged for thirty-six hours. The Italian column was stretched for ten miles along the road, and at first it had only a tiny British flying column against it. On paper the Italians were in an overwhelmingly superior position, but once again the surprise and vigour of the British attack seemed to throw them into a state of hypnosis from which they never recovered. The British fought the battle on the basis of supreme mobility. It was fatal for them to settle down in any one spot and form a strong-point, for the Italians were immeasurably stronger in gun power. British tanks raged up and down the Italian column, keeping a constant current of confusion and destruction rippling along its whole length. Once a squadron of tanks raced the whole ten miles of the battle-field, firing all the way, in order to replenish their petrol and ammunition, then shot their way back again.

The Italians began to fight desperately and bitterly, and this time they did not surrender. Had they at any moment fought scientifically they must at least have been able to back their way out. But they could not even do that. Impossible as it may seem, the little British column got the big Italian army trapped in the middle of a flat open plain.

Once the Italian tanks massed for a counterattack that might have been serious, and British sappers just managed to lay a mine field in front of it in time. A large contingent strove to escape by a track leading down near the sea-coast, but the Second Rifle Brigade spread itself out over three and a half miles and resolutely blocked the way. Gradually, in fighting so swift-moving and confused that a complete tactical picture is simply not possible, the Italian force crumbled. Prisoners began streaming into our lines. General Tellera himself was hit by a bullet and died on the field. And on the afternoon of the second day Headquarters received the thrilling message: "Bergonzoli is in the bag. What do I do now?" The reply was sent: "Good work. Now get Graziani."

By nightfall on the second day the battle was no longer a battle but a fitful splutter of isolated engagements. Early next morning the Italians rallied all their tanks and made one last desperate thrust. But it faltered and broke on the defences which the British had got together during the night, and that was the end. At nine o'clock the message was sent: "The enemy has been completely eliminated."

The battle-field was a fantastic ten-mile trail of wreckage. Even now the blowing desert sands have not covered it all, and as men drive by along the coast road, they can still dimly visualize the fearful slaughter of that day. Only the bodies have gone, and a few odd things which the Arabs considered valuable. But there still remain the tanks, guns, lorries, uniforms, flags, petrol drums, hand-grenades, rifles, hillocks of ammunition, and an unbelievable amount of what is neither more nor less than rubbish.

In the little one-horse village of Solluch I saw the final scene of all this. It was a shabby, tawdry place at the best of times and today the rain had turned it into a sea of mud. Crouching miserably beneath the trees were thousands of prisoners, and a bare white cottage near by was brimming with colonels, brigadiers, and generals. I counted six generals but I looked in vain for the one I wanted to see. Finally someone directed me out into the yard. And there at last, sitting hunched up in a closed car, was Bergonzoli.

But the beard that had bristled so fiercely that day at Andorra in the Pyrenees had no life left in it now. The gleam in his eye was quenched. His face was grey and haggard with misery. He was no longer "Electric Whiskers," but just a broken old man who had failed. It was impossible not to feel sorry for him, for he had undoubtedly fought better than any of the others. His eyes lit up for a moment when I talked of Spain, and for a little he dwelt nostalgically on his triumphs then. But he shrank back into misery again when he looked out of the car at the grey rain falling softly into the muddy yard which was his prison.

He told me at last how he had escaped from Bardia. All our wild surmises had been wrong. He had simply walked out on foot with his entire staff. He said, "I passed close to your men while they were lighting fires and cooking and digging trenches but no one seemed to take any notice. We hid in caves by day and walked at night and it took us five days to reach Tobruk. I had to jettison my

Staff Major who was a stout man and couldn't stand the pace. But all the rest of us got away safely.

"I escaped from Tobruk in the last available plane and from Derna in a baby Fiat. But this time I was not so lucky. We delayed our departure too long for we did not believe that you could cut us off. You were too quick for us and too strong."

A day later he and the other generals were flown back to Cairo in a Bombay transport plane. I wanted to go too for I had no clothes, no typewriter, no food or bedding and it was extremely doubtful whether any of our despatches were getting back. In any case I was desperately tired. So I tried to get a trip with the generals. Three of us wanted to go and there was only one place so we had to toss for it. I won but somehow in the confusion I did not get the place and the Bombay went off without me. Eddie Ward of the B.B.C. and I were left standing there, feeling we might remain there for weeks for there were no organized communications. But a chance remark overheard in a bar an hour later put us in touch with the pilot of a Blenheim. And with his help we managed to hitch-hike our way back to Cairo.

CHAPTER 7

Assignment in Greece

So WAVELL's gamble came off, with unbelievable success. In sixty-two days a great army had been destroyed. There were 133,295 prisoners in our hands and a stupendous quantity of war material lay strewn over the desert we had conquered. It had cost us all in all a little under 3000 casualties. How was it possible that so few should defeat so many so quickly? The answer was important, for whichever way things went there was still plenty of fighting to be done in and around the Mediterranean.

In the last analysis Wavell's army won because it was overwhelmingly superior in the only two spheres where it could be superior: in quality of leadership and quality of individual fighting troops. It was on this superiority that Wavell had gambled so heavily and so well. Victory came through non-material, impalpable things, largely qualities of the mind: through a disciplined audacity, an intuitive awareness of when and where risks could be taken, a sure instinct of success, a knowledge, still only half-formulated, of how to handle the desert, a capacity for taking advantage of the enemy's mistakes. A lot of it could be classed as sheer guts. And the enemy's mistakes, which were numerous and profound, gave the British again and again the opportunities they were seeking.

From start to finish Graziani had been wrong. In the first place his Intelligence Service was hopelessly inefficient. There was no excuse for that, for British G.H.Q. was in the capital of a non-belligerent country, a country with an Italian population sixty thousand strong, with neutral but pro-Axis Legations functioning (the Vichy French, for instance). It should have been a wonderful field for Fifth Column work. But at no time can Graziani possibly have appreciated the pitiful smallness of Wavell's forces. He had no inkling of the attack on December 9. It must admittedly be difficult to run an accurate Intelligence Service for a nation with a natural propensity to florid exaggeration, where the reports of a patrol or an air raid can never be taken as literally true, where wishful thinking has been developed to such an art. But the Italians need not have failed so abjectly.

Next, Graziani's handling of the desert was wrong. His spray of luxury camps round Sidi Barrani was utterly inappropriate to the circumstances. He should have seen the weak point in it long before the British did. But he was blinded by the magnitude and brilliance of his own plans, by the weakness of his Intelligence Service, by sheer military disability.

Then, when the crust of their positions had been broken, the Italians showed an unbelievable incapacity for organizing the most rudimentary resistance. They were, it seemed, paralyzed by the swiftness and energy of the British movement. Troops with any innate fighting qualities could at least have saved themselves from being captured. But the Italians were led like sheep to the slaughter.

Graziani's next mistake was his experiment in the fortress-area theory. As he handled it, it was almost bound to fail. He condemned whole divisions to a passive, negative role behind fortifications, and just left them sitting there. What could he hope they would do? Did he intend ultimately to bring a mobile armoured force into the field, attack the British in the rear, and raise the siege? He never showed any signs of even contemplating it.

Mechanically, too, the fortress-area theory was dubious. It involved spreading the defenders equally round, say, thirty miles of perimeter; and it permitted the attackers to throw the full concentrated weight of their fire power against one mile. With this enormous local superiority the attacker was almost certain to make a penetration. And once a penetration had been made and exploited the fortress was punctured, the rest of the perimeter was exposed to attack from the rear, the whole defensive system collapsed. That had been proved convincingly enough at Bardia. It was then sheer madness to try the same thing again at Tobruk.

Having flung away the bulk of his forces, Graziani at last looked facts in the face. He realized that Cyrenaica was almost certainly lost to him and that he could not save it by defending first one place, then another. But he still had that large, well-equipped army with which he fled southward from Bengasi. He could have put that into the field to meet the small, tired British forces which came against him, and he should have had a very reasonable chance of defeating them in open battle. Yet even that he dared not do. He must by now have lost all confidence in his men and in himself. His only thought was flight.

And having chosen flight, it was criminal incompetence for the Italian generals to let themselves be trapped. The most elementary reconnaissance precautions could have warned them. But right to the last they blundered, and the British adroitly took advantage of every mistake they made.

A very large proportion of the blame must be borne by Marshal Graziani himself. For these were mistakes of principle, of theory, of grand strategy, not local, temporary blunders but the wholesale misconception and mismanagement of a campaign. He was a spectacular general with as high a reputation as anyone in the Italian army. But an analysis of his rise to fame is very significant: he had ruthlessly quelled the Tripolitanian revolt, cruelly occupied Cyrenaica, crushed the Senussi (the Libyan Arabs who belong to a peculiarly austere Moslem sect), led the Southern Italian armies to victory in the Abyssinian War, and finally staged one of the most horrible massacres of contemporary history when patriots tried to kill him in Addis Ababa. All these were colonial campaigns, waged against primitive, under-armed peoples. And Graziani had made the mistake of trying to wage a colonial campaign against Wavell.

This whole first Cyrenaican victory, and in particular Graziani's mistakes, offered material for the development of a new technique of desert warfare. Tremendous emphasis had been laid on the importance of mobility. Graziani had been strongly place-conscious — he had instinctively tried to cling to Sidi Barrani, Bardia, Tobruk. British experience showed that possession of tracts of territory meant nothing. The vital thing was to stay unceasingly mobile, with the irreducible minimum of fixed points and permanent installations. It meant cutting kit and comforts to the bone, and it called for extreme motorization and the development of special transport equipped to carry large stores of petrol and water.

The campaign hinted strongly at the fallacy of the fortress-area theory, and at the value of quick, accurate information. It seemed to show that anyone who took an initiative stood an almost disproportionately good chance of getting away with it. It offered only negative clues as to the best method of defence in the desert, for the Italians had always failed. But it stressed strongly the importance of absolutely first-class war material.

In the desert tanks and trucks and guns had to stand up to much harder conditions than in a European theatre of war. Workshops and repair facilities were necessarily rare and sketchy. If the machines were not composed of first-class materials and workmanship — special designs for the desert were obviously desirable — then breakdowns were certain and a whole campaign might be endangered. Wavell's army of the winter of 1940 was very much better equipped than the army of the summer of 1940. All through the autumn convoys had been rounding the Cape of Good Hope and unloading tanks and guns and trucks in Suez and Port Said. The army finally went into battle not inferior to the Italians in quality of arms. The enemy had nothing comparable to the British infantry tanks. Their field guns could not touch the British twenty-five-pounders. All the way through our smaller trucks were more successful than the heavy-weight Italian Diesel burners. Against the Italians our war-machines and equipment, even allowing for the discrepancy in numbers, were just about good enough. But that only proved that Italy was simply not a first-class military power. Against a German army the British equipment would have been useless.

In this first campaign the air forces had played only a relatively minor role; the British because it was so small and embryonic, the Italian because its commanders seemed to have little notion of how they ought to use it. The British were now flying Hurricanes, Blenheims and Wellingtons, technically better machines than the Italians had. But Air-Marshal Sir Arthur Longmore had to split his forces between East Africa, the Western Desert, and Greece; and that meant that each of the three sub-forces was dangerously small. He conceived it the function of the R.A.F. in the desert to neutralize the enemy air force, and it was done with a success that left the British ground forces almost entirely free of serious air attacks. The Italian fighters and bombers were sought out and destroyed not so much in the air as on the ground. They were pinned to their air fields by systematic raiding, and when they did succeed in taking the air, they would only venture out in great circuses of bombers, heavily escorted by fighters, which dropped their bombs all together without any apparent relation to what was happening on the ground.

There was an inspiring "Dawn Patrol" atmosphere about the R.A.F. squadrons in the desert in those days. They were living an uncomfortable hand-to-mouth life in dusty huts and tents, and if ever they met the enemy they could always count on being heavily outnumbered. Yet there was a casual, happy-go-lucky, almost schoolboy air in their bars and mess tents; a passion for nicknames, a love of absurd trophies, a style of conversation that was to a great extent highly specialized slang, a tendency to extravagant understatement when they spoke of their exploits. They had some very pretty air battles. Both sides were using biplane fighters until the arrival of the Hurricanes and they relied more on aerobatics than on speed. In fact, the Hurricane found itself at a disadvantage at first — it was too fast. The pilot would find that he had shot straight through the battle and out the other side while the Gladiators and Capronis were still whirling in fancy twists and spirals. The Capronis developed a technique of doing an abrupt side-slip when chased by a Hurricane, and the Hurricane then found that the tables had been turned and it was itself now being shot at from behind by the Caproni.

But very soon the monoplane fighter dominated the air. It was a domination based on quality rather than quantity, and it was still all on a very small scale. But there was enough air experience in that first campaign to show that the Italian air force was no more a really serious factor in the war than the Italian army.

ii

While the bells were still ringing out for the capture of Bengasi, Wavell was wrestling with fresh problems. So far he had not made a mistake. But now came questions of even greater range and scope than those he had faced before, questions whose purely military aspect was complicated by difficult political angles.

Three fronts had to be covered:—

First, in Italian East Africa there was a campaign already in full swing. On January 19 British troops under General Platt had invaded Eritrea, and things were going favourably. It was certainly desirable to finish what had been so well begun.

Second, there was the desert front. True, an army had been destroyed, but only half Libya had been conquered. Tripoli still remained.

Third, there was Greece. Britain had pledged help to Greece if she were attacked. And even as Bengasi fell, Greece had asked Britain to honour that pledge.

All three fronts had strong arguments in their favour. East Africa had a special political significance for South Africa. It had just been settled, not without opposition, that South African troops should serve outside the Union, though not outside Africa. Abyssinia was an ideal front on which to use them. And in view of the tricky internal political situation which Field-Marshal Smuts was trying to handle, it was highly desirable that the South African forces should start off with a quick, spectacular, and, it was hoped, a not too costly victory.

Away down on the confines of Tripolitania, the desert army

were waiting for the order to go ahead. It was true that their transport desperately needed overhauling, Bengasi Harbour was not capable of handling great quantities of supplies, weapons were worn out and no replacements were available. But the men of the army felt ready to try it. During those few days I spent in Bengasi after it fell, I had listened to the arguments for and against a dozen times, and always the arguments in favour of going on had won. It seemed then as though the whole of Tripolitania lay wide-open to us. Patrols had already scouted ahead as far as Sirte. The Italians were said to have no proper defensive line even round Tripoli, and the troops there were thought to be low-grade units doing duty as frontier guards on the Tunisian border.

Probably it would not have been so easy as that, for already the Germans were ferrying across an Armoured Division from Italy. Even now the Afrikakorps warehouses at Buerat were bulging with stores. Yet it is doubtful whether the Germans were ready to fight, whether they had had any training at all. And the prize was so tremendous.

There were some who caustically asked, what was the use to us of eight hundred more miles of desert? But the answer was clearly this: we were fighting not for deserts, but for the Mediterranean. The rapidly evolving relationship between air power and sea power made it axiomatic that whoever was to control the waters of the Mediterranean must control the air above it. And that could only be done by possessing fighter air fields along the coasts.

So primarily it was for its landing grounds that we needed the far-flung coast-line of Libya. But there was also the subsidiary argument that the complete elimination of the Italian Empire in Africa would greatly increase our freedom of action and release whole armies for use elsewhere. And if Libya were not eliminated now, it was morally certain that the whole campaign would have to be fought all over again. For Italy and this time Germany too would send across reinforcements until a powerful new army was built up.

Then there was Greece. In the face of the world Britain had promised aid to Greece and now Greece wanted it. All we had given Poland was a declaration of war against Germany over the radio, and the world was waiting to see what we would give Greece. The Greeks had said, in effect, "We want help, but — please — not just a token force. If you send anything, send us a real big army." They had hoped for something like half a million men, and had finally settled for a minimum of six divisions.

On paper Wavell barely had troops enough for one of these fronts. He saw that he must stretch them to cover at least two. Three was out of the question. But which two? It was a question which he in his purely military capacity could not be asked to solve. Anthony Eden and Sir John Dill, Chief of the Imperial General Staff, flew out from London and Smuts came up from Capetown. There were conferences all up and down the eastern end of the Mediterranean. General Wavell, Admiral Cunningham and Air-Marshal Longmore gave their opinions. There were talks in Athens, meetings with Turkish statesmen in Cyprus. And in the end Greece got it, Greece and Abyssinia. Once more Wavell was obliged, almost certainly against his military judgement, to take a gamble on Cyrenaica. This time he lost.

The arguments in favour of Greece were presumably overwhelming at the time. But it was my opinion then, and it still is, that we were wrong to go to Greece. For we could not send a force as large as the minimum the Greeks had asked for. And the British Empire then was in no state to afford mere heroical gestures.

The Greeks, that spring, were still fighting with epic courage up in their mountains. But they were nearing the end of their reserves of men and material and strength. Italy had had six months in which to recognize her mistakes, rectify them and start anew. Mussolini then had a reasonable prospect of beating the Greeks that summer — a prospect sufficiently reasonable to make him refuse the indignity of German help. The Germans were planning their attack on Russia, and they certainly did not welcome the notion of unnecessary additional fronts in Europe at that moment. They had no reason for fighting the Greeks. The Greeks might have held up the Italians, but they could not be considered a potential menace to Germany. A British army on European soil was entirely another matter. That was something the Italians could almost certainly not handle. Germany *had* to step in.

So, I believe, the British step precipitated the German march into Greece. It was argued afterwards that the British had slowed down the German programme by holding up the Wehrmacht in Greece. But the contrary is more plausible. The Germans entered Greece because the British had gone there, and they could hardly have advanced quicker had there been no British troops there at all. It was a question of days, that campaign, not months.

Finally, there is the question of our moral obligation to answer Greece's appeal. We were fighting, among other things, to uphold the sanctity of treaties and a standard of international decency. And it would have been very hard for us to break our solemn word to Greece and refuse the help she asked. But the point is we did not send the help she asked. We sent a force so small that its defeat was inevitable. We left Greece with nothing to thank us for. Her fate could not have been more terrible had no British soldier ever set foot on Greek soil. We lost part of the force we did send and all of its equipment—equipment which England herself could barely spare at the time and which could not be easily or quickly replaced. Those, remember, were desperate moments. Russia was not yet in the war. America was not in the war. Britain was fighting the Axis alone, and Britain could not afford to make costly gestures in the interests of her prestige abroad. In the event, Greece would have been better served had Britain kept her Middle East armies intact and concentrated on hastening the end of the war as a whole.

But that is all largely a personal opinion. Much of what happened could not have been accurately foreseen at the time the decision was taken to send troops to Greece. The German strength was still being under-estimated, and it was hoped that the Yugoslavs might come in on our side. The great thing was to have an army in Europe again. If Hitler was planning an invasion of England, then a British army advancing through the Balkans might provide a very important diversion. Perhaps the Turks would come in with us too. Down in this corner of the Balkans we might start such a blaze as would sweep all over Europe and bring us to the gates of Berlin. There was a negative angle to it as well. The Germans were incontestably massing armies in Rumania. But we did not then know for certain that their function was to invade Russia. There was a possibility that they might be destined for a drive down through Turkey to take the Middle East position in the rear. The Greek expedition would meet this threat half-way and perhaps stifle it altogether.

So, during that spring of 1941, the Middle East was fermenting with incipient activity. There was a wholesale reshuffle of divisions. Already in December the Fourth Indian Division had been removed from the desert to make way for the Sixth Australian Division, and sent down to Abyssinia. Now the Sixth in its turn was whisked back from the Tripolitanian frontier and sent across to Greece. The First New Zealand Division followed it. Both the Australian and New Zealand Governments had given their permission for their troops to be used in Europe. The seasoned Seventh Armoured Division came out of the desert and was shipped north across the Mediterranean. General Sir Henry Maitland Wilson was given command of the whole expedition. Everywhere training and equipping was going on apace. British gunners and technicians and auxiliary services were being groomed for action in mountains instead of deserts. Next on the list to go were the Seventh Australian Division and then the Polish Carpathian Brigade. But before they got over there it had become tragically obvious that there was no point in their going. And even if they had gone it would still have been a very small army, barely four whole divisions—much smaller than the minimum the Greeks had asked for.

There was an absurd pretence of secrecy about the whole thing. The German naval and military attachés in Athens were there to meet every British convoy as it arrived at Piræus. German diplomats strolled through the New Zealanders' camps, chatting to the men. Everybody knew. The American papers were full of it. But until the last minute we talked about the Greek expeditionary force almost in whispers, referring to it as the "W Force," and I was not allowed to ask my newspaper whether I should go with it.

But obviously I had to go, for this was now easily the biggest thing in the Middle East. On March 21 I wrote what I thought to be my last message about the desert — the Italian garrison in the tiny oasis of Jarabub, deep down inland along the Egyptian frontier, had finally surrendered the squalid mud village, the belt of scrawny palm trees, and the Senussi religious college which it had been defending for months.

CHAPTER 8

Three Defeats

In the sparkling, exhilarating air of Athens, my spirits revived. For the Greeks were taking their war with gaiety and humour. There had come to them in this hour of peril a deep personal dignity and self-assurance which would survive any military defeat they might suffer. They could be beaten as a nation, but they were spiritually insured against being beaten as a people.

This was inspiring, and so was the consciousness of being once more back on European soil. Athens that spring was fantastically lovely. No city is more superbly set. On three sides it is cupped by thyme-covered hills and on the fourth it looks down to the wine-dark sea. Away out beyond Salamis and Ægina the mountains and islands are banked in purple waves. The sunshine was pale-gold and warm and the breeze that blew down from the mountains smelled of pine trees and eucalyptus.

For the moment we just waited: waited for the British Expeditionary Force to finish arriving or for the Germans to declare war, whichever should happen first. And meanwhile it was strangely exciting to watch men in British, Australian or New Zealand uniforms climbing over the white marble ruins of the Parthenon, or strolling among the orange trees of Constitution Square. Eddie Ward and I went out for a week-end to Sunium, where the temple of Poseidon rears its pale columns on a flower-strewn headland. Cutting through the dark sea below it, where Attic pilots used to cast their propitiatory garlands, came convoys of British merchantmen and slim grey destroyers escorting them into port.

But even while we waited our hold on Cyrenaica was already crumbling. Three British armoured cars patrolling down beyond

Agedabia had met and passed three German armoured cars on the main road. All six had slithered to a standstill and then deployed symmetrically into the desert according to textbook tactics. In a series of formal movements they succeeded in disentangling themselves and the British cars sped off home to report that the Afrikakorps was now in the front line.

On May 24 the Germans occupied El Agheila and established a foothold in Cyrenaica. A few days later they were seen driving eastwards into the desert in a big powerful column. The British were at first not alarmed. It seemed so improbable that the Germans or anyone else could try to reconquer Cyrenaica so soon. "Just reconnaissance," they said when the reports came in.

But the Germans meant business. In all Cyrenaica there were now only the Ninth Australian Division and elements of the newly arrived Second Armoured Division from England. Wavell had stretched his resources to provide armies for Greece and Abyssinia and Cyrenaica had been left almost bare. Against the tiny British force there, the new German commander, General Erwin Rommel, now borrowed Wavell's tactics. He had little more than one armoured division, but he used it with extreme mobility, extreme speed and extreme concentration of fire power. The British were simply not strong enough to challenge the Germans in open battle. If they lost it would be the end of Egypt. They had no option but to retreat.

It was a swift, confused retreat. Rommel split his forces, sending one column curling back to the sea-coast to occupy Bengasi and the other due east to bypass the Green Mountains. The British in Bengasi had to race back along the coast road to avoid being cut off. Demolitions were spasmodic and unsystematic. One British armoured unit had to abandon its tanks because its fuel dump was blown up too soon. There were misunderstandings and mishaps and mistakes. But there was no real battle for the British forces had not been geared for defensive action.

The Germans were in Bengasi on April 4. And the day after Generals O'Connor and Neame, the senior British commanders, were cut off by German motorcyclists and captured while their staff-car was held up in a traffic jam. General Gambier-Parry was unexpectedly trapped down inland at Fort Mechili and taken in his tent. It was all going as badly as it could go.

But in Athens we paid little attention to all this, for bigger things were happening. Early on the morning of Sunday, April 5, the sirens wailed to announce that Germany had declared war on Greece and Yugoslavia. In an hour crowds were demonstrating outside the German Legation and parading the streets. When I went out to take a despatch to the censorship office I was seized by a cheering mob and chaired on their shoulders. But there was a touch of hysteria about this enthusiasm now. They had honestly hated the Italians and had marched out against them with gladness and confidence. But for Germany they felt a certain respect. Remember, the Greeks had had years of totalitarian government under Metaxas, and it was not hatred of Fascist dogma that inspired them to fight Italy. It was a deep-seated traditional dislike, a local Mediterranean fear and jealousy, and in the last resort a defence of their independence. Their hatred for Italy was emotional, not intellectual, and they could not have the same feeling about Germany. Moreover they were intelligent people, and they knew that the German army was not the Italian army.

And so that morning there was a false note in the popular enthusiasm, a subconscious subterfuge to tide them over the first realization that, unless the British pulled some miracle out of the hat, this was the end. Now they were beaten.

So when the wireless that evening gave the news about Cyrenaica, our minds had no room to digest it and appreciate its seriousness. We were standing on the roof of the King George Hotel watching the German bombers dive onto the harbour of Piræus. They made three attacks and in the third they put a bomb fair and square into a lighter laden with 250 tons of TNT. That explosion was beyond any description. When I drove down next day every house round the water-front had been blown backwards and twelve ships were still blazing in the port.

On April 12, when the Yugoslav army had already been split and destroyed and Salonika had fallen, Rommel's Afrikakorps by-passed Tobruk and came on to Bardia. But there the German momentum petered out and they came to a standstill. For one thing they were only a small force and their supply lines had become dangerously stretched. For another, the retiring Australian division had gone into Tobruk and shut itself up inside the perimeter. And that not only gave Rommel a permanent threat to his flank, but robbed him of the only supply port east of Bengasi.

So, even faster than it was conquered, Cyrenaica was lost. The losing of it cost us little in men and Rommel's success could not be compared with Wavell's for Wavell had destroyed an army. But the threat to Egypt was there again. Our first step towards real control of the Mediterranean, including air control, had been retraced. Most of the transport and equipment we had captured had been lost again, in addition to new equipment of our own. And the whole campaign would have to be fought all over again, this time against Germans as well as Italians.

ii

It was a bitter blow, and even the men fighting in the mountains of Greece had time to recognize it. One day near the Pass of Thermopylæ I found myself sharing a slit trench with a New Zealander and an Australian. The New Zealander was dark and quiet but vehement when he spoke and he was called MacGregor. The Australian was tall and narrow-headed and lantern-jawed and he said his name was Peter. Our trench was in the corner of a field of growing corn and the cliffs of the pass rose dizzily above us. We had been there most of the morning, for German bombers were fooling about overhead all the time. And we fell to discussing some news we had heard on the radio about Cyrenaica.

Peter said, "I fought for all those places and I hate to think of them being lost again. How could it happen?"

I suggested: "We haven't enough troops to do everything. If we had stayed there we couldn't have come here."

MacGregor said: "Why did we come here? I volunteered to fight. But I object to being used as part of a political experiment."

I said: "It wasn't just a political experiment. It was largely a military experiment."

"A political guinea-pig," said MacGregor, searching for metaphors, "a bit of cheese in a military mousetrap."

"No," I said, "things might have turned out quite differently. Supposing the Yugoslav army had had a chance to organize proper defence, supposing Turkey had come in, supposing a lot of things."

Peter said: "Yes, supposing. But they should have been able to foresee all this."

I said: "If they could have foreseen all this, they would not have sent us here."

A plane droned over us machine-gunning and we ducked as the line of explosive bullets came fizzing through the cornfield.

"The bastards," said Peter. "Anyway, I don't like to think of the Germans being in Derna. I was in the attack we made along the beach, when we came into the Italians' fixed lines of fire. I lost a lot of friends."

"Were you there?" I said. "I was up on the cliff. That was bad, wasn't it?"

"Yes, that was bad," said Peter. "But not nearly as bad as this."

MacGregor opened a tin of sardines and passed it round with a water bottle full of wine.

"Do you think we shall get out of this?" he asked.

I said: "It's too early to talk of that. We are going to hold a shorter line from Thermopylæ to Delphi. And then I suppose we can hold the Isthmus of Corinth, and then somewhere in the Peloponnesos and then Crete."

He persisted: "But we shall have to try and get out in the end, won't we? It's just a matter of simple mathematics. We know how strong we are ourselves and we know what we are up against. It's straight mathematics. Either we stay where we are and all get killed or we retreat and try and get away."

"That sounds a little defeatist," I said.

"No," said MacGregor. "It isn't defeatist. It's just a matter of knowing how things are. It doesn't make any difference to the way I fight. I don't think my side as a whole is going to be defeated. But I am sure that we here are going to be defeated."

I saw four bombs fall from an aeroplane that flew over the edge of the cliff and they landed with dull thuds on the road just near us. "Duds," I said and stood up to look but they pulled me down again just as the bombs exploded.

"They are dive-bomber bombs with a sort of delayed action," said Peter. "It's a pity we haven't some dive bombers."

MacGregor screwed up his eyes and gazed across the flat blue water towards the mountains of Euboia. "There's a Hurricane," he said.

"I don't believe it," said Peter without turning his head. Then he looked at me and added, "I try hard to be fair about the R.A.F. I know perfectly well they have few planes and few air fields and they're hopelessly outnumbered and they're operating nearly all the time. But when you don't ever see them, you get to feeling they aren't there at all. I know I ought not to feel bitter but I do feel bitter just the same."

An old Greek shepherd, with a wrinkled face of great character and dignity, came wandering past, grumbling because his flock of sheep had been machine-gunned. Peter looked up at him and said, "Poor bastard. I don't suppose he knows what it's all about at all. You know, I still can't help worrying about Derna."

iii

The detailed course of the fighting in Greece is irrelevant to African campaigns. Only the beginning and the end are important — the quantity of men and arms that went there and the quantity that came back. Into those limits must be compressed the tragedy, and the bright flashes of individual glory, that marked the last days of April, 1941. A bare statement of figures must cover those last hours in Athens when the Greek women, who might have been bitter and resentful, came to us weeping in the streets and kissed us good-bye. Statistics must conceal these things: the anguish, almost the shame, of leaving these people who must stay and face the enemy while we might go; the long drive through the scented Greek night, past the blazing air field of Eleusis, over the Corinth Canal, down into the Peloponnesos; the long day crouching in another cornfield while the German planes bombed and bombed and dived to drop mines into the harbour from which we must evacuate; the sight of a whole countryside filled with men deliberately destroying their trucks and cars, blowing out the barrels of their guns, pushing their tanks over cliffs, burning their petrol and stores, tearing up their blankets and bedding, reducing everything they had to a rifle and one tiny haversack; a Major sitting on a wall in the evening sunlight and telling us, "If you are bombed on the way to the harbour you will keep your ranks; anyone who falls out will be left behind; you will carry your wounded and leave your dead"; the long cold wait lying in utter darkness on the cobbles of the quayside and the sudden news that our ship had run aground in the harbour and we couldn't go; and the wild relief when we are allotted to another vessel; sleeping under a mess-room table in a freighter while bombing raids alternated with the burial of men who had died of wounds aboard; the almost miraculous safe arrival in Crete; and a thousand other memories and impressions that go to make up the full story of that evacuation.

The figures that mattered as far as the African front was concerned were these. General Wilson took just about 60,000 fully armed and equipped men to Greece. About 45,000 men got out with their rifles and whatever clothes they happened to have on their backs.

Then at the end of May there was Crete where the Germans, in the most futuristic exhibition of warfare so far, tried an experiment in air invasion. Crete, too, was in a great many respects a British mistake. There was a case for defending Crete — and Crete might have been defended and held if there had been sufficient preparation. There was a case for abandoning Crete and evacuating all our forces there with their equipment. But there was no case at all for half-defending it.

When the survivors came back from Crete, an exhausted friend of mine called on me for a bath and a meal and a bed. Afterwards we talked deep into the night. And in the morning I wrote an article which I am still astonished that the censors passed. I said: —

> Crete must not happen again. It was not only aeroplanes we lacked, it was foresight. The Battle of Crete was lost not this May but last November. We occupied the island so that we could use Suda Bay as a naval base. But no serious attempt was ever made to fortify it.
>
> No shore batteries were set up and no system of prepared defences established to protect vital spots. For a few months the old last-war monitor *Terror* was in the bay as a floating fortress, but she was taken away around Christmas.
>
> Maleme Air Field was built in a few weeks, but in the ensuing months there were no attempts to make underground hangars, which alone could have protected aircraft. Even when whole squadrons of fighter planes were destroyed on the ground in Greece, nothing was done to improve protection at Maleme.
>
> After six months in Greece we had not got enough air fields even for our few planes. But within three weeks of occupying the country, the Nazis had taken into use landing grounds which we had rejected as unusable. [The most important of these was in the island of Melos.]
>
> A senior air-force officer yesterday said: "The Germans are quite ruthless. All male Greeks between the ages of 15 and 30 were conscripted to build air fields. The British don't do that — they behave too much like gentlemen."
>
> Crete has shown once again that we cannot afford to behave too much like gentlemen.
>
> In the circumstances Crete was untenable. Even Suda Bay was hardly worth anything to the navy after Nazi planes started a systematic series of blitz raids this spring. Warships just lay there as targets.
>
> Already on May 12 [the attack on Crete started May 20], our Intelligence knew that the invasion was being prepared. Troop

carriers stood wing-tip to wing-tip on the Greek air fields. An airborne division was massing in Athens. Something was going to be invaded, and it did not need much imagination to realize that Crete was going to be the victim.

There was time to pull out. It was quite clear that we could not supply air protection even for our two small air fields. But it was decided to fight.

Our men fought more bravely and took more punishment than any other troops this war. No one can charge Crete's defenders with having let the side down. They did all and more than could have been expected of them. But even the best troops get depressed when for days on end they see only enemy planes. They feel that they are being let down. And they start fighting solely to save their own lives and not to beat the enemy.

In the end, out of 27,550 men who defended Crete, 14,850 came back to the Middle East. Virtually all their equipment was lost. The navy had sustained losses so serious that from that moment the balance of naval power in the Mediterranean was against Britain. The air force had lost planes on the ground when the attack had first started and had lost more later by trying to fly Hurricanes across from Sidi Barrani with extra petrol tanks.

On the credit side we could point to the tremendous price the Germans had paid for Crete. They bought the island and its air fields for much more than it was worth. But they had to have it, for it still lay there as a potential British springboard back into Europe, and Hitler needed to have his hands free to attack Russia in the summer. The Nazi Intelligence Service had placed the defenders of Crete at about five thousand, and as soon as they started attacking, they found out that it was going to be a bigger thing than they anticipated. But having once begun, they had to go through with it. And they poured in transport planes and parachutists until it was certain that they had used all their immediate reserves. That at any rate was at least a temporary guarantee of immunity for the Middle East.

Finally Crete had taught us lessons. And the main lesson was not, as seemed obvious at the time, the details of Germany's aerial invasion technique. The main lesson was the paramount importance of fighter aircraft and the protection of air bases. If we could have maintained fighter aircraft over Crete, then those parachute planes and gliders and troop carriers could never have reached the island. If Maleme Air Field had been properly defended, the troop carriers could never have got down. The lesson was rammed home again in Singapore, and later in Malta. But Crete should have been sufficient.

CHAPTER 9

The Restoration of an Empire

ONLY down in East Africa had things been going well this spring.

As far as the main Mediterranean theatre of war was concerned, the Abyssinian campaign was a negative one. Its objectives were the elimination of the Italian armies there, the consequent freeing of British armies for service elsewhere, the making safe of the Red Sea for British convoys. The conquest and possession of this huge block of territory, which is about the size of Alaska, could lead to no positive or decisive results. But sooner or later it had to be undertaken.

It proved a campaign of great tactical complexity and fascinating incidental detail. It reflected many aspects of the Western Desert Campaign: always the smaller force beat the bigger force; prisoners and booty were taken in relatively enormous quantities; fortune invariably seemed to favour the side which took the initiative; and the British proved again that superior leadership and training could compensate for an apparently crushing discrepancy in numbers.

The savage hills of the almost legendary empire of Ethiopia were the background for the fighting and the British fought with allies to whom the spear was a more natural weapon than the rifle. Yet in this particular campaign we borrowed and used three of the most modern weapons that the Germans had perfected: the Fifth Column, propaganda, and blitz tactics.

The Fifth Column was organized with a whole-heartedness and skill that were most un-English. Even as Italy declared war, eleven trained runners crossed the borders into Abyssinia bearing in their cleft sticks letters inscribed in Amharic script on strong linen parchment. They took them to eleven powerful chieftains, who read that they might have money, arms, food and ammunition from the British if they sent mules to the Sudan to fetch them. Hot on the heels of the letters came a little band of men cryptically referred to as "Mission 101." They were led by a bald-headed, bespectacled enthusiast called Colonel Sandford, though for purposes of disguise he took the name of Fiki Mariam, or "The Love of Mary." With four colleagues and two wireless sets, he penetrated far into the interior of the country to organize resistance among the native *patrios.*

Sandford made contact with a powerful Prince called Dejasmatch Mangasha, and together they collected mules to go and collect arms from the Sudan. They organized attacks on the Italian communications. Photos of the Emperor and inspiring proclamations began to pass from hand to hand. British air raids convinced dubious patriots that the British were really strong. Sandford and his colleagues eluded the Italians so adroitly and so spectacularly that they acquired a half-mystical reputation of being uncapturable. The Italians detailed General Nasi, who had a knack of dealing with the Ethiopian population on friendly terms, to quell the growing Fifth Column menace. But Sandford, penniless and almost foodless, kept the whole Gojjam Province seething on the verge of open revolt.

All this time the British were building up forces. To the original seven thousand troops in the Sudan Wavell had sent the Fourth Indian Division, and later on the Fifth. West African troops had come across from Nigeria and the Gold Coast. The first South African Division came up from the Union. Free French and Free Belgians increased the swelling total. In the air Hurricanes supplemented the out-of-date Welleseleys.

It was still a ridiculously small force with which to attempt the invasion of a mountainous country double the size of Texas, held by some three hundred thousand trained troops. But all Wavell's campaigns had to be gambles, and those that he had tried so far against the Italians had been magnificently rewarded. Moreover, incalculably valuable psychological data had been secured in Cyrenaica. The processes by which Italian morale crumbled had been carefully studied. It was realized that Italian Intelligence Officers built their appreciations on the basis of over-enthusiastic reports, and relied on purely mechanical calculations about how long certain demolitions would hold up the enemy, to what extent certain routes were passable, how many men could hold a fort for how long. They ignored the apparent miracles that brave, determined, highly trained men can accomplish.

So the war was planned with the full knowledge that the British would always be fighting against superior numbers and probably superior arms. The details of this campaign, as of the Greek campaign, are irrelevant to the course of the Libyan campaigns as a whole but they are too interesting to be passed over altogether.

Broadly speaking the strategical plan can be simplified down to one tremendous pincer movement—the longest, thinnest, quickest pincer movement in all military history. From the north and from the south the two arms of the pincer clove the country clean in two. And when they met on the sugar-loaf peak of Amba Alagi the victory had been gained.

The Northern pincer, under General Platt, drove eastwards into Eritrea on January 19 with the object of turning south at Asmara, and the first serious battle was before the town of Agordat. Here fair-haired General Lorenzini, a melodramatic figure who had somehow got himself nicknamed "The Lion of the Sahara," opposed a bold front. He had been ordered officially from Rome to restore the faith of the Italian and colonial troops in themselves, for "at Agordat must be fought the battle that will seal the fate of Italy in East Africa." He was promised full air support; and there lay the crux of Platt's first success. For the new Hurricanes smashed Lorenzini's Savoia bombers before they ever left the ground, and the Italians lost the protection they had most counted on.

The odds on the ground were then three to one against Platt, and he found the figure remarkably encouraging. Taking a psychological tip from the Western Desert, he boldly weakened his

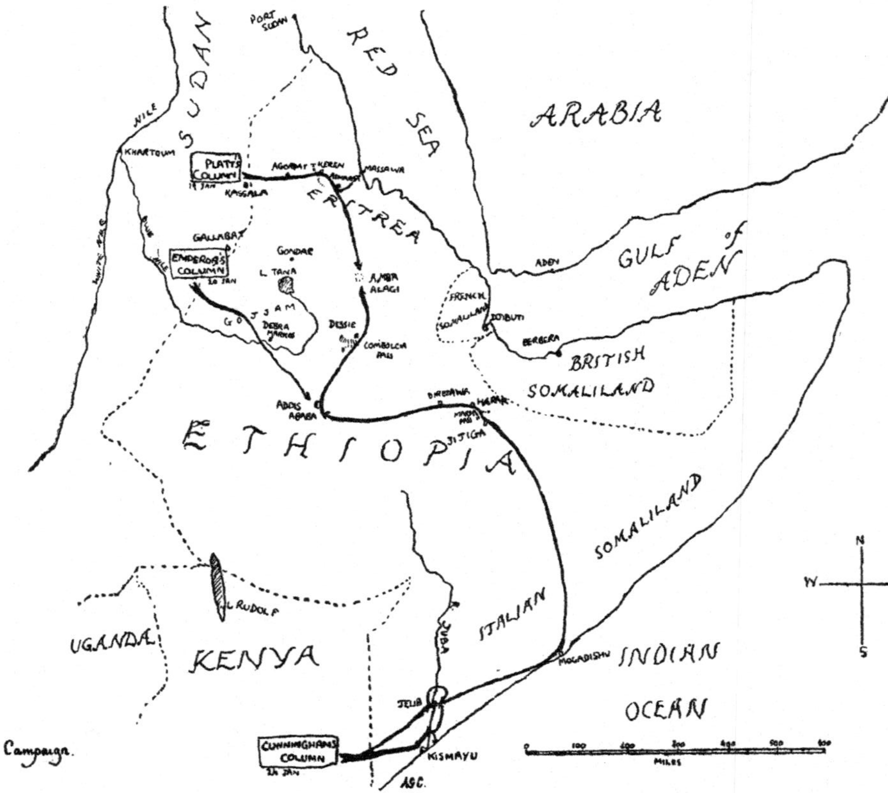

The Abyssinian Campaign.

front and threw his force round the flanks in a threat to the Italian communications. Very hard fighting secured a firm immovable footing for his right wing, and on that the whole line swivelled. The heavy infantry tanks came in as the final argument. And on February 1 Lorenzini abandoned Agordat and fled.

Then General Frusci, Italian commander in the North, gathered everything he had on the huge bare rock wall called Keren. The only way up to the plateau behind it was a gorge, and this the Italians blocked by clowing up two hundred yards of cliff. Crack Italian troops from every corner of East Africa were summoned at urgent speed — they were not even allowed time to say farewell to their families or sleep on the way. Artillery crowned every height. This was to be the last bastion. And the British probed fruitlessly for a way round it.

As always the British were inferior in numbers and for once their equipment was too modern. They were very highly motorized and what they really needed for this terrain was mules. But Platt thought he would try a frontal attack at once. He selected a point called Sanchil which dominated most of the Keren ridge and sent the Cameron Highlanders swarming up by night like monkeys to take it.

They just failed. The Italians turned their guns straight down over the cliff edge and tossed down their hand-grenades to burst shatteringly among men clinging for dear life to a little hand-hold in the rock. But the Camerons got a ridge well over half-way up and they held that and never let it go again. It was from that day called Cameron Ridge.

This was on the left of the blocked gorge. On the right Platt tried again. Then he tried left and right simultaneously. But it could not be done. It was not humanly possible to climb those precipices in the face of such fire and stay there and send down the wounded and bring up food and water and ammunition and sleep there and still have time to fight.

So Platt sat back to work it out. There was no way round, so Keren must be attacked frontally. Therefore it would have to be on a really big scale, with heavy casualties, and it would mean a month of steady preparation. Perhaps in the end the plan of attack would have to include the blocked gorge, which had not yet been tried. But in any case it must be a big attack, and the supplies must be arranged immediately.

All transport was mobilized to go and fetch food and ammunition from the bases. Mule companies were sent for from Cyprus. A small marauding column of Indian and Free French troops began to drive down the Red Sea coast from Port Sudan, forming a menace to Keren from the north-east. And in the meantime the propagandists went to work.

Big loudspeakers were rigged up in the front lines and the Italians heard operatic excerpts alternating with bulletins of depressing news. Leaflets were dropped by the R.A.F. and pamphlets smuggled round. News of British successes in other parts of East Africa began to make the Italians uneasy about their rear-guard. The British Fifth Column inside the country spread rumours and alarm. And in a trickle which sometimes swelled to a stream deserters began to come across.

On March 15 Platt was ready again. The attack began with a long, fierce mutual artillery barrage while the air was charged with the sullen heat of a thunderstorm that would not quite break. Once again Sanchil, on the left, could not be taken, though the Camerons still held their ridge. But on the right Indian troops fought their way to a point called Fort Dologorodoc and held it. They stayed there for ten days and beat off eight fully mounted counterattacks while food and ammunition were dropped them from the air. The officer commanding them tried crazy tricks with his artillery to disconcert the enemy, such as making every gun fire simultaneously one round on the same specific target. And in one of these fancy barrages blond Lorenzini got his head blown off.

The Italians by this time were nervous and exhausted. Their casualties from air and artillery bombardment were high and some of their native troops were dangerously near mutiny. But they were still more numerous than the British and had infinitely better positions.

On March 25 Platt put the second part of the plan into operation. He already held points well up the cliff to the right and left of the gorge. He now proposed to shoulder his way up the gorge itself.

The striking forces massed in a railway tunnel and well before dawn they poured out and into the mouth of the gorge. By midday they had battled their way past the blockage on the left-hand side, and the Indians had stormed down from Fort Dologorodoc and cleared the defences on the right-hand side. The block was under heavy and incessant shell fire and the sappers had to bring up their explosives in "I" tanks. But on the evening of the twenty-sixth they blasted the block away and the door to Keren was open.

It did not last long then. White flags waved from Sanchil and three dead Camerons were found on the highest point. Prisoners dribbled back down the gorge and native troops deserted in units. The "I" tanks were through Keren and beyond. That morning the Duce sent the Duke of Aosta a telegram congratulating him on the heroic defence of the pass. The Duke had to cable back that it had been lost.

But the success had not been cheaply won. The Fourth Indian Division alone had lost nearly three thousand men. It was easily the bloodiest battle of the whole African war to date, as far as the British were concerned. But it was decisive.

There was another mountain position behind which was naturally even stronger than Keren and the Italians made a pretence of defending it. But there was no heart left in them now. Platt knew they would not hold and he agreed to send the Fourth Indian Division back to Egypt to buttress the little army that was retreating before Rommel. On April 1 Asmara, capital of Eritrea, was occupied and the signal that was sent to Khartoum about it emphasized that this was NOT repeat NOT an April fool.

A mobile mopping-up force contemptuously called "FLIT, the Fly Killer" (this army loved light-hearted nicknames—General Platt's staid private plane was always known as Mrs. Clutterbuck), turned south to chase the Italians into Abyssinia. But only a small remnant had gone that way. The bulk of the survivors of Keren were waiting to surrender at the Red Sea port of Massawa. And Massawa was captured in a mad sequence of theatrical anticlimax.

The commander there was one Admiral Bonnetti. He had seven destroyers and as the British approached he sent them all off on those desperate, heroical missions which Italians love to plan. All seven failed abjectly. The navy sunk one outside Massawa. Two ran aground and two were sunk by the Fleet Air Arm when they tried to attack the fuel tanks of Port Sudan. And the remaining two were supposed to attack Suez and were similarly accounted for.

Since he showed such spirit it was thought Bonnetti might start destroying Massawa Harbour and scuttling the ships in it. So the British telephoned him from Asmara and told him not to. If he did, they said, the British would not be responsible for feeding the forty thousand Italians in Asmara.

Bonnetti asked Rome. And Rome said go ahead and scuttle. So the British attacked. They broke through the road blocks and stormed down the mountains to the sea. Bonnetti put up a white flag and then pulled it down again. So "I" tanks shot their way into the town.

Bonnetti was sitting sulkily in a deck-chair by the harbour when they found him. He tried one more gesture. He took his sword in both hands and banged it across his knee. But it would not break so he flung it disgustedly into the sea. The crowning humiliation came when the British fished it out again and bent it back to normal.

From Asmara the northern pincer pursued General Frusci and his remnants southwards towards Amba Alagi. But by then Platt knew that he had lost the great race to Addis Ababa. For the outsider, General Cunningham, coming up from the south, had already won it.

ii

General Sir Alan Cunningham, brother of the Admiral, started out from Kenya on January 24, five days after Platt had launched his invasion of Eritrea. His forces were West, East and South Africans, and he set the pace for his advance with a blood-stirring order of the day which ended "Hit them, hit them hard and hit them again."

The Italian penetration into Kenya was rolled up quickly and the frontier of Italian Somaliland was crossed at two points. The enemy at this stage was distance and deserts, not Italians. On February 14 British African armoured cars drove easily into Kismayu, a port which was once British but which had been ceded to Italy fifteen years ago. Still no real engagement had been fought. Gradually it became plain that the Italians were planning to stand along the Juba River. And the crossing of the Juba is one of the great key battles of this East African campaign, as Keren was for the northern pincer.

Cunningham's force reached the Juba opposite Jelib, which was the focal point of the Italian resistance. The river here was some two hundred yards broad and bridgeless, and Italian troops were dug in along both banks of it. It looked a very strong defensive position. And then Cunningham discovered that the Italians had failed to do something which is elementary in defending rivers. They had retained no large mobile force well in the rear to stage a counterattack. All their men were along the banks.

Here, then, was a possible solution. Parties were sent out to tap along the banks until they found weak spots. On the left a crossing was found at Mbonga, thirty miles upstream. And fifty miles away to the right, down towards the mouth of the river, a possible place was discovered by the column which had captured Kismayu.

In collapsible canoes and in the face of considerable resistance the right-hand party got across by the morning of February 18. The left-hand party crossed a day later, but the Italians, still expecting a frontal assault at Jelib, were behindhand with their counterattack. The two flanking forces swung round inwards and met on the Mogadishu high road eighteen miles behind the Italians at Jelib. Then they attacked from all sides. Bewildered by the speed and the surprise of Cunningham's manœuvre, the Italians were thrown into confusion. The black troops deserted and the white surrendered.

That night — February 22 — as he pored over his maps, a wild, mad idea came to Cunningham. He began working out figures and distances. A certain psychological factor — an estimate of the way this particular Italian army would react in certain circumstances — played a large part in his calculations. In the end it seemed to be crazy, but possible. And he cabled to General Wavell asking permission to try and reach Harar.

Now Harar, the second city of Abyssinia, was 1054 miles from Jelib, greater than the distance from New York to St. Louis, Missouri. But it wasn't a distance you could just do overnight in a train. There was only one road, and that probably not a very good one. It was hostile country all the way. And Cunningham's was a very small force. But he got permission to try it.

Mogadishu, the capital of Somaliland, was 275 miles away but Cunningham made it in three days. Rich booty and thousands of prisoners fell to him, but he scarcely paused to look at them. Mogadishu to him was not a city, but a usable port which might shorten his enormously elongated supply lines stretching back to Kenya. The only booty that interested him was 350,000 gallons of motor spirit.

On March 1 the Nigerian mobile column moved out of Mogadishu with Italian gas in its tanks. It swung onto the great Strada Imperiale which drives north towards Abyssinia. And for sixteen days it never stopped going. It raced headlong through bare white sand and bush-speckled desert and squalid villages and was gone again before the gaping natives had made up their minds to cheer. When the Italians tried to stop it they were just blasted out of the way. Once or twice supply difficulties or mine fields or a pocket of resistance made it pause. But it kept up an average of better than forty-five miles a day, not just touring, but fighting. It was a mad, unorthodox, swashbuckling advance which broke all the rules. Against a calm, determined, well-trained enemy it would have been suicide. Against the Italians it worked.

As they heard of the British advance, the Italian Seventieth Brigade, which were garrisoning British Somaliland, realized they were being cut off and began to panic. They pestered Headquarters until they obtained permission to evacuate Berbera. But it was too late. The British got to Jijiga first and the Seventieth Brigade just disintegrated. It was never heard of again as a unit. And on March 16 a force from Aden sailed into Berbera and the Union Jack flew once more over Government House.

At the Marda Pass between Jijiga and Harar, where the desert rears up into a savage range of mountains, the Italians at last turned and fought. The place was admirably chosen and the hills were already tunnelled and wired and camouflaged and mined for defence. A searchlight swept the approaches by night. It was a formidable position.

Cunningham searched vainly for a route round the flank, then decided on a frontal attack on March 23, which would allow for the arrival of reinforcements. But news came that the enemy were planning to withdraw and the attack had to be staged two days early, without reinforcements and without proper preparation. It went in as a straightforward attack, a real infantrymen's and gunners' battle right out in the open, and the Nigerians made progress slowly and at the cost of casualties. They had one stroke of luck on the left wing, when a chance shot set fire to some dry grass and flames drove the Italians off a vital hilltop. But mostly it was hard straight fighting and when night fell the thing was still not settled. The Nigerians slept among the hills, in crannies of the rocks or curled up in the grass, and crawled out in the chill morning ready to do battle again. But the enemy had gone.

Then the Italians suddenly began to play for time. They did it not by fighting, but by demolitions and quibbling and pointless parleying. There was quibbling about the surrender of Harar. An envoy from the Duke of Aosta flew to Diredawa and parleyed evasively. And the reason soon became plain enough. Up in the Mediterranean big things were happening. Rommel was preparing to retake Cyrenaica, British troops were landing in Greece. At all costs Wavell's armies must be kept split. The maximum total of troops must be kept occupied in Ethiopia. Orders flashed from Rome to Addis Ababa to delay the final conclusion by every conceivable means.

So while Cunningham's troops scrambled across the River Awash, where the single-span bridge had been tumbled 200 feet down into the gorge below, the Italians thought of a clever plan. They threw Addis Ababa to the wolves. They marched their armies out of the city and then saddled the British with the responsibility of protecting the civilians, including women and children, left behind. That, they reckoned, would tie up a good part of the small British army.

So it was that the spearhead of Cunningham's forces found themselves, not resisted by the enemy, but hurried on. The civil authorities sent out to invite them into the city as quickly as possible. The vanguard was escorted on its way by armed Italians on motorcycles. The Italian police force was drawn up five miles outside the city, awaiting orders. The British found themselves jostled ahead by the very people who ought to be stopping them.

Major-General Wetherall, the Divisional Commander, entered Addis on the morning of April 6. It was an untidy, haphazard entry which staggered the Italians by its lack of formality. The Fascist authorities, with uniforms and decorations and bodyguards, had staged the whole thing neatly and impressively. The typically British reaction was to do the whole thing in a casual, offhand way as quickly as possible. The only British show of force at that unsatisfactory ceremony was a single armoured car, parked in the shade of a tree, flying a home-made Union Jack. In the centre of the patch of grass was a flag-pole from which the Italians, in their zeal, had already removed their national flag. And at this point General Wetherall relented and gave the onlookers one little touch of the theatre. He had the Italian flag hoisted again and saluted with full military honours. Then it was hauled down and the Union Jack was run up in its place.

That was the end of an advance of 1725 miles in just fifty-three days. Divisional Headquarters had moved no fewer than twenty-one times during those seven and a half weeks. Thousands of the enemy had been killed, wounded or dispersed in the bush, and over twenty thousand had been captured. Hundreds of thousands of square miles had been added to British-controlled territory. And the British fatal casualties in the last thousand miles just about ran into double figures.

In Addis there were thousands of tons of oil, great stores of foodstuffs and medical supplies, a fine wireless station and signal material of immense value. But Cunningham's army did not stay long. To an extent the Italians' ruse had worked, for a number of troops had to be left behind to garrison the place. But the tiny force which drove on north was nevertheless big enough to finish off the campaign. A five-day battle was fought at Combolcia Pass to decide the fate of Dessie. It sounds absurd to call it a battle when only ten South Africans were killed in it, but on the other hand the Italians lost eight thousand prisoners and over fifty guns. Then the way was open to the Duke of Aosta's last stronghold.

The two great British pincer arms finally met on the shoulders of Amba Alagi, a ten-thousand-foot peak where the enemy Commander-in-Chief had entrenched himself with the remnants of his army. It was wild, chaotic country, and the fighting ranged over and around a whole series of summits and ridges to which the British gave names like Fin, Pyramid, Elephant, Whaleback. No tactical description is possible without a relief-model of those mountains, and even then the attacks and counterattacks, the feints and withdrawals would be bewilderingly complex. Roughly, General Platt's forces worked their way into the Italian defences on three sides and the South Africans, supported by Abyssinian patriots, attacked on the fourth. Gradually the Italians were driven higher up the mountain and deeper into their caves. On May 16 the Duke of Aosta sent out General Volpini to negotiate surrender, but Abyssinian villagers murdered him. There were further parleys and a brisk exchange of white flags. And on May 18 the Duke of Aosta marched down with his men, past a guard rendering full military honours, into captivity.

So where the two great prongs of the pincers met it was finished, all except for the mopping up. A campaign of great brilliance and audacity, great endurance, and great rewards. And on the Italian side of missed opportunities, inefficiency, and just plain inferiority in quality. Apart from the "I" tanks, the British produced no weapon which was overwhelmingly superior to anything the Italians had. And there was no single engagement in which the Italians had not been superior in numbers. If there was any one constant factor that contributed outstandingly to the British success, it was the British commanders' determination never to lose the initiative. The Italians were on the defensive from start to finish. And on the defensive, as Libya had shown, they are not good.

The great pincer movement stole most of the limelight in Abyssinia. But all the time there had been other minor columns thrusting in, all of them fighting successful battles against superior odds, struggling through savage, almost unexplored countrysides, filling the pages of their war diaries with a wealth of picturesque personal details. And one of these columns was particularly important, for the Emperor Haile Selassie, King of Kings, Lion of Judah, was leading it.

This column started out from the Sudan around the same date as the other two and struck due east into the province of Gojjam. On January 20 the Emperor's personal flag was ceremoniously broken in a dried river-bed just over the frontier. With him he had a propaganda unit, two Ethiopian battalions, and a vast herd of fifteen thousand camels laden with newly minted Maria Theresa thalers — the only coinage all Abyssinians will accept. Their way lay through an atrocious landscape and at times the Emperor and his notables had to get out and themselves help to build little stone causeways for their trucks.

Their progress was slow but steady. The Italians surrendered fort after fort as their lines of retreat were systematically threatened and all along the route patriots flocked to the Emperor's standard. Debra Markos might have held, but the swift approach of General Cunningham's army from the south precipitated the withdrawal of the huge garrison there. And on April 6 the Emperor's standard was raised over its twin forts and Ras Hailu, a shrewd old Prince with dyed hair, rows of Italian decorations and an ambiguous past, came to make formal obeisance.

For a month more the Emperor's force was chasing the Italian Colonel Maraventano who, with 8000 troops, was scouring the Gojjam looking for a loophole to escape from it. On the tableland of Agibar the Italians were finally pinned down to battle while old Ras Kassa sat on his shooting stick and cheered his side on. The attacks were fierce, but Abyssinian nerve war by night wore Maraventano down in the end. And one morning, under the barrels of three Bren guns, his 8000 Italians were disarmed of their 170 machine-guns, seven mountain guns, two mortars, 15,000 mules and 300 horses.

On May 5, exactly five years to the day after Marshal Badoglio had marched into Addis Ababa, the Emperor Haile Selassie rode down from the hills and reclaimed his capital. The first victim of Axis aggression had been liberated. It made excellent propaganda. But it wasn't quite so simple as it sounded, for there was a tricky ethical angle to it. The Italians had undoubtedly provided Abyssinia with a number of fine roads and badly needed hospitals and schools. And when the British gave the country back to Haile Selassie, the Italians said that a nation on the road to prosperity, culture and civilization had been hurled callously back to barbarism.

It is to be hoped that this is not so. It is profoundly to be hoped that Abyssinia has not been sacrificed on the altar of democratic symbolism. For Abyssinia is not, and never has been, a democracy. It is theoretically a monarchy and practically a loose federation of tyrannies, in the Greek sense of the word. Abyssinia may have the Government its people wants, but no one has yet asked them. And if they are not to have the Government they want, it is important that the Government imposed on them should be appropriate. For unless the new Government is demonstrably better than the Italian régime, how can the British justify the change?

Haile Selassie is an exceptionally intelligent and enlightened man.

He knows as well as the Italians did the importance of schools and hospitals. It is to be hoped that he will be able to introduce, by whatever means he has at his disposal, the reforms which the Italians had started imposing by force.

CHAPTER 10

Wavell's Farewell

IN SPITE of Amba Alagi, British fortunes in the Middle East touched their lowest ebb in June 1941. Whichever way he looked from Cairo, north, south, east or west, Wavell saw trouble.

Consider the position. On the Egyptian frontier stood now a German army, a small one but a good one, where Graziani's huge white elephant had stood before. And sixty miles over the frontier was Tobruk with a division or more bottled up inside it. It was not certain yet whether Tobruk could hold or not. If it fell, it would be another spectacular disaster. And even if it held, it was going to prove difficult and expensive to supply.

To the north German planes were already operating from the air fields of Crete. Cyprus lay undefended, with a wide flat plain where parachutists and transport planes could easily get down. Already it had had its first air raids. In Syria trouble was only just beneath the surface. General Dentz, the French commander there, had sold himself utterly to the enemy. And it was now confirmed that German planes were stacking up on the French military air fields. In Iraq a revolutionary puppet called Rashid Ali, with Berlin pulling the strings, had already raised a revolt in May. It was quelled easily enough and Rashid Ali appealed in vain to the Germans, who never espouse an obviously lost cause. But it showed that the seeds of trouble were there.

In Persia German agents and Fifth Columnists were going through the old familiar motions. The whole Nazi propaganda machine in the Middle East was being controlled from Teheran. Trouble could come from there any day. And down south in

Abyssinia it was proving difficult to spare any troops for other fronts. For one thing there were at least two big pockets of Italian resistance still uselessly but annoyingly holding out.

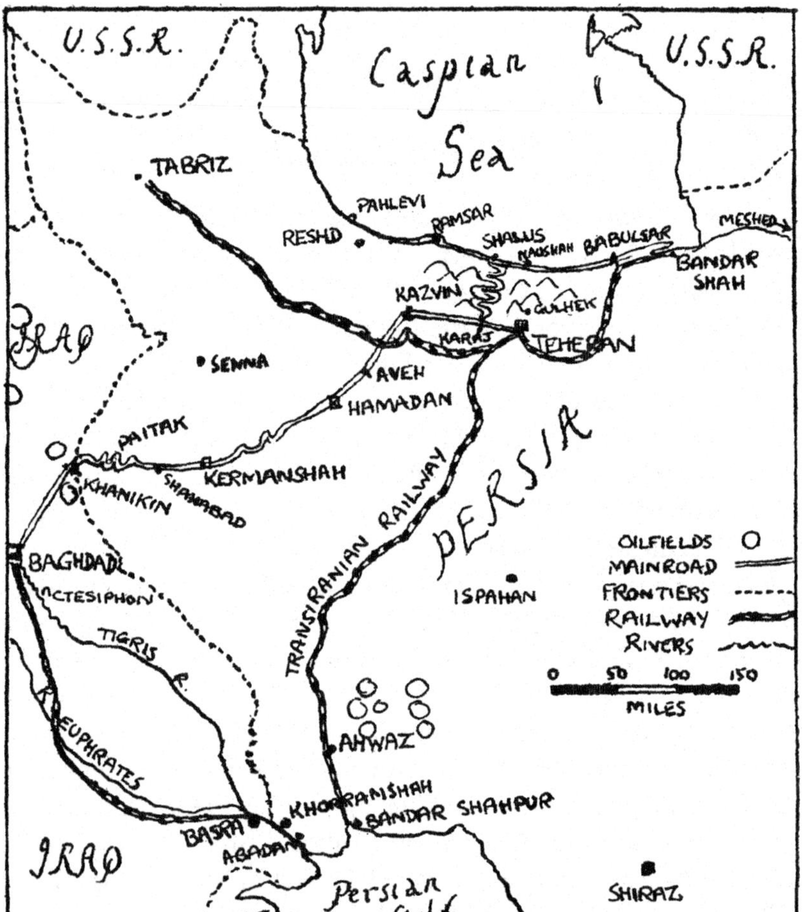

Persia

This line-up of Greece-Cyprus-Syria-Iraq-Persia looked particularly menacing. Obviously the Germans were feeling out the possibilities along it. There were half a dozen possible prizes they might be after—an attack on the Middle East position from behind, seizure of the Suez Canal, capture of the Iraq and Persian oilfields, an offensive against the rear of the Russian Caucasus defences. On the face of it it did not look very practicable—in particular the first step from Greece to Syria would be enormously difficult unless the Germans marched through Turkey. But the Germans had a habit of doing things which looked impracticable.

It was not a pretty picture, and Wavell had only meagre resources with which to face it. A skeleton force was holding off Rommel in the desert. The troops who had returned from Greece and Crete had to be completely re-clothed, re-equipped, and re-armed. Divisions were hopelessly tied up in Tobruk and East Africa. The R.A.F. had reached an all-time low. The navy had fought its last great purely naval action off Cape Matapan and had been cruelly mauled rescuing the army from Greece and Crete.

But something had to be done. The best form of defence is attack—a stitch in time saves nine—the foolish old English proverbs are sometimes true. As Wavell looked round the map he saw that Syria was the most important and the most alarming link in the chain of trouble around him. The time had come to take firm action. And on Sunday, June 8, a small army under General Wilson marched north across the border from Palestine.

It went diffidently, almost casually, not expecting any serious resistance. But a very grave psychological miscalculation had been made. It was not recognized that at this time the French national character was complicated, out-of-gear, and as raw as an open wound. In the mind of every Frenchman were bitter shame and bewilderment about what had happened in France. And the little army the British sent against them in Syria was an insult. It was as though the British had said, "Oh, the French aren't serious, they can't fight, you can beat them with anything." And when Wilson's army appeared the French said, "We'll show them we can fight, we won't let them get away with this."

So there started a horrible, fratricidal campaign. There could be little glory in it for anyone, only regret and shame. The Germans judged Syria a lost cause and sent no aid, so it was just French against British and French. It was probably an additional mistake to put the Free French into the fighting line at all. For Spain had shown that there is no war so bitter as a civil war, when each side regards the other as traitors.

It went slowly and painfully up in Syria, though the Anglo-Franco-Australian force under Wilson continued to advance. Reinforcements, especially of guns, had to be sent up. Wavell found he had not a man to spare anywhere. And in an attempt to iron out some of his other difficulties he tried a sudden, bold coup in the Western Desert.

The operation started on June 15. A very large force of new "I" tanks was rushed straight from the quaysides at Suez to the desert. It was to be largely a tank battle outside Bardia, and its object was to smash Rommel's armoured forces and relieve Tobruk. There was some dispute between the army and the air-force Intelligence Services about the enemy's tanks: one said a certain group of vehicles were trucks and the other said they were tanks disguised as trucks. But in any case there was good hope of success.

The tanks duly stormed their way onto the escarpment above Sollum and took Fort Capuzzo. The German tanks engaged them and a big mobile battle took place in the dust and the heat of that June week-end. The British edged forward across the south of Bardia, but they could make no great penetration. And the Germans produced some reserve tanks and started to outflank the British.

In the end, on the second afternoon, the British were forced back off the escarpment. They left behind them, in the enemy's hands, the greater part of their tanks and many wounded. There had been miscalculations and mistakes. One battalion of tanks was left for ten minutes exposed to the enemy's anti-tank gunfire while the Commander hesitated about what to do next. In the last analysis the British had simply been outfought.

It was, indeed, a moment of appalling seriousness. There were no reserves and Egypt then lay wide-open to Rommel. There was nothing in the way to stop him. This action made little impression at the time, for it only lasted two days, and it was soon forgotten by the rest of the world. But it was in fact one of the most dangerous things that ever happened to the British in the Western Desert.

In the end what saved Wavell then was the mere existence of Tobruk. We did not know it at the time, but we discovered later that Rommel was almost exaggeratedly sensitive about any threat to his flank. He could not bring himself to drive ahead into Egypt while Tobruk remained in British hands behind him. Tobruk was a millstone round his neck. And about that fact was built the strategy of Britain's next desert offensive.

This was Wavell's last Middle East campaign. For at the beginning of July he was suddenly sent to Delhi to take over the India Command, and the C-in-C India, General Sir Claude Auchinleck, came to Cairo in his place. Before Wavell left he called the war correspondents together and in the conference room at G.H.Q. he reviewed his year of command. He went into no great detail but as he spoke I glimpsed how oblique, how ambiguous, how fantastically involved had been the problems before him. He had found the Middle East in a state of acute danger, and by precarious virtuosity and audacity — not straightforward men and arms, but bluff and deception — he had at first won through. And then in the winter all these new problems had crowded in upon him with their contorted political angles, and he found bluff could not work any more. The plain military threads of supplies and men and equipment and Intelligence would not be woven into a smooth, straightforward skein of warfare. They were knotted and tangled up with questions of politics, morale at home, and a dozen extraneous circumstances which resulted in inadequate equipment and insufficient men. And so, in spite of smashing both Italy's colonial armies, Wavell left the Middle East in possibly greater peril than he found it. No one knew for sure, but it seemed as though his removal to India was in the nature of a disgrace after the defeats of the spring. But we hoped not. For the curious thing was that, in spite of Greece, Crete, Cyrenaica, Wavell still retained the respect and affection and confidence of the troops in the Middle East.

And then a strange thing happened. When Auchinleck arrived

the processes which Wavell and others had set in motion went on working by their own momentum. Gradually Syria was won. Tobruk was being supplied. Reinforcements of guns and aircraft and men were reaching the desert. And by September, when Auchinleck then looked north, south, east, and west from Cairo, the picture was utterly different from that which Wavell had seen. Nothing very spectacular had happened. But the whole orientation was changed.

Geographically the war in the Middle East had shown a peculiar tendency to return to the status quo. Graziani had advanced into Egypt and retreated again. The British drove through to Bengasi and were driven back. We sent an army to Greece and evacuated it. We occupied Crete and surrrendered it. Syria we had lost to Vichy and regained by force of arms. Iraq was barely saved from a coup d'état. Persia was occupied by British forces when the Germans were ripe for action there. Abyssinia alone was the brilliant exception that proved the rule.

Germany's declaration of war on Russia on June 22 was, of course, the big new factor in the situation. The whole centre of gravity had changed. The threat to Cyprus, Syria and Iraq was a threat no longer, and anyway it had been nipped in the bud. The Middle East position had, in fact, very nearly cancelled itself out. After the far-flung complexity of that first year it had all been simplified down to the point where the British were only facing the Germans and Italians on one front—the Egyptian frontier. The great lines of communications which had radiated out from Cairo to so many distant armies had been snapped one by one. Auchinleck now need only look west, along the coast of Africa, to one single front.

And so in the autumn of 1941 the Middle East took a deep breath, shook itself, and set out to begin all over again.

CHAPTER 11

The Rats of Tobruk

THE STORY of the desert during the summer of 1941 is the story of Tobruk.

In the middle of April the Australian Ninth Division, retreating at top speed through Cyrenaica, had stopped inside the perimeter defences of Tobruk and turned and fought. From the Germans' point of view it was not a fully staged attack on a fortress, but an incidental attack on some defences. The Commander of the Twenty-first German *Panzerdivision* was convinced that he could get the place easily. He attacked strongly. But when he ran into difficulties he swerved aside from Tobruk and drove on to the frontier in pursuit of the rest of the British army.

For fifteen anxious days the Australians, under the command of General Morshead, redug the defences and drew up their plans. Then on May 1 Rommel made the biggest attack he ever did make on Tobruk. His forces were at that time not very great and this was his first desert campaign. He had left himself only a little time to spy out the ground and reconnoitre the enemy defences. And he picked a spot on the south-west boundary which was naturally strong and strongly held.

The German attack, when it came, was a powerful one. But the Australians had improvised a supple, resilient form of defence and they deliberately allowed the German tanks to make a penetration. Then they rushed mobile anti-tank guns from all the near-by sectors and formed them up in a corridor on either side of the enemy thrust. The Germans found themselves suddenly caught in a blistering crossfire and they turned back and relinquished the attack.

But they retained a dent they had made in the perimeter, and this "bulge" or "blister"—or if you prefer it "salient"—stayed there until Tobruk was finally disengaged.

Now it may well be argued that the Australians, in repelling these two attacks, justified the Italians' fortress-area theory. But there are these points to be considered: Rommel was new to the desert and so were his men. They were not numerous or experienced. Part of the German forces had to be detached to keep at bay the British forces along the frontier. The attack was quickly planned and quickly staged. And the Australians met it with a supple, mobile form of defence inside the perimeter, not with the rigid, outward-facing fortifications of the Italians. The Australians had proved that, given certain circumstances and a bold, intelligent defence, these fortress areas need not necessarily collapse even when a penetration has been made. They had proved that in a modified way the fortress area can be useful in the desert, for while Rommel had not been prevented from thrusting ahead to Bardia and the frontier, he had been prevented from marching on into Egypt afterwards. Tobruk, the first British experiment in the theory, was already paying dividends as far as defence was concerned. It still remained to be seen whether the place could have any more than a purely negative value.

In May Rommel sat down to besiege Tobruk. He gave up land attacks and tried the air. The Stuka dive bombers and high-level bombers came over in layers. Night and day the harbour and the little white town rocked under the impact of the explosions. The enemy planes only had fifteen miles to fly. The defenders of the southern perimeter could actually hear the bombers warming up their engines at El Adem before coming to bomb Tobruk.

Geographically the Tobruk area was twice the size of the District of Columbia and the shape of a wooden clog standing level and with the toe pointing to the right. Tobruk itself—a plain white town of one-story stucco buildings arranged in half a dozen criss-crossing streets—lay with its back to the open sea, facing south across the inlet which forms its harbour. From it one metalled road ran east to Bardia, one west to Derna, and one south to El Adem Air-Port.

The defences ran in a semicircle from coast to coast, concentric rings of barbed wire, tank traps, trenches, mine fields, concrete pill-boxes. Dotted all round were high look-out posts like ships' crow's-nests, from which artillery observers could survey the countryside. The whole was divided into two levels by the steep escarpment which ran right across it, parallel with the sea, a mile or so inland. Nothing grew there except in a fertile little oasis down by the shore called the Wadi Auda, where the Public Relations Unit had its camp.

Tobruk had no fighter protection. Its own air fields inside the perimeter could not possibly be used, and the Egyptian air fields were too far away. It only had its anti-aircraft batteries to fight off these cascades of planes. Between April 9 and July 31, for instance, actual bombing raids totalled 437. Forty-eight of these were dive-bombing attacks, 277 were high-level daylight raids and 160 were at night. It was calculated that 458,000 pounds of high explosive had been dropped during the day raids, and 320,000 pounds during the night.

Yet in the face of this Tobruk was not only fed and maintained but it was turned into a dump. The navy ferried in shipload after shipload of food and petrol and ammunition which was stored against the day when an army advancing from Egypt should need it. More than eighty tanks were brought in. Thousands of tons of matériel were unloaded at night on the battered quayside by workers who retired into caves when the bombers came. A complete repair workshop was established. Tobruk settled down to a noisy, hectic routine.

Lord Haw-haw called the defenders "the self-supporting prisoners," and "the rats of Tobruk," but Rommel gave up trying to take the place. He built the "Achsenstrasse," a forty-mile bypass road round Tobruk, so that his convoys could get through to Bardia. He brought up siege guns — long-barrelled 155-millimetre French guns and even a 210-millimetre cannon. He pounded the harbour with shells and bombs and of course he sank a ship now and then but Tobruk never starved.

They lived a life there of simplicity so stark, so primitive, that its rhythm was even governed by the phases of the moon. For it was only on a few black moonless nights that Tobruk had contact with the outside world. In the dead of those black nights, men would stand on the quayside, straining their eyes into the darkness, seeing and hearing nothing until voices hailed them from just twenty yards ahead across the water, and they saw the faint phosphorescence of the inky sea as it swished round the bows of a destroyer. Then men would stream ashore and march away, and others would embark in a swift, steady exchange. Newcomers would be afraid to talk aloud, so near did the enemy seem. They jumped when they were told to and marched ahead into the opaque darkness when they got the order, obeying blindly like children because they were in a place with rules of its own which they did not understand.

Few of the men in Tobruk ever had a roof over their heads. They lived in a picnic not as a reaction or an escape from civilized life, but merely because there was no civilized life. They were almost unimaginably devoid of luxuries. Strip life of everything that makes it worth-while, and you will have the standard of living in Tobruk. The water was scanty and brackish and the tea tasted salty however strong it was made. The rations were just a means of keeping alive in the most economical way and Vitamin C came in little white pills. Beer appeared once in a blue moon—there is the story of the only Tobrukian who ever achieved a hangover. His unit decided to make one man thoroughly happy instead of getting a tantalizing mouthful each, so they drew lots for the entire ration. On one famous occasion two tins of beer were issued to every man in the garrison, and the sounds of rejoicing were so loud that the Italians uneasily doubled their sentries, then ordered "Action Stations" all night, and finally laid down a non-stop artillery barrage, just in case.

The nearest they ever got to women in Tobruk was when they cut pictures of film actresses out of old magazines, or painted the names of their girl friends on their trucks. No Tobruk sock was ever darned by a woman's hand, no button was ever properly sewn on. They never saw a tree or a flower or bought themselves a drink or sat round a table to eat a meal, or heard a note of music. They very rarely had much to read, for shipping space was worth its volume in gold. But they got their mails and parcels, and that was a bigger comfort to them than anything else. I still think one of the most pathetic stories of the war is the one about the private in Tobruk who unwrapped a parcel from England and out tumbled a tin of bully beef. For bully beef was one of the very few things they did have in Tobruk, perhaps the only thing in the world that was infinitely more precious in England than there.

The surprising thing is that they did not go crazy with boredom. There were front-line positions which could not be reached in daylight, and the outposts had to crawl there before dawn and just sit and wait all through the torrid day for evening to relieve them. It is a wonder that sand-storms and bombings and eternally salty water and boredom did not drive them to despair. But there was not a moment when Tobruk's morale was not higher than Cairo's.

These men grew tough and lean and seasoned. The summer suns burned them the colour of shoe leather. They bathed in warm sea and played football and organized sports. Gradually their bodies grew accustomed to this hard living and monotonous eating. The raids caused astonishingly few casualties. Men said that they got used to the bombs much more easily than to the flies. And there were even people who claimed that they liked the place.

Towards the end of July and the beginning of August, British, Indian and Australian patrols began to take the offensive. At first they went out just to obtain information. They checked up on the dispositions of the enemy fortifications and the changes in his position. Then they found that it was rather more effective to destroy enemy observation posts and strong-points than merely to plot them on their maps. Next they discovered that Italian morale was beginning to crumble as the night raids continued. Finally the patrols realized that they themselves enjoyed the business.

As a rule each raid provoked a hysterical artillery barrage big enough to stop a division. Sometimes the Italians wore out their guns and used up their shells for two hours on end. Then the patrollers would silently rise from the dug-outs where they had been waiting and carry on with their job.

One Indian patrol attacked and took four enemy positions in a night. An Australian patrol spent a whole day outside the perimeter in a captured strong-point and then came home to read about its own exploits in the daily paper, *Tobruk Truth* (or *Dinkum Oil* to Australians). The best patrol story of all was that of the eighty Italians who stood one night watching Tobruk being shelled, rubbing their hands and exchanging congratulations. So intent were they on watching that they did not hear a faint shuffling in the sand behind them. In fact, they heard nothing at all until an electrifying war-cry made their blood run cold. They spun round to see the moonlight gleaming on Australian bayonets. Most of them were so horror-struck that they did not even try to flee..

Amateur "Bush Artillery"—cooks, orderlies and such like—doing stunts with guns captured by the Italians from the Austrians in the last war, was another of Tobruk's features. The first salvoes of these patched-up cannons seem to have caused consternation. Puzzled German gunners ranged feverishly, trying to contact this mystery battery which their Intelligence had failed to locate. But the "Bushmen" were able to keep up their hobby for weeks and were finally given a place in the line.

At the end of August the garrison was relieved. The Australians came out, all except one battalion, and they were replaced by the Polish brigade, the Thirty-second British Army Tank Brigade, the King's Dragoon Guards (with armoured cars) and men from the Black Watch and an assortment of British country regiments. General Morshead handed over to General Scobie.

The Poles livened up the pace at once. Their pleasure at the prospect of fighting Germans could hardly be restrained. Sometimes a deafening clamour would break out at night from the Polish sector and men would stir uneasily in their sleeping-bags and wonder whether the Germans were attacking. But they soon got to understand. The Poles were apt to interpret a patrol as an offensive. Or someone had thought they had seen a German. Or simply the Poles had felt like having a barrage.

A friend of mine once went to the Poles to explain to them where the enemy's guns lay. They listened politely but without enthusiasm while he pin-pointed the Italian batteries. Then he mentioned a German battery.

While he was still speaking three Poles left the tent at the double. Outside he heard urgent words of command. And before he had finished talking the Polish guns were in action, all aimed at the Germans.

When he could hear himself speak, the Englishman showed the Poles where an Italian division was being relieved. Again they listened politely. Then he pointed out three German sentries. Within a couple of minutes the three bewildered sentries had gone to ground with a hail of fire screaming about their ears. The Italians were left in peace.

As the summer wore on the defence system was worked out with elaborate detail. The place was divided up into interdependent sectors and all the defences were designed to swivel round to the flank or the rear and form a new front inside the perimeter at a moment's notice. All signal wires and communications were duplicated by alternative routes so that if one line were cut another could instantly be switched on. There was a complex technique of mutual assistance among the closely interlocked subdivisions of the front line, and forces for counterattacks were always held ready in the rear.

And Tobruk was also being groomed for offence as well as defence. All its defenders knew that the fortress was to play its vital part in the winter offensive—for it was morally certain that there would be a winter offensive. The tank force mounted up and the caves became stuffed with food and petrol. The nightly patrols were recognized as rehearsals for the day when the garrison should really break out in earnest. From being an isolated remnant of a retreating army, Tobruk increased in stature and confidence as the summer burned on. It became the forward outpost, the vanguard of a new army that was growing daily stronger away in Egypt. And when Russia came into the war, Tobruk was the extreme left wing of an Allied front that ran from its own sun-parched patch of desert to somewhere on the Arctic Ocean.

So the epic of Tobruk was built up, out of a multitude of human details all co-ordinated towards one end. A life that had been stripped nearly beyond its bare essentials grew somehow rich and dramatic on this barren soil. The Rats of Tobruk became almost proud of their prison and they cursed it with a certain affection. But their greatest hour was yet to come.

CHAPTER 12

Crusader Is Planned

In the autumn of 1941, while Tobruk was busy getting ready, preparations for the winter offensive were taking final shape back in Egypt. The campaign was given the code name "Crusader."

For months Britain had been sending to the Middle East, in Winston Churchill's words, "everything we could lay our hands on." The stream of supplies was flowing evenly now, and the war matériel was steadily improving in quality. The British press had been clamouring for action and on November 6 Joseph Stalin spoke publicly and significantly about "opening up a second front." But General Auchinleck, the new Commander-in-Chief, set himself stubbornly against being hurried. He had picked out the crucial lesson from the turgid campaigns of Wavell's year—you can gamble against the Italians, but you cannot gamble against the Germans. This time, for the first time, the British were to go into battle not inferior to the enemy either on land or in the air.

There was the usual general post among the troops. All the Australians were sent back to Palestine and Syria. And into the desert came two South African divisions (one fresh from its triumphs in Abyssinia), the New Zealand division, rather more than one Indian Division, and the Seventh Armoured Division. This now consisted of the Seventh Armoured Brigade, equipped with old British cruiser tanks, and the Fourth Armoured Brigade using the new fourteen-ton American Stuart or "Honey" tanks. Five weeks before the battle began the Twenty-second Armoured Brigade arrived in Egypt with its new British Valentine and Crusader tanks, and was brigaded with the Seventh Armoured Division.

Added to this was the force in Tobruk under General Scobie,

which was now named the Seventieth Division. And the whole thing was turned into a completely separate command, entitled the Eighth Army, and put under the command of Major-General Sir Alan Cunningham, the hero of the southern pincer in Abyssinia.

Cunningham was a ruddy-faced, blue-eyed, outspoken man, and it was natural that after the East African campaign the South Africans should admire him greatly. It is probable that their recommendation carried weight with Auchinleck when he came to choose a commander for the newly-formed Eighth Army, which included South Africans.

Not only British but also American equipment for Cunningham's army had been flowing in during the summer. The first shipment of American matériel had arrived on Independence Day and I drove down to watch it being unloaded at a spot on the Red Sea coast where the turquoise-blue water met the sunburned desert in a narrow fringe of green palms.

Freighters with Stars and Stripes painted all over the hull hung almost motionless in the translucent sea. The heat made colours dance maddeningly before the eyes and the horizon shimmered with mirages. But on the waterfront yelling sweating Arabs, with their white-cotton nightgowns girded about their dusky loins, were unloading and unpacking crates with an energy which it hurt to watch.

British soldiers, American technicians and Egyptian dockers were working in shifts all round the clock to handle the stuff. Someone invited me aboard one of the freighters and there I got my first look at the new American tanks. They were stowed as neatly as a child's box of bricks, with coils of wire, tyres, medical stores, even packages of boot polish filling every nook and cranny round them. When they were unloaded they came out so neatly and cleanly you expected to hear a pop like a champagne cork. The tanks were chunky, high-built, old-fashioned-looking things, bristling with machine-guns, small but fast and comfortable.

Tanks and lorries were being unloaded, unpacked, assembled and driven away to the overhauling yards with what seemed to me uncanny efficiency. But that was only the first fine careless rapture. Soon matériel started to arrive faster than it could be handled. Valuable shipping space was lost because ships, laden sometimes with bombs and explosives, had to lie for days at anchor waiting to be dealt with. There were strikes and troubles among the Egyptian labourers, and the unloading went far less swiftly and efficiently than had been hoped.

Nevertheless tanks, guns, motor-vehicles, equipment and supplies of all sorts were coming in. And simultaneously the R.A.F. was achieving air superiority in the Middle East.

The process was planned and organized from one small group of offices in Cairo, but the wires that were pulled from there stretched right round the world. Air-Marshal Arthur Tedder, small, dynamic, bright-eyed, was the brains behind it.

From his spacious, map-hung office in Cairo, his pipe almost always between his teeth, Tedder steadily built up the Middle East's strength in the air. America sent Marylands and Tomahawks at first, and then followed up with Bostons and Brewsters and finally Kittyhawks. From Britain came more and more Hurricanes, Blenheims, Wellingtons and Beaufighters. New air fields were carved out of the desert. Pilots and ground staffs grew from a mere handful to a whole army. Bombs and high-octane aviation spirit, guns, ammunition and spare parts arrived in a swelling stream.

Throughout those warm golden autumn days they were working hard at Cairo G.H.Q. And probably no one harder than Auchinleck himself.

Little enough was known at that time about Auchinleck's capabilities as a commander-in-chief. We had the bare biographical details: fifty-eight years old; born of an army family; went to an army school; service in the Indian army; fought in the Middle East in the last war; more service in India; commanded the British force at Narvik; had the Southern Command in England; appointed Commander-in-Chief in India; nicknamed, naturally, "The Auk." People said he was popular and energetic, which is the sort of description you apply to a society hostess. He was certainly a fine figure of a man—tall, very well set up, brown not-very-tidy hair, and extremely striking light blue eyes. But as to ability, we did not know much.

He held a press conference almost as soon as he came to the Middle East in July 1941, and we all sat round a big table and asked him questions. He replied frankly, not very fluently but confidently and with quick intelligence. Unfortunately he made a remark about Britain needing American man-power which got headlines in the American press and after that, I think, he was a little afraid of us. At any rate, we did not see him again.

It was soon clear that he was indeed energetic, hardworking, and clear-sighted, with no little firmness of character and no fear of shouldering responsibility. It became fashionable to say that he was a talented General but not a genius, that he was certainly a good Corps or Army commander, but had yet to prove himself a Commander-in-Chief. That was probably true—in any case it was as much as anyone could say at the time. But he inspired confidence, his decisions were clear-cut and firm, and he was immediately liked and trusted by those who worked with and under him.

Every morning Auchinleck would drive from his white house on green Gezira Island to the wire-encircled section of a Cairo suburb where he had his office.

G.H.Q. Middle East had by this time become an untidy sprawling growth, tightly tied together with red tape. It had started in a hotel. Then moved into a vast new block of flats. Presently it incorporated more flats. Then a big villa. Then it engulfed a whole street. Finally it became a district and they flung a barbed-wire entanglement round it and posted sentries at the entrances. For one whole block the entanglement ran along one of Cairo's main streets, and the plans for beating Rommel were forged with clanging trams and camel caravans and all the clamorous hurly-burly of Egyptian traffic passing by a few yards away.

But inside G.H.Q., if you could get past the Cypriot sentinels at the gates, you received an impression of improvisation and makeshift. Its greatest admirers admitted that the place was unwieldy and over-complicated. The atmosphere was that of a big department store valiantly carrying on during alterations. You might find a shirt-sleeved brigadier working in a kitchen. Next door, in a partitioned-off bedroom, operational plans would be under discussion round secret maps. You would find yourself constantly passing through bathrooms, which formed the passages between the different flats. Everywhere you came up against boarded-up doors and corridors.

It was hard to realize that the campaigns in Libya, Abyssinia, Greece, Crete and Syria had been planned and organized in this jumble of offices amid the luxurious, hot-house atmosphere of Cairo. For in its spare time G.H.Q. was living a life of costliness which staggered people fresh from war-time England. Cairo apartments were palatial and their prices would have been spectacular in London or New York. Usually a few officers clubbed together and shared the rental, for their wives and families had mostly been evacuated. And naturally these bachelors and grass widowers were fair game for every housekeeping racket anyone could think up. Prices in the shops were already soaring wildly but they became still more outrageous when they appeared in the officers' housekeeping books. Cooks were making fortunes. Merchants who soaked firewood and melons in water to make them weigh heavier came into their own.

But if you had the money you could buy comfort. You could have bacon and eggs, plenty of butter and English marmalade for breakfast. Gas for your car was unrationed. When you joined friends before lunch on the green lawns of the Gezira Sporting Club, your Scotch whisky cost you only half what it would have cost in Scotland. You could stroll across to the club dining-room and eat your fill from a cold buffet which always had unlimited chicken, game-pie, boiled and roast beef, ham and chops.

The weather was still warm enough for you to put on your smart gabardine uniform and take an expensively gowned girl to dine beneath the stars at an open-air cabaret show, with glamorously shaded lights and slick waiters.

There were times when this luxury produced raging attacks of conscience. These usually started with a letter from home or something read in the paper, and people would begin to wonder why they should be enjoying this comfort and safety when their families were being bombed and going short of things. Suddenly Cairo's pleasures would turn to ashes and one would feel an insatiable longing for home.

But it was difficult to blame Cairo. It was the capital of a fertile and non-belligerent country. There was no reason why it should not be safe and comfortable. And it was worth remembering this: Cairo had already been the headquarters of five full campaigns on five different battle fronts. Some were victorious, some tragic, but none were comfortable. And from these five campaigns men came back to Cairo on leave. Cairo could not give them their homes, which was what they really wanted. But it gave them the next best thing—comfort, food and drink, hot baths, entertainment and colour, and a breath of relief from the war.

ii

That was the background against which the new offensive was being planned. And as a warm and sunny October merged into a warm and sunny November, I went down to the desert to see the actual stage being set.

I went by the old familiar road—the journey which I hoped I had done for the last time about a year before. But before I had gone a hundred miles, I saw that things were different this time. Far more eloquent than any statistics of our reinforcements was the altered face of the desert itself as I saw it in this drive westwards. The change compared with a year ago was hardly describable. Then you had found scores of miles of utter emptiness. Each camp was a little circumscribed area complete in itself. You met an odd vehicle every five miles or so and a rare convoy was a matter of twenty or thirty vehicles. If you saw a plane, the odds were that it was an enemy one.

But this time I drove for mile after mile through an uninterrupted sprawl of camouflaged tents and dumps. The bare landscape had become a vast canvas suburb alive with activity. I do not suppose any road in Britain was carrying as much traffic as this one desert highway did during the last few weeks before the campaign opened. We had to force our way for more than an hour through an unbroken convoy of brand-new anti-tank guns, twenty-five-pounders, supply lorries, trucks of every size and weight, armoured cars, Bren-gun carriers. This was quite a different sort of army from the one Wavell had had. I began to feel very optimistic.

I was just about a week too early for the offensive. It had been postponed for a few days at the request of the South Africans, who were not quite ready. It was still warm enough to go about in shirt and shorts, and at least once a day we bathed. I cannot believe that there is better bathing in the world than along this coast — a soft dazzlingly white sandy shore, warm blue sea with a bottom shelving down steeply so that you are out of your depth in about fifteen yards, rocks to swim out to, sunshine for sun-bathing. In addition we had the clean, satisfying freedom of bathing naked.

Gradually other war correspondents appeared and our camp by the sea-shore began to fill up. This time we had tents to sleep and eat in, all properly dispersed, counter-sunk and sandbagged. I shared sleeping quarters with Alan Moorehead and with James Holborn of the *Times* and in the evenings we would invite a fourth to come in and play bridge by the light of a hurricane lamp. We visited the NAAFI depot and bought additional stocks of tinned foods for the coming days, and called on friends whose camps were near by. We were encouraged to write as little as possible so as to avoid drawing attention to the fact that we were all gathering in the desert.

By the eve of the offensive I had formed a pretty complete picture of the dispositions of the two armies. The British front line started on the coast some miles west of Buqbuq and swept down in a long shallow curve inland to the oases of Siwa and Jarabub. This time there was to be no question of attacking straight along the coast. The enemy's positions round Halfaya and Sollum were much too strong, for one thing. The coast was to be left to the Indian Division which, backed by extensive mine fields, would operate as a containing force in case the enemy tried to break out eastwards. Farther south the New Zealand Division would advance in a curve clockwise, outflanking the Halfaya positions and reaching the main road beyond Bardia. Farther south still, starting from Fort Maddalena, the Seventh Armoured Division was to launch the main thrust — a great swing north-westwards in the direction of Tobruk. Simultaneously the defenders of Tobruk were to break out south-eastwards. Right down below them were two South African Brigades which were going to move up on the left flank of the Armoured Division.

The Indians and New Zealanders were lumped together as Thirteenth Corps, and the Armoured Division and the South Africans as Thirtieth Corps — a circumstance which led to a good deal of verbal confusion and tongue-twisting. The Second South African Division was to be held in reserve.

The whole thing was planned on a far bigger scale than Wavell's campaign. For months South African and New Zealand engineers had been extending the railway line past Mersa Matruh in the general direction of Fort Maddalena. Sometimes they had progressed as much as two and a half miles a day, and all the time matériel was pouring up along it. Lorries had been churning back and forth along the track to Siwa and on to Jarabub for weeks. The German reconnaissance patrols had observed the multiplicity of tracks and had deduced that if the British did make any attack, the main thrust would come from these two oases. Enormous forward dumps of food and petrol had been established way ahead of the troops, and carefully camouflaged. The new tanks were sent forward. The air force had established a complete chain of new air fields and had prospected the terrain for future landing-grounds miles behind the enemy line. South African armoured-car patrols continually swept the strip of no-man's-land dividing the two armies, charting mine fields, collecting information, keeping the enemy from probing our preparations.

The security problem was handled with subtlety. The Italians had been tricked last year into thinking we were stronger than we in fact were. This time we had to make the Germans believe we were weaker. But it was quite impossible to conceal the fact that we were building up our strength. So instead of making a secret of it, we shouted it out loud—and then gave Rommel reason to think it was bluff. There is almost incontrovertible evidence to show that our offensive was a complete surprise to the Germans. They almost certainly argued that our preparations were getting all this publicity either because they were not nearly so big as we pretended, or because we were not anything like ready yet. One or two minor points may have helped to deceive Rommel as to our zero hour. We missed the rising moon, and attacked when there was no moon at all. Auchinleck, on the eve of the battle, took a quiet trip to Palestine. German reconnaissance planes had discovered that the new railway was not finished. In addition, Rommel was intent on plans of his own.

General Erwin Rommel, Commander of the German Afrikakorps and C-in-C of all the Axis forces in Libya, only got as far as Company Commander in the First World War, but he won the "Pour le Mérite," Germany's Victoria Cross, so he must have been good. He was a professional soldier, an infantryman, but after the war most of his fighting was done in the streets in the early turbulent days of the Nazi Party. He hitched his wagon to Hitler's star; and as the Nazi Party rose in power he was able to leave political gangsterism for a series of respectable military instructional posts. Shortly before this war began he was made Commandant of Hitler's own headquarters, and then in France he commanded the Seventh German Armoured Division. Again he must have done well, for he earned the Oakleaf addition to his Ritterkreuz. Finally he was sent out to Africa to help the Italians. A sturdy, square-faced, firm-jawed man, he had a reputation for great daring and swift decisions. He had shown these qualities in the spring of the year when he turned a raid into an offensive and swept us clean out of Cyrenaica. He had failed to take Tobruk, but he had fought very successfully elsewhere. He was clearly a General to be treated seriously.

Under his command Rommel now had the Fifteenth and Twenty-first German Armoured Divisions, numbering about 8000 men each, all extremely highly trained, equipped and mechanized; the German Ninetieth Light Infantry Division; the Italian Ariete ("Battering Ram") Armoured Division; and the Italian Savona, Pavia, Trento, Trieste, Brescia and Bologna Infantry Divisions, all of them somewhat small divisions averaging probably less than 10,000 men each. The three armoured divisions were supposed to have 135 tanks each.

All the summer the enemy had been fortifying the steep escarpment which curls in from the sea at Sollum and then sweeps away obliquely inland from Halfaya Pass. Twice I had lain on our side of no-man's-land and watched the plumes of purple smoke rise into the heat-laden air as German sappers blasted away the rocky earth. They were building gun emplacements, concrete pillboxes, underground shelters, protected machine-gun nests and miniature fortresses. Guarding this line Rommel had put his Twenty-first Armoured Division under Major-General Ravenstein, and the Italian Savona Division. The rest of his forces were more or less grouped round the Tobruk perimeter. Rommel was not happy about the Italians—he knew as well as anyone that they were his weak spot. But he gave them plenty of barbed wire and plenty of guns and prayed that at least they would be able to hold their positions against a numerically inferior enemy.

All the summer, doggedly and very expensively, Rommel had been getting in supplies and reinforcements. Convoy after convoy was sent across the Mediterranean from Italy, and day after day British bombers, submarines and warships were out trying to stop them. There were moments when only two out of every five ships were getting through at all. Often vital cargoes had to be repeated three or four times before they actually reached the forces in Africa. The task of keeping Rommel supplied with what he wanted in the right quantities must have turned hair grey in Italy.

As the time of the offensive drew nearer, this supply route was being attacked along its whole length. New superweight bombs fell on Naples, where a good deal of the men and materials were embarked. A dozen harbours in Sicily and along the railway line which skirts Italy's toe were systematically raided. The ships were attacked at sea and hardly a day or a night passed without a bombing raid on Tripoli or Bengasi where the supplies were unloaded in Africa. And all the way up to the front the roads were being raked by low-flying fighters with heavy cannons. It was all an integral part of the preparations.

In the second week in November a small British cruiser and destroyer force got in among two Italian convoys in the Central Mediterranean. Without any loss to themselves the British warships sank eight supply ships, one ammunition ship, one destroyer, and left a ten-thousand-ton oil tanker blazing from end to end. In fact, both convoys were completely wiped out.

A couple of days later another naval force caught another Italian convoy and two sailing ships were sunk, and two armed merchant cruisers and two supply ships were damaged. The Prime Minister, in his telegram of congratulation, had every reason to describe this as "a most important and timely action." It was reasonable to think that Rommel had lost something important which he could not hope to replace before the offensive began.

But despite all this opposition Rommel had been able to collect a force big enough to launch an offensive himself. He had decided that Tobruk, for six months a festering wound in his side, must be taken. When he made this decision, he must have been quite convinced that we were in no condition to attack from Egypt. He calculated he could get into Tobruk and clean it up before the British had time to react behind his back. It seems that he originally planned to launch his offensive on November 14, which was his fiftieth birthday, but for some reason—possibly sand-storms—he had to put it off.

His plans were known—to the defenders of Tobruk they had become quite obvious. Auchinleck had to decide whether to wait until Rommel was embroiled in Tobruk and then hit him hard and swiftly in his rear, or choose his own moment for the attack. The trouble was, we did not know when the Axis zero hour was. We might have had to wait for a fortnight, and you cannot, in desert warfare, maintain four divisions at their secret action stations for a fortnight. So Auchinleck decided to go ahead.

CHAPTER 13

Tank Battle

ON THE evening of Sunday, November 16, all the war correspondents in the desert were summoned to meet General Cunningham. In pitch-darkness we stumbled through the camp, picking our way among slit trenches and tent ropes, to his underground headquarters scooped out of the sand-hills. There we sat round a plain bare trestle table and drank whisky-and-sodas while he told us what was going to happen.

Zero hour, he told us, would be before dawn on Tuesday. We should start with superiority in the air; almost certain superiority in tanks, slight inferiority in manpower. He was absolutely confident of success, and he thought the Italian morale would collapse quicker than ever as soon as the Germans cracked.

"We are going to drive deep into Libya," he said.

As we felt our way back to our tents in the darkness we discussed it together and most of us had been struck by the same point: most of us felt that the official optimism was being pitched just a little too high.

We rose before dawn on Monday and packed up our bedding rolls, our kitbags of clothes, our stores of food and drink. I was in a party with Alan Moorehead and Richard Busvine of the *Chicago Times*. We were allotted a Humber staff car, two ten-hundredweight trucks, three drivers, and an officer, to conduct us. The idea was to go as far forward as possible in order to be in position when the show started.

In the cold morning sunlight we passed through the furrows of rubble which had once been the streets of Mersa Matruh and at the road fork which is now known officially as Charing Cross we turned left and headed inland. Then after a few miles we swung right, parallel with the sea again, along a great corridor between two mine fields, almost the same way we had gone when we were beating Graziani a year before. Again there was that first bitter taste of dust in the mouth and again for one minute I was back in Spain, standing on the ring of naked hills round Teruel. But this time the sensation was weaker and shorter, for all last winter's dust had intervened and the desert was conquering Spain.

We stopped for a quick snack and everyone was quietly taking stock of what the others chose to eat, where and how they ate it, how seriously they took lunch. We were still the separate elements of a party, not yet merged together, and no one had yet come forward as the acknowledged cook, the self-appointed keeper of the rations, the washer-up. I had been on many trips with Alan before, but not with any of the others. We should have to go through all the birth pangs of a routine.

We bumped on westwards, driving circumspectly to save the vehicles and make the journey a little less uncomfortable. Sometimes we glimpsed the new railway, and once a train came steaming towards us across the empty desert. If I had seen it a year before I should have known I was mad. But now it was a common thing. At Piccadilly — a cross-roads graced by a copy of London's Eros made of four-gallon petrol tins — we had to turn left. And from there on we got lost. We were trying to find Eighth Army Battle Headquarters, where we should be told the location of Thirtieth Corps Headquarters, and it ought to have been easy. But we asked and asked, followed up clues and false trails, compared map references, searched for signposts. We found R.A.M.C., R.A.S.C., R.A.O.C., every possible sort of unit, but no one had so much as heard of Battle Headquarters.

Then towards dusk we came to two mighty air fields. American Marylands were slipping down out of a pale, apple-green evening sky, strolling back in twos and threes from a raid. The dust spurted in two yellow jets from their wheels as they landed, and they taxied away to the side of the fields until the horizon seemed ringed with them. Then someone showed us the tents of Battle H.Q. sprayed over the desert a mile away.

It was too late to go on — the light was going fast. We decided to spend the night and wait for the first reports back from the front line in the morning. Then we would write stories, get them away by the first available plane, and go on forward ourselves. In inky darkness we unpacked our camp-beds, put them up on the leeward side of the car, unrolled our bedding, and pushed ourselves into our sleeping-bags.

Away out ahead of us in the blackness an army was waiting to go into battle, each unit at its carefully plotted position. I could picture the men — I had seen them often enough — moving around restless and impatient, wishing it would begin. They would be joking in whispers, rather tensely and absent-mindedly, for their minds were pitched a few hours ahead in the future and the present was just a blank interval of waiting.

At nameless points which were simply map-references, different headquarters would be checking over their final arrangements or trying to snatch a few hours' sleep. Every man and every machine was ready to play its part in the intricately devised plan — as elaborate and exact as a ballet-dance — which was on the eve of being put in motion.

The centre of gravity of the air force had swung from Tedder's softly carpeted Cairo office to a tent in the desert. Here Air Vice-Marshal Arthur Coningham — a tall, dark, six-foot New Zealander — was preparing to wield the pliant, finely balanced instrument which Tedder had forged him. He had a reputation for dazzlingly brilliant flying and dazzlingly brilliant wisecracks — a man of action with a rapier-like mind. He did not know then that he had got air superiority — he could not know it until he put it to the test. But he had planned to get a flying start by an all-out blitz on the enemy's air fields all this Monday night. The army had asked him to provide two clear days without serious air opposition.

But quite suddenly all his plans had to be scrapped. Something happened which was not on the programme. Heavy rainclouds obscured the stars. A wind rose. And the most spectacular thunderstorm within local memory burst upon the desert.

Up to the north and west vivid jagged flashes of lightning tore the sky. Gradually it spread round the horizon till simultaneous flashes were flood-lighting the desert with a cold, weird radiance. The thunder mumbled and murmured and roared in long growling cadences, and burst overhead with a crack like a bomb. For some time we argued stupidly whether this was really thunder and lightning or a series of terrific bombing raids. But then the rain came drumming down on our sleeping-bags, a sharp penetrating rain which hissed into the desert dust. I tied and buttoned and strapped up everything I could and got well inside. During a lull I pushed all my possessions underneath my bed, then dived under cover again. From Alan and Richard came murmurs of complaint and loud rousing curses. It was uncomfortable enough for us, but it was infuriating for Coningham. Not a single plane took off that night.

But they were off again in the morning. Before dawn we heard the engines warming up on the great air fields beside us. When it was light enough for us to crawl from our sleeping-bags and examine our own private damage, hundreds, literally hundreds, of planes were shuttling back and forth in the sky around us.

The desert smelt clean and fresh, washed all over by the rain which had for the moment settled the dust. I had not suffered badly. My bedding had proved more waterproof than I had dared hope and there was only one point, near the foot, where the water had soaked through. But Richard had spent the last few hours of the night holding his body out of a puddle which had somehow formed right inside his sleeping-bag.

We propped up everything to dry in the weak morning sun, and went down to get the news. Everything, we found, was going sweetly. Sappers had been out ahead of the troops in the darkness, putting mines out of action with delicate groping fingers, and dragging away great skeins of the barbed-wire frontier fence. When zero hour came men had climbed into their trucks, the rain gleaming on their mackintosh capes and steel helmets, and driven straight forward into Libya. Tanks, armoured cars, Bren-gun carriers, lorries, were now miles inside enemy territory, advancing without opposition. Up on the coast the six-inch guns of the navy had shelled the enemy's positions at Halfaya and Sollum while the thunderstorm was still raging. And as dawn came twenty-five-pounder guns on land took up the barrage.

There were two other items of news, one good, the other — well, no one quite knew whether it was good or bad. The first was that the thunderstorm had done what Coningham's planes had not had a chance of doing: it had kept a large proportion of the enemy's air force on the ground by turning his air fields into bogs. Derna and Gazala, where the dive bombers were concentrated, appeared to be particularly bad. The other piece of news was that Rommel was in the process of shifting his forces. There was a surprise move westwards from Bardia, and the Twenty-first Armoured Division seemed to be in it. In point of fact Rommel was just concentrating his forces for his attack on Tobruk.

Otherwise all seemed to be going well. The King had sent a stirring message to the troops and General Cunningham had issued an order of the day. We wrote our messages and packed up hurriedly, eager and impatient to get on ahead.

Everything was racing forward as hard as it could go over the firm dry surface which last night's rain and the morning's sun had produced. We wasted a lot of time following a compass bearing when we might just as well have joined in the general stream. We reached the place where Corps Headquarters ought to be only to find that it had packed up and left. All day we blundered on, stopping, asking, consulting, but always going steadily west. A Brigadier took us some of the way. Then we were able to follow a new telephone line. We passed through a gap in the frontier wire — Mussolini's great fence was always known simply as "the wire" — and skirted the ruins of Fort Maddalena. And at last we were in Libya.

The tracks of the leading vehicles had long since been obliterated by the mass of transport that had followed them. You could still see that this Libyan desert had been smooth and flat and hard a few hours ago. But already it was furrowed into countless parallel ruts which were spreading and spreading as convoys diverged farther and farther from the central axis in search of a fresh, firm route.

It was extraordinarily exhilarating, that first day in Libya. Our Humber had already broken down, so we had piled everything into the ten-hundredweights and I was in the back of one of them, sprawled on the baggage. It was sunny and warm, if you could keep out of the wind, and we were racing ahead, mile after mile into enemy territory. But the really exciting thing was the air. It was filled with British planes. Tedder and Coningham had got the air superiority they had been striving for. In Greece I had found out what it was like to be attacked all day long by enemy planes and never see one of your own. But nobody had told me how fine the opposite was. Nobody could have told me — it had never happened.

To-day it was happening. Whole shoals of fighters went careering by, glinting like little silver splinters in the sun. Bombers cruised steadily overhead with their fighter escorts fooling all round them. It had become almost second nature with most of us to stop the truck and run when planes appeared, but today we could sit tight and admire them. I think everyone's spirits rose to a higher level then than in any campaign so far.

We still did not get anywhere that day. We asked everyone but no one knew. A common answer was: "Sorry, I'm a stranger here myself." Often we would be given totally conflicting directions by several different people, all of whom claimed to know quite definitely. And again and again we listened to a vague, complicated description which always ended with: "You couldn't miss it if you tried."

We always could. By evening we were still nowhere. But we did meet someone who gave us the welcome news that battle had not yet been joined — we had not missed anything. So we finally settled down to camp and we found we were furiously hungry. In the darkness I groped for half a dozen cans of food, selecting them haphazard, and opened them into our stewpot and heated the mess over a small spirit-stove in the cab of the truck. It was not very tasty and it was apparent that our staff work had been bad as regards cooking facilities. But we gulped it down without remark — all we really cared about then was catching up with the battle.

The cold woke me early in the morning and I lay until dawn planning a reorganization of my bedding. We got breakfast and shaved and packed with numb, inexpert fingers — we had not yet got into the rhythm of the thing at all. Then we set out once more on our quest. Again the sky was full of planes and great convoys of lorries cruised steadily across the desert, all going the same pace and keeping even distances, like a convoy at sea. We zigzagged back and forth chasing clue after clue. Everyone else had explicit orders to follow and just followed them. No one could help us in our search for a specific unit. But towards noon a Colonel gave us a bearing and we thought we were really getting warmer. Our new course lay almost due west and soon we were running through an uncannily empty stretch of desert. We must have covered ten miles when we were suddenly hailed from behind a little hillock. One of the sleek new sand-coloured Crusader tanks was lying there with the Commander's head sticking out of the turret.

"Where are you off to?" he called.

"We are trying to find Corps Headquarters."

"Well, you're going straight into a battle."

He was right, too. Now that we had stopped the engines of our trucks, we could hear the thudding of guns not far over the horizon ahead. The Tank Commander climbed down and strolled over to us.

"They're fighting an Italian armoured division," he told us. "That blasted thing — " waving his foot at his tank — "broke down so we missed the show. But apparently there's going to be a second instalment, so we'll be there for that."

For the first time we got some picture of what had been happening. As soon as it crossed the frontier, the Seventh Armoured Division fanned its three brigades out north and west in three striking columns. The Fourth Brigade, with American tanks, went straight north, the Seventh Brigade went north-west, dead for Tobruk, and the Twenty-second moved up on the left flank.

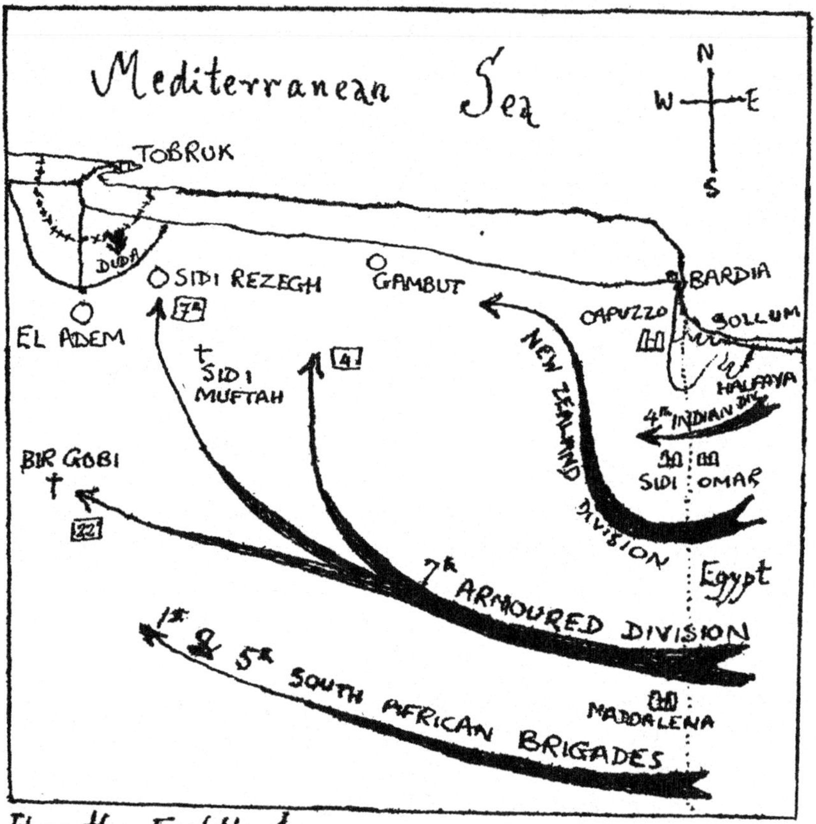

How the Eighth Army attacked November 18

We had caught up with the Twenty-second, who had just finished fighting the first battle of the campaign. Rommel, it seemed, had expected any British attack to come up from Jarabub Oasis towards Tobruk. So he had prepared a strong defensive position at El Gobi—a junction of desert tracks south of Tobruk—and stationed the

Italian Ariete Division there. The Twenty-second, cruising forward over the desert, had bumped into a concentration which looked like a big bunch of lorries. But it turned out to be an extremely strong, cleverly camouflaged anti-tank position. The Twenty-second veered off amid a hail of shells and engaged the Ariete, which offered battle with its full complement of 135 tanks.

In a quick careering engagement the Italians were forced to withdraw. Their first brave battle array degenerated into flurried shooting and incoherent manœuvrings, and they were said to have lost 45 tanks. But we had lost some too, and in the accounts I heard there was an implied suggestion that the Italians had put up rather a stiffer fight than Italians usually do. Moreover, they had come back for more. They had got reinforcements — apparently including a battalion of Germans — and the battle was going to be re-joined at any minute.

The Twenty-second directed us to Seventh Armoured Division Headquarters — we must have bypassed the Corps miles back — and off we set once again. But we missed our way again and drove right across the British front to the Fourth Brigade which was on the right wing. We found the American Honeys just making their debut. Rommel had detached a force of rather over 100 tanks from his Twenty-first *Panzerdivision* and had shot them south into the desert to make a fighting reconnaissance. In the golden evening sunshine they met the Fourth.

ii

The first shots snapped out just as we arrived and we grabbed our tin hats and clambered on the roof of a car to try and get a view of it. The Germans were coming on in one great stretched-out column, moving fast. The Americans went in to meet them weaving, zigzagging, making full use of their forty miles an hour to minimize themselves as targets. There was something in it of a naval battle, something of a mediæval cavalry charge, but all speeded up madly as you might speed up a cinema film.

Then they met and intermingled and there was utter, indescribable confusion. There was noise — the quick, jarring crack of tank guns firing, the pulsing clamour of mighty engines going all out, the rasping squeaking clatter of the tank treads, the grinding of the gears. There was dust — a hundred separate cyclones of whirling choking yellow dust. There was smoke — the thin bitter smoke of explosives and the exhaust smoke from a couple of hundred raving engines. There was flame — the quick stabbing flash of guns firing, the red-black blaze of a tank set on fire. There were grotesque firework displays when a shell got in among a tank's ammunition or Very lights. But there was no pattern or design of coherence about it at all.

Inside that frantic jumble tanks were duelling with tanks in running, almost hand-to-hand fights, firing nearly point-blank, twisting, dodging, sprinting with screaming treads and whining engines that rose to a shriek as they changed gear. As each new tank loomed up ahead, gunners were swinging the muzzles of their guns automatically, eyes strained behind their goggles, fighting through the smoke and dust to discriminate friend from foe. Men told me afterwards that they were not even conscious of the two-pounders going off almost in their ears, so tense was their concentration.

The battle swung away and back again, careering across five miles or more of desert. To us it was just a greyish-blackish-yellowish fog shot with flame. But inside it men were lying in agony, waiting helplessly with the acrid stench of shellfire in their nostrils and the deafening clamour in their ears, waiting till it should stop, till night should come, hoping the ambulance would find them. Tanks got on fire, exploded, men ran or crawled from the wreckage and tried to get out of the battle before someone ran them over or the criss-crossing shells got them. After the initial charge it had become crazy–free-for-all, all rules, all conscious tactics and training and drill forgotten, nothing left but a blazing instinct to kill before you were killed yourself.

There was one moment's respite in the battle when a German petrol and ammunition column hove in sight over the horizon and the enemy tanks drew off and clustered round it like wasps round a honey-pot. It looked a wonderful target, but we could not attack. The Germans, standing still, with steady gun platforms and heavier guns, could have picked off our tanks before we could have got into position. They finished their re-fuelling and re-engaged. We stood watching, but seeing little and understanding nothing, until the sun went down redly behind us and it was too dark to see any more.

When dusk fell we went back and found Seventh Armoured Division Headquarters. At last we were somewhere where we wanted to be. We met Eddie Ward of the B.B.C.—a very fine descriptive broadcaster who had been my companion on almost every Middle East campaign—and he suggested that we should camp the night with him.

Headquarters was only a very short distance from the front line so it went into "leaguer" after dark. All the "soft" or unarmed transport gathered in a ring—much like the circle of wagons from which the American pioneers defied the Red Indians—with armoured cars stationed all round as a defensive screen. We were hungry and cold and for some reason Eddie was sure we were going to be bombed; he said there had been three German reconnaissance planes over that day. But I made some hot soup and we wrapped ourselves up in our blankets and munched biscuits and argued about the theory of the leaguer. Was it as good against bombers as against Red Indians? There was the unnerving consideration that one bomb could now wipe out pretty well the whole Headquarters.

All along the horizon where the battle had been, silver star shells rose and fell in jerky flight. Tracers skidded along just above the skyline. Coloured Very lights rose singly or in pairs and distant orange flashes meant that the twenty-five-pounders were firing. We could hear quite clearly the rumble of moving tanks and vehicles. Both sides were re-grouping and jockeying for position in preparation for the morning. The German recovery services were hard at work on the fifteen tanks which the Honeys' guns had knocked out and ambulance parties were groping in the darkness, guided by the groans and shouts of the wounded.

Before we went to bed we got news of the central column — the Seventh Armoured Brigade. Against little or no opposition it had pushed miles ahead, almost to within sight of Tobruk. Its tanks had stormed and taken Sidi Rezegh Air Field, which lies near the forty-mile "Axis Road" girdling Tobruk, and they had destroyed something like nineteen planes, twelve of them yellow-nosed, gull-winged Stukas. Now it had flung out guards and was spending the night on the air field.

I slept soundly until a double burst of Bren-gun fire woke me almost in panic at four-thirty. But it was only the Headquarters' alarm clock. The leaguer had to be dispersed and the whole camp moved before first light in case enemy planes came to bomb it. As we dressed we could still see Very lights, star shells and tracers to the east. And when we moved off, our armoured cars glinting ruddily in a garish sunrise, the battle had started again.

This was the third day of the campaign, and we still had not found Corps Headquarters. What was much worse, we had not written a despatch for two days. We decided we must at all costs get ourselves straightened out.

By good luck we struck a Liaison Officer who was going our way, and we followed him doggedly over fifteen miles of rock-seamed mud-flats. And so at last, shortly before lunch, we reached Corps. For the first time in the campaign we were able to relax a little.

We shaved and washed (as much as you can wash in a mug of water you have already shaved in), and opened some cans for a leisurely lunch. We aired our bedding, which was still damp from that first torrential night, and Richard did some sewing. We dug ourselves slit trenches at a suitable distance from the trucks. And at a convenient moment we strolled over to the Intelligence van to get the news.

This was the position on the third day: the four British divisions had wheeled into Libya in four concentric curves. The Indians, nearest the hub, had scarcely moved at all. The New Zealanders were edging forwards slowly. The Armoured Division was deeply engaged. And away on the left flank the South Africans were racing swiftly ahead. Only the Armoured Division had done any fighting. Its three brigades were still stuck out like three fingers: the Twenty-second on the left had had two battles with the Ariete and apparently routed them; the Seventh had beaten off an infantry counterattack on Sidi Rezegh; and on the right the Fourth, in a second engagement, had held firm against 130 German tanks which were said to have withdrawn with the loss of thirty more tanks and nine caterpillar-wheeled troop carriers. Rommel, it seemed, was in the process of uniting all the tanks of his two armoured divisions somewhere between Bardia and Tobruk, and was jabbing in all along the British line in the hope of finding a weak spot.

As we walked back to our trucks we discussed the situation. I think we realized right then that it was not going to be quite such an easy victory as we had been led to expect. Alan argued that we were wrong to split our armoured forces, that Rommel was doing the smart thing by uniting his. I still felt it was a mistake ever to surrender the initiative in the desert.

We had all heard the first whispers of the thing that the whole desert was soon talking about — the fact that our tanks were seriously out-gunned by the heavier German tanks. In the message I wrote when we got back, I said warily: "Only preliminary actions have been fought so far. It is too early to hang out your flags yet. There are other, stiffer battles to be fought before the enemy's forces are broken."

We slept that night at Corps, and next morning we learned that the big battle had started. We thought it was almost certainly the key battle of the campaign, and possibly the biggest single tank battle in history. The Germans had broken off their fight with the Fourth Brigade and made a bee-line for the Seventh, which was semi-marooned up on Sidi Rezegh. The Seventh had moved forward to meet the oncoming Nazis and had engaged them at about 9.30 A.M. The Fourth and the Twenty-second were moving up to help. The battle-field was about thirty miles south-east of Tobruk and my map showed a Bedu tomb there called Sidi Muftah.

Muftah is the Arabic for "key," and I thought this was an appropriate name for the battle, but it came to be known as Sidi Rezegh.

Of course we wanted to get up there, and we set off with someone who was supposed to be going to the Fourth Brigade H.Q. But I

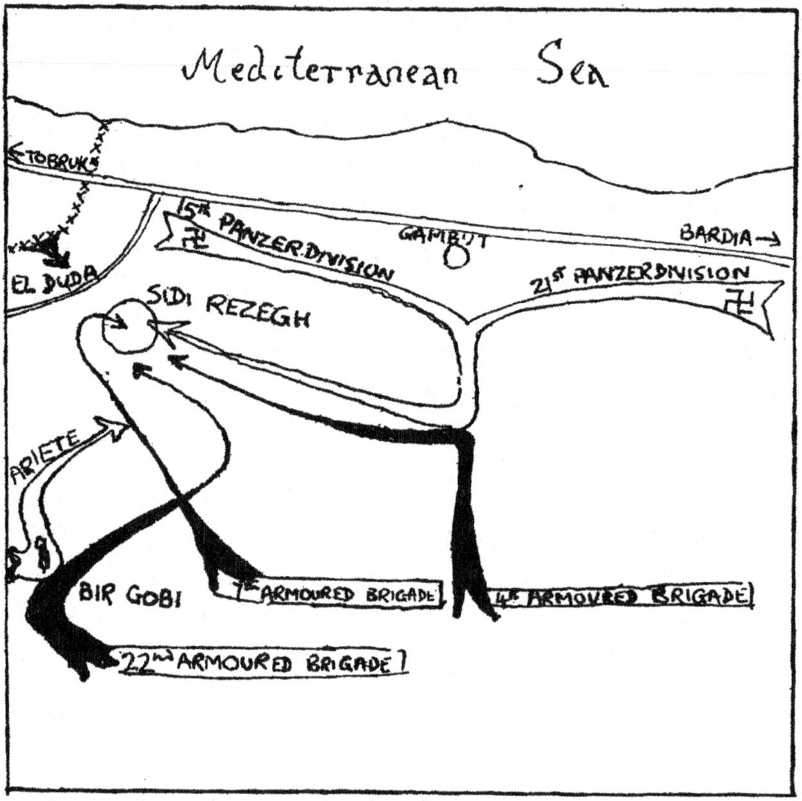

The Battle of Sidi Rezegh.

never understood our peregrinations that day. Certainly we never reached the Fourth. I was in the back of one of the trucks still, almost immovably wedged in, and I did not know what questions were being asked every time we stopped, or what answers we were getting. I sat trying to shield my left ear from the icy wind and my nose from the dust which whirled back upon us. When it got too unbearable I closed my eyes and let my imagination produce an antidote. Nearly always the scene which filled my mind was the same. It was a grassy ride through the wood which lies just outside the back-door of my home in England. On the left beech trees and oaks sprang from a carpet of blue-bells and primroses. On the right, by a convenient seasonal anachronism, fully grown bracken covered the swelling hillside. I watched the rabbits playing and the squirrels collecting nuts in this conventionalized setting. And then some extra big bump would awaken me again to the chill, empty, beige-and-blue world of dust and discomfort.

In the late afternoon we caught up with Seventh Armoured Division Headquarters and got the news. The Seventh Brigade — and the Seventh Support Group, seasoned veterans who had had more experience than anyone living of desert tank warfare — had been holding out since the morning against the entire German tank force. If any single unit had to take the brunt of the Nazi onslaught, this was certainly the right one to do it. After two hours of bitter fighting they had wirelessed to the Brigadier commanding the Seventh asking him how he was getting on. He had replied: "Quite happy, but would like to know when the others are coming."

So would everyone else. The plan was for the Seventh to hold the Germans and for the other two brigades to strike them. But where were the other two brigades? They had not very far to come — not much farther, in fact, than the Germans. The Fourth, it turned out, had bumped into a well-defended enemy transport column and had spent some time mopping it up. The Twenty-second was supposed to be on the way. But they both seemed agonizingly slow.

It may have been some organizational defect which caused this delay. The Twenty-second, completely new, both tanks and men, to desert warfare, may have encountered unexpected difficulties. But at tea-time the Seventh was still fighting with unimaginable gallantry and the other two brigades still had not come.

The Seventh was outnumbered and out-gunned and it had not very many tanks left. It was just hanging on like grim death. With it was the Seventh Support Group — riflemen and gunners who I suppose had done more fighting than any other unit in the British army this war. Now once again they were in a tight spot, and their Commander had been earning himself the V.C. by two days of matchless leadership.

The story of Brigadier Jock Campbell during those two hellish days was the story of the whole Seventh Support Group, for again and again he led them personally into battle. Several times he leapt into his staff car — a station wagon with the roof sawn off — hoisted his blue flag and led a tank charge. Never did he fail to get as far forward as the farthest tank. It sounds a crazy thing for a brigadier to do. But there was not an ounce of bravado in it; what he did he had to do for there was no one else who could have done it.

Twice on the first morning the Germans attacked the air field from the east, the second time with over sixty tanks. The Support Group was in grave danger of being overrun and pushed right off the ground it was holding. Campbell seized his staff car, raced away to the north-west corner of the air field and collected every tank he could find. Then he took them into battle. He had to go with them, for only he knew just where they had to attack, and he stuck his blue flag in the top of the car and went before them like a beacon.

Twice that happened. Then the third time the Germans tried to run right past the British positions on the southern flank. Again Campbell drove in search of tanks. This time he could only get twelve and seven of them were shot into flames within a few minutes. But somehow the enemy were driven off and Campbell led his five remaining tanks back into camp again.

That was the first day. Dawn of the second day showed the German tank force lined up a thousand yards away to the east, re-fuelling. Instantly the Support Group blazed into action. Campbell took off his coat and worked like a madman at the guns. He used his huge strength to help swing them round and he even did some loading himself. Then he climbed on a limber and stayed directing their fire. The German re-fuelling column slipped away at once and took refuge down the escarpment to the north. One by one the enemy tanks began to follow it in order to fill up with oil. Again Campbell went into action like a tornado. He collected another of his scratch tank forces and charged out with it. Then he drove back and climbed on a derelict Stuka to direct operations. Again he helped to man the guns, for there had been casualties among the artillery officers.

Then came the really big attack, the attack that nearly brought the Seventh Brigade to its knees. It came from the west, and there were more than a hundred German tanks in it. The fighting boiled up in an inferno of sound and fury until the smoke and dust were as thick in the air as a London fog. Something like twenty-seven aeroplanes were blazing round the landing-ground as the result of stray incendiaries. It was impossible to see anything clearly. And when the Fourth and Twenty-second Armoured Brigades finally did come on the scene a little later, they had no idea where to go.

So Jock Campbell showed them. Back in his roofless staff car, his blue flag gleaming in the smoke, he took the Twenty-second into battle, yelling, shouting, literally hurling rocks at people to make them go faster. Then he went back for the Fourth. Men who were there told me he seemed like one possessed. He was everywhere all the time, running from tank to tank, banging on the steel doors, encouraging, helping, giving orders, directing fire. "Everyone feels about six times as good when he is about," one of his officers said. It was while he was out in the open rounding up individual tanks that something hit him in the side underneath his right armpit. But he got the V.C. for it all — an almost unknown honour for a brigadier — and there was not a man in the Support Group who did not think he was worth it.[1]

Now that the other two Brigades had arrived, the battle became stupendous. There must have been something like five hun-

[1] In February 1942, Jock Campbell was promoted to Major-General and given command of the Seventh Armoured Division, and a few days later he was dead. He died in the senseless, trivial way V.C.'s so often die — a car smash in the desert, only a few miles from where he led his tank charges.

dred tanks engaged. Low-built Valentines and Crusaders, greenish-yellow Honeys with their knobby turrets, older battle-worn British cruisers were interlocked with German Mark Twos, Threes and Fours — powerful black-grey monsters with their white crosses conspicuous on their sides. Until the sun went down we listened to its din rising and falling as the battle swayed and careered back and forth across the escarpment top. Sometimes it was ten miles from where we stood, sometimes plumes of purplish smoke were blotting out the horizon. No one could assess just what was happening. No one was able to get from or through or round the battle to bring a report. The ether was throbbing with a crazy jumble of radio messages from tank to tank — "Get out of my way, damn you, you're blocking my view"; "I'm coming up on your left"; "Don't look now but I think you're being followed." By the time the radio reports had been pieced together the situation had entirely altered.

As night fell the two forces drew apart. Ambulances and stretcher parties came forward to succour the wounded who had been lying there while the fighting stormed round them. Recovery units came up to drag away the knocked-out tanks and do running repairs. Petrol and ammunition columns appeared on the scene. And the tank crews had a little leisure to wipe the dust and grime and smoke and sweat from their faces, bathe their bloodshot eyes, moisten their parched throats and rest their deafened ears.

As we leaguered for the night, the din calmed down to a fitful throbbing over the horizon. Richard got out a tin basin and a big bottle of Eau-de-Cologne and "did" his feet. Then it began to rain and the driest place was in bed. I strapped up my "valise" over my head and slept.

A fine rain fell all night, wetting everything and turning the desert surface to the consistency of cold cream. And in the pallid washed dawn of Saturday, the battle began again. The British had brought up field artillery during the night and now the twenty-five-pounders were firing hard. Sometimes when the battle swept near them, they had to shorten the range until they were firing over open sights, aiming straight into the melee whenever they could get a clear view of the enemy tanks. The rounded thump of the guns came clearly on the morning air, mingled with the sharper crack of the tank guns and sometimes the regular rattle of machine-guns.

An officer was driving back to Corps Headquarters, so we sat down in the cabs of the two trucks, with our typewriters on our knees, to write despatches. There was a general theory at that moment that Rommel was on the run — that he was trying to whip his tank forces through the gap to the west before our Armoured Division joined hands with the defenders of Tobruk, who had already made a sortie. It is just possible that he really was on the run. But when he was cornered he began to fight, and fight both well and skilfully. And from that moment he went on fighting.

Then we set off for Sidi Rezegh.

CHAPTER 14

Flight into Egypt

THAT morning the tank battle stopped being one continuous engagement and broke down into a series of sharp skirmishes. Our initial impetus had now spent itself, and this was the turning point of the first phase. No one could say who had won so far—only exact figures of tanks knocked out and tanks still in action could have supplied the answer. But we were still holding our ground and Rommel had certainly not been decisively smashed. It looked pretty even.

By the time we reached Sidi Rezegh something vaguely like a front line had been established and infantry and artillery were in action. Then towards sundown the Germans counterattacked.

I stood watching on a slightly shelving slice of desert. In front of me ten blackened, burnt-out tanks were lying about and I saw with a little shock of horror that they were all British—new Valentines. They had been caught re-fuelling and shot into flames. At the foot of one of them was a simple grave with a makeshift cross and yesterday's date. Sodden kitbags and clothes were still smouldering. In my nostrils was that chemical smell of burning you always get on a modern battle-field.

In front of me, across the deeply rutted ground, big shells were thumping down. The Italian artillery outside Tobruk had swivelled round its heavy guns and the shells threw up great billows of rose-red and mauvish smoke, making a marbled frieze all along the horizon. Livid flashes jerked out along the ridge as our guns replied. The rattle of machine-gun fire sounded like a chorus of giant typewriters.

Out from among the smoke and flame wound a long sluggish column, half-blue and half-khaki — the first prisoners. They were half-German and half-Italian and the Germans looked curiously unheroic in their shoddy, stained canvas uniforms.

While we were watching them march away into the distance, I chanced to look over my shoulder. They told me afterwards I said in a conversational voice, "There's a nice bit of dive-bombing." But in point of fact I cannot remember saying anything at all. Thirty-five dive bombers were milling around just behind us, poised to swoop.

Lying flat on my stomach, pressed as close to the ground as I could get, I watched their performance in profile. They dived so steeply it seemed impossible they could ever get up again. As each one's bomb burst, the next one tilted its nose downwards, and the remainder circled round awaiting their turn. The bombs shook the earth and came cracking across the desert with a noise that made me stuff my fingers in my ears. I tipped down my head, wincing from the sound, and found that my nose was resting on a complete fossilized jellyfish. I noted, rather bitterly, that this place was once at the bottom of the sea.

Then three Stukas came racketing along on top of me, just a few feet from the ground. The air sang with bullets — ours and theirs. One of the planes was rocking crazily, and the pilot's face had a grim frozen look as he went over my head. Abruptly just a couple of hundred yards behind me he hit the ground in a tremendous pillar of flame. He must have been hit during the bombing, and a Bren gunner standing beside me had given him the *coup de grâce.*

We got to our feet, laughing a little hysterically with relief, bubbling with eagerness to explain just how it had looked to us. Eddie Ward had been lying beside me, and that was the last time I saw him. We parted with some trivial remark about our supplies of clean socks.

We walked over to the A.C.V. — the Armoured Command Vehicle — and sat down on the ground, talking with the officers. Inside, directing the battle, was "Strafer" Gott, with whom I had traded biscuits for water down at Fort Mechili the winter before. Now he was a Major-General commanding the Seventh Armoured Division but he still looked more like a bishop than a soldier, with his silver hair and friendly blue eyes. Only the great firmness of his mouth marked him down as the man of action.

I looked at his map and tried to assess the situation. The Germans, with tanks and infantry, had just retaken Sidi Rezegh. The air field was still visible through glasses, about four miles away, with the carcasses of wrecked aeroplanes all round it. But the Germans had got it and the South Africans were trying to push them out again.

Shells were still biting into the lip of the escarpment, and occasionally a loose one plunged down among the vehicles dispersed around us. But no one seemed very worried. We decided to camp down in a nice open patch of desert where we could keep an eye on the A.C.V. With the dive bombers fresh in our memories, we dug ourselves deep, narrow slit trenches. The Conducting Officer, eager to help, started erecting Richard's bed and broke a vital strut. I got out my pots and pans and set about compiling a stew while it was still daylight.

We had had our dinner and were sitting on our beds drinking tea when someone noticed that the A.C.V. had gone. We looked round and found that practically everything had gone or was going. Transport was streaming back through us from the north-east, shepherded by Bren-gun carriers and armoured cars. Sometimes as they passed men tossed us jokes which we could not catch. But it seemed prudent to pack up and get under way.

The German counterattack was spreading. A detachment of their tanks had broken loose and was marauding along our flank. Unarmed transport vehicles began scurrying this way and that like a flock of sheep with mad dogs at their heels. As it grew darker we could see the tracer shells flying, and the red, white and green Very lights which the German tanks used for signalling to one another. We drove on warily, following the main stream, straining our eyes to avoid the slit trenches which the troops had dug wherever they camped, until I had lost all sense of direction. It was impossible to know whether to be alarmed or not. We finally found ourselves with an Ambulance Unit attached to the Fifth South African Brigade, and there we put up our beds and lay down on them fully dressed beneath our blankets. A screen of tanks and armoured cars was supposed to be between us and the enemy and I lay and let a confused murmur of explosions from the direction of Tobruk lull me to sleep. The last thing I remember was a little Sergeant-Major explaining how sixteen British tanks had held off forty-five German ones. I did not hear where.

We were awakened well before dawn and we started off south-east at once, hoping to contact some headquarters. It was imperative to know what had happened. Our movements always depended on accurate knowledge of the situation, and since yesterday evening we had lost track of events completely. We found the Headquarters of the Seventh Brigade, and they told us they had exactly four complete tanks left out of their original 150. Now they had been withdrawn from the battle. We went on, following the divisional axis backwards. It was a bright sunny morning and the white racing clouds made moving islands of shadow on the desert surface.

We found Seventh Armoured Division Headquarters, but there was no sign of Eddie, or of the others who had been with him. We supposed they must have been lost in last night's mix-up. The news generally was confused and not very encouraging. An Italian tank force was making a stab at our left flank and the South Africans were fighting it off. We got out our typewriters and began to write stories telling all yesterday's news. I was on my second page when the whole camp began to pack up urgently. Little groups of trucks began to race through us from the left. The sound of firing boiled up over the horizon and within a few minutes the squat black shapes of German tanks had appeared.

We packed with the rest and fled. We were a headquarters, not a fighting unit, and there was no point in staying. We bumped a few miles at full speed across the desert, then stopped and sent out a couple of Bren-gun carriers to reconnoitre. The scare seemed to have died down again. We sat in the sun and resumed our stories.

No more news came in, so we packed again and went on to Corps. For the second time since the campaign began we had an hour or two of leisure. I laid all my bedding in the sun to air, and picked through my sleeping-bags for fleas — little brown shiny creatures, not particularly agile or intelligent, but clever at hiding themselves. I rearranged my bedding, putting underneath me a shepherd's sheepskin coat I had bought in Persia, for I had a theory that it was the cold striking up from below that froze me so early in the morning.

That night we saw strange lights hanging in the sky over the battle-field and rather uneasily we invented theories about what was happening. But nothing could be done until the morning. Richard and Alan and I went to bed, lying side by side with the truck at our heads so that all together we formed a letter E, and talked. Not seeing one another, but looking upwards at the stars, we advanced the most extravagant theses and defended them. We dusted off opinions and ideas we had not used for years and gave them an airing. We began by trying to teach Alan some astronomy, but he comes from Australia where the sky is doubtless different, and all he knew was a constellation called the Pot. Richard and I thought he must mean the Great Bear, which Americans call the Dipper, but he did not. As far as we could gather he meant Orion's Belt. From astronomy we went on to poetry in a ludicrous argument about Wordsworth. With the fighting still throbbing faintly over the horizon, we tangled ourselves up deeply in metaphysics and quarrelled acidly about art. In the end we pared things down to such a refinement of subtlety that we argued furiously about the principles of argument, and Richard and I had to decide that Alan's logic was not sufficiently exact for dialectics. Then Alan took refuge in Cartesian first principles and we subsided into sleep.

In the morning we got news which made it plain that the tide had for the moment turned against us. The biggest single fact which emerged was that the Fifth South African Brigade had been completely disintegrated.

All Saturday the Fifth had fought at Sidi Rezegh and on Sunday morning it had to beat off a whole series of attacks from almost every point of the compass. The really big onslaught came quite suddenly in the afternoon after a very heavy artillery bombardment. A tidal wave of tanks swept into the Brigade. They came on seven abreast and ten deep, shooting as they came. The anti-tank gunners used up every round they had and then stood helpless. Right past Brigade Headquarters the enemy thundered, picking up the Brigadier as a prisoner on the way. Helpless, bewildered riflemen were herded like cattle before the oncoming tanks. Staff officers took refuge under the A.C.V. until an incendiary shell set it on fire. Then they too were captured.

The Germans were already rounding up the prisoners when tanks from the British Twenty-second Brigade came to the rescue. As they stormed into the camp, utter confusion broke out again. The Germans dived for the South Africans' slit trenches. The South Africans made a concerted break for freedom. For a few minutes it looked as though the tables might be turned. But the British tanks were too few, and towards dusk the Germans got the upper hand again.

Groups of South Africans were still managing to escape. Individuals were lingering behind and then making a dash for it. The Brigade-Major got away like this, and in the course of a nine-mile hike to safety he had to lie in a slit trench while a German tank went clean over him. All that night and all next day by ones and twos members of the Fifth were turning up at other units. But the Brigade could not be said to exist any more. When all heads were counted, it was found that the total casualties, including prisoners and missing, were just over 3800. The prisoners included Eddie, Anderson, Denny, and five South African war correspondents.

The enemy, it was said, had lost 45 German and 11 Italian tanks in this attack. But those fine figures of tank losses in the early days of the battle turned out to have been very misleading. Two or three British tanks might be firing simultaneously at an enemy tank when it was knocked out, and all of them would claim it separately. Many of the tanks reported as "knocked out" only needed a couple of hours' work on them to make them usable again. The German recovery services were working very well. And the result was that while we were claiming to have inflicted staggering losses, the Germans always seemed to turn up with more tanks than they ought to have had.

The pace was getting fast and furious now, and the operational maps were a grotesque jumble of arrows and figures and numbers in coloured chalks sprawling crazily across the south-east of Tobruk. Some units seemed completely cut off on the map though in fact no one is ever quite cut off in the desert. Germans and British were often occupying the same slice of desert alternately five or six times a day.

It seemed unwise to move from Corps Headquarters until things became clearer and I sat down quietly in the sun to write a letter home. Richard was in the cab, sewing on buttons. Alan had gone off with a spade and a roll of toilet paper. Suddenly all sorts of transport started streaming through the camp. It had happened twice before during the morning, but this time seemed to me subtly different.

"I think this is the real thing," I told Richard.

He looked at the passing lorries for a minute, then diagnosed it swiftly.

"Yes," he said. "Let's get going."

We packed with a speed which was rapidly being born of practice, and flung everything into the trucks. Alan came racing back with his spade. We drove over to where other members of our unit were camped.

"What's the panic?" they asked. "Intelligence will tell us if anything's happening."

I desired them to take a look at Intelligence. Intelligence were busy throwing the last of their luggage into their A.C.V. and the driver was revving up his engine. At that moment a shell burst just where our trucks had been parked. Another screamed through the camp itself. We scrammed.

The whole Headquarters galloped away over the desert in a swirl of dust. Odd units and convoys saw the A.C.V.'s rocketing by and joined in. Great fleets of lorries came cruising over the horizon, all the trucks moving evenly in perfect formation, with fighting close behind them. Sometimes one convoy would meet another obliquely and they would interlock and disentangle themselves again in a choking cloud of dust that nearly obscured the sun. Often enough they could not disentangle themselves completely and each convoy would race on with bits of the other attached to it.

All we knew then was that enemy tanks had broken through. They had got in behind our hard shell of armour and were wreaking havoc among the "soft" transport. It was a case of the wolf and the flock of sheep again: the sheep had stampeded—it was the only thing for them to do. They were simply moving out of the way of the battle. But it was both undignified and extremely inconvenient.

We ran for a couple of hours and then stopped to take stock of the situation and have something to eat. We had lost the A.C.V. we had tried to follow and had attached ourselves to the Corps Headquarters Signals. Almost before we had had time to open a can of something, shells started to fall among us once more. Either we or the battle had taken the wrong direction.

We moved off again while the noise of the firing grew and then receded. On the horizon rose a black column of smoke where a driver had set fire to his lorry rather than let it fall into enemy hands. Throughout the afternoon we drove steadily on towards Egypt. Once a whole host of planes set us running from our vehicles, but they turned out to be British. I began to wonder whether we should have to get right out of Libya, whether there would be enough gaps in the frontier wire to let all this urgent transport through, whether the Germans would realize what a fine dive-bombing target they were likely to get at the wire.

Towards evening we were part of a smallish column, perhaps

thirty vehicles, grouped round the Signals A.C.V. There were a Bofors gun which would not fire, a tank which needed repairs, a couple of Bren-gun carriers and the rest trucks. The sun had already set when we reached the wire and I noted that it was too dark for dive-bombing anyway. Someone in a staff car met us and shepherded us through the gaps — back into Egypt. We ran on a few miles farther and then gathered into close leaguer, hoping to Heaven we were safe.

Alan and I were asked to drive round shouting "All officers to the front of the column." An extraordinarily varied group turned up. We seemed to have caught up fragments of every unit in the desert. Here and there sergeants appeared, saying they were the senior man of their unit present. But gradually things were sorted out and some sort of defence system organized. Very lights were going up all round us and somewhere guns were firing. So we knew the enemy was not far away. There was no reason at all why he should not be in Egypt itself.

I got out my stove and put it in the cab of the truck and cooked a hot stew, for the night was bitterly cold and we were feeling lost and very depressed. On that evening of the twenty-fourth, I confess I thought we had probably lost the whole campaign. Of course it was possible that the New Zealanders up in the north were doing very well, that our armoured forces were still round Tobruk, that the position was nothing like as bad as it looked. But enemy tanks were certainly on the Egyptian frontier. We had been fleeing for about six hours, and the whole desert seemed to be fleeing with us. I knew it was only soft transport which had been stampeded, but it meant a colossal muddle at the best, and the psychological effect of the retreat was very strong.

I lent a blanket to the Commander of the damaged tank which had come with us. From him I heard more explicitly what all the tank people had been talking about for the last three days. The German tanks, it turned out, were both more heavily armoured and more heavily gunned than ours. The Mark Threes and Mark Fours both had more fire power than anything we had. We found ourselves up against the Mark Threes' 50-millimetre guns firing 4½-pound shells and the Mark Fours' 75-millimetre guns firing 15-pound shells. The best we could do was a 37-millimetre cannon firing two-pound shells. It was like pitting destroyers against cruisers. It meant that the British had to start every battle with a sprint of half a mile under fire before they could fire back.

We worked out the mathematics of the thing. Supposing the German advantage is 800 yards (the penetration of the 4½-pounder and of the 15-pounder is much the same, though the effect of the latter is far more devastating), and that the British are advancing at 20 miles an hour, it gives the Germans 80 seconds grace. That means they can fire between 12 and 15 rounds before we can reply effectively, and for those rounds the Germans can remain stationary and have steady gun-platforms — unless, of course, our covering artillery forces them to keep on the move.

Now supposing the Germans get a hit with one shot in 20, which is not over-optimistic, a body of 100 German tanks would score between 65 and 70 direct hits in the 80 seconds during which the British were unable to fire. And supposing that it takes on an average two direct hits to knock out a tank, rather over thirty of our lighter tanks must expect to be knocked out before they could get within effective range of the enemy.

In fact, if we were to join battle on equal terms with the enemy, it meant that we must start off with something like a 30 per cent superiority in numbers. It seemed a grave handicap. We had been countering it partly by using our twenty-five-pounders to give very strong covering fire. But it remained a handicap. Of course our military authorities had known and expected it. It was one of the risks they were prepared to take. But I think it came as a surprise to most of the men inside our tanks.

That night was one of the coldest I remember in the desert. Alan and Richard curled up in the car, and I unrolled my bedding and made myself a sort of nest on the ground by the wheel of the truck, but none of us could sleep.

In the morning we all moved on fifteen miles into Egypt and

then sent out a reconnaissance patrol. We found that Eighth Army Battle Headquarters was just a mile or two away over a rise, and our particular party decided to go there. The rest moved on to a place where the Thirtieth Corps was rallying and regrouping.

We were welcomed with unfeigned relief when we reached the Public Relations tent at Army H.Q. Only one other party of war correspondents had turned up so far, and there was a certain note of anxiety. Everyone shook us warmly by the hand, congratulating us on our escape. The correspondents who had been working back at Headquarters and had not been up at the front tried to find out from us what had happened, but they really knew more than we did. We went off to our trucks to write despatches, for an aeroplane was leaving for Cairo within an hour. While we were writing the mail arrived. Alan got a rise in salary. I got a demand for so much income tax that I still cannot believe it is true.

ii

The enemy tank force which had chased us back into Egypt had turned north and was now somewhere around Sidi Omar, one of the frontier fortresses. According to some versions it was the bulk of the German tank strength, but others declared it was only the Ariete Division. In either case it was clear that Rommel had tried a desperate gamble. He had broken through the hard crust of our advance and had split our army clean down the middle as you might split a pear from the narrow end. Tanks followed by motor transport had shot their way through the mass of unarmed vehicles which were maintaining our fighting forces. In a country of roads and fields and hedges it would have been disastrous for us. But here in the desert great masses of motor transport simply melted away as the Axis column clove through. The material damage done was not serious.

Though he did not know it, Rommel had all but succeeded. He failed, it is true, to distract us away from the main focal point—Tobruk—and possibly scare us right out of Libya. But his marauding tank column finished up only four miles from our main supply dump. If he had got in among that there is no knowing what might have happened. By the grace of God he missed it.

Nevertheless the confusion was indescribable. Commanding officers had lost their units and applied to the R.A.F. to help them find them. Thirtieth Corps Headquarters got split in two and part went north and joined the New Zealanders while the rest went south into the desert. General Gott's Headquarters travelled right through the enemy lines at night and came away with prisoners. People were being captured and escaping and being re-captured and re-escaping. A staff officer in one British Headquarters looked up and saw a tractor chugging through the camp towing a wireless truck. "Not one of ours," he remarked and bent to his work again. Then his head jerked up again in a wild surmise. "Good God, it's Boche," he yelled, and they caught it just as the German driver was hoping he had got away with it. That sort of thing was happening all the time. Men were captured by Germans using New Zealand lorries, then re-captured by New Zealanders in German lorries. Libya was a madhouse.

Operational maps now looked like surrealist masterpieces. Staff officers were going crazy trying to keep track of the manœuvrings and countermanœuvrings of the two closely interwoven armies. Even quite early on there had been no fewer than five fronts running down inland from the coast between the west of Tobruk and the east of Sollum. But now the armies were also interlocked in layers running east and west. It made no sense at all. All preconceived text-book notions went by the board. The proper technical terms hardly existed to describe what was happening. The campaign was making up its own rules as it went along.

Once already Army Headquarters had been warned to get ready to leave at half an hour's notice. Thirteenth Corps, up in the north, was virtually cut off, though individual people were managing to get through. Quent Reynolds arrived from up there with a hair-raising story of running the gauntlet through a midnight battle.

The very first night we spent at Headquarters eight tanks churned up to my bedside — we were sleeping on the very outside edge of the camp — and I honestly did not know whether they were going to be British or German. I thought the chances were about fifty-fifty. As the Commander's footsteps crunched over the gravel towards me I began to rehearse German phrases in my mind in the hope of bluffing him. He asked me the way in English, and we exchanged identifications suspiciously. Then, I think, we both breathed a sigh of relief. I know I did.

It took some days for the men to sort themselves out. A scratch tank force was collected and sent off to fight the enemy's flying column. At Sidi Omar the Indian Division engaged it with twenty-five-pounder guns and mauled it badly. The R.A.F. pounded it incessantly. Finally Rommel called it back to Tobruk, where he urgently needed tanks.

It is just possible that Rommel lost the campaign by sending out that flying column. It was an "all-or-nothing" gamble, and he drew nothing. He might, of course, have got away with it — he probably never realized quite how nearly he did. But had he retained those tanks at Tobruk he still had a hope of beating our depleted armoured forces in a straight fight. It was the second time that Rommel showed himself an instinctive gambler. The first time was when he reconquered Cyrenaica nine months before.

Gradually life in the camp settled down again. We heard fragments of news that we had been too busy to collect up in the battle front. A British parachutist force had made a sensational and very nearly successful attempt to trap and kill Rommel in his own Headquarters on the eve of the battle. The Twenty-ninth Indian Brigade had crossed 270 miles of utterly waterless desert from Jarabub and occupied the Italian oasis of Jalo, deep inland more than two hundred miles south-east of Bengasi. With their terrifying battle-cry "*Ya Ali,*" the Indians had stormed the fortress and now they were holding it as a constant menace to the coast road south of Bengasi. Meantime up north the Fourth Indian Division had had a very hard fight to take the two frontier forts called the

Omars, but the New Zealand Division was pressing forwards along the coast towards Tobruk. But in Bardia and the Halfaya fortifications strong Axis forces were still holding out.

So it was not quite so hopeless after all. Certainly things had gone nothing like so well as Cunningham had hoped and planned. Rommel, though taken by surprise, had shown no signs of collapsing in bewilderment as the Italians had done the previous winter. But nevertheless British forces were still up there fighting round Tobruk, and Rommel's showy thrust back to the frontier had failed. The Eighth Army had not yet definitely lost, and while there was life there was hope.

The sorting-out process was going ahead briskly. The only tank brigade with any strength left was the Fourth — the one with American Honeys — but the Twenty-second was being re-equipped as fast as possible. Thirtieth Corps had more or less got itself straight again. And on November 27 came great news — the New Zealanders had joined hands with the Tobruk garrison on a bleak shell-scarred patch of desert called El Duda.

Alan, Richard, and I were eager to be off to the front again now, but our conducting officer had left us, and technically we were not entitled to move. So we turned to Major Randolph Churchill, the British Premier's son, who had caused a sensation by arriving with Eve Curie, then corresponding for the *Herald Tribune*. She sat there typing in the sunshine, a neat figure in slacks and a snood, the only woman for something like three hundred miles in any direction. She discovered the disadvantage of this when Randolph had to drive her four miles out into an empty patch of desert and wait discreetly with his back turned.

Randolph agreed to conduct us to the front, and we set off once more into Libya. The going by now was atrocious. Half the desert surface was permanently in the air, a gusty, gritty fog, and lorries ploughed slowly through a rutted morass of dust. At one point we passed a little pen made of barbed wire which was half-filled with German prisoners. And it was there that I first heard the great Moscow legend.

A German officer, a truculent man with a villainous Saxon accent, asked me if I had heard that Moscow had fallen.

"No," I said, "I don't think it has."

"Oh, yes, indeed, it has," he replied. "Of course your papers wouldn't admit it — they never do until several days after the thing has happened. But it's true. We have had it announced officially."

At the time I simply did not know. But later I discovered that Rommel had announced the fall of Moscow in a special "Order of the Day." I don't know why he did it. It may have been a propaganda move to hearten — or to shame — his troops, but I do not think that up to that time they were in such desperate need of encouragement. But Rommel had announced it, and most of the prisoners we took believed it.

We lurched on through the dust and reached the Seventh Armoured Division just before nightfall. We cooked our stew that evening in the approved desert style: you cut a four-gallon petrol tin in half with a jack-knife, fill one half with sand, pour petrol on it and set it on fire. Then you cook in the other half. It is a quick simple method but you must finish by sundown, for the fires can be seen for miles.

The rattle of Bren-gun fire woke us startlingly at four-thirty next morning and Churchill came across to tell us to pack quickly. General Gott was just going off to the Fourth Brigade and we could come too. We were only allowed to take one truck, so we put ourselves and skeleton baggage into that and left the rest in the care of one of the drivers. Then, still half-asleep, we bumped off across the desert.

The rendezvous was at dawn, and we just made it. Gawky tank silhouettes showed everywhere against the paling eastern sky where the sun was about to rise. The cold struck through to the bone. The tanks were wet with dew and the chill metal numbed men's fingers as they packed up hastily. They would probably be in action within an hour. But they had already been in action so long that it had come to seem the natural condition of their lives. They stretched themselves, hunted for lost socks and mufflers, opened packets of dry biscuits, did a thousand trivial things. They shouted from tank to tank using Christian names, joking, cursing, borrowing things, asking questions. There was nothing whatever to suggest they were setting out to face death.

As the sun rose I met Brigadier Alec Gatehouse — a huge brown-faced man with a jutting chin and a hawk-like nose. Days ago he had lost all his personal kit and he was dressed in a grey rug tied round his waist with a leather strap, a white Palestinian sheepskin coat, and a black Tank Corps beret. He had been in action more or less continuously for about ten days. Most of his staff seemed to have been captured at least once and escaped after fantastic adventures. But they gave their orders quickly and precisely and there was nothing forced or nervous about their jokes.

I asked him about the American Honeys he had been using. He thought they were fine. He told me, "Their speed is just what we want, and mechanically they are first-class. Their armour's good too — I have seen Honeys take six direct hits and still stay in action. But they ought to have a bigger range — and of course a bigger gun."

We moved off north up into the Rezegh battle-field. Tanks were sprayed all about us, advancing warily, testing out each new horizon, the commanders raking earth and sky with field glasses. Ahead of us the Brigadier's white coat stuck out of his turret like a beacon. All the time he was talking with his tanks, giving orders, asking for information. Several reports had to be verified. One was that the German tank force had been reduced from 74 to 41 the day before, and the Brigadier had grave doubts about this being true.

The general lay-out was something like this: on our right was another British tank force with which we were co-operating. On our left South African infantry were advancing to attack. Somewhere an absolutely vital convoy of ammunition and food was being got through to the New Zealanders up in the north. An enemy convoy was reported to be cutting through from east to west on its way out of the Bardia pocket.

Heavy gunfire burst out suddenly on our right, with other duller explosions beyond it. For some minutes we argued, analyzing the sounds. Then we saw that the twenty-five–pounders were shooting up the German convoy. Something like three thousand unarmed motor vehicles were streaming by with 25 tanks skirmishing protectively behind them. Gatehouse could hardly restrain himself from attacking them. But he had other jobs to do and he could not leave his position. He sent off a handful of tanks to investigate and we heard the deep throbbing barrage of anti-tank fire which met them. A message was flashed back to the R.A.F. notifying them of this fine target. And the twenty-five–pounders fired away, picking off vehicle after vehicle out of the huge, dust-enshrouded column as it wound past.

Then there fell one of those mysterious hushes which sometimes fall on battle-fields. The sun shone warmly, and you could even hear the birds singing. The only sounds of war came from a burning tank whose ammunition was exploding in a series of sharp metallic cracks. Someone produced a pack of cards and we began to play three-handed bridge in the back of the truck.

Richard was losing badly and somewhat indignantly when suddenly everything began to move at once. Field guns began firing just to our left. The whole battlefront seemed to swing westwards. Twenty-five–pounders, light ack-ack guns, ambulances, armoured cars came bumping obliquely across us. Tanks fussed up and down on the left wing while on the right they swung out in a great arc northwards.

We raced along behind the Brigadier, bumping across a battlefield which seemed familiar. Then I recognized the burnt-out Valentines I had seen about a week before, and the blackened debris of the Stuka that had nearly crashed on top of me. The tanks threaded their way among slit trenches, German petrol cans, fragments of clothing, charred trucks, piles of shell-cases and green ammunition boxes, and all the mess and litter of war. We passed a little graveyard with pathetic wooden crosses and a monument of shiny four-gallon petrol tins. Then we stopped and ate a few biscuits. The New Zealanders' convoy had got through, we learned, and the South African infantry were getting into position for their attack.

Then the situation was suddenly turned upside down. A truck dashed up to the Brigadier's tank. The Brigadier jammed on his earphones and rapped a few words into the mouthpiece. A German tank force was attacking us in the rear.

At that moment they began to come in sight — sixteen squat black shapes just topping the horizon like the superstructures of battleships. They streamed down into a saucer of flat desert between two shallow ridges and the battle began. I saw the British tanks moving fast on the right, zigzagging and weaving their way forward so that they could bring their guns to bear. The German Mark Fours were firing their 75-millimetre guns and scoring hits at fifteen hundred yards. There was little point in the British firing their two-pounders until they were within eight hundred yards.

Back and forth across the hollow the guns spat. Sudden pillars of smoke rose where the shells bit into the dusty earth. Something burst abruptly into flames and streamers of jet-black smoke began to trail away on the wind. Dimly I could see tanks manœuvring crazily about one another as though performing some strange minuet. One lurched drunkenly as a direct hit got it and then reeled to a standstill.

Jets of flame stabbed the smoke as the twenty-five–pounders went into action just to my left. Their deep full-bodied whang rattled the doors of the truck. They dropped their shells straight across the battle-field and the German tanks scurried this way and that like ants to avoid them.

It was growing almost too smoky to see. But here and there gusts of wind blew aside the curtain of smoke and revealed little cameos of the battle — a tank blazing, a little group of men running, a gun being unlimbered, an ambulance plunging forward. The leading battery of twenty-five–pounders came racing back, the guns bouncing among the stringy grey tussocks of scrub. The tanks drew off to give the artillery free play. Then aircraft dropped stick after stick of bombs right in the front line, cutting us off from sight of the enemy with a great white screen of smoke. The din rose and fell, not a continuous throbbing roar but broken sequences of explosions and reports which jerked the attention brutally from point to point. Sometimes you could fancy there was a real pattern woven into it, a free counterpoint of rhythms — machine-guns firing in bursts, sticks of bombs crashing down one . . . two . . . three . . . four . . . five, troops of guns firing in four-time — a battle composition something like those realistic Straussian symphonies where you are supposed to hear the teacups rattling in the kitchen, or peasants yodeling on the Alps. But mostly it was just noise.

Ten British tanks abruptly broke out of the smoke and swung diagonally across to our rear. The whole thing began to look like utter chaos to me. But the Brigadier knew just what was happening. He gave his orders in a swift coherent sequence, each phase of the battle dovetailing into the next. I felt that as long as he was there it was all right. He told us we were almost certainly surrounded by the enemy, but I was not able to take it seriously.

Then I noticed that the gun muzzles were pointing higher. The enemy was withdrawing and the range was lengthening. "Nine thousand yards," someone shouted. Other, purplish shell-bursts started to creep across the plain towards us. When they became uncomfortably close our foremost batteries moved. But it was the enemy's last gesture, just intended to cover the withdrawal of his tanks. As the sun went down blood-red behind the German lines, that day's battle was over.

Of course, it was not much of a battle. But it was a more or less typical day in the lives of these tank brigades. They had been in bigger battles and in smaller ones. Sometimes they had had to fight all day instead of just all afternoon, and sometimes they went twenty-four hours with nothing much more serious than a skirmish. But this was the fabric of their existence, the way they lived, the way things could suddenly happen and upset their plans and force them to fight at a minute's notice in quite the opposite direction. And the afternoon's engagement had shown me for the first time the new technique that was being evolved to counter the enemy's superior gun-power, the use of agile, accurate 25-pounder guns, beautifully handled, to engage the enemy and keep them on the run until our tanks could get within range and fight on more or less equal terms. Of course the terms could never be quite equal as long as the enemy was answering two-pounder shells with 4½- or 15-pounders. But at least both sides could fire.

It was getting dark and all our food and bedding was back at Seventh Armoured Division Headquarters. We moved off cautiously, for the Brigadier had been serious when he said we were surrounded. But we got through safely enough in the gathering dusk, and ran back south-west following a compass course we had been given. Unfortunately our Headquarters had been dive-bombed during the day and had been forced to move. We wandered for hours in the darkness, cold, tired, and hungry, and only a fluke led us to our destination in the end. For supper Randolph produced some fresh eggs he had brought from Cairo and I hard-boiled them. I wanted to use the egg water for making tea, but the drivers said I must not, it would result in warts on the stomach. While we were arguing about this someone came out of the mess and told us that General Cunningham had been relieved of his command.

CHAPTER 15

Change of Command

THE NEWS was so extraordinary that I did not believe it. We argued about it until we went to sleep, and next day we drove back to Army Battle Headquarters to see what we could find out. There were rumours, but no one knew anything definite. Whatever the truth, it was being kept a dead secret.

What had, in fact, happened was this: on November 22 Auchinleck, at the suggestion of Air Vice-Marshal Coningham, had come up to the desert. For three days he had worked beside General Cunningham. On the twenty-fourth there had come the great enemy break-through down to the border. Just what happened inside G.H.Q. that day is a story which will have to wait till after the war to be told. But things must have looked pretty black. On the twenty-fifth Auchinleck handed Cunningham this message:—

> During three days at your Headquarters I have seen and heard enough to convince me, though I did not need convincing, that the determination of your commanders and troops to beat the enemy could not be greater, and I have no doubt that he will be beaten. His position is desperate and he is trying, by lashing out in all directions, to distract us from our objective which is to destroy him utterly. We will *not* be distracted and he *will* be destroyed. You have got your teeth into him. Hold on, bite deeper and deeper, and hang on till he is finished. Give him no rest. (The general situation in North Africa is excellent.) There is only one order, ATTACK AND PURSUE.

Next morning, flying back to Cairo, Auchinleck thought the thing over very carefully. On his arrival he conferred with, among others, Mr. Oliver Lyttelton, the Minister of State. And the same day he wrote a letter to Cunningham, relieving him of his command, and appointed Major-General Ritchie to command the Eighth Army with the rank of Lieutenant-General. Cunningham flew secretly to Alexandria to stay with his brother, the Admiral, and then went into a nursing-home. But before he went, he formally drew attention to the consequences that might ensue if we did not withdraw from Libya.

Auchinleck's action was, of course, a stroke of amazing boldness. Its significance was far more profound than just the changing of the army commander. In a situation of great peril, he had taken a gamble as serious as any Wavell ever took. He took it against the advice of his army commander, and if he lost it almost certainly meant complete and utter defeat for the Eighth Army. There is no doubt whatever that in the end, by his courageous decision, he saved the situation at that moment and turned what could have been a humiliating reverse into a victory. It must have cost him a lot to do, for he himself had appointed Cunningham. And then, supposing Cunningham turned out to have been right?

At Army Headquarters I waited a day, wondering what to do. Something of a lull seemed to have set in at the front and the events of the past ten days were being digested in my mind into some sort of coherent picture. I decided to fly back to Cairo and write a critical summary of it all, explaining what had happened.

A cold stinging rain was falling when I left the desert. It was horribly bumpy and for the first time in my life I was air-sick. But in Cairo it was sunny and warm, and I tasted gluttonously the exquisite joy of that first hot bath and a meal I had not cooked myself and a bottle of wine and clean linen sheets in bed.

But next morning Cairo, with its atmosphere of tinselly, complacent glamour, appeared a vivid contrast to the stern facts of the desert. People seemed to me shockingly over-optimistic. When I looked over the back numbers of the newspapers, I was horrified. I discovered for the first time that the campaign had started in a glare of uncritical publicity. We had heard in the desert the speech with which Mr. Churchill had inaugurated the offensive, and I think every officer I met up there in the firing line had deplored it. But even so we had none of us realized quite how high the expectations had been raised back in England. Arm-chair strategists, for the most part quite incredibly misinformed, had fought the battle for us and made us win almost before we had started. There were stories about American twenty-eight-ton tanks smashing through the German armour, stories about Rommel having eight hundred tanks, and a dozen other such misconceptions. At the daily one-thirty conference for journalists in the censorship room in Cairo, Brigadier Shearer had supplemented the communiqué with information and an interpretation which the local correspondents cabled home to swell the chorus of optimism. I felt my stories from the desert itself had been late and tame and useless and I wondered dejectedly whether it was really worth while going up to the front to report.

It took me a little time to realize that all this was largely inevitable. Our high estimates of the enemy tank losses had been published, but not a word about our own losses; we could not publish them without giving away information. It was more or less the same with the air. The plain facts, as known to the newspaper reader in Cairo and London, were that we had captured most of Marmarica, relieved Tobruk, and destroyed an immense quantity of enemy tanks. It all added up to a victorious picture which I, fresh from the battle-field, could hardly recognize.

Nevertheless I thought it must be plain now that things had not gone according to plan (a few days later Mr. Churchill openly announced the fact). So I wrote the despatch I had been planning. My idea was that in staging this campaign we had made three dangerous mistakes: one of equipment, one of strategy, and one of tactics.

The equipment mistake was in facing the Germans with tanks lighter in both armament and fire power than their own. Quite clearly we had gone into the campaign with our eyes open — we *knew* we were pitting lighter tanks against heavier ones. But there must, I supposed, have been some factor which was likely to compensate for this disadvantage. It was true that we were superior in numbers, and that most of our tanks had more speed than the enemy's. Possibly we also assumed that our tank fighters were better than the Germans. But I did not think that any of these factors was sufficient to warrant the confident optimism with which we started out. Of course, it was easy to be wise after the event. But I thought one could have been wise before the event. One does not, after all, have to be an expert to realize that it is desirable to meet fifteen-pounders with fifteen-pounders — or with something heavier.

The answer, I suppose, was this: that if we were to fight this campaign at all — and I think there is no doubt we were bound to fight it — we had to do it with the equipment available to us. It took five months to get the Eighth Army together, and once the matériel had started flowing down the long pipe-line from Britain and America, it was too late to make last-minute changes. You can say, if you like, that someone ought to have sent us out heavier tanks in the beginning. That may be true. But I do not see how Auchinleck could have refused to fight until he had got heavier tanks. Do not forget that we did in the end drive Rommel back to the confines of Tripolitania, and that had we waited we might have lost Tobruk and then, perhaps, Egypt.

The strategical mistake, I thought, was the surrendering of the initiative to Rommel. Of course, that might not have been intentional. But from what General Cunningham said to us on the eve of the battle it seems to have been our plan; and it is a fact that within a few days of the beginning of the campaign it was Rommel who was darting about making attacks, and it was we who were on the defensive. Our moves became conditioned by what he did when it ought to have been the other way round.

The tactical mistake, which was intimately bound up with the strategical mistake, seemed to me to be the splitting of our tank forces into three. That statement, too, may be an over-simplification of the facts. But we did give Rommel the opportunity of meeting each of our Brigades separately with a superior force of his own.

Even separately our Brigades gave a very good account of themselves. How much better might they not have done all together? Mustered into one powerful column, they could have retained the initiative and done the attacking. They in their turn might have beaten Rommel's divisions one by one — certainly the Ariete started by being entirely isolated. But split up as they were, our Brigades had an extremely difficult task and so did the men handling them. During the first few days it never seemed certain whether the Fourth was even under the orders of the Seventh Armoured Division at all. There was a period when it was directly under Corps.

We had, indeed, lost many more tanks than most people guessed in those opening rounds. And often enough the Germans remained in possession of the field and so recovered not only their own semi-damaged tanks, but ours as well. It is true that we could better afford to lose tanks than the Germans could, but it was apt to make our victories look rather Pyrrhic.

There were other points which seemed to me of importance. For once, I thought, we had underrated the Italians. On quite a number of occasions the Ariete Division had given a surprisingly good account of itself. The stiffening of Germans which Rommel had planted in the Italian motorized and infantry divisions seemed to be doing the trick. We had half-counted on the Italian morale collapsing quickly, but on the contrary it appeared stronger than usual.

Then Rommel turned out to be a general of unusual calibre. There was a swashbuckling, very un-German quality about him which enabled him to take great risks, to throw out daring tank columns to rampage back into our lines, to improvise swiftly and skilfully. It was said that he spent too much time in the forefront of the battle, that he never knew what was going on. But there was little evidence that this was doing him much harm. And he probably counted on his forces being so well-organized that they largely ran themselves. It was said, too, that he was boastful and exaggerated in his claims and his reports back to Berlin. Well, that is a quality which fits in well with his gambler's nature, and it must be admitted that he did on occasions have something to boast about. There is no need to turn Rommel into a hero, but there is no sense in not estimating your opponent at his highest value.

I wrote a message embodying some of these points and comparing the German tactics and equipment with our own in a general way. But I quickly realized that I was not going to be allowed to send it to London at the time. The issue had not yet been decided, for one thing. It was much too early to start analyzing the campaign. What I had written struck an inopportunely jarring note. I had to put my despatch away, hoping to be able to use some of it later.

ii

One other thing I checked up on in Cairo — the air situation. I saw Air-Marshal Tedder and heard from him how the theory and practice of air superiority was being developed. For this was a historic occasion. For the first time this war a British army had gone into action with local air superiority.

It was an elusive, almost indefinable thing, this air superiority. It was certainly not based on numbers of planes, for the enemy had more than we did — the fighter ratio was three to one in his favour. It was not based entirely on quality of planes, for the Messerschmitt 109F, which the Germans were using, was a better fighter than anything we had. There is no evidence that the Germans ever ran short of petrol, though there were moments when they were uneasy about it. In the end it seemed that air superiority rested on the same two factors which had given Wavell his victory over the Italians — leadership and men. In this case it meant the way in which the air force was handled, and the personal, individual quality of the fighter pilots. It was very heartening to know that we had this especial sort of superiority over the Germans in the air, for we had not as yet proved that we could achieve it on land.

Air superiority meant, in the last resort, ability to do what you liked in the air — to carry out successfully the offensive operations you had planned. And certainly in the first week of the campaign the R.A.F. had been able to do this. But achievement of air superiority was not enough. It had to be maintained, and the Germans were making a real bid to regain control of the daylight air. They were fetching more bombers from Crete and Greece, fighters were flying across from Europe with big blue-painted auxiliary petrol tanks, transport planes started a daily service from Athens to Derna, and others flew from Sicily towing gliders filled with urgently needed supplies.

Early on Tedder and Coningham realized that they could not sit back and let their original plans go ahead. Almost from hour to hour new plans had to be made. A dozen experiments were tried and the results either rejected or accepted, and Tedder flew constantly back and forth between Cairo and the desert controlling the swiftly evolving situation. Theory and practice were born and superseded a dozen times in those days. And all the time it was being emphasized that you must never stand still and think you have got the answer — you must plan and improve and prune your technique and material ad infinitum.

Those were exciting, pioneering days. For the pioneer the past and the present are known, the future is only a vague question-mark framing the plans he has made; and often enough he visualizes as his final goal something much simpler and nearer than the real goal implicit in what he is doing. So in this campaign it was not realized how experimental, how rudimentary was the evolution of air technique. In point of fact all that was being done was the collection of data. A theory and a technique would ultimately emerge, but this was the first time Britain had had air superiority over a battle-field, and Britain did not really know what to do with it.

Tedder and Coningham showed their qualities in this situation. For they were prepared to be bold and experimental and completely open-minded. They tried anything and everything. They pushed their advanced landing-grounds far, almost dangerously far, forward. They tried out one squadron of Hurricanes equipped for carrying small bombs — the birth of the fighter-bomber as a kind of mobile artillery. The theory of dive bombers was being scrupulously examined, and the comparative merits of the fast fighter armed with heavy cannons were being recognized.

The theory was still maintained that the job of the air force was to engage and destroy the opposing air force. But almost imperceptibly the air force was getting mixed up in the battles on the ground, and that gave rise to new problems. The question of army–air-force co-operation came irresistibly and rather cantankerously to the fore. The matter had been given a certain amount of theoretical attention beforehand and experts had been flown out from London to offer advice. But the whole technique was in its infancy. The very term "army–air-force co-operation" contained in itself an implication that the R.A.F. was normally non-co-operative. The Air Liaison Officers, who were experimentally appointed, often found themselves treated with jealousy or amused indifference. Tedder very clearly recognized that mutual goodwill was the first essential of real co-operation, and he described the ideal to me as "a happy marriage in which neither partner is dominant." But all that he did could not break down a certain inevitable resistance to change and innovation. More than once — as was unavoidable on so chaotic and changeable a front — British troops were bombed by the R.A.F. There grew up in the army a feeling that co-operation ought to be much more exact and intimate and speedy and that the air force ought to be forced into it, even to the point of incorporation. And on the other hand, the air force began to resist this trend, not so much with the perfectly sound arguments at its disposal, as with a blank refusal to permit the subject to be discussed at all.

The arguments on both sides were bitter but futile, for the whole technique was still in a primitive stage of development. The important thing was that the ground troops were becoming intensely interested in the air and the air force was growing increasingly interested in the ground. A method of co-operation must inevitably be worked out, but there was as yet not nearly enough evidence to show that the best method was the incorporation of one branch in the other. On the contrary it was probable that only a completely air-minded, and therefore autonomous, air force could retain air superiority and make full use of it. The experiments and mistakes and arguments of this campaign were merely the birth pangs of a new technique.

Very striking was the increased interest of the pilots themselves in the ground. Up in the desert I had gone to visit a friend on one of the advanced air fields from which fighters operated. We sat on a couple of collapsible chairs slap in the middle of a flat disc of desert circumscribed by the yellow obscurity of a small-scale sand-storm. It was almost too thick to see the slim shapes of the Tomahawks standing all round us. Here and there a revving propeller fanned up the dust into a whirling tornado which filled our eyes and ears and noses and got through our closed lips to grit against our teeth. Half a dozen planes painted like sharks with grinning jaws landed and the pilots strolled casually over swinging their helmets. They were all caked with dust and reddened and blistered by the sun. Some, who had been operating since dawn, went off to get breakfast and wash and shave in a mugful of cold water. The rest got out camp stools and began to talk shop in their slangily technical language.

All that they said referred directly or indirectly to what had been happening on the ground. They discussed new methods of protection which they had been trying out over the Tobruk troops on El Duda. They mentioned the timidity and vulnerability of Stukas against an enemy with air superiority, and they spoke of the very fine barrage which British troops on the ground were now putting up against low-flying aircraft. They compared notes about the best method of assisting a land force that was attacking and the best methods of self-identification for trucks and troops. They had noticed so much that was happening on the ground that it was clearly going to be worth training fighter pilots to do incidental reconnaissance.

None of these points had been settled yet — it was solely a phase of collecting experience. The great thing was that we had at least begun — we were for the first time fighting a campaign in which army–air-force co-operation was possible; for we had achieved air superiority. The perfected technique of handling it must come later.

iii

The day after I had discussed all this with Tedder, I realized that I must be getting back to the desert. Alan was also in Cairo and for want of more convenient transport we decided to travel by train.

It was, I think, the most unpleasant journey I have ever made — and in the course of a journalistic career round Europe I have made plenty. The train left at midnight, and Cairo's blacked-out station was thronged to bursting with men in full kit, buffeting their way about, cursing, shouting, stumbling. An Egyptian porter succeeded in smashing my thermos flask before I had even got as far as the barrier. I left the remains there, stacked at the foot of an iron pillar. We fought our way to a couple of places in a first-class carriage, and sat there all night getting colder and colder. Goodness knows what the train did in the course of the night, but by morning we had only gone about a hundred miles. We bought newspapers at a station and found that Japan had declared war on America. All day we trundled on through the desert, reading, eating and talking. In the evening we came to a halt where I thought we had to change. No one else changed there, which seemed strange, and there was no one to ask. We hovered indecisively for the few minutes that the train stopped, then decided to get out. I threw our baggage out piece by piece as the train began to move and then I picked up an egg which I thought was hard-boiled and jumped out myself. The jerk of landing made me crush the egg, and it was not hard-boiled. It got over everything with a stickiness that was hardly credible, and for days I was scraping bits of yellow off my great-coat.

But there was a fire in the little hut at the station, and a Yorkshire Sergeant told us we were right to get off, our train would be along in a few minutes. He let us go into his tent to eat our sandwiches and he made us a cup of tea. We felt things were getting better. But his conversation was all about German air attacks on trains and we watched a raid on Mersa Matruh while we were talking. And when our train came in, we found it was loaded partly with petrol and partly with ammunition.

We got settled in the brake-van, and the train ran straight off the rails. We watched shivering while a gang of blasphemous New Zealanders tried to put things straight, but it got too cold and we went back to the brake-van and tried to sleep. In the morning, more dirty and dishevelled than ever, we found ourselves still benighted there. We decided to abandon the train.

We walked to the road and cadged a lift back to a place where we knew there was an air field. All day we stayed there trying to get a seat in a plane going forward—*anywhere* forward, we did not mind. But a sand-storm was raging and very few planes were going anywhere at all. The best we could get was a promise of a place in a hospital plane the following morning. (We could travel in hospital planes because we were unarmed and counted as civilians.) Cold and miserable we went to bed on the floor of a tent.

We did get the hospital plane, but only just. We circled around for an hour or more in the cold dank darkness before dawn looking for the air field, which was some way away from the main road. We had lost ourselves completely when we suddenly drove straight on to the runway just as our plane was taxiing down for the take-off. It was our one stroke of luck. The plane, flying circumspectly, for another hospital plane had been shot down the day before, took us nearly to Army Headquarters and the rest of the way was easy.

We had not been there an hour before Richard arrived. He had left Cairo just about three hours before. It had taken us three horrible days.

CHAPTER 16

Tobruk's Nineteen Days

For nearly a week now the fighting had been growling and muttering sullenly round the south-east facet of Tobruk. There was nothing very violent or spectacular about it — both sides had fought themselves almost to a standstill during those tremendous first ten days. It was difficult to point to any one circumstance and say "That is what made Rommel decide to retreat at this point." But by the end of the first week in December his troops were filtering back westwards along the main road towards Derna and three days later Tobruk was completely free.

Four things influenced Rommel at that particular moment.

The first was very simple. British armoured forces discovered and destroyed his most important dump in the Tobruk area. He was left unable to maintain his whole army in the front line.

The second thing was the knowledge that he had already used all his reserves and could expect no more in time. The British meanwhile were re-grouping their forces and bringing new tanks up to the battle-field every day.

The third thing was a new and beautifully appropriate development in desert warfare. The British commanders dug right down to the fundamental principle of the desert, to the rule that everyone up there sooner or later comes to recognize: use the desert, make the desert help you, play the desert's game. They organized the "Jock Columns."

This was a buccaneering, marauding, piratical sort of game which Englishmen took to like ducks to water. They discovered a talent and a liking for it, a heritage, I suppose, from four centuries of pioneers, explorers, travellers, colonists, eccentrics, individuals. Brigadier Jock Campbell had invented it and given his name to it. An officer would take an armoured car or a tank, a few trucks, a handful of men, and disappear into the blue. For as long as his food and fuel and ammunition lasted, he would harass the enemy in a series of fast hit-and-run raids all over the map of Cyrenaica. These columns spied out weak spots and hit when the enemy was least expecting it. They never stayed to fight and they never risked getting caught. They were so small that reconnaissance planes scarcely ever bothered about them. They would sweep in under cover of a sand-storm, or at night, or from behind a bluff, and shoot the tail end of an undefended convoy to bits. Or they would put an ambush on a road and get a couple of staff cars. The enemy never knew where they were or how big they were or what they were doing. They made it impossible to tell whether they were part of a big, serious force, or merely a tiny patrol. They went where they liked, without specific orders or time-tables, and did what they liked. And I think most of them thoroughly enjoyed it.

This was true desert warfare — something that could never be done in a country like France or England or the jungles of Malaya. It was making a friend of the desert, this taking advantage of every opportunity this peculiar battle-field offered. And it was something against which the Germans found it extremely hard to hit back. Maybe for psychological reasons, because they had definitely not got that heritage of exploration and adventure, the Nazis showed up badly as patrollers. Their taste was for mass action, well supported. They felt nervous and defenceless and lonely when they were sent out in tiny groups into the desert. There was a German report found near Tobruk, written by a senior officer, which said that the British had forgotten more about patrolling than the Germans had ever learned.

The fourth thing which impelled Rommel to retreat was the unflagging, indomitable resistance of the Tobruk garrison.

ii

Tobruk was finally disengaged on December 10 after nineteen days of battle.

It was a great and heroic story, a perfect climax to the seven months of waiting that had preceded it. The fighting itself had the simplicity of strategical outline and the complication of personal detail of trench warfare. For throughout nineteen days it raged within a few featureless square miles so that it is possible to concentrate nineteen days of human bravery and endurance and suffering into the words "The Seventieth Division fought its way out to Duda and held it." The battle could only be properly described by dividing the ground into squares and giving a play-by-play account, as of a football game. And even that would be misleading, for sometimes twelve hours' savage fighting left the two sides in the same squares they started in.

On November 18 men with earphones in the signals room at Tobruk heard the single word JAM over the wireless. And then they knew they had just forty-eight hours more in which to prepare, for JAM meant that the Eighth Army had attacked and the Rats of Tobruk were to burst from their prison exactly two days later. Then when the opening stages of the main offensive moved less swiftly than was expected, their zero hour was postponed for another day and night. The sortie was made on November 21 at half-past six in the morning.

Almost everything there was in Tobruk had been mustered for the first assault. Massed behind that mile-long front on the south-eastern perimeter, waiting to go forward, were sixty-eight "I" tanks and possibly fifty cruisers. They were to lead the attack with the King's Dragoon Guards in armoured cars and the Black Watch, and behind them British infantry regiments were drawn up ready to advance. Away to the west the Polish Brigade was awaiting the signal to make a noisy, spectacular feint.

Until two o'clock in the morning the Germans swept the ground with great searchlights. And then, just as the sappers were wondering how on earth they were going to do their work in that glare, the lights were snapped off. It was an unaccountable stroke of luck. The sappers wriggled forward and cut their own wire and laid eight bridges across the anti-tank ditch. The Germans themselves had already partly lifted their own mine fields, for by an incredible coincidence this was the exact spot which Rommel had selected to make his own attack on Tobruk.

The first tanks rumbled across the bridges at six-thirty sharp. They went forward in high heart that morning, the Rats of Tobruk. This was the justification of all those months of endurance and preparation and toil. Sharing the honours with them, though far away in space, were the first Rats of Tobruk — those Australians who had held the place all through the torrid, shadeless, fly-ridden summer. This was Tobruk's hour. The Black Watch advanced to the brave skirl of bag-pipes, a Major in kilts piping them into battle, just as he had piped them into battle in British Somaliland and Crete. It was a touch of mad, incongruous pageantry to fit a great occasion.

But right from that first minute the fighting was bitter. The Germans already had plenty of guns in position, ready for their own intended attack, and they straightway laid down a thick, accurate barrage. The Fourth "I" tanks and the Black Watch stormed their way through it and split their forces to attack the position called Tiger both frontally and behind. They found it defended by Germans, not Italians, deeply entrenched with plenty of guns. Some of the Black Watch pushed too far ahead and began to take heavy casualties. The Major with the bag-pipes fell wounded, and there was a ridiculous scene at the Field Dressing Station when wounded German prisoners tried to find out what he wore under his kilt.

But they got Tiger. A handful of tanks edged round behind it and found three or four thousand Germans at the mercy of their guns. The Tank Commander scratched his head for a moment; he could not massacre the lot in cold blood while they were trying to surrender, but he had no infantry with him to take them prisoners. So he just left them to be picked up later — the battle was lapping fiercely round them and they had little chance of getting clear away.

That day Tiger, Butch, Jack and Jill — the Australian nicknames

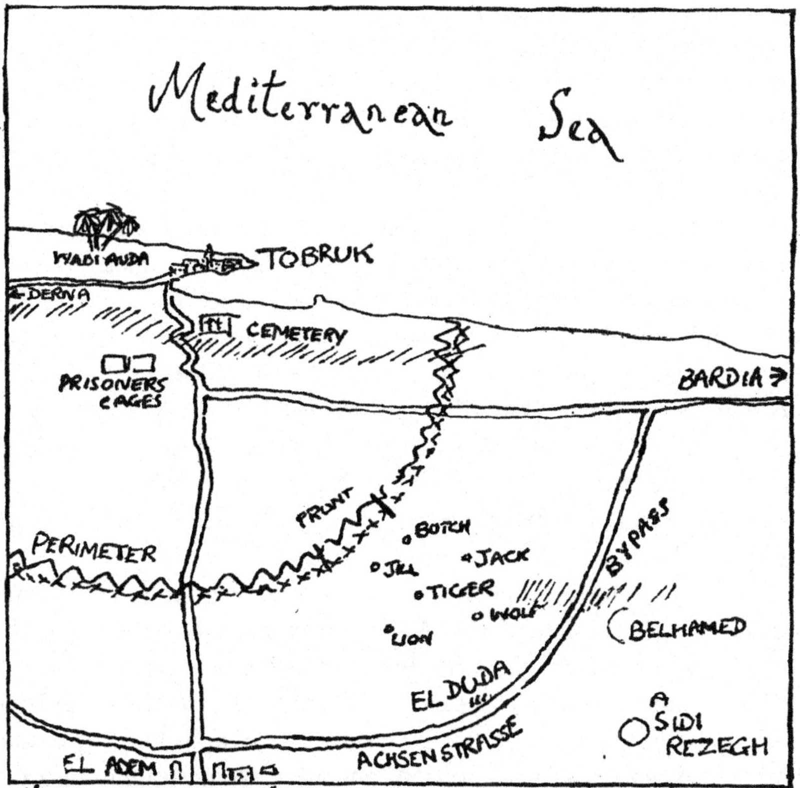

The battle of El Duda.

of the four enemy positions which were the key to El Duda — fell into our hands. The fighting had been very heavy and not without casualties. One troop of twenty-five-pounders had fired seven hundred rounds per gun in thirteen hours. Upwards of forty thousand shells had been fired altogether that day and there were guns whose barrels became literally red-hot. But two positions, Lion and

Wolf, remained to be taken before the road to Duda was open.

Lion fell on the afternoon of the second day, while the Germans were putting down a barrage from their heaviest guns. One of their 210 shells fell slap in the middle of a column of German prisoners.

On the twenty-third men driving up to the front out from Tobruk saw the first batch of German prisoners marching down to be embarked for Alexandria by sea. They hated the idea when they discovered what was going to happen to them. For six months they had been hearing that their dive bombers were making that the most perilous journey in the world, and now they were going to do the trip themselves.

The next day the British tanks were withdrawn for refitting. For over seventy-two hours they had been fighting almost without rest. The crews had hardly had time to eat. Desperately they needed sleep and a wash and a short respite from battle. And their tanks had been driven nearly to the limits of endurance. If things had gone well out there with the rest of the Eighth Army, Tobruk should have been relieved by now. In quiet moments they had heard the clamour of battle from Sidi Rezegh direction, but it came no nearer. For the moment, at least, the Rats would have to fight on alone.

The Royal Horse Artillery brought up their guns to Tiger and shelled a long stretch of the Axis by-pass continuously while the tanks were away, and on November 26 Wolf was taken.

That meant the way was clear to El Duda. The tanks came back from their overhaul and the crews from a stupor-like sleep that had wiped away their exhaustion, and they went straight into the attack. The R.H.A. gave them covering fire as they zigzagged seven thousand yards slightly downhill and then up on to Duda Ridge, but they were fully exposed the whole way, and it was a very gallant charge. Fortunately the enemy, for some reason, were disconcerted. They apparently had not expected the attack and they could be heard shouting wildly on their radio blowers: "Look out, they're coming this way . . . where's the crew of that gun . . . send up some tanks immediately." They did not react quickly enough to stop the attack, and in a final tornado of machine-gun fire the Northumberland Fusiliers won a firm footing on the heights.

But soon the German artillery fire grew very heavy. With shells splashing down all round them, the British commanders held an urgent conference. Should they hold onto Duda or not? They decided to get the infantry up and try it. Still under heavy fire the Essex Regiment came forward and dug itself in. The foremost units of the New Zealand Division, with a battalion of "I" tanks, was reported to be at Belhamed, only a short distance away to the east.

That night, for the first time, Tobruk shook hands with the rest of the Eighth Army. A British Colonel led a squadron of "I" tanks and a battalion of New Zealand infantry slap through the enemy lines, destroying their gun positions on the way, and reached El Duda.

It was a moment of high drama. They met with a salute and a handshake and did what they could to celebrate the occasion fittingly. A carefully hoarded Union Jack was run up on the leading tank. The Brigadier commanding the Thirty-second Army Tank Brigade hauled down the silk stocking which he had vowed to fly from his wireless mast until Tobruk was relieved. But there was tragedy there too. For someone had to tell the Colonel that his own son had been killed, fighting magnificently, on Duda the day before.

That was the first contact. But it was not until two days later that a real corridor was opened. On the night of the twenty-eighth a long column of motor transport and the whole headquarters of the Thirteenth Corps moved into Tobruk, and the General commanding the Thirteenth Corps made his wisecrack: "Tobruk is relieved, but not half so relieved as I am." It was in fact absurd to speak of the operation as "The Relief of Tobruk." The Rats themselves always referred to it as "The Relief of the Eighth Army."

On the twenty-ninth the Germans lined up three columns to attack Duda. One came from the south, one from the north-east, and the main one from the west. This westerly column overran the Essex Regiment, swept aside the machine-gun and anti-tank gun positions, and got a footing on the Ridge. The corridor for a moment was closed, but a counterattack with tanks was organized, and the Germans were flung back again. A New Zealand Bren-gun carrier picked up Major-General Ravenstein, Commander of the Twenty-first *Panzerdivision,* who had not heard that the German attack had failed. (They put him aboard a ship for Alexandria, and he was torpedoed by his own air force and finally washed up on the shores of Egypt clad only in his pyjama top.)

Next day Rommel's flying tank column was whistled back from its tour to the Egyptian frontier and attacked the New Zealanders at Belhamed. It was a bitter, sanguinary business in which the New Zealanders had bad losses, and this time the corridor really was closed. But the men of Tobruk still held Duda, and with a floating balance of twenty-five or thirty tanks, the defenders beat off constant German attacks for six days.

Rommel flung in his armoured forces from every direction. Time and again he deployed his favourite technique, using tanks economically in intimate and skilful conjunction with his powerful anti-tank guns. He battered away incessantly and on December 4 he made an attack so determined that it was probably his last desperate bid to dislodge the defenders of El Duda and possibly even take Tobruk. But the Rats, entrenched among so many derelict tanks that most of them were now being charted as landmarks on maps, held firm. And next day Rommel began pulling back his forces west of Tobruk. On December 6 the Poles, after fighting hard for a week, suddenly found nothing opposite them but Italian stragglers. The Duda defenders moved on to Sidi Rezegh and made contact with the rest of the Eighth Army. By the ninth, they had got El Adem with its vast air field. And on the tenth the Axis bypass was renamed Democracy Lane and the Rats of Tobruk were rats no more.

If at any time these men had failed and given way, it is almost certain that the whole campaign would have failed. But they had behind them the accumulated strength of all those months of waiting and looking forward, and the knowledge that they were fighting their way out of a Tobruk existence into a future where they would get leave and fresh water and fresh food and beds and women and the impossibility of being bombed. A sort of mass claustrophobia drove the Rats of Tobruk out of their holes in an impassioned fury. On some of those nineteen days they took bad casualties, but they never dreamed of turning back. Their really bad moment was when the corridor was snipped in two and there was a chance that the Eighth Army had failed them. But they weathered that and held Duda until the Eighth Army had weathered its own crisis. And on the glorious tenth of December they could walk all round their perimeter and never hear a shot fired.

iii

There was a complete German-tank workshop down by the sea near Tobruk. Its occupants must have left it in a hurry, for thirty-eight tanks and thousands of dollars' worth of machinery were lying about untouched. But far more interesting than the machines were the little tents and huts lying round about. For they gave, for the first time, a cross-section of how the Germans lived in the desert.

I knew well enough how the British treat the desert. They simply pretend it is not there. They make no concessions to it whatsoever, they neither fight it nor conciliate it. If a thing can happen in the desert it happens, if not it is simply omitted. The British soldier is not faddy, he does not worry about his diet, and if he can be sure of strong tea with sugar in it and enough bully beef and biscuits, he is not likely to complain seriously. He sleeps wrapped in blankets on the ground, and his wardrobe is small and practical. He lives, in fact, the life of the desert and only in the rarest cases does he try to improve or beautify it.

At Nibeiwa Camp a year ago I had seen how the Italian treats the desert. He tries to make it habitable. He builds little houses with stones and lays out flower gardens where nothing will ever grow. He brings his smartest uniforms and his insignia and his perfumes and his best crockery. He drinks wines and brandy and bottled mineral water and he eats pretty much the food he would eat at home. He hates the desert and he can only bear it when he makes it as much like Italy as he can.

But the German, I found, instinctively fights the desert. Scattered all round was evidence that Nazi scientists and technicians and experts had been working hard on antidotes and palliatives for this place which they conceived to be so terrible and unnatural. The Tropical Institute at Hamburg had designed special uniforms and equipment and in some cases had given the troops special hot-house training there before sending them out. Everything had been thought of and guarded against. The moment he stepped ashore in Africa the German soldier was given a little book warning him against the dangers of the women, the vice, the dirt, the disease, the vermin, the heat, the water, the dishonesty of the natives, the peculiarities of the climate. In the Quartermaster's stores I found food powders, body powders, vitamin pills, energy tablets, mouth washes, eye lotions, special sand goggles, water-purifiers, insect powders.

Their food was undeniably good. They had delicious brown full-corn bread wrapped in cellophane and silver paper; rich succulent Frankfurter sausage—the kind you hang from the ceiling and cut a piece off whenever you feel like it; plenty of fresh lemons; wine and beer and orange syrup; tinned fruits; chocolate; little hard bricks the size of a match box which boil up into thick pea-soup; dried vegetables which look like straw but come up into a rich minestrone soup when boiled in water. It was all of good quality too. His family might have been faring badly at home, but the Nazi soldier at the front was eating exceedingly well.

He even got real coffee. In one hut I found the table spread with little packages, each containing perhaps an ounce and a half of genuine coffee beans. Someone had been doing up his Christmas presents for the packets were addressed to people all over Germany. Probably he had been saving up his rations for weeks.

I wandered on through the camps, looking at letters, pay-books, magazines, newspapers. The letters, too, reflected the German horror of the desert. Those from home overflowed with sympathy for the men fighting in "that terrible, terrible place." Those from the desert were filled with an almost morbid home-sickness for the green hills of Northern Europe, and with hair-raising descriptions of the horrors of Africa. No wonder Ravenstein had to send a complaint back to Germany asking for something to be done about the extraordinary number of men who succeeded in not returning to Africa after their home leave.

It was true enough as British propaganda claimed that the Germans loathed the desert. But we made the mistake of thinking that therefore they would fight badly in it. By a judicious blend of propaganda, organization, training and discipline, the Germans had produced an exceedingly good desert fighter, and it was absurd and unwise to pretend the contrary.

As we were leaving this camp a British salvage squad arrived to see what they could do with the damaged German tanks. They had just picked up a prisoner—a blond, bewildered youth who told me he had only been taken because his comrades forgot to wake him up when they left. We spoke German and he could not make out what I was. He must have finally got the idea I might be some sort of Fifth Columnist, for he sounded me gently on the prospects of escaping. But he was horrified when I told him where the front line was now. He thought he had been captured by a local fluke, and that his own forces were still close at hand.

They went on picking up stragglers along this coast for days. Two men who were chasing pigs—the Germans had kept live pigs to eat their garbage and provide them with pork—routed forty indignant Germans from out of a cave. One of the pigs was roasted in a derelict tank and eaten on the spot.

CHAPTER 17

Decision at Gazala

Now ROMMEL was moving westwards slowly and in good order. He had resolved to cut his losses and keep some sort of force in being, in the hope that somewhere, sometime, he would get the chance of building it up and using it again. He was obliged to abandon the mixed German-Italian garrisons in the Bardia and Halfaya positions along the Egyptian frontier; but they were still performing a useful purpose in pinning down large British forces, and they might eventually be made the basis of a big counter-attack, as Tobruk had been for the British.

The maps we saw at Headquarters were getting cleaner and simpler. British mobile patrols had now cleared the whole area between Bardia and Tobruk. They only found little knots of ragged, cold, hungry men who either surrendered on sight, or satisfied honour with a brief flurry of rifle fire. Duda and Rezegh had become clean, blank spaces on the map, and in real life rutted, evil-smelling expanses of desert speckled with derelict tanks. The retreat had begun.

But where would Rommel stand? Mostly we talked of the Derna-Mechili Line, for it was there that the Italians had put up very nearly their best fight the previous winter. Some thought there might be heavy fighting up in the green hills of Jebel Achdar and the most optimistic suggested that Rommel would run right to the confines of Cyrenaica and stand again near El Agheila.

Almost no one thought of Gazala. There had never been a line there before, and somehow we all expected history to repeat itself. But in fact a strong Italian rear-guard force, stiffened by German infantry and supported by the remaining tanks, was taking up its positions at Gazala in a series of well-prepared defence works with concrete gun emplacements ten feet deep and cleverly planned machine-gun posts.

Gazala, of course, was not a town or a village or even an oasis. It was another of these geographical fictions, so common in the desert, which spring from the necessity of giving names to places where things happen. At a point where a long inlet of the sea almost touches the foot of the escarpment the Turks had built a little fort and the Italians two air fields, and that was Gazala. The main road wriggles past at the foot of the cliff, but there is a rude track which spirals up it, and that was where the Gazala Line began. It ran south, threaded along a series of barely perceptible rises and ridges, then swept away west in a big curve and finally faded into the desert.

Rommel's tank force, it was calculated, could not now be much more than fifty or sixty strong. But he never seriously risked it in battle again. It was the end of the phase of mighty tank clashes. He kept his tanks closely together and made use of their superior gun-power to keep out of range. He would sit hull down just over the skyline, taking pot-shots at the British tanks, and then retire swiftly when they came too close. Or he would try and lure our tanks into strong, camouflaged anti-tank positions. His was a swift-moving, ultra-mobile force which he flung about the desert so that we were never quite sure where it was going or what it was doing. But he wisely avoided a face-to-face clash. The campaign began to take on a new character — less intense, more spread out, more orthodox. And it gained a background — the main road, the sea, a few villages, an oasis or two; little enough, in all conscience, but better than an utterly featureless slab of desert.

With this simplification of the battle, the Eighth Army was itself simplified. Thirtieth Corps became almost a fiction, for it was now just one huge South African division which encircled Bardia and Halfaya like a vast horseshoe. In the front were all the tanks — now lumped into one force called the Fourth Brigade —

the Indian Division, the Polish Brigade, and one New Zealand brigade.

Thirteenth Corps Headquarters had flung its rash of scattered tents and vehicles across the desert a little inland from the old Turkish fortress of Acroma, and for a few days we settled down there to do a spell of almost normal war reporting.

Our party now was taking on the intimacy, the self-sufficiency, of an expedition to Tibet or the North Pole. In our two trucks we had the ingredients of a quite complicated existence that could be prolonged for weeks. We had whittled our baggage down to our personal minimum in the circumstances. That is to say, our possessions consisted in each case of the same solid core of basic necessities, plus a crust of moral rather than physical necessities—luxuries which we valued more highly than necessities. Thus, Richard allowed himself his large flagon of Eau-de-Cologne, and I put a high value on my pillow-case. Alan's main concern was his cigarettes, and often he would spend long periods planning his supplies, questioning people and suggesting trips to distant canteens, when to me the impending shortage was a matter of complete indifference.

We had a new Conducting Officer whom we called Kim, and he and I undertook the cuisine. He operated a primus stove in the blacked-out truck, while I used an ingenious little German apparatus I had found, rather pompously called a *Sicherheitsfeldkochgestell,* which ran on solid methylated spirit. Alan organized the blackout and the lighting and seating arrangements inside the truck. Richard, who has had plenty of luxury in his private life, voluntarily undertook to do the washing up. That is pretty nearly the nastiest domestic chore in the desert, for the plates are greasy and you cannot afford any water and usually it is bitterly cold and often enough you cannot see. But Richard took his place in our routine as washer-up and grumbled about it surprisingly little.

News was scarce until the attack on the Gazala Line started. One day we came on a nice bit of Italian flamboyance, an order of the day about the Trento Division which, as far as anyone knew, had not yet been in action at all. This document, however, claimed:—

> Since the beginning of the present gigantic fighting the Trento has offered an impassable wall of steel to all the desperate attacks of the enemy, delivering lightning blows which have once more snatched the initiative from the enemy's hands. Now that definite victory seems to be at hand, it continues to fight.

We also found a German proclamation which made it quite plain that on December 2, a day or two after Cunningham had been relieved of his command, Rommel definitely believed he had won.

One evening the wind changed ominously and we had to move all our camp round to get protection for our beds. While we were eating our meal, little gusts of rain pattered against the side of the truck and driving clouds obscured the stars. The night was a succession of drenching showers. Every few minutes I had to heave myself about to dissipate the puddles which formed in the hollows of my limbs. Sometimes it stopped and I went to sleep, then the steady drumming of rain on mackintosh would wake me again, and from my comparative comfort I would pity the men in the firing line, huddling under rugs and greatcoats, with tin hats on for shelter, or crouching in the cold damp cabs of their vehicles.

At dawn the wind began blowing from the sea and a dust-storm started. It got into our beds and our clothes and our food before we could pack anything up, and there was no shelter from it. We put on goggles and flung our things together, planning to shake them out later, and got under way in the hope of finding somewhere where the storm was less thick. Convoys of vehicles were cruising warily across the desert through a howling yellow fog, each truck keeping the tailboard of the truck ahead always in sight. It cleared only in patches where the rain had been heavy enough to turn the dust into a pasty mud which guns and tanks and lorries were churning into foot-deep ruts.

It was a horrible day for fighting, but when we got to Corps Headquarters we found that the big Gazala attack was on the point of starting. Under cover of the dust-storm, the British tanks had been sent right round the Gazala Line towards Bomba, so that the German tank force and the Italian infantry were sandwiched between our tanks and our front-line infantry. The idea was that the British tanks would either engage the Germans and force them to fight, or drive them on to the British guns. On the map, at any rate, it looked like a beautiful situation.

A Liaison Officer was going to Polish Headquarters and we followed him through the wild windy day with the dust whirling in continuously through the cracks of the doors and up through the floorboards of the car. Once we saw a little knot of civilians—Bedouins striding across the desert with a small flock of camels, the women's bright-coloured robes blowing out like banners in the gale.

We passed through the New Zealanders who told us that zero hour was 3.30 P.M., and that the Poles were going to open the attack by advancing between two New Zealand battalions. A Maori Sergeant warned us to keep our ears open for the war-cry of his countrymen going into battle. He said they were hoping for a night attack, with knives.

Then at last we found the Polish Headquarters, and it seemed to me strangely far forward for a Brigade Headquarters, almost in the front line in fact. But it turned out that General Kopanski, the Polish Commander-in-Chief, liked to see for himself what was going on. He was standing there on the front edge of his little clot of trucks when we arrived, a small, deceptively gentle man. His transport was a motley collection of British, Australian, German and Italian vehicles, but all he cared about was the red-and-white Polish flags flying on them. There was always something peculiarly exciting about these Poles, a certain tinge of chivalry and fanaticism that was curiously exhilarating, and their enthusiasm for killing Germans was unbounded.

As we stood talking to Kopanski, the artillery barrage was opening up. From all round behind us batteries of twenty-five-pounders were firing, and the shells were bursting along a ridge a mile or so ahead of us. The smoke rose lazily into the air, until it was caught by the howling wind from the coast and dragged away across country in a great slanting screen. In front of us the Polish troops were strung out in parallel lines across the landscape, waiting to move, lounging among the tussocks of camel scrub until zero hour struck. Guns were steadying and concentrating their fire, playing their shells accurately on the enemy front line, rather less than two miles away from us. The Italians started a nervous, tentative counter-barrage, dropping a shell here and a shell there, but not doing any harm.

With an impatient movement Kopanski tapped his watch and held it to his ear to make sure it was still going. Suddenly the quick pop-popping of automatic weapons began to rattle down the line until the air was singing with bullets. A low-flying enemy plane was dodging in and out among the scudding clouds and everyone was firing at it as it came along. Almost at the same moment Kopanski looked up from his watch and said, "Thirty seconds to go." All across the plain ahead of us men were getting to their feet. They stretched themselves, as men always seem to do before going into battle. For a moment they hunched their shoulders against the wind and their greatcoats blew out stiffly behind them. They turned up their collars and tilted their tin hats to windward. Then they hoisted machine-guns onto their shoulders or picked up their rifles and held them across their bodies. Dead on time they started to move.

They had to walk across a little dip, then over a shallow ridge, then through another hollow, and onto the skyline. Then they would be in action. They went slowly but very steadily. They were so close that there was no need to use field glasses to watch them. There came a moment when the entire horizon ahead of us was covered with an almost unbroken hedge of men, silhouetted blackly against the billowing, wind-driven clouds. The Italian barrage grew more excited, more erratic. "They aren't getting much serious opposition yet or they wouldn't be standing up," Kopanski murmured.

Almost as he said it a shell cracked down at the right-hand end of the line and when the ginger-coloured smoke had cleared away about fifty yards of the line was gone. But a couple of seconds later the men sprang up again from the ground where they had thrown themselves and continued their steady march.

The whole first line with its patrols sprayed out before it went down over the skyline. Kopanski began to use his field glasses. "It makes a nice change for the boys after being cooped up in Tobruk," he said in a musing, perfectly serious voice. I looked round at him with a quick query, but he really meant what he said.

From over the ridge machine-guns began to fire in quick, stuttering bursts. Then came the sharp whiplash crack of rifles. Each sound arrived detached and clear on the driving wind. The front line was at close quarters with the enemy now, but the rear units were still breasting the rise onto the skyline. Perceptibly the whole tempo of the battle quickened.

Inside a canvas lean-to attached to a truck beside us, an artillery Major was rapping orders down a telephone in rich consonantal Polish. The guns behind us paused in their steady firing to increase the range. Then they started again and their shells went whimpering over our heads almost non-stop. Sometimes the wind would drop for a second and the noise of the guns would reach us with a redoubled loudness that made us jump.

By this time all the men had topped the ridge and gone down into battle. On the left a battery of anti-tank guns bounced forward over the hummocky ground and disappeared. Then a despatch rider came bumping out of the smoke ahead and gave Kopanski a message. The Polish guns suddenly began firing right over the front line onto the enemy batteries.

The machine-gunning began to extend left and right on the Polish flanks. The New Zealanders were in action, and the Indians too. The engagement was general all along the front. But the sun started to go down gaudily among heavy rainclouds. Darkness came earlier than usual and a chill wind set us shivering. We had to get back and find our camp and write our stories. We shook hands with all the Poles we could see and drove off.

While we drove back to Corps, Richard began telling us a long fairy story which took place entirely in New York night clubs. He was still telling it during supper when someone came over with the news that things were not going so well. Away on the left wing the Fifth Indian Brigade had been completely overrun by a German tank force. The Buffs, who were part of the Brigade, had lost very heavily though they had made a very gallant stand. No one quite knew just yet how serious the situation was.

A German prisoner had warned the Buffs that they were going to be attacked by a hundred and fifty tanks during the afternoon. They hardly believed it, but they made every preparation they could for an emergency. And after lunch the attack duly came. There were only twenty-five tanks instead of a hundred and fifty but they came with lorried infantry and mobile guns behind them. They overran the Buffs' batteries and charged straight through the camp. The Buffs' Colonel, who had been wounded, telephoned to Division. "I am afraid this is the last time I shall speak to you," he said. "They are right on top of my Headquarters now." Then there was a snap as he broke the wire.

But in the end the Buffs' stand was not in vain. The Germans who attacked them had to report that their losses made it imperative for them to return and refit. They withdrew and then the way was open for the Fourth Indian Division to advance.

Quite suddenly there was success in the atmosphere again. A sort of instinct built up out of a thousand tiny symptoms put the whole desert in a winning mood. We felt it too, and we thought we would leave the inland desert and try the coast. For if there was a break-through, the best place was on the main road. The road was empty and untouched, and as we bowled along in the yellow winter sunshine we toyed with the idea of coming back here after the war and seeing the desert from a peace-time angle. Alan suggested we should get a concession for running tours to the battlefields, and contract with some Japanese firm to stock the place with cheap mass-produced articles which the tourists would be allowed to loot. We wove extravagant fantasies round the possibilities. We thought big things could be done with parachute troops in desert warfare and we laughed insanely at the idea of nuns and tram-conductors bustling back and forth across this ridiculous landscape.

We found dumps of empty German petrol cans, and stopped to help a Czech ambulance driver who had run out of gasoline and was trying to get some by emptying the dregs of about five hundred tins into one. Then we drove on to Gazala Air Field, which was Gambut all over again: a great graveyard of wrecked planes. While we were driving round, someone stopped us and told us that demolition squads were blowing up bombs. Almost as he spoke six five-hundred–pounders burst all together straight across the air field from where we were standing. They went up in an eruption of flame and a great spout of purple smoke which kept rising and rising into the still air, and the noise almost blew me flat on my back. It must have made a wonderful story for the Italian gunners who were dropping their shells over the escarpment only a little way ahead.

We went on and found the New Zealanders, and we knew we had come too soon. For as yet they were not advancing. As far as I could see they were just letting the Italians retire. Men sunning themselves in slit trenches and bomb-holes round the air field showed me where the enemy's shells had been landing at daybreak. All day, they said, the bursts had been retreating westwards, and now they were splashing down harmlessly into the low-lying dried-up riverbed ahead. It seemed certain that the foremost Italian batteries had been withdrawn, and if that were true it meant the whole Gazala Line was cracking.

We cruised back along the shore, passing through half a dozen deserted enemy encampments. As always we could distinguish the Italian camps by the incredible quantity of letters and picture postcards lying about, and by the smell, which was subtly different from that of the Germans. I do not know what it was — garlic, perhaps. We found a water point which still gave clear sweet water, and I picked up two bottles of the Italian mineral water which is called Recoaro and which, in the desert, makes all the difference between enjoying a drink and not enjoying it. I kept collecting German papers and throwing them away again, for usually they were shockingly boring. But there was one high-brow Berlin weekly which had a brilliantly scurrilous article on Winston Churchill and his family.

We camped down by the shore among some small, brilliantly white sand-hills, miles away from anyone. It was delicious to get the clean tang of the sea in our nostrils instead of smoke and dust, and we took off our shoes and socks and paddled about childishly in the fine silver sand. We felt we were somehow playing truant from the war, just for one night; we were so remote that there was not the slightest possibility of our being bombed, and we hardly bothered to black out.

The artillery back at Gazala had stopped. We theorized about this lazily, lying in bed side by side. Then with the sea murmuring and splashing on the shore about fifteen yards away, we went to sleep.

Back at Corps in the morning we learned that our instinct had been right. The Axis forces had slipped away from the Gazala Line during the night. That was why the artillery fire had ceased. Now they were streaming back along the main road to Derna and down south towards Mechili, with all our forces in hot pursuit.

Rommel, as skilful in flight as he was in attack, had wormed his way out of what might have been a fatal trap. He must have had a shock when he found that the British Armoured Brigade had got around behind him in a sand-storm and nearly reached Bomba. It seemed that he had the choice of fighting our tanks, which outnumbered his overwhelmingly, or running forwards onto the anti-tank guns and twenty-five-pounders of our infantry and artillery. But he managed to do neither. Using his speediest tanks and never letting the British tanks get within range with their two-pounder guns, he played for time until our petrol was exhausted. Our tanks had to fall back to re-fuel, and in that interval Rommel smuggled out his own tanks and his whole Italian holding force.

It was cleverly done. There was no chance of his holding out, for the Polish and New Zealand attack I had watched two days before had already cracked the Gazala Line, and Rommel knew that those Italian infantry divisions would not hold. He made a very slick get-away.

We sat down quickly and wrote despatches, for we were impatient to join in the pursuit. While we were writing two great armadas of bombers with attendant clouds of fighters boomed past overhead on their way to attack the retreating enemy. Around us everything was packing up and moving forward at a hectic pace. It was one of those wild swift intervals when one army chases the other as fast as it can go from one battle-field to the next. We bumped on westwards, threading our way through unit after unit. The whole plateau was seamed with parallel trails of dust which never had time to settle. We passed Maoris, Indians, Czechs, Poles, New Zealanders, and men from every part of the British Isles, packed into lorries and going as hard as they could. Tanks, Bren-gun carriers, ambulances and staff cars wound their independent way among the huge convoys. Hot pursuit like this is an exciting business that tends to go to the head and everyone was mad-keen to push forward.

We only stopped when we found ourselves among a milling throng of Polish vehicles at the top of the corkscrew, hairpin-bent mountain track leading down the escarpment to Gazala Bay. We argued bitterly for some time but finally we agreed to go down it. It looked to me the perfect dive-bomber target. Two great Italian artillery tractors were lying on their sides at the two sharpest bends, and trucks were having to edge their way round them, reversing half a dozen times. Traffic was moving with agonizing slowness and more and more trucks were arriving at the top and having to wait. We were held up countless times on the way down, and it was almost dark when we reached the bottom. Silhouetted against the yellow evening sky we could still see great rows of vehicles waiting to start down, and the rocks re-echoed with shouts of abuse and encouragement in fierce, sibilant Polish.

We found General Kopanski in a truck tucked under the cliff, and he told us about the attack which we had seen launched a couple of days before. In one great charge that evening the Poles had stormed their first objective. All night through they had lain out there among the camel-thorn, wrapping their greatcoats round them. And in the dawn they had assaulted again, with unquenchable spirit, and finished off the job. Their dead lay buried around a lone fig tree near by, to keep them safe from Bedouins and desert foxes. But they meant to dig them up again and send them to lie beside their comrades in the cemetery at Tobruk.

The Poles had taken fifteen hundred men of the Seventh Bersaglieri, with a complete anti-tank battery and full equipment. The Bersaglieri's Colonel was sobbing in a staff car not two yards from where we were talking. "He's terribly upset," Kopanski said. "It would be kinder not to disturb him."

We went off to camp for the night. The stunted bushes were popping all round us as amateur sappers cleaned up hand-grenades and minor booby traps. The Gulfs of Bomba and Gazala lay wonderfully blue and still in the evening sunlight. Chattering Arabs were picking among the useless rubbish and carrying away squalid little bits of loot on overladen donkeys. A group of Italian soldiers came drifting along the road by themselves, trying to find someone who had time to take them prisoners. But the Poles were only really interested in Germans.

ii

The next thing was Derna. But we were still geared to the pace of the slow, hard-fought advances of the early part of the campaign, and neither Alan nor I could believe that it would fall immediately. Subconsciously we remembered the unexpected delay of the previous winter, and we clung to the view that Derna was a difficult place to take.

In any case we had to go back to Army Headquarters to write

our despatches and draw rations. While we packed up a Polish ack-ack gun on the cliff chased two Messerschmitts picturesquely round the sky with pink tracer bullets. And I turned Alan's sleeping-bag inside out and laid it on a thorn bush and showed him how to catch the nimble brown fleas that were living in it.

At Army Headquarters, while Alan was opening a Christmas parcel from Australia containing a plum cake, we heard the rumour that Derna had fallen. I could not believe that I had missed it again — for the second year running. But the news was confirmed at Tmimi, a bleak spot where Corps Headquarters had just settled in. The Italians had run clean through Derna and out again the other side. The Indian Division had strolled in as though on holiday. Fighting their usual rear-guard action with dynamite, the Italians had blown up the serpentine road leading down the cliff to Derna, and the equally serpentine road leading up the cliff the other side. The capture of the place was just a simple job for the sappers.

So the Derna-Mechili Line was not going to be held. It meant the chase was going to be fast and furious now. There was talk of a line at Barce, a line at Bengasi, a line at Agedabia. But I do not think many people seriously believed in any of these lines. Rommel himself with his tanks and a great mass of motor transport had chosen the shorter, more southerly, infinitely more difficult route through the desert via Mechili. It meant he would come out on the main road somewhere south of Bengasi, and it seemed unlikely he would then wheel north up into Jebel Achdar, which he had so pointedly avoided. There at Tmimi, just after we had got the news, I wrote, "To-day's guess is that they won't stop running until they have cleared right out of Cyrenaica."

CHAPTER 18

Bengasi Christmas

THE DYNAMITED road up the escarpment beyond Derna was still impassable, so we had to go back to Martuba and then make a circuit round inland. And at this point Richard left us. He had finally come to the conclusion that, since he worked for an American paper, he ought to go to the Far East. Singapore, he argued, was more important than Bengasi. So we handed him out his bedding and some food and drink and left him to find his way back to Cairo. We were genuinely sorry to see him go, for he had fitted smoothly and easily into our party and there had been no serious quarrels at all. Moreover, he did the washing up.

As we said farewell to him, we heard that the German *Panzerdivision* had raced off south across the desert and left an Italian rear-guard at the fort of Mechili. The campaign was falling curiously into rules and habits — it had by now become almost etiquette for a retiring armoured column to go by Mechili and leave a rear-guard to fight an action there. This time the R.A.F. dropped tons of bombs on the fort, but the Italians seemed to be holding on remarkably well. All one night their lights were blazing from every window. But next morning British tanks found the place gruesomely empty. Every light was full on. And scattered about just where they had died were the bodies of over a hundred Italians. The living defenders had slipped away.

We left Richard and drove up onto the great reddish plateau of Martuba. At Giovanni Berta, a little pointed hill with a castle on top, we happened on the final stages of a small engagement with the Italian rear-guard, which, having put up a good show, surrendered happily.

After by-passing the ruined road beyond Derna, we went on as fast as we could, cutting across to the southern round. It became absurdly like last year. Fewer of the colonists' houses remained occupied this time. The surface of the road had been worn rather more threadbare by a year's war traffic. There were more derelict vehicles strewn along it than before, and many had the palm-and-swastika emblem stencilled on them. The traffic signs all had German versions added. But these were minor shades of difference in a background that basically had not changed at all. It seemed ludicrous that two different campaigns should look so exactly the same.

But it became downright farce when we stopped and Alan ran back down the road laughing and said, "The ambush is there again."

"The ambush?" I said, dumbfounded.

"Yes, the Italians have staged it again in almost exactly the same place as before."

It argued an almost inconceivable lack of originality on the part of the Italians. But I suppose someone had remembered there had been a pretty successful ambush there last year, so why not try it again? This time it had not been quite so good. The leading British armoured cars had had time to dodge back before much harm was done. Only one had been hit. But the Italians were there with field guns and anti-tank guns at a spot where the road curved between steep, tree-covered banks, and they could not be outflanked.

I went and looked, without perceptible emotion, at the scene of last year's ambush (the new one was a little farther on). There was nothing to show for it now but some rotten wood and rusty iron thrust into the bushes by the road, and a few shell-cases. But I found the shallow groove where I had lain and expected death, and I tried in vain to remember just how I had felt. Then we drove back a couple of miles and camped for the night in the same colonist's farmstead where our wounds had been treated the year before. The Italians, too, had used it as a hospital, but the Arabs had turned it into a shambles of broken glass, spilled medicines, smashed instruments and torn muddy bandages. We swept a room clear and put up our camp-beds and spent the night. When we woke next morning the ground was white with half-frozen dew and the ambush was still in place.

We hung about all morning waiting for some twenty-five-pounders to come and clear it up. Then about midday a staff captain drove up the road and slap into it. Before anyone could stop him he had disappeared on the other side. They could hear his exhaust fading into the distance but not a shot was fired. Men looked at each other in amazement and then scrambled for their vehicles. The Italians had packed up and stolen away, so quietly that no one had heard them.

ii

Christmas Day dawned fine and the countryside had a faintly European, civilized look. We left Barce through orchards just coming into blossom and ploughed fields where the red earth lay in big moist clods. The farmhouses here were white and completely cubic, as though a child had made them with a box of bricks. There was a village with a big market-place, and at the back of it a sort of super-simplified Renaissance church set between two colonnades at the top of broad steps, which was quite charming. The colonnades framed a sweeping chocolate and blue-green landscape with clouds that looked like some background in a picture by Bellini.

Where the road curls down to Tocra, through a tangle of ravines that provides Cyrenaica's loveliest patch of countryside, the Italian engineers had done a great job. They had blown up the highway at a point where it was a mere shelf on a precipice, and there was nothing left but a vast stretch of scree which looked like the aftermath of an avalanche. There was no hope of rebuilding it, so the sappers had blazed a very makeshift trail up over a neighbouring spur and down a sort of mud slide to the main road below. Nothing could possibly have come up it.

Now the road to Bengasi was wide-open to us. We hummed

down through the squalid little fishing village of Tocra, with its mammoth ruined walls, and out into the flat, coastal desert again. The whole world was out looting in the sunshine. For mile after mile along this road the Italians and Germans had left dumps of food and drink and petrol, and every Arab man or woman old enough or not too old to carry a sack was pillaging furiously. Urchins rushed to the roadside and clapped at us ingratiatingly, and Biblical-looking shepherds wrapped in rugs and carrying great staves looked gravely at us from the midst of their sheep. But we stopped for nothing — we wanted to see Bengasi.

We came to the native quarter first — shapeless, whitewashed mud cabins with men sitting in the sun and women uncording their bales of loot, and goats and children picking about in the garbage. Most Arab native quarters always look as though they had gone through a bad bombing, for their architecture is slipshod and rarely completed, and there was nothing specially ruinous about this.

But then we drove on into the European quarter. I thought back to the first time we had marched in — the fresh, gleaming streets lined with trees, the sparkling white houses, the civilians in European dress, the exhilaration and the triumph. Now it was a ruin. There was not a soul in the streets. A dead horse lay twisted in the gutter. Every window was shattered and every door barred. The roadway seesawed up and down over half-mended bomb craters, and palm trees and lamp standards lay uprooted or drooped drunkenly. Every house was ripped and scarred with shrapnel. Iron shop shutters were torn and twisted by blast. The fair white walls were blackened by fire.

There was that same stench and dirt and desolation that you always get in a town which has come straight out of the firing line, where the damage has never been repaired or the debris removed, where no one is even trying to live.

We went to the Hotel d'Italia where we had lodged the first time, but it was closed and deserted. A big bomb had split it clean in two and tons of plaster and iron girders had spilled out crazily into the square on either side. With a silly sort of persistence, like travellers looking for rooms in a town which they know is absolutely full, we drove on to the Berenice Hotel, which used to be Bengasi's luxury hostelry. But that too was empty and derelict, its windows blown out and the ground floor still smouldering. Last time it had been Italian G.H.Q. This time the Luftwaffe had had it and in the lounge the floor and tables were littered with parachute kits from which the valuable silk had been cut away. The German pilots had tried to gut the place before they left.

Outside on the water-front a solitary British armoured car was parked, and the crew were cooking their Christmas dinner on the pavement. The whole roadway all round was filled-in bomb craters. Again and again the Italians had had to renew the railway lines which ran alongside the harbour. There was not even one small stretch of the stone balustrade left standing and one by one the ornamental columns had been blown away. From the water itself funnels and masts and hulls were jutting grotesquely. The top of a big dredger was sticking up from the very middle of the harbour. This had been Rommel's chief supply port and the R.A.F.'s chief target. Only the Cathedral, which was plumb in the middle of the target area, seemed to have been spared a serious direct hit. It looked like either astoundingly accurate bombing or else a miracle.

The armoured-car crew hailed us, wishing us a Merry Christmas and offering us wine. We joined them on the pavement and they told us the story of how Bengasi had been entered this second time.

Two armoured-car patrols had been first in on Christmas Eve. One came from the south and one from the east, and they had met each other, with mutual surprise, in the middle. Neither had had to fire a shot. They could not tell for certain which had been there first, so the honour was shared by common consent among the King's Dragoon Guards, the Royal Dragoons, and the South African armoured cars.

While we drank rather vinegary Chianti out of cracked tea-cups, we heard of the terrible journey they had made to reach Bengasi. Their car was still spattered to the windscreen with the glutinous red mud which the wheels had splashed up. For mile after mile they had slithered and skidded and dug themselves in until their racing engines boiled and everything they had was coated with slime. Hail and sleet and rain had beaten steadily against them, turning desert tracks into swamps and swamps into lakes. Truck after truck had had to be towed or pushed out of axle-deep mud.

Once they picked up an R.A.F. pilot who had been living in the desert ever since he had crashed. He had seen armoured cars in the distance, but he could not tell whose they were so he tossed a coin for it. It came down heads. So he went across and they were British.

The patrol coming from the east had finally reached the top of the escarpment and seen Bengasi lying white and still in the distance. They slithered down the winding track on to Benina Air Field and paused to gasp at the wreckage there before driving on into the town. They told us Benina beat all records for air-field cemeteries.

So we drove out to see it and counted the 117 wrecked planes round its vast water-sodden expanse. Many stood quite whole and perfect save where wandering Bedouins had broken in and stolen the neat black cases containing the pilot's emergency rations. Some of the workshops looked as though the mechanics had just gone away to lunch, and the big stores of pale-blue high-octane aviation spirit were untouched. We wandered round, trying to assess the enormous value of the matériel that had been left behind. Then we drove into Bengasi again and renewed the sharp impact of anticlimax which those forlorn, shell-shocked streets gave us.

Yet there were people who were happy here, men whose eyes shone with uncontainable joy. We found some in the hospital—wounded British officers and men, who had been left behind by the Italians. They were lying in their little cots bubbling with happiness, talking furiously and bombarding us with questions, celebrating the best Christmas they would ever have. And out in the street I met a shock-haired, raw-boned Greek who had just got himself out of prison. He had escaped from Greece to Africa in a little boat and had landed just a few miles inside enemy territory. He firmly believed the Italians had been starving him to death. "I was a fat man," he said and showed me the waist-band of his pants to prove it.

In the main square a leather-jacketed Italian policeman, directing traffic with a look of quiet bewilderment on his face, told us that the war correspondents and photographers were all living in a big block of flats near the railway station. We found them there unpacking in the courtyard, choosing apartments and moving in, while two Italian friars looked on and gave helpful information. Someone was going round issuing invitations to a cocktail party for the evening.

Alan and I picked a ground-floor apartment that had apparently been a police station and we swept it out and re-arranged the furniture and set up our beds. Faintly, almost imperceptibly, a feeling of Christmas and conviviality began to creep in. We wandered round to one another's apartments borrowing things, accepting drinks, exchanging gossip. Strangers who picked their way past in the ruined streets shouted "Merry Christmas" and we shouted back from the windows, although it could not possibly be a very Merry Christmas for anyone. There was a minimum of peace and goodwill roundabout it.

Alan and Kim and I pooled our resources with Geoffrey Keating and Russell Hill and Freddie Bayliss, the Paramount photographer. We had among us two turkeys, a tinned ham, two tinned Christmas puddings, and one of the Italian friars gave us a bottle of Chianti. The problem was how to cook the turkeys. We suggested boiling them in a hip-bath, cooking them on spits over a bonfire, or coating them with mud and building a fire round them. But we finally cooked them on the huge derelict kitchen range in the Hotel Berenice.

Bits of the kitchen were still smouldering round us where the Luftwaffe had tried to set fire to it. Strewn about the greasy floor were big bricks of German dried vegetables, packages of pea-soup tablets and something in tins that must presumably have been edible but looked, tasted and smelt like sawdust. Everything was indescribably dirty and the fumes from the burning made our throats tickle and our eyes water. We stuffed bits of furniture into the grate but we must have done something wrong for the top of the stove got red-hot while the oven remained icily cold. So in the end the turkeys were fried. They were put in flat trays on top of the kitchen range and basted continuously with tinned ration margarine. I stayed there long enough to make a stuffing out of an onion, a tin of sausages and some herbs I found, then I left Kim and Freddie in charge and went back to our flat to write my story.

In a way it was a difficult story to write for it was the story of an anticlimax. There was a feeling of futility where there should have been jubilation, of pity where there should have been triumph. There was no satisfaction in the knowledge that all this destruction had been wrought by us in straight warfare. All one saw was the destruction and emptiness and desolation, and it was a depressing sight in itself although it may have been excellent as a means to an end. There was nothing to do but write a straightforward description of the place.

Aeroplanes swooped overhead and an ear-cracking racket broke out all through the town. The Germans had sent over bombers to drop mines in the harbour and every man in the streets who had a fire-arm was shooting vertically into the air. The shots re-echoed theatrically among the hollow shells of the buildings and a light ack-ack gun barked away steadily on the water-front. Then there was silence again and a messenger came to tell me the turkeys were just done.

It was a really good meal by any standards — eaten by candle-light off tin plates on the counter of a captured police station, but none the less a first-class meal. There was lacking in it the finesse, the gastronomic punctilio of purist cooking, but a Christmas meal is essentially hearty, and this was undoubtedly hearty. For six weeks we had been living on tinned things inevitably mixed with sand and usually prepared and eaten in the dark. To-night we stuffed ourselves without any pretence at manners, just eating as much as we could possibly force down.

When we could walk we went visiting round the other flats. There were about four basic parties permanently in progress, and people drifted round from one to another as the fancy took them. We accepted what drinks we were given and sang all the songs we could think of. There was a moment of mad Bacchanale in the courtyard when two processions carrying glasses met and intermingled in an orgy of folk-dancing. The singing got better and better as our throats loosened and our dinners digested. There developed what the Germans call *Stimmung*. The sense of anti-climax receded and it seemed not such a bad Christmas after all. And at the right moment, before the party had a chance to go stale on us, Kim led us out into the cool wet night air and back to our police station to bed.

Next morning, seen through a hangover, Bengasi looked worse than ever and we felt an urgent need to get out of it. In any case we had to discover what was happening down south. No one could tell us whether Rommel had in fact pulled right out of Cyrenaica, or whether he had turned to dig himself in as soon as the pursuit weakened. A suspicion had begun to spread abroad that perhaps he had not been so decisively beaten as we had at first thought.

We drove out of the town and down through the dull uncompromising desert. Here and there, at intervals of several miles, we found trucks and tents and men lounging about or cooking or shaving in the thin sunshine. They gave the air of being a forgotten scrag-end of the army. All the urgency had gone out of the campaign. There was a feeling that the spot light had been turned off and the show was finished. The little Arab shepherdesses grazing their camels and goats and sheep seemed to be the proper actors on this stage, not the soldiers.

Beside a little mud village called Magrun we lunched with an armoured-car patrol on an air field, and they told us what news there was about the enemy. There had been no Battle of Beda Fomm this time. In a swift orderly retreat Rommel had taken his troops and tanks slap across the desert and reached the coast about a hundred miles south of Bengasi. Then he had turned round and dug himself in just south of Agedabia. Many of his Italian-infantry units whose transport had broken down had been evacuated by ship from the beaches. But the Germans had all stayed. Their positions were thought to be strong and just before Christmas Rommel had launched a counterattack with thirty-seven tanks and overrun some of our gun positions. As far as anyone could tell me he had met with insignificant opposition.

So that was the situation. Rommel was still in Cyrenaica, still offering fight. We were opposite him with a force that amounted to little more than patrols. I remember it was then we started to joke in an unbelieving way about the possibility of a real counterattack, the possibility that the events of the previous spring might be repeated. I do not think any of us genuinely supposed that such a thing could really happen. But I find an underlying sense of uneasiness in the despatch I wrote that day, phrases such as "Rommel's counterattack was probably only to raise the morale of his troops, but it is significant that he did take the offensive"; "The Nazis are clearly unwilling to abandon the whole of this province before they are forced to do so"; "Rommel still has not fought that famous last battle we have all been talking about for six weeks."

We almost all of us decided to return towards Cairo next morning. It was becoming impossible to send our despatches back in anything under four or five days. We were all very tired. Unlike men serving in regular units, we had had to make all our own arrangements, do all our own domestic chores, get our own information and make our own plans, and be continually on the go between the front line and various headquarters in order to send off our despatches. We got all the help that could be given from the Public Relations Unit, but in the nature of things we had to work most of it out for ourselves. Our food and our clothes were nearly exhausted. But worst of all was the feeling that we had written ourselves dry, that there was no more zest in the campaign.

Geoffrey Keating invited me to ride with him in his "Passion Wagon," a vehicle he had had constructed in Tobruk. It was, in fact, a station wagon with the back seat removed and a spring bed fitted in — the smallest, neatest caravan imaginable. We moved out of Bengasi in an impressive file of cars. All along the road Arabs were standing holding up handfuls of eggs, and Geoffrey and I started collecting them. We paid for them with handfuls of sugar and we had got something over five dozen when we discovered that we had lost the whole of the rest of the party.

It took us two hours to discover that our colleagues, learning it was impossible to get up the escarpment at Tocra where the Italians had blown it, had gone on north to try and find a way round. Geoffrey and I started after them and immediately the Passion Wagon broke down. Among other things it had run out of oil. We got stupidly indignant that the others had not waited for us. I climbed on the roof and gazed up the coast through field glasses while Geoffrey prowled round the Passion Wagon discovering new things wrong with it. We found that while we had no food with us, we had the bedding belonging to four people, but not including our own. Finally we cruised back to Tocra to borrow something for lunch, borrow some oil for the Passion Wagon, and wait for the others.

We waited for hours but no one came. And in desperation, late in the afternoon, we stormed the pass. Nothing was going up, but heavy ack-ack guns were slithering down and they were not improving the surface. But Geoffrey and I were savagely determined. We collected about twenty Indian troops, turned the whole affair into a joke, and made them cart us up bodily. The spinning wheels flung great gobbets of red mud around, but the Indians dodged them, laughing like children. In ten minutes we were bowling along the good road to Barce.

At the Barce Hotel Alan had left a note saying they were trying to get to Giovanni Berta for the night. The sun was setting behind us as we flung up the Barce escarpment after them, the Passion

Wagon purring angrily. We passed Tecnis in growing dusk, and Maraua in the last of the twilight. The country was deserted, and somehow very chic and orderly with its stunted evergreen bushes bordering the fine metalled road. It grew steadily colder and more difficult to see. We could have used lights with complete safety but the Passion Wagon had none. We decided to stop and camp in one of the little white farmhouses which flanked the road at intervals on either side.

The first we tried must have had a couple of platoons in it. There was hardly standing room. The second was being systematically looted and burned by some Bedouins. In the third we found all our missing colleagues.

We made a brilliantly dramatic entrance. They had lit a tremendous blaze in a wide old-fashioned hearth and were sitting round in the ruddy firelight stirring stews, making tea, drinking whisky. As we ate the stew they gave us, we heard how they too had found it impossible to drive any farther along the dark road and had decided to choose the first likely farmhouse. By an absurd coincidence we had chosen the same one. We sat round for a long time talking, enjoying the warmth and glow of the fireside, the pleasure of having achieved the day's destination after it had seemed impossible we could do so, the agreeable consciousness that this particular phase of war and discomfort was nearly behind us. Then we put up our beds like a dormitory in a clean room and went to bed.

Next morning someone tipped us off that an attack was just going to be launched against the Axis forces still holding out in Bardia.

CHAPTER 19

Night Fight for Bardia

We passed through Tobruk in a sand-storm and, I think, an air raid. It certainly sounded like one, but the whirling dust was so thick we could not see more than a few yards, and no one we met along the road was any wiser than we were. But it was sunny again when we climbed the escarpment above Bardia and camped with a South African Brigade. They told us that we were just about in time for the attack. Zero hour was to be 6 A.M. on New Year's Eve.

I was specially anxious to see the attack on Bardia, for this was Rommel's first experiment in the fortress-area theory. It was by no means certain that he was trying it willingly; he had been obliged to leave that large garrison behind when he was prized away from Tobruk and forced westwards. But all the time as he retreated he must have been contemplating the possibility of an early come-back. And if Bardia could hold out for a month, for a few weeks only, then it might play a vital role in the counter-attack he hoped to make, just as Tobruk had been vital in Auchinleck's plans. The precedents on the subject were not very clear: twice the Italians had only been able to hold fortress areas for a couple of days; on the other hand the British had spent six months in Tobruk. But Rommel must have thought that, given a little luck, Bardia had a chance.

The place was nothing like so well garrisoned as when Bergonzoli held it. It was thought to contain about six thousand Axis troops, probably one fifth of them German. They had no air protection, and probably not more than half a dozen tanks. But in their seventeen miles of perimeter they had plenty of guns of all sorts. The defences were shorter and deeper than a year before and they were very well planned. Concrete anti-tank gun positions gave a tremendous cross-fire on every point of approach, and hundreds of miles of wire had been used in the entanglements. The defenders had plenty of water, plenty of food, plenty of petrol and ammunition, and anything they really urgently needed was being sent by plane from Crete.

General de Villiers, commander of the Second South African Division, thought he might quite easily have a tough nut to crack in Bardia. He talked to us about it in his heraldic tent — a small, square erection which looked as though it might have been used in the Crusades — the evening before the battle began. He was going to attack with the first British army tank brigade, but all the infantry and all the artillery except for one Polish battery were to be South African. He had one large division but he could not use the whole of it, for in addition to attacking Bardia he had to contain the Axis forces in Halfaya. Nevertheless he was confident he could pull it off. He was a stocky ruddy-faced man who had been Police Chief in the Union, and he was clearly accustomed to making detailed, comprehensive plans and putting them into execution.

Militarily it was going to be very small beer — less than a division on either side. Bardia was nothing — one street of single-storey white-washed ruins tottering on the brink of a cliff above a tiny harbour. But the whole world had heard of it. It had, in fact, been the very first enemy town or village which the British Empire had captured by force of arms in this war. The Australians had made their debut here and now the South Africans hoped that they could repeat the performance. They needed a quick, rousing, bloodless victory in the Union for they had still not been able to announce the full details of the rout of the Fifth Brigade at Rezegh. This was no side-show for General de Villiers.

It was a wild cold night when we went to bed and I snuggled into my sleeping-bag feeling sorry for the men who were going to attack in the morning, and wondering if the defenders of Bardia had any idea of what was going to happen to them. Then I fell quickly asleep and it seemed only a minute later that the concerted roar of scores of guns jerked me bolt upright in my sleeping-bag. It was four-fifteen exactly. Left and right across the desert the muzzle flashes flickered and blazed with a livid glare that lit up the under-sides of the low clouds. The din re-echoed with a full deep-pitched note that seemed to reverberate in the pit of one's stomach. The truck which sheltered our beds quivered and rattled without stopping. It was easily the biggest barrage the campaign had produced so far.

The moon had set and it was dark and bitterly cold. The heavy dew was freezing crisply on my groundsheet. I buried my head in my bag again and tried to sleep despite the din. It was no use getting up, for there was nothing to see. But I knew that way out ahead, working with numb, chilled fingers, sappers were carving pathways for the tanks to go in. Bren-gun carriers had taken them a good distance towards the enemy. Then they had had to walk and the last couple of hundred yards they wormed their way on their bellies, steering a careful course among the harsh, prickly camel-scrub, dragging their tools and explosives with them.

First they blew in the sides of the anti-tank ditch — it turned out to be ten feet deep instead of the three feet they had anticipated — and levelled it into a shallow causeway for the tanks. Then they opened gateways in line after line of barbed-wire entanglements. Then they made safe corridors through the thickly strewn mine fields. I can imagine few jobs which need greater courage.

Little parties of infantry who went with them were cleaning up the first pillboxes, pouncing on sentinels and outpost parties holding the outermost lines of defence. They worked in cold and darkness with our shells spraying the enemy strong-points just ahead of them and the enemy all round them firing machine-guns on fixed lines. But just as the first faint light of morning glimmered over Sollum, they sent back a message that half a dozen safe passages had been made for the tanks. And they had not lost a man doing it.

All this time the tanks were moving up to their battle positions and we heard the harsh steady hum of their engines as they clattered through the camp. They picked their way carefully, following special routes to avoid churning up the telephone lines. Men's breaths were like smoke in the frosty air as they passed.

At six o'clock the noise reached a new peak of intensity. The gap had been made down to the south-east of Bardia town, pretty much where the Australians had gone in a year before. But up to the north-west one South African Brigade was staging a noisy, showy feint. Some genius with a grasp of German psychology had laid shiny empty petrol tins in neat rows across the countryside. The Bardia look-outs had noticed them uneasily the night before, and now the rising sun burnished them rosy-red. If they had had any purpose at all, the Germans could have worked it out. But they meant absolutely nothing. And the German gunners, utterly bewildered, dumped salvo after salvo on them as hard as they could go.

At six-thirty I got up and crept to a ridge from which I could look down over the battle-field. It was getting lighter and the gun flashes were less blinding, but their bursts were very clearly visible, drifting lazily along the skyline. Tracer shells were leaving curious parabolas of smoke arched above the rising sun. The tanks as they moved in to the attack were just faint smudges of smoke creeping across the desert. But the sharp cough of their guns and the crackle of machine-gun fire came clearly and incessantly on the morning air. The tanks moved steadily on, straight through the enemy's fire. This sector was being held by the Genoa Cavalry, armed to the teeth with automatic weapons, and they were fighting back hard. But, as every other Italian unit had done before them, they gave way in the face of an attack strongly pressed home. They surrendered the two strong-points they were holding and by the time a garish sunrise had brought full daylight to the battle-field, the tanks had won through and the infantry was pouring in behind them.

It had taken just about an hour to effect that initial break-through. In the approved fashion the perimeter had been punctured, as with a sharp instrument. Once more the fortress-area theory was being disproved. The South Africans were jubilant and de Villiers described it as a "pure text-book operation."

Then came a lull, for the next phase of the attack was billed for dusk. An incipient sand-storm began to blow in fierce cruel gusts. The non-combatant Zulus stood about miserably, wrapped up to the eyebrows and wearing tin hats on top of thick woollen helmets. My companions decided to go straight on to Cairo. So I teamed up with a South African correspondent and we shut ourselves in our car and shaved and opened a tin of bully and settled down to read year-old magazines. I was beginning to feel that I could endure just about two more days of the desert and that was all.

The General's A.D.C. came across to take us to the front. We drove across country to Capuzzo, now a gaunt shapeless ruin with a brand-new German cemetery beside it, and down the main road to Bardia's outer defences. Guns were firing from behind us and shells were thumping down in a great arc between us and Bardia town. For half an hour we tried to diagnose and analyze the shell bursts but we could not make head or tail of the situation. For one thing the front seemed a good deal too near us and in the wrong direction. Once again we had to drive away from the battle in order to find out what had been going on right in front of our eyes.

There had been counterattack — a counterattack which the South Africans had not seriously expected. The German commander — he turned out to be a certain Major-General Artur Schmidt — had reacted bravely and skilfully after a very bad start. He had at first been deceived by the Third Brigade's feint in the north-west. While the British tanks had been cracking through in the south-east he had rushed up his guns and his best troops to face the noisy, mysterious menace in the opposite direction. That was why the first phase had gone so easily for us.

But Schmidt swiftly discovered his mistake. He swung everything round and rushed it down to the south-east again. Every gun and every man he could use was flung into an impromptu line across the fortress area. Field artillery began firing from deep ravines running down to the sea, and anti-tank guns were dug in with feverish haste. Schmidt hurled his shock troops against the Kaffirian Rifles, who were temporarily occupying a weak section of the line, and gained himself an improvised front where he could use his massive concrete strong-points and pillboxes.

There was just a faint undercurrent of uneasiness among the South Africans. The counterattack was not in the least serious, but it delayed the hopes of a quick, smashing victory. The South Africans still held one third of the Bardia area. But they had been pushed back to a line parallel with and south of the main road leading to Bardia from Egypt, and the plans would have to be altered. The night attack would have to be postponed for twenty-four hours.

Next day we waited around in the worst sand-storm I had ever experienced. You could see perhaps eighteen inches in front of you. The dust got through your closed lips and sifted down your back and into your ears. Every two or three minutes it collected in little pellets in the corners of your eyes. Men fought their way through it, blundering over tent ropes, their faces like beige-plaster masks. The mess tent was blown away right under our noses, just as we were going in to have lunch. I found myself trying to suspend all my faculties, to reduce my consciousness to the minimum, to concentrate on just enduring it until it stopped.

It did stop towards evening, and in its stead came sharp, icy rainstorms driving in from the sea. We sat huddled in the car, wondering whether the rain would make the ground too wet for the tanks to operate and postpone the night attack again. We had planned to walk out into no-man's-land and watch it start at ten o'clock. But it clearly was not going to be pleasant.

Then the squalls dropped, and a bright moon began to sail in and out of the ragged clouds. We walked over to the General's tent to fetch his A.D.C., who had promised to come with us, and found that the attack was still on the programme — the ground was still firm enough for the tanks. The General told us to wait in his car and play with the wireless if we liked. I turned the knob, and one of Handel's Concerti Grossi flowed out into the night like a great stream of silver and gold. It was the first note of music I had heard for months and I sat in the darkness almost hypnotized with pleasure. There was a mighty rolling adagio, and then a fine bold fugue, and they dragged me away in the middle of it to come and see the battle.

We took a compass bearing and walked forward into the darkness. Everything was quite quiet now, a sinister expectant hush. We could see nothing, but we knew that within the compass of our eyes, had it been light, ten thousand men were waiting to fight. Once a squall of sleet sent us staggering back and drove against our faces until we could not feel. Then it settled down to a thin, drenching rain. We passed a battery of twenty-five–pounders and the gun crews were getting ready to go into action. Their tin hats and waterproof capes gleamed wetly as they moved about the emplacement with shoulders hunched up against the cold. We walked on, following a telephone line that led to an observation post.

At nine–forty-five the rain stopped and we were suddenly walking in full moonlight. Simultaneously splashes of flame leaped up round three quarters of the horizon as our guns began to fire. A few seconds later the shells bursting completed the circle. The battery just behind us warned us each time by its livid flashes to brace ourselves for the shock of the noise. We walked on and on, reached the observation post, and passed beyond it. At a point where the first wire entanglement of the perimeter defences was a dark blur across the landscape ahead of us, we sat down. We knew that the enemy strong-points which were the main objective of the attack were there just in front of us, and that the battle would sweep across us as though we were at a race meeting.

Ten o'clock was zero hour, but a slight heightening of the noise was the only thing that marked it. We sat there shivering, and I uncorked a bottle of South African ration brandy—rich fruity stuff that seemed to roll with a slow smooth warmth through the veins. The fighting was still well away to the right of us, a meaningless confusion of explosions. It seemed to me to be moving very slowly.

Then quite suddenly, in rapid crescendo, the battle surged right up to where we sat. We heard the din of the British tanks, first as just a distant rumble, then as a grinding, clattering roar rising and falling in pitch as they revved up their engines. They had taken their exhausts off and were making all the noise they could.

The enemy anti-tank guns were firing with quick thudding bursts and the rocky ravines threw back the sound like a mighty roll of drums. Their shells described white sparkling parabolas against the dark storm clouds. The tanks were using crimson tracers which scudded along the horizon and ricocheted high into the air when they hit something.

Then the brittle rattle of machine-guns showed us the infantry were there too. They spouted their rosy tracers this way and that across the battle-field, crossing and re-crossing the enemy's fire. The fighting was going past us in profile, and you could follow quite clearly how the infantry were held up at one point, then smashed their way through and took a position from which they could enfilade the enemy and clear a passage for the unit on their right.

Gradually the trajectories of the tracer shells grew flatter as the tanks and infantry advanced and the range shortened. There was an abrupt lull on the left and for a few minutes the shooting was all one way. The enemy were retiring on their next positions. Then it all started violently again.

Sometimes the moon would sail out into a clear patch of sky and everything stood forth with eerie clarity. It was fantastically lovely and totally unreal—Walt Disney in a serious mood. The tanks surged along like great silver-glinting mastodons amid cascades of flaming shells. Bursts from the twenty-five-pounders stood like slowly blossoming avenues of trees. One had a brief, crazy impression of smoke and movement and coloured flame, then the moon slid away again.

Once an enemy munition dump went up with a thunderous double explosion, and later a great fire started which rose and fell luridly across the battle-field. Just to our right infantry stormed a strong-point in a fierce burst of hand-to-hand fighting. Machine-guns firing at very short range raved away like pneumatic drills, then abruptly stuttered into silence and with quick yellow flashes of flame hand-grenades began bursting.

The tanks surged on ahead, sweeping their path clear with spitting bursts of fire, then dodging swiftly to mask their movements. All over the place the enemy began firing green Very lights. And then a sudden weird silence struck us almost like a blow. The field guns had all stopped firing and until then I had not realized how tremendous their noise had been. The barrage on the final enemy strong-points had been lifted, and the infantry were going to assault them.

It happened in a bewildering tornado of flame and noise. I lost all track of what was going on. The tanks must have run clean past some of the points before they opened fire, for the bullets were flaming in every direction. The Italians, with Germans manning the important gun positions, fought their hopeless battle with unusual tenacity. The South Africans had to struggle for every yard of ground they gained, and storm every position they took.

But then the fury gradually drained out of the fighting and we knew these main positions had fallen. Stiffly we started to walk back. We followed the telephone wire to the battery and were challenged by a sentry who was so astonished that we had to prompt him. Then we took a bearing and walked on. I was desperately tired, and I could not stop myself tripping over the tussocks of scrub. Twice we blundered into the wrong camp, and I knew that if we went wrong again I should just lie down where I was and sleep. But the next camp was the right one.

A Liaison Officer was flying off early in the morning and would take our despatches with him so we decided to write at once and have done with it. We blacked out the car with blankets, stuck a candle in a bottle, and forced ourselves to stay awake and type. The keys of the typewriter were dancing in front of my eyes and my fingers were fumbling stupidly as I wrote the last words. I handed the stuff in without attempting to read it through and went to bed.

We slept a long time — much too long. The sun climbed round the corner of the car and shone into my eyes and I woke to find it was after nine o'clock. We were still dragging on our clothes when someone strolled across and told us that Bardia had thrown in the sponge. At eight-forty-five two German officers had driven out with flags of truce and asked when General Schmidt could wait on General de Villiers. He was told ten o'clock, and not to be late, otherwise the battle would continue.

The meeting took place just inside the perimeter wire, on the road. Schmidt was punctual, faultlessly turned out, meticulously correct. The morning was cold and blustering and the British and German Generals climbed into a station wagon and discussed terms sitting together on the back seat. The Italian Generals thrust their heads through the windows, making excited comments and suggestions, but Schmidt took not the least notice of them. He alone was surrendering Bardia. He scanned the list of conditions and accepted the lot. But he put his finger on one point and said, "It is no good my signing that — I have already given orders that everything inside the perimeter be destroyed. It's too late to stop it now." Then he drove off to pack his bag for captivity.

We continued in to Bardia, and there we saw how the demolition orders had been carried out. Underground petrol dumps were blazing with hundred-foot-high flames. Great billows of black smoke were drifting miles out to sea. Every few yards there was a derelict lorry blazing or smouldering or smoking. Even petrol cans were swollen and split by fire. There did not seem to be so much as a tent left.

Bardia town was a derelict version of what it had been the winter before. The only big change I saw was the complete collapse of the western end of the church. But every house was a little more dilapidated and shell and bomb splinters had stripped away most of the white stucco in the main street. Our Public Relations house, where the correspondents had lived a year before, still had P.R.G.H.Q. painted up on it and someone had added in English *To Let.* I stood on a barrel and rubbed it out again.

Prisoners were appearing from everywhere. Squads of Germans and Italians marched up the curling road from the harbour and congregated on the terrace outside the town gate. A group of Italians stuck up a white flag beside the roadside and tried to surrender to all who came past, but for a long time everyone was too busy to bother about them. Here and there Germans marched unattended in neat orderly gangs along the road. Huge blue and khaki columns trudged through the rain up to the barbed-wire prisoners' cages. Their final total was 1804 Germans, 5278 Italians, and 900 mixed wounded.

In the street of Bardia an odd thousand British prisoners were going mad with happiness. They were ragged and cold and hungry and most of them had grown beards for they had not been allowed razor blades. But two of them produced a gramophone and a whole group began to dance for joy—a rare and curiously moving sight. They climbed over Bren-gun carriers and armoured cars, and shook hands with everyone they met. We produced what rations we had and they sat on the curb and wolfed everything they were given, for they had been kept very short of food.

We drove back to Headquarters and I found General de Villiers had kept a seat for me in the special plane which had been ordered to take Schmidt away from El Adem next morning. So I went and camped alongside the air field and once more we blacked out the car and wrote stories by candle-light. Overhead we could hear the German bombers going in one by one to bomb Tobruk.

I got to the plane next morning just as Schmidt arrived. He walked through the mud and rain stiffly, his sand goggles pushed up above the brim of his hat and a big khaki cloak concealing his crimson lapels. His cropped grizzled hair and very pale blue eyes and rat-trap mouth were perfectly in character and he had that almost instinctive arrogance which inevitably hallmarks a Prussian officer.

He had shown it the day before at the surrender, when he suavely ignored the Italian commanders. Then he had been stiff and meticulously correct — the complete portrait of a General surrendering a city. But now, in the plane, he was a prisoner of war. When he caught someone's eye, he smiled and tried to appear cheerful. But mostly he sat thinking with vacant eyes and his leathery face fell into lines of shame and misery.

I do not suppose he was an enthusiastic Nazi from the political point of view. But he was a professional Prussian General and he had lost his battle in as downright a fashion as anyone ever can. If he had been Japanese he would have committed hara-kiri. Now his mind was running on excuses and explanations and justifications. Ever since his capture he had been telling British officers why he had lost. He hinted, and he was no doubt right, that he could never hope to hold Bardia with so many Italians under his command.

What it really came to was this: with a few battalions of Germans and Italians, without tanks and without planes, he had failed to hold a few square miles of desert and a wretched fishing village. It was not very important in a war which had engulfed almost the entire globe. But it was bitter shame for Major-General Artur Schmidt, the first German General to run up a white flag and surrender his city to the British.

For the whole of the rest of the journey back to Cairo he sat there musing, his pale-blue eyes watering with cold. He smiled just once — when his batman, a stolid Rhineland lad with a round rosy peasant face, was violently air-sick.

ii

On January 12 the Transvaal Scottish Regiment attacked and took Sollum in a small, fiercely fought engagement. All they got was a few score prisoners and some ruined houses strung along the curve of a miraculously blue bay. But Sollum's possession completed the circle which the South African troops had drawn round Halfaya.

Halfaya is, properly speaking, not a pass but a steep winding road climbing the escarpment just to the south-east of Sollum. It gains its strategical importance from the fact that it is the only way up the escarpment at the coast, apart from the main road at Sollum. The Germans had fortified a whole area of cliff, plateau and ravines all round it, and now between five and six thousand Axis troops had barricaded themselves in there behind an enormous mass of artillery. They had even taken the turrets off the "I" tanks which the British had lost in earlier actions, and sunk them in concrete to provide armoured gun positions. A whole row of these straddled the main road a little short of Sollum.

It was, of course, a dog-in-the-manger position. The defenders had no possibility of being rescued, and no possibility of attacking. They had neither planes nor tanks, and they were defending nothing but themselves. The only value they had to anyone was a nuisance value. But under the leadership of the Reverend Major Bach they were holding out gallantly and obstinately. Perhaps if Generals Buttafuoco and de Georgis, who were also there, had been in charge, they would have surrendered long since. But the German, though a clergyman and only a Major, was in command of all Italian and German troops and he decided to hold on.

They were nearly starving in Halfaya. Their meagre rations had been cut to the bone. Transport planes flew across from Crete in the early mornings and dropped them great sacks of provisions—raisins, boiled sweets, British bully beef, chocolate—but they could not feed five thousand men. And even shorter than food was water. They put out every cup and plate they had to catch dew and rainwater. They tried to strain the sea through handkerchiefs and sand, and they set up amateur distilling plants. Even that possibility went when they lost Sollum for they lost access to the sea.

The South Africans shelled them and the R.A.F. bombed them, but they had good caves scooped out of the cliff face and their casualties were not very high. What they feared more than anything else were the "Henderson Cocktails," a secret weapon invented by the South Africans. It consisted of a Diesel oil barrel filled with explosive, bits of old metal and a seven seconds' fuse. The barrel was simply rolled over the cliff face and it exploded into the caves as it ricocheted its way down.

But in the end it was hunger and thirst that broke them down. There was never any need for us to launch an attack that must have proved very costly. Major Bach, who had won the Ritterkreuz and the Iron Cross for capturing Halfaya on May 27, 1941, surrendered it unconditionally on January 17, 1942. A great booty of guns and ammunition fell into our hands intact. We sent 2126 more Germans and 3351 Italians to the prison camps.

With Halfaya fell a little isolated outcropping of resistance called Point 207. It had, as a matter of fact, very nearly surrendered earlier. At the New Year, when Bardia was falling, a man came out of Point 207 with a large white flag. But by an evil chance a twenty-five-pounder shell dropped just near him before he had gone twenty paces, and he scuttled back to safety and never re-appeared.

CHAPTER 20

Recessional and Post-Mortem

WELL, that looked like the end of the campaign. Churchill rounded it off in a speech. Some 11,500 Germans and 13,000 Italians had been killed or wounded, 36,500 Axis troops had been made prisoners. Eight hundred and fifty enemy aircraft had been destroyed, and 386 tanks. We had lost 18,000 men, but we had got Cyrenaica. We thought we could call it a campaign.

But, of course, we could not. That constant tendency towards the status quo came into operation again. The old game of military pingpong began once more. Rommel swept forward and re-engulfed most of the territory he had lost. The unhappy, bewildered inhabitants of Cyrenaica changed their masters for the fourth time in little more than a year. In a swift, confusing withdrawal, the British fell back nearly to Tobruk.

On January 7 Rommel had started to withdraw from Agedabia. Under cover of a dust-storm he pulled his army back along the road towards Tripoli. It looked at first sight as though he were pulling right out of Cyrenaica now that Bardia had fallen. But near El Agheila he turned and dug himself in once more in exceedingly strong positions. Heavy rains came down and turned into impassable marshes all the flat ground in front of him. His sappers laid mine fields. And he began to refit.

He got tanks — not many and not very good ones, but more than enough to double his tank strength. Some came along the main road from Tripoli, some were landed by shallow-draft boats on the beaches beside him. He had a good month for convoys — something like 89 per cent of Axis shipping got safely across the Mediterranean in January. He re-equipped his troops as far as he could and sent for more petrol and ammunition. For just about a fortnight he worked with feverish haste. Then on January 21 he sent out three strong armoured columns to make a tactical reconnaissance.

The results surprised him even more than they surprised us. For we had only the thinnest of protective screens to stop him. One armoured brigade was scattered through a huge area, supported by armoured-car patrols. There was one Indian Brigade across the road south of Bengasi, and the rest of the Fourth Indian Division farther north round Barce. That was about all the fighting troops we had. We were deeply engaged in solving our supply problem, building up lines of communication, establishing dumps to enable us to maintain large bodies of men down there and prepare a thrust against Tripolitania. We could not yet use Bengasi as a port, the main roads were still being repaired in places, heavy rains had turned the desert route to mud, much of our transport was exhausted. Rommel caught us just at the moment when our dumps were piling up nicely, and when we still had very few troops to protect them. His tactical reconnaissance was swiftly reshaped into a tentative offensive.

He managed to seize the main road and edge our forces off it into the sticky marshland all the way along. Tank after tank was stuck in the mud and had to be abandoned. Many broke down mechanically in these cruel conditions. The Germans had made their first moves in a blinding pea-soup sand-storm which baffled reconnaissance and we had not known how best to meet them. The swamps and even lakes which the heavy rains had formed tended to split up the forces engaged, and Rommel at first fanned out his columns and obliged us to do likewise. It was a tactical picture of great confusion with the initiative in the enemy's hands.

Rommel was still wondering how far he dared go. He took Agedabia with negligible opposition. There were rich dumps ahead, and a chance to regain the prestige which the German army had lost through his withdrawal. He decided to take another gamble and forge ahead as far as he could.

He suddenly flung all his armour into one big column—bigger

than any single British column — and sent it driving through our scattered forces. He branched right from the main road and thrust up diagonally inland, very nearly capturing our whole Thirteenth Corps Headquarters at Antelat. On petrol won from the British, he raced on to Msus, an old Turkish fortress covering a convergence of desert tracks just seventy-five miles south-east of Bengasi. The air force did its best to stop him, bombing and machine-gunning his columns until the wrecked lorries were numbered by hundreds. But his initial momentum combined with the lack of any serious opposition on land carried him through. The Luftwaffe was surprisingly absent in these early stages. According to one theory Rommel grounded his planes to provide petrol for his transport, but that hardly takes account of the fact that high-octane aviation spirit is ruination to lorry engines, and German tanks run on Diesel. Another suggestion was that he was short of bombs. But whatever the truth, dust-storms and rainstorms proved of more value to him in those first days than his own air force, and he proved that you can win through against complete air supremacy if you have sufficient predominance on land.

At Msus Rommel paused for consolidation and thought. He had been advancing fifty miles a day and he desperately needed to stabilize his position. In addition he had to decide on his next move. He could do three things: he could withdraw to his line at El Agheila, satisfied with the remarkable success of what had only been intended as a raid; he could press on eastwards to the key fort of Mechili; or he could turn west and make a grab at Bengasi. He chose, almost inevitably, the third course. He was not the man to retire before he had probed all the possibilities of the situation. He was still getting no serious opposition, and there was plenty left for him to do. He probably argued that if the British did mass forces to oppose him, they would mass them at Mechili and try and block him there. But he could not go forward and meet them with Bengasi still in British hands behind his back. So he turned west to Bengasi, knowing he was quite safe as long as he kept the road open for a withdrawal to his El Agheila Line.

He sent his Italian tanks up the main road from the south and the German tanks with lorry-borne infantry in from the west. A small flying column was despatched round north to occupy Regima, on the Barce-Bengasi road above Benina, with instructions to put blocks across the main road and surround the town. The Seventh Indian Brigade, posted south-east of Bengasi, were the only troops on hand to defend the place, and their case was hopeless. All our most important installations had been removed from the town, and the sappers had completed their demolitions. The Seventh had one clash just south-east of Bengasi and understood that it was up against tanks with which it could not cope. The Brigade Commander decided to try and fight or bluff his way out of the trap.

He slipped down in between the Ariete Division and the German *Panzerdivisions* by night. The forces roundabout were at least four times as strong as his brigade and he never ought to have got away. But when morning came the brigade was racing through the desert eastwards, all safe except for a few trucks that had broken down, with nearly two hundred miles to go to safety. They took no notice of strong enemy columns, and annihilated weak ones. They never fired at puzzled German aircraft which came and looked at them. Just once or twice they had to fight their way through when someone discovered beyond doubt that they were British, but mostly their bluff worked. Their compass course took them straight to Mechili and they arrived safely with prisoners from a convoy they had surprised.

Rommel entered Bengasi on January 28, capturing two companies of infantry and a few oddments. The remaining brigades of the Fourth Indian Division retired up the escarpment at Tocra, blowing it behind them, and into the Green Mountains. For a week longer they retired, travelling at night and fighting by day. Rommel made no attempt to chase them up the coast road. He went back eastwards into the desert and then sent up his columns by little roads running due north into the mountains at Tecnis, Maraua, Slonta, Giovanni Berta, and an action had to be fought at each place.

This retreat was swift, but supremely orderly. Time and again the Germans were ambushed as they came through the mountains. Bren-gun carriers covered the sappers who blew bridges, laid mines, destroyed roads. Sometimes the pursuit was so hot that the engineers heard the enemy vehicles being blown up on the mines they had just laid. On this northern route every vehicle left behind and every dump was destroyed. At Giovanni Berta the Libyan Arab force held the Germans in a brisk guerilla skirmish while sappers went down into Derna, blew the escarpments, smashed the jetties, and cracked the ship in the harbour clean in two.

At last, between Gazala and Tmimi we rallied all our forces and fought. That was the biggest battle of the whole withdrawal and an enemy submarine struck a bizarre note in it by coming to the surface and taking part in the German artillery barrage. But this time we stood firm and the Germans came no farther. By February 4 the two lines were roughly stabilized, one at Tmimi and one at Gazala. We had, I think, done to Rommel exactly what he had done to us. We had withdrawn so fast that we had run him to a standstill. He now took over all the problems we had had down at El Agheila, and for the moment, at least, he could attack no more.

We had suffered serious losses of matériel in this withdrawal — we had had to abandon or destroy a very fair proportion of the matériel we had destined for the drive against Tripoli. We had lost more tanks than we could afford, plenty of petrol, food, ammunition, vehicles. We had lost greatly in prestige at a moment when we could ill afford it, for the Libyan campaign had had stupendous publicity and was being used to offset our disasters in Malaya. Most humiliating of all was the fact that we had let exactly the same catastrophe happen two years running.

In prestige the Germans gained as much as we had lost. In matériel they lost if anything, for we left little of value behind and what they did get they used up in the course of their advance. But they got Bengasi back as a supply port and they recaptured nearly all the big air fields of Cyrenaica, from which they could raid Egypt. It was a bitter blow to us.

It is difficult to believe that the withdrawal was unavoidable, that there was bound to be a moment when, if he attacked, Rommel would inevitably drive us back. It was, in the main, the supply problem that beat us, for we were unable to maintain an adequate force down south of Bengasi. The Fourth Indian Division tried it, and they had to retire to Barce for lack of supplies. Perhaps it was inevitable. But if it was not, then the fault clearly lies with the organization of our supply system. Possibly the contingency was not sufficiently foreseen and the supplies were not there ready to be moved up. Perhaps the condition of our transport could have been better. Maybe we were too slow in getting Bengasi Harbour into working order. Possibly the answer was big fleets of transport aeroplanes. I have a cynical suspicion that somehow the Germans would have managed it.

But there is one mistake we did make, and it may have been crucial. We went off the offensive without going on the defensive. We did not dig ourselves in and make fortified positions, which is something the Germans always do even if they only intend to spend a couple of days in a place. We merely flung out patrols and left it at that. Had Rommel's reconnaissance columns come up against strong, well-prepared anti-tank positions they might never have tried to come any farther, and we should have had time to organize a real resistance.

ii

What had been wrong with this campaign, the only serious fighting the whole British Empire had undertaken since the defeats of the spring? Clearly it had been expected to succeed brilliantly. All round the world people thought back to the officially sponsored optimism of the first days. There was an outbreak of theorizing, argument, criticism and analysis. It was vitally important to discover just where mistakes had been made.

To start with, the campaign clearly had to be fought. Morally Britain needed an active battle front. Strategically she needed to wipe out this steady threat to Egypt, this southernmost German army which might one day be the basis of a great thrust through to the east. The maintenance of Tobruk was costly and precarious, and the loss of it would be sentimentally, tactically and diplomatically regrettable. There were political and press agitation at home, hints from Russia, pressure by the Dominions. We had to fight Rommel.

But to capture Cyrenaica was not going to be enough. Economically the place was a liability. Geographically the only thing that could be said for it was that its possession would bring us much closer to Malta and Italy from the east, should the doors be closed to us in the west. Strategically experience had shown that the rival armies in North Africa, based respectively on Cairo and Tripoli, were like two springs coiling and uncoiling opposite one another. The one which was uncoiled could never stand the strain for long, for the coiled one always gathered new impetus and drove it back. The lines of communication were, in fact, too long and the back-and-forth process might continue indefinitely. The only hope was either to make one supreme effort and smash right through to the enemy's base, or to destroy the opposing army utterly and finally in the field. We needed either to take Tripoli, or break Rommel. We did neither. Like Wavell we ended up with half-measures—merely the occupation of Cyrenaica.

There were thus two points at which we failed this second time: at the beginning when we did not break Rommel completely and at the end when we stopped short at Agedabia.

In those first ten days of the campaign the two tank forces fought one another almost to a standstill. But not quite. Rommel's army had been worn away very badly round the edges, but the essential nucleus was still there. Rommel knew that we could and would send up reinforcements, and he knew he could expect none in time. His position was strategically ridiculous, for he had something like two divisions bottled up in Bardia and Halfaya, and Tobruk was jabbing constantly into his side like a knife. If we could have pressed our victory home he was beaten then. But before we were able to do it he had gone racing for safety with what forces he had left. Gazala, in retrospect, was merely a delaying action in which the

Italians were thrown to the pursuing wolves to keep them occupied. There was only one refuge then for Rommel — the marsh-defended cliffs of El Agheila, where he could turn and face us, where his communications would be halved and ours doubled, where he could lie and lick his wounds until he was strong enough to fight.

And there came our second failure. We let him do it. I do not think in the circumstances we had very much choice but at that moment there was still a chance of polishing him off. If we could have sent a strong enough force hot on his heels and never let him stop running we could, I believe, have smashed him. But all those "Q" problems came into play — lengthening supply lines. Bengasi unusable, exhausted transport. We could not produce the petrol, food and ammunition for a large pursuing force. We could only send off a skeleton column, and Rommel turned and dug himself in.

At that point, having failed to smash Rommel completely in battle, and having failed to polish him off in pursuit, we had two alternatives. We could turn back, form a line, say, a little west of Tobruk or even at the Egyptian frontier, hand Cyrenaica back to him if he wanted it, and set about beating him again. Or we could try to organize a drive through to Tripoli, taking the risk that he would counterattack us before we were ready. We chose the latter, and bolder, course, and it proved to be the wrong one. We were duly counterattacked and we were driven back for the same reason that we failed to go on: our inability to maintain and supply a large force so far from our bases. Rommel at certain points had much luck, and he exploited it with boldness and skill. That must have been a lovely little campaign for the war correspondents on the other side.

The key phase of the whole thing was of course the first ten days, when in mighty tank battles we tried to destroy Rommel completely and failed to do so. All the rest flowed logically from our failure to succeed then. And the reasons for our failure were, I think, the ones I outlined when I came back to Cairo at the end of November and tried to analyze what had happened. It all boiled down to quality of tanks and the way they were used.

Standing back and looking at events now that the tumult had died down, it was plain that the German tanks had been better than the British. Better, that is, in the sense that the more heavily armed and armoured tanks must always be better when it comes to a straight fight. It was absurd to pit the British and American tanks with their 37-millimetre guns against the Mark Threes with their 50-millimetre and the Mark Fours with their 75-millimetre weapons and pretend that the terms were equal. To do so was grossly unfair to the British armoured brigades. The Valentines and Crusaders were good enough tanks of their kind. But they were designed for reconnaissance in a country with plenty of cover, not for battle in the open desert. They proved mechanically delicate in desert conditions. They needed inordinately tender maintenance, and their percentage of break-downs was much too high. The American Honeys were tougher, and they had speed. But all of them ran on high-grade petrol which rendered them far more liable to catch fire than the Diesel-burning Germans.

The Germans showed brilliant skill and much courage in their tank-recovery organization. Lame tanks were dragged from the battle while the firing was still on, tended in a mobile workshop almost on the spot, and flung back into the fight next day. Our recovery units worked themselves to exhaustion, but they simply were not organized like that. They were like doctors in a sudden epidemic — they had far more patients than they knew how to deal with. It was his superiority in this sphere that enabled Rommel to appear each day with slightly more tanks than we thought he could possibly have.

Tank fighting essentially includes anti-tank fighting, and here again the Germans had great superiority. Their 50-millimetre anti-tank gun was a fine weapon. It was a low-built model — a good deal lower than our two-pounder — and the men who handled it could dig it in and camouflage it until it was practically invisible. It was much more difficult to knock out than our higher, more conspicuous weapon which too often showed up as an exposed target. The Germans, too, had their big 88-millimetre all-purpose anti-aircraft and anti-tank gun, which proved a really formidable weapon. We had nothing quite corresponding to this, though we could and did turn our Bofors light ack-ack guns against tanks in an emergency.

But it was the British twenty-five–pounder which stole the show. It is hardly an exaggeration to say that this agile, accurate, reliable gun really saved us in the Libyan Campaign. The twenty-five–pounders were beautifully handled, especially by the Royal Horse Artillery, and time and again they saved the day. They kept the German tanks dodging about on the move while our tanks got within range. Traversing rings had been fitted to them so that they could easily be swung round. They minimized as much as was humanly possible the danger of that half-mile advantage the German tank guns had. They even took on German tanks alone and drove them off with serious losses. It was a costly, improvised technique which our tank brigades were forced to develop and only suitable for an emergency. The guns were conspicuous objectives and they could not be easily dug in. They fired a relatively high trajectory shell which did not allow anything like the same margin of error in range as the low-flying anti-tank gun shell. They were bulky to move, and so was their ammunition. But I never heard anything but unstinted praise for them.

Those were the weapons with which those critical ten days were fought, but there was a big difference in the way the two sides used them. Rommel adopted the best tactics he possibly could to baffle our obvious intentions. He instantly concentrated his tanks and for the most part commanded the whole force directly himself. The result was that he had the biggest single force in the field, for we had split our tanks into three separate brigades, and he began to dictate the moves. He never fought an action with a small body of tanks unless he was certain the opposition was insignificant. He avoided risking his tanks in dangerously even battles, and he never wasted a thing. Often enough he came out not to fight, but to lure our forces on into strong anti-tank positions. He always used tanks and anti-tank guns in intimate co-operation. He must have been very well served by his recovery, petrol and ammunition columns, and his *Panzer* troops were clearly highly trained and able. He had learned the lessons of the desert painstakingly and thoroughly. Personally I think Rommel fought that battle just about as well as it could have been fought, which was a good deal better than we had bargained for. His one mistake, in the end, was the single occasion when he deliberately split his forces and sent the Ariete down into Egypt.

Between the courage and skill of the British and the Germans there was honestly, I think, not a great deal to choose. Man for man we may have been better, but it was hardly ever a question of man for man. It was tank for tank and unit for unit. The British inevitably produced more instances of individual bravery and resource, but the Germans through discipline and organization produced better team-work. The desert did, in fact, bring out with fascinating clarity the racial characteristics of the two nations. For the desert scrapes away the incrustations of civilization and leaves only the most primitive factors bare. Men are reduced from the things that make life worth living to the things that make life possible. The only ingredients are food and drink, warmth and cold, sleep and health, safety and death. Not even sex. And the consequence is that basic racial tendencies that are often obscured and distorted by a mass of traditional, cultural international usages emerge into the open and are given free play.

Thus the Germans' sense of the sanctity and naturalness of belligerence, their urge to sink themselves in the mass and be a cog in a big machine, certain distorted Nietzschean qualities reaching back into the dark mists of Teutonic tribalism, were displayed in full nakedness. Rommel instinctively massed his tanks, and it was not only good tactics but good German psychology to do so. He was naturally division-minded where the British were brigade-minded. He knew Germans fought better when they had plenty of their comrades around them, when they felt themselves part of something big. A wounded German officer lying beside a British officer in a field hospital near Tobruk said, "I don't think we could ever get our troops to advance in small groups behind tanks as yours do."

But in the mass they fought with a ruthless self-sacrifice that took no count of losses, and was dictated, I think, not by any passionate belief in their cause, but by passionate deference to the reality of war.

The Germans were good in the mass but at the other end of the scale we gained. Against mass-produced men we opposed as mixed an army as you could find. We had men from the United Kingdom, New Zealanders, Maoris, South Africans of British origin and Afrikaners, Australians, Poles, Czechs, and members of half the races of India. They differed in race and colour and language. But they had one thing in common — they were not mass-produced, they were individuals. It meant that when a very small force was needed — a commando force or a patrol or a Jock Column — we could produce it and the Germans could not. The Maoris positively liked night fighting. Indians took naturally to the fast semi-guerilla warfare of the desert. Men from the Dominions all had pioneering in their blood. The New Zealanders had a special revenge to take for Crete. The Poles, with their fanatical hatred of the Germans, would go in against anything.

None of these men felt unhappy when they were not fighting in the mass, as I think the Germans did. And the ability of the individual soldier to take the initiative and think for himself enabled us to recover time and again from sticky positions. Our patrolling and our Jock Columns were worth whole divisions to us. But it was when we came to divisions that the Germans surpassed us. We were much too apt to prefer small units.

Yet in the last resort it was, as of course it always is, the unsung common soldier who pulled us through. The men who with never enough sleep and never a hot meal, no water to wash in and no time to change their clothes, in cold and in sand-storms, night and day were prepared to go on fighting tank battles against tanks bigger than their own. All the men of the ancillary services whose jobs are all toil and no glory, dust without palms, who drove their lorries of food and fuel and ammunition through dive-bombing attacks and artillery barrages right up to the front line to keep the fighting forces going. The individual sappers who went out alone and unprotected to make straight the paths for the tanks. Signallers, Red Cross workers, a thousand others. And above all the Rats of Tobruk, who broke out of their fortress to smash their besiegers and without whose help the Eighth Army would, I think, have retreated to Egypt after the first week's fighting.

As for the Italians, I realized more and more that they were simply not interested. Those long greeny-blue columns of scruffy unshaven prisoners were composed of peasants and shopkeepers, waiters and factory workers. They liked Italy's martial glory very well when it stayed in their newspapers, but none of them wanted it in their private lives. Rommel organized his tactics so as to throw as little responsibility as possible on the shoulders of the Italians, for he knew he could not afford to depend on them.

Yet even so we underrated them. We tended to dismiss them from our calculations altogether, and you simply cannot dismiss sixty or seventy thousand men, especially when they are equipped with good guns. Anyone will put up a fight if he knows he is fighting for his life, and this we did not appreciate. We did not allow for the stiffening of Germans in the Italian divisions. We did not realize that the Ariete Division was going to fight twice as well as any Italian tank unit had fought under Graziani. Italians are not good soldiers by German standards, but they are not completely despicable.

But if we had made mistakes in this campaign, we had a wonderful opportunity to learn from them. We had an immense amount of raw material for dissection and analysis. The very fact that things had not gone easily had helped, for a hard-fought fight is inevitably more instructive than a walk-over. Our tanks had fought the Germans' tanks in straight combat, our infantry had fought their infantry. For the first time in this war we had captured their camps, their dumps, their workshops, their documents and their generals. We had met them on the offensive and on the defensive, on land and in the air. We had been forced to study their tactics, their methods and their equipment not merely theoretically, but in action. The desert had proved a wonderful operating table, with the absolute minimum of extraneous and irrelevant circumstances to influence and confuse the issue.

Of the lessons we were offered some were deeply technical and many were very secret. But none were too trivial for consideration, for some time or other this desert campaign had got to be fought over again, and we needed to know all that could be known. There was value as well as interest in what we discovered about the food, the clothes, the literature of the German soldiers. For the most part, for instance, the British troops were surprised to find the enemy eating so well. The rations captured in German tanks were more varied and more appetizing than the eternal bully, biscuits and tea which formed the staple diet of our tank crews for days on end. I have no doubt that these desert *Panzer* troops were pampered beyond any other German troops, and far beyond the civilians at home. Probably their rations were neither so copious nor so rich nor so costly as the British rations. But they were extremely well planned and, just as a matter of personal preference, I preferred the enemy's.

On the other hand our clothing proved very much better than theirs. The professors who had worked out the Afrikakorps' uniform had concentrated on fighting heat rather than cold. It had seemed more natural to send the warm clothes to Russia and the thin ones to Africa. And the result was that the Germans fought this campaign in cheap drill uniforms, and overcoats that were not even as warm as they looked. Some warm clothes they did have, for we once found a store of long underpants and gloves and sweaters—real wool, not milk and nettles—but there were not enough for everyone. And they were very short of blankets.

But there were not many things they were short of, despite that long list of sunken shipping. Somehow or other Rommel had kept his supplies extremely well balanced. It is likely that the Germans were in grave danger of running short of petrol. Orders enjoining strict economy were captured, and we never found a large quantity of fuel on any air field. Two or three times they left behind about five hundred gallons of high-octane aviation spirit, but five hundred gallons is nothing to a fighter squadron, and it is improbable that they had been able to take any away in their precipitate flight. But there was still no evidence that they ever did quite run short.

For the most part they had planned well for the desert, these Nazis. Their staff cars might look gawky and old-fashioned, but they had been specially designed, sprung and fitted. You could go as fast as you liked over rough ground in their tinny little runabouts with Volkswagen engines. Too often our staff cars were ordinary models designed and sprung for British or American roads.

There was something worth noting in all the German equipment —their little green bivouac tents, their petrol cans, their groundsheets, dozens of specially designed desert gadgets. They used far more signs and notice-boards than the British did and thereby probably saved a great deal of time and petrol, for nothing is easier than to get lost in the desert. They did more digging in than we did, and on the whole their dispersal and road discipline were better.

There were endless new lessons to be learned. But the campaign reaffirmed all the old main principles of desert warfare. It put the emphasis once again on speed, on complete mobility, on concentrating overwhelming fire-power on the vital point. It confirmed the value of expert patrolling, of secrecy and surprise, of quick and accurate intelligence. It brought out more than ever the supreme importance of tough, mechanically sound vehicles, of a first-class Army Service Corps, and above all of swift, unfailing supply services. It showed how the desert reduces fighting entirely to quality of men, materials and leadership, for there are no geographical accidents, no canals or buildings or bridges, no Fifth Columns or civil populations, nothing but earth that has already been ruthlessly scorched by nature.

Even despite the retreat, the campaign had ended in our favour. Rommel had lost more than we had (though it was worth remembering that his reinforcements had a sea trip of 300 miles, ours of 14,000). Tobruk, the costly strategical anomaly, had been disengaged. The menace to Egypt had been pushed a full hundred miles farther back. We had once more shown an offensive spirit and we could claim to have won Cyrenaica in a fair fight, even if we did hand it back again. We had ended up with a stronger line than we ever held at Sollum, where there was in truth no line at all facing west.

In February 1942 there came a miracle to the desert. Heavy rains fell, quickening seeds that had lain there maybe for years, and bringing them up flowering extravagantly. Men were pitching their tents in great fields of asphodel. One evening I walked for half a mile through dwarf night-scented stock and the fragrance as my boots crushed it was almost tangible. There were dozens of plants I should have been proud to have in my garden, luxuriating fantastically where there had always been just black earth. And in this incongruous loveliness, the two armies were still facing one another across a thick slice of flowery no-man's-land, waiting for the next swing of the desert pendulum.

CHAPTER 21

Spring Interval

FIVE full times now the pendulum had swung across the desert.

The land itself was grown scarred with trenches and shell-holes and ruts and garbage dumps. Thousands of fighting vehicles had been brought thousands of perilous miles by sea to be destroyed in a few minutes in this wilderness. Its barren dust was soaked with sweat and blood. Thousands had died and thousands more had been led into captivity defending it. The very weather had grown worse, for now every little gust of wind would lift the loosened surface into the air and whirl it away in a sand-storm. And yet nothing whatever had been achieved.

It was becoming a joke, a bitter, grim joke. Already the Paris radio was referring to Cyrenaica as the "Promenade des Anglais." And the joke was all the more pointed when it was realized that neither side wanted this desert that both were fighting for. The British wanted just a few square miles of it, room enough for air fields along the Mediterranean Coast. To Rommel it was mere vacant space, a vacuum, through which he must pass on his way to the Nile. And now the pendulum had swung to rest at what was probably its point of equilibrium (Wavell told me once he regarded Gazala as the natural front line). The two armies were disposed with the improbable symmetry of an artificial war-game—each side had two ports (Tobruk balancing Bengasi, Alexandria balancing Tripoli), each had a single well-made road and hundreds of miles of coastline. There was even a balancing of oases for patrolling inland—Siwa against Jalo, Kufra against Murzuk. Rommel had infinitely the shorter sea route for his supplies, but it was infinitely

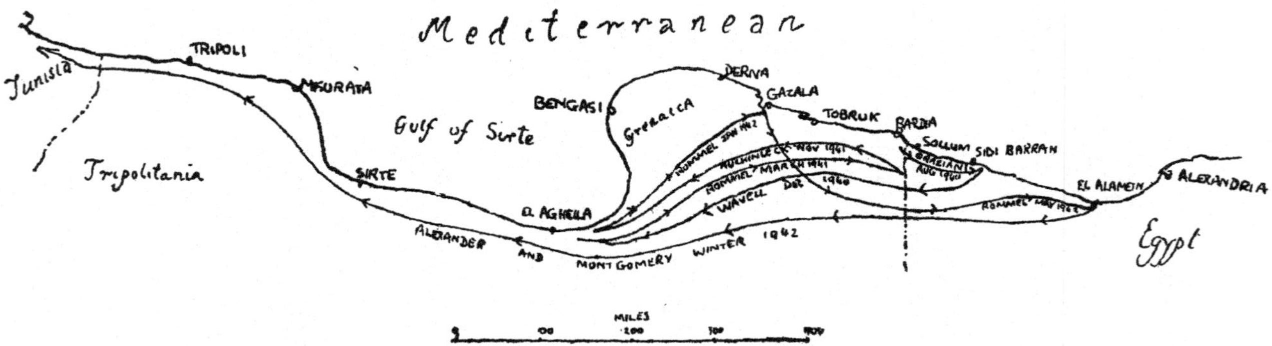

The Pendulum.

the more dangerous for Britain had Malta right in the middle of it as an air base.

Rarely in history have generals and armies had a second chance to fight their battles over again. But in the desert it was happening all the time. Each new offensive started in almost the same circumstances as the last one, but with the accumulated wisdom and experience of all that had gone before. So that now certain trends and principles and processes were beginning to emerge, a set of rules which made it possible to predict what would almost invariably happen in a known combination of circumstances.

Thus the typical desert campaign could now be simplified down to two separate parts. It might be compared to a tadpole or a comet. There was first of all a solid, concentrated core or body of very intense fighting, usually with tanks. And then there would be the tail of the tadpole or comet when the winner chased the loser at frantic speed across Cyrenaica. Graziani (once) and Rommel (twice) had done the chasing without having previously fought the battle, for the British would not stay and fight it. Wavell and Auchinleck had won the battles, but they could not chase their beaten opponent far enough. They had to stop for lack of breath and the beaten opponent, who was now back on his home ground, was able to make a swift recovery.

So during the spring of 1942, both Rommel and Auchinleck had their minds on two things. First it was necessary to win the battle; and then to be able to stay the course in the ensuing chase. Tanks, therefore, and supplies.

A great armaments race now started. To the arid Gazala plateau, where the spring flowers were shrivelling in the first summer suns, flowed two great streams of war material. One came from the factories of Germany, over the Alps, down through Italy and across the Mediterranean. The other poured from the factories of Britain and America in a mighty sweep round Africa and up the Red Sea to Egyptian ports. Auchinleck started with a triple handicap. First he had this longer supply route. Second, reinforcements destined for the Middle East had already been diverted to the Far East; ten thousand men who should have been in the desert disembarked in Singapore three days before it fell, and scores of fighter planes and pilots had gone that way. Third, the British tanks and anti-tank guns would have to be not only renewed but changed. The whole world now knew that the British tanks were simply not good enough against the Germans. New types would have to be sent out.

Auchinleck reasoned and pleaded and argued. He *must* have something with a gun as powerful as the guns of the Marks Three and Four. He *must* have something bigger and better than the two-pounder anti-tank gun. And he *must* have it quickly. The British Armoured Divisions could not any longer be frittered away because they had inferior equipment. Tank battles must be fought properly, on equal terms, not with wild, improvised, suicidal tactics.

Britain had no tank she could send out. Only the Churchill was big enough for Auchinleck's purpose, and the Churchill was in the throes of growing pains. Its design still had to be greatly modified. So Britain applied to America, and America sent General Grants with a 75-millimetre gun as powerful as the Mark Fours. The Grant was not a perfect tank, but it was so much better than anything else in the desert that the British tank men cheered uncritically when they saw it.

In the matter of the anti-tank gun, Britain could be more helpful. For there was a brand-new six-pounder just going into production, and by the middle of the summer, it was calculated, copious supplies should be reaching the Middle East.

While these things were on their way out, Auchinleck undertook to comb through and tighten up the whole fabric of the army. He began to try experiments in organization and co-operation. A new technique was evolved for infantry against tanks. The relationship between infantry and artillery was basically overhauled. The captured German petrol and water containers were taken over as a going concern. The desert traffic system was re-organized, and sign posts became much more frequent. Scores of huge new tank transporters arrived, and this was really important: for it meant that in the first place there would never be a repetition of what had happened to a certain extent during Crusader, when a large proportion of British tanks became unserviceable on the road before they ever reached the battle-field; and it meant in the second place that tanks crippled in battle could be removed and repaired in the minimum time. These transporters might result in a doubling of the effective British tank strength during a battle.

Meantime Tedder and Coningham were working on the huge mass of data which the R.A.F. had collected during the winter. They were seeking to draw conclusions from it, to evolve a technique which would utilize to the utmost superiority in the air.

The first decision they made was a revolutionary one. They decided to throw overboard the old negative theory that the function of an air force was to neutralize the opposing air force. And in its place they put the positive proposition that a very large part of an air force's function was to take part in the battle in co-operation with the troops on the ground. They no longer thought of co-operation as the dovetailing of two jobs, but as collaboration in one job. And partly as a symbolic gesture, partly for the sake of efficiency, Coningham decided to abolish his own separate camp and move in alongside the Army Commander in the Army Commander's camp. That was a very bold and important step. It meant that the Air Force had got over its fear of being manœuvred into incorporation in the army, and was now sure of the validity of its own arguments. Tedder and Coningham were too honest and intelligent to resist a development that was obviously inevitable. And they threw themselves heart and soul into the problem of immediate co-operation between air and ground troops.

The most important technical innovation in the air worked out during these spring months was the development of fighter bombers. The squadron of Hurricanes which had carried bombs during the winter was regarded as an almost unqualified success. And progressively the Hurricanes, Tomahawks and Kittyhawks were adapted as an answer to the German Stuka.

Rommel, too, was busy with his reinforcements, but he had none of these problems of technique and development. His *Panzerdivisions* were part of a complete military theory worked out before war started, and still holding good. His tanks, anti-tank guns and fighter planes were still better than any the British had brought against him. The need for improving them did not arise. So his problem was merely that of bringing shiploads of replacements across from Europe.

And here Malta began its long, terrible martyrdom. For Malta was the obstacle to Rommel's shipping, the one base from which Britain could operate anything besides long-distance bombers against the Axis supply lines. So a formidable German-Italian air force was concentrated in Sicily. And week after week Malta's few concentrated air fields were bombed and bombed until it was almost impossible to operate any aircraft from them. It was a race, and the Germans wholeheartedly threw everything into it. Rommel knew there would be a certain moment when his preparations would be further ahead of Auchinleck's than at any other time. And at this optimum moment he proposed to attack. He utilized the one great factor in his favour — the shortness of his sea route — which meant that the quicker he could build up his strength, the further ahead he would get. Time was on Auchinleck's side — time to get plenty of the right sort of matériel round the Cape of Good Hope. And to shorten this time to the minimum the Germans set out methodically to neutralize Malta's striking capacity, and thus to get the greatest possible amount of their own reinforcements to Africa in the shortest possible time.

Malta held out, dazed and bleeding, under the rain of bombs. But the German plan succeeded so far: the tiny island was in fact neutralized as a striking base. And the tragic thing is that it need not have been. As in Crete, it was not possible to give adequate protection to the aircraft on the ground. Had underground hangars been built when it was still possible to build them — and digging is easy in Malta — hundreds of planes would have been saved. A fighter screen could have been maintained over the island. Fighters could have escorted badly needed convoys into port. But no underground hangars had been made, and of course after the blitz started it was no longer feasible to make them. A scheme had been proposed for constructing them before the war, but it had been turned down as too expensive. In any case, war with Italy was not seriously contemplated. And if it did come, then Malta was not thought to be tenable anyway. But that scheme for underground hangars would have paid for itself a hundred times over during the blitz of this spring.

So in the desert both sides were urgently girding their loins for the next round. But it was a dull period as far as news was concerned, entangled in a web of secrecy and security. And early in May, as an antidote, I drove down to the almost legendary oasis of Siwa to collect one of the most romantic stories that the desert has produced.

ii

Siwa itself is romantic enough. It is one of the Western Desert's few genuine oases—a sudden riotous explosion of palm trees and gardens in the midst of an utterly dry wilderness.

You drive there through two hundred miles of empty landscape so unchanging that you have no sense of progress at all. You are the centre of an unvarying disk of flat brown gravel, walled in with mirages and domed by a brassy sky. Then quite abruptly you dive down into a maze of grotesque limestone hillocks which look like something off the moon: little symmetrical hills the exact shape of haystacks, and layers of creamy stone covered by a dark rind of gravel like a gigantic cheese. Then you writhe down between two table-topped hills and see a long greeny-blue blur of palm trees stretched across the desert like a bruise.

There is such a sense of remoteness that you wonder anyone ever found the place. Yet in ancient times the temple of Jupiter Ammon was here and Alexander the Great came to consult its oracle. Cambyses sent fifty thousand men to attack it, and the whole fifty thousand were engulfed and buried without trace by a sand-storm. Even now it claims to produce the world's best dates.

To-day some four thousand mysterious people live there, speaking a language which has only two numerals, 1 and 2 (they use Arabic for the rest), and lovely onomatopœic words like *tahhah-huthh* for a cough. Centuries of inbreeding have left them docile and lazy. For just two months of the year they tend their palm trees, arranging the necessary marriages (for dates have sex), and for the other ten they just watch them grow. Their fields are tiny areas of fertility where springs of sweet water have burst through the sour glittering crust of the salt-marshes. Their cities consist of fantastic mud skyscrapers. As each house collapses another is built on the ruins, until Siwa Village has become a circle round a huge pinnacle of rubble that is no longer usable. Their virgins wear circular certificates of engraved silver round their necks, and no woman would dream of wearing a dress without a row of olive-green embroidery at the throat.

All this, and much more, make Siwa exotic enough. But in addition it was, at the time I visited it, the Headquarters of the desert's most secret unit — the Long Range Desert Group.

This was originally another of Wavell's makeshift improvisations. The vast interior desert of Libya had to be patrolled. The Italians might be planning all sorts of things down there — raids across the Sand Sea into Egypt's south-western oases, air attacks on the Sudan and Lake Tchad, and so on. And they certainly were using air bases far down in the south in order to reinforce their aircraft in East Africa. But Wavell could not afford long-range bombers to patrol all this area. So there came into being small but extremely mobile motor columns, capable of remaining self-contained for weeks and travelling two thousand miles without re-fuelling.

They were all experts. Major Ralph Bagnold, a great amateur desert traveller, was in charge of them. And it was found that New Zealanders, with their solid common sense and their pioneering traditions, made particularly good patrollers. They had to be able to cross the world's biggest area of sand dunes — generally regarded as totally uncrossable. They must be able to steer by the stars through country that had never been mapped. They must be capable of choosing their route by diagnosing the texture, colour, drift, ripples and curvature of the dunes. And they must be temperamentally able to make huge journeys behind the enemy lines where there was no conceivable possibility of help.

They did not look different from other men when I met them down at Siwa. They were, perhaps, a little deeper tanned than most, and their eyes had a slightly strained, far-away look which comes from constantly watching horizons in steady glaring sunlight. When they came in from a patrol they were bearded and dishevelled. But when they had tidied themselves up and come out to drink their gin-and-limes on the terrace of their Headquarters, there was nothing to suggest that they were doing the desert's most daring job.

Their first patrols had crossed the Sand Sea into Libya in August 1940, in heat so intense that men vomited and became delirious. Then they were in the flat Libyan interior, where there is not a pebble to break the monotony for hundreds of miles, where an obscene fauna of vultures and snakes and insects lives exclusively on migrating birds which fall lifeless in the heat. By day they hid from the sun beneath their tarpaulins, by night they checked their position by the blazing African stars and travelled. They mapped every desert track the Italians were using. They captured the official mail from Kufra and the Italians never knew what had happened to that particular convoy. They found the transit air field for enemy planes going to Abyssinia and destroyed the petrol and bombs there. Once they took a camel in the back of a truck, used it over an otherwise impassable area of soft sand, and brought it back again.

Soon they knew that the Italians had no offensive plans down in this desert. So they started being offensive themselves. They laid mines on the desert tracks. They charged into desert forts and usually got saluted by the sentry who knew, as a matter of certain fact, that there could not be any enemy within five hundred miles. They attacked garrisons and carried off prisoners. The Italians stopped all normal desert traffic. Only heavily armed convoys were allowed to circulate. All garrisons in the interior of Libya were reinforced. Daily air patrols over the desert were started. The L.R.D.G. grinned and went and did it again.

Their two most spectacular exploits in their first year were both in conjunction with Colonel Leclerc's Free French columns operating from Lake Tchad. A British patrol under Captain Clayton crossed the whole of Libya diagonally to meet the French. Then they drove up north together and raided Murzuk and three other oases in the Fezzan District of South-west Libya. On their way back they joined with the Free French in an attack on Kufra, the only inhabitable place in all South-east Libya. Clayton himself was captured, but four of his companions—two of them wounded—escaped and walked 210 miles to safety in ten days with nothing but one tin of jam and a two-gallon tin of water between them. Colonel Leclerc went on and captured Kufra.

In the summer of 1942 the L.R.D.G. was helping to prepare for the coming winter campaign. Here and there the patrols were continually scooping up a couple of prisoners for information and identification. At least once Italian aircraft landed beside them and gave them an easy capture. Once near Misurata they erected a road block and collected a lorry crew and left behind a couple of mines to blow up the next passer-by. They charted *wadis* and escarpments and corrected errors in maps. They sought out flat patches of desert as future landing-grounds for the R.A.F. They counted the trucks passing along the coast road and lay for hours watching camps. Once a patrol camped in the darkness and when the moon rose they found they were bang in the middle of an Axis lorry park. They destroyed eighteen vehicles before anyone found them.

They had to be desperately careful. They had to bury every cigarette end and matchbox even in the remotest desert. All sorts of minor accidents could foil them. Once they had to return because a stray bullet punctured the petrol tank of one of the trucks. Another time because somebody got appendicitis. Another time a patrol was bogged for six hours within sight of Tmimi Air Field, and only just dug itself out in time.

Then the winter offensive began. And when a week later Rommel sent his flying tank column back to the Egyptian frontier, the L.R.D.G. got new orders. They were told to "attack, take offensive action wherever you can." And so they started attacking.

Near Magrun, south of Bengasi, a patrol drove right round an Axis car park tossing hand grenades into each vehicle. Another drove down the main street of Solluch like armoured cow boys, firing right and left into Italian tents and barracks. Ambushes were laid everywhere. The road flowed red with wine when they shot up a food convoy near Maraua. Near Agedabia they turned back traffic in both directions for a whole evening. At night they drove down the main road with headlights full on to meet Axis convoys and riddled the trucks with their tommy-guns as they careered past.

They got so used to being bombed that they would drive through Stuka raids looking up at the sky and twirling their steering wheels to dodge the planes and bombs. They took astonishingly few casualties. And they finally got their own back with one of the most dazzling exploits — co-operation with parachutists in a night raid on all the Axis landing-grounds between Agedabia and Sirte. They destroyed at least one hundred planes in a single night.

There was one curious aspect of this long-range patrolling. Why did the Germans not do it? The achievements of the British patrollers were so obviously worth while. And it was known that Rommel had a desert expert on his staff — a Hungarian called Almaszy. Yet there had never been any sign of a German attempt to copy the L.R.D.G. The implication was that the Germans could not do it. They were temperamentally unsuited for a job which required so much individualism, such liveliness, so much thinking for oneself.

CHAPTER 22

The Cauldron

THE BIG old Bombay jolted awkwardly down to earth and I woke from my doze and looked abstractedly out of the window. Then the noise of the engines died away and I realized that the pilot was yelling to me.

"This ought to be Gambut," he said, "but it doesn't look very much like it. I'm afraid I'm a stranger in these parts. Do you know where we are?"

I stepped out into the thick glowing heat of the day and looked round the landing-ground. It was utterly deserted and empty save for a few piles of wreckage round the edge. As a landscape it was completely meaningless. And then I had a queer little stab of familiarity and I realized where I was.

"This is no good," I shouted up to the pilot. "It's Sidi Rezegh."

This was the place for which we had fought so bloodily six months ago. Today it was a silent, indifferent, characterless patch of wilderness. And now we were going to start fighting bloodily again for some other patch of wilderness a few miles away. It was with a sense of bleak futility that I climbed back into the Bombay and directed the pilot how to get to Gambut.

It was May 26, and Rommel had won the armaments race. Under cover of the ceaseless air attacks on Malta, his convoys had got across. In April he had shot forward strong columns and established forward dumps and strong-points between Tmimi and Gazala. I had added all the little facts up carefully and now I had come up to the desert again backing my judgement that Rommel would attack just before the full moon at the end of May.

The British, too, had been building up fast, but they needed just a little more time. They had been very very careful not to hustle Rommel. Their propaganda talked naïvely of the impossibility of fighting at all in summer, the overpowering heat, the insoluble water problem. Rommel was supposed to get the idea that the British, at any rate, had no intention of launching an offensive. But Rommel smiled and went ahead with his plans.

At Gambut the war correspondents were camped in a patch of desert exactly like any other patch of desert. It lay between the road and the sea, alongside the Headquarters camp of General Ritchie who was still commanding the Eighth Army. And here I was shown the strategical situation on the map.

For once it was delightfully simple. The British were holding one straight line running inland from the blue bay of Gazala. Up by the sea were the First South Africans, commanded by talkative, picturesque General Dan Pienaar. In the middle was "Fifty Div."—the British Fiftieth Division, the first all-English infantry division to fight in the Middle East. Its men spoke the slow, soft broad speech of the North Country. And on the left, where the line faded out into the desert, the Free French Brigade was dug in round an old disused Bedouin well called Bir Hacheim. Behind this line the British First and Seventh Armoured Divisions waited as a mobile counterattacking force. And the other South African Division was in reserve in Tobruk. All the New Zealanders and Australians had been taken out of the front. The Fourth Indian Division was on its way up again.

Rommel could either attack this line frontally or else go round it to the south. We sat round the sticky trestle table in the mess-tent that night and weighed up the chances. The people at Headquarters, I found, were very confident. They argued that we had beaten Rommel last winter, and the improvement in the British army since then had been much bigger than the improvement in the Axis army. We had these new Grant tanks which could fight the Mark Fours on equal terms. We had the new six-pounder anti-tank gun which was thought to be extremely good, although

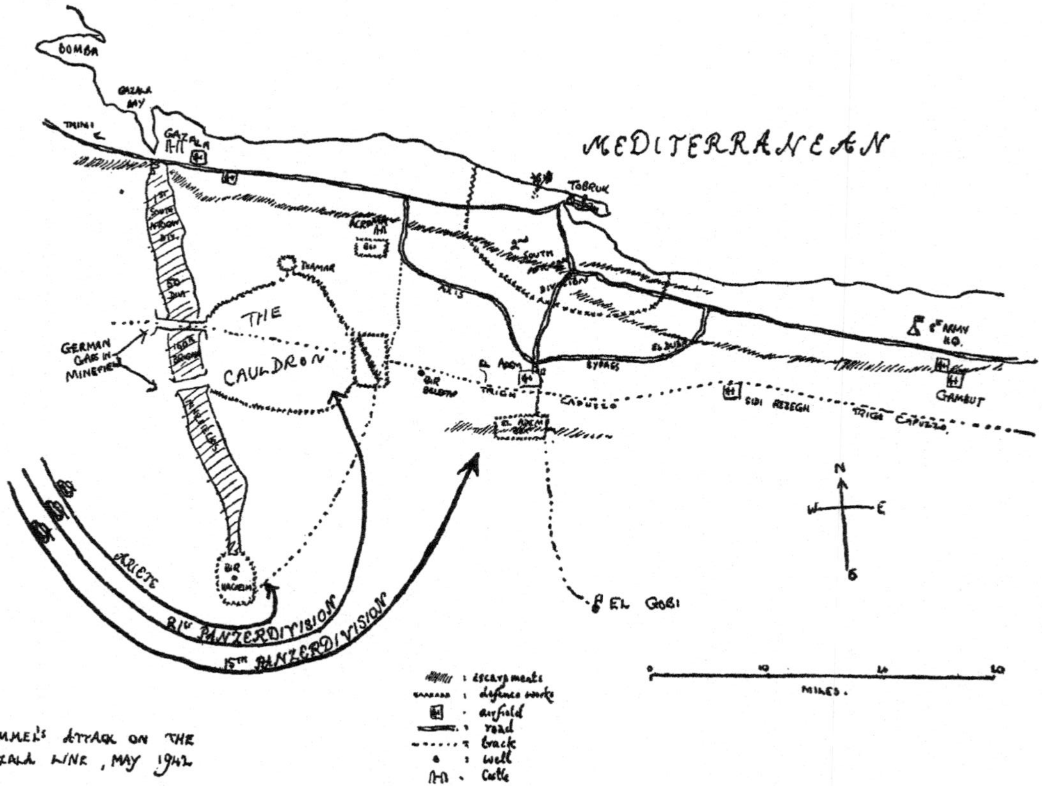

ROMMEL'S ATTACK ON THE GAZALA LINE, MAY 1942

unfortunately only forty-two of them had so far arrived in the desert and there had been no time to train anyone in the use of them. We had this enormously improved tank-recovery service. And there was every chance that the R.A.F. would this time not only have air superiority, but know exactly how best to use it.

Against this Rommel had very few innovations—there were slightly longer guns on some of the German tanks, and the Italians had a self-propelled gun on a tank mounting called a *semovente*. It was true that Rommel had more tanks than last winter, for he had added an extra regiment to each of his *Panzerdivisions*. And he had as many as ninety of the formidable 88-millimetre guns. Moreover he was going to launch the offensive, so he would have the advantage of gaining the initiative right away. But he had no Tobruk to help him, as we had had during the winter. On paper, at any rate, the superiority should lie with the British.

They were still arguing about it when I yawned and said good night and groped my way out into the moonlight to go to my tent. Someone shouted after me, "Put the tent flap back so that the light doesn't get out. The Luftwaffe's insomnia raid should start any minute now." And it started, in a cascade of machine-gun bullets that looked like golden rain, before I had gone ten paces.

This was a new technique the Germans had adopted. The idea was to give their enemy as little sleep as possible before the coming offensive. They sent bombers out with instructions "Go where you like, attack what you like, drop a bomb here and a bomb there, just keep the enemy awake." I went to bed in my tent, but there were never less than two bombers cruising low over the camp and I knew sleep was going to be impossible. I wandered out into the luminous moonlight and watched. Then someone popped out of the ground and offered me the unoccupied arm of the L-shaped trench he had dug. So I rolled myself in my blankets and lay in it and it was tight and warm and the earth kept shaking down onto me when the bombs landed, but I had such a sense of security that in the end I slept very well.

Next morning after breakfast I went across to Headquarters to see the Intelligence Officer. He was briskly sticking pins into a map and altering all his coloured-chalk markings. "The balloon's gone up," he said.

"You mean Rommel has attacked?"

"Yes, there's a tank battle going on now this side of the Gazala Line."

"Oh. . . . How are we doing?"

The officer frowned and drew a big curved red arrow round Bir Hacheim.

"It's all in a shocking mess now," he said. "Come back this evening and we shall be able to tell you more."

What in fact had happened was this. Rommel had decided on the regulation opening gambit—the sweep down into the desert round the southern end of the enemy line. On the night of May 26 two hundred and fifty of his tanks had clattered off down south and by-passed Bir Hacheim with twenty-five miles to spare. On the morning of the twenty-seventh they were driving up due north behind the Gazala Line.

They came in three great prongs, the Ariete on the left, the Twenty-first *Panzerdivision* in the middle and the Fifteenth *Panzerdivision* on the right. His plan was immediately obvious. First he wanted to nip off Bir Hacheim, forge a pathway through the mine field above it, and so get himself a shortened supply route. Then his main German tank forces would assault and occupy Tobruk. And then the infantry divisions in the Gazala Line would fall easily into his hand, for they would be hopelessly cut off. He was counting on a blitz decision. He had only three days' petrol and water rations with him and he reckoned that that, plus any stores he might capture, would see him through. These were bold, blitz tactics. And they did not work.

The first thing that went wrong was Bir Hacheim. Seventy Italian tanks appeared in front of the Free French, made a demonstration of force, and suggested that Bir Hacheim should surrender. The French, with whoops of joy, manned their beloved seventy-fives and fought. Probably at no time in the whole war had

Frenchmen fought with such a will. And pretty soon they were radioing Headquarters that thirty-five Italian tanks were blazing in front of their positions.

Next, neither of the German *Panzerdivisions* got its objective. The Twenty-first was going for Knightsbridge, a fortified rectangular compound outlined with barbed-wire and mine fields which the British had planned as the pivot of their defence, and the Fifteenth was aiming for the air field of El Adem. But the British tank forces intervened.

They had been warned to stand by at five o'clock in the morning, when the first dew was falling on the tanks. They got into battle formation and waited while it grew light. By breakfast time nothing had happened. Then suddenly the German *Panzers* came over the horizon like a solid black thread that grew gradually thicker and thicker. They came shoulder to shoulder, stretched across a good mile of desert, and the massed roar of their engines beat shatteringly on the ears of the waiting British.

They came on cautiously, but the British had been told to hold their fire until one thousand yards, so there was only the noise of the Germans' engines. Then at a thousand yards the twenty-eight-ton American General Grants fired their first shots in anger.

So, on the great rocky plateau south-west of Tobruk, the opening tank battle of the new campaign began. It was a very different thing from the tank battles of the previous winter, when the German tanks stood foursquare and stationary and firing hard while the under-gunned British cruisers waltzed frantically in, trying to get within range before they were hit. Now the two sides were ranged almost symmetrically and there was little movement. Only occasionally the formations shifted slightly within themselves as tanks were knocked out or forced from the field, and there was movement where the tank-recovery units darted in to carry off some crippled vehicle. It came down to a duel, to a contest of guns and gunnery and armour. The gunners in the Grants watched their tracer shells whizz like golf balls smack into the Mark Threes and saw the sudden dull rosy glow which meant a direct hit.

This was a real gun! And they felt their tanks lurch and quiver under direct hits from the enemy and they knew they were behind some very fine steel indeed. Still the terms were not quite equal, for the British were still using plenty of the lighter-weight tanks with two-pounders, and the Grant's gun was not well-placed, it had not enough traverse. But this was a far better tank force than any Britain had put into the field this war. The first engagement lasted about an hour and at the end of it the Germans withdrew.

So Rommel's first great thrust was parried. It had not been cheap or easy to do, and his initial momentum had carried him a little farther than we had hoped, but now the sharp edge of his impetus was blunted. The battle began to crystallize down into a great, tangled, swift-moving engagement up and down to the east of the Gazala Line. Sometimes the fighting lapped all round the edges of Knightsbridge and then drained away, leaving its defenders high and dry again. Rommel thrust wildly and fiercely, trying to strike some blow that would be mortal, still trying to get his blitz decision. It was still entirely in the stage of a tank battle. The Gazala Line simply stood firm and waited to be attacked from either direction.

ii

I set off at once to see what I could see on that first morning. Already little ripples of confusion and alarm were spreading out from the ragged fringes of the battle. The air was thick with dust, and the roads choked with vehicles. No one had yet had time to work out the geography of what was going on — no one could say whether this road was safe or that track was cut or El Adem was in our hands. I took the Axis by-pass and suddenly, on El Duda itself, I met the enemy. I lay on the hot stones, while lizards darted over my bare legs, and peeped over the brow of a little rise at the Nazis. From somewhere behind our guns were shelling them, and as the shells fell they kept sorting themselves out and reorganizing their dispersal. Two or three trucks were burning with a steady red-black flame. That seemed pretty serious — Germans on

El Duda. Our main supply dump was only half a mile behind where I lay. But they were only a small isolated party, not the main body. And next morning they were gone again.

All across the Tobruk area there was what looked like a full-scale retreat. Trucks were jostling their way back eastwards to safety, and rolling stock was being pushed back along the newly laid railway line. But if you looked carefully you saw that there were no guns or tanks or fighting troops among them. They were simply empty lorries—"soft transport"—and they were clearing the floor to leave room for the battle. The drivers' faces were so caked with dust and sweat that they looked as though they were wearing beauty specialists' mud packs. Most of them had tinted goggles to keep out the glare and the dust, and with their tin hats on they looked sinisterly inhuman.

During those first few chaotic days I used to go back and sleep the night in my hole while the Luftwaffe kept up its insomnia raids above me, and spend the day looking for the battle. It usually meant a quick easy run to the edge of the known fighting arena, then a cautious groping forward, for the battle might be anywhere.

One morning, for instance, a grimy Major strolled across and said, with that exaggerated casualness British officers adopt in moments of excitement, "Oh, I shouldn't go on if I were you. They shell anyone who shows himself. I've just had my observation post blown up." So we had to go round another way. We drove warily ahead, watching the antics of five planes until they suddenly began to sow a long line of bombs just ahead of us. Five minutes later we ran madly from two harmless Tomahawks. It was a difficult problem, this identification of aircraft, because you got spots in front of the eyes if you looked at the sky for more than ten consecutive seconds. Everywhere men were lying under trucks and tractors, and each time I spotted them my mind would automatically suggest "enemy aircraft about." But they were sheltering from the sun, not from planes, using the only shade that can be found in the desert. And yet, by some queer meteorological fluke, these first days of battle were not so unbearably hot as we had expected. The sun at midday, it is true, shone down with a heat that was like a red-hot drill boring into your head and eyes. But there was a cool breeze from the sea which made the sun just endurable.

Worse than the heat was the dust. Each truck drove about in its own private cloud and when two trucks met each tried desperately to steer to windward of the other in order to avoid his dust. Here round El Adem, where there had already been so much fighting, the whole of the top-soil had been churned into dust and most of it was permanently in the air. Seen dimly through it were layers of wreckage which could be analyzed down into their component campaigns. For instance, the green-brimmed Italian sun helmets were two years old, the Italian Caproni fighters a year and a half, the Stukas one year, and so forth.

The battle was always a faint throbbing of sound and a sudden blossoming of smoke and flame just beyond the horizon. But occasionally it flung forth dangerous tentacles of combat. One afternoon near Acroma a couple of armoured cars, going flat out, tore across the road ahead of us with trails of dust wreathing out behind them. After them came squat black tanks, grinding steadily along, spitting little jets of flame and dropping shells around their heels. We stopped and turned our cars, ready to flee. Beside us a signaller was lounging against a telegraph pole. He had just tapped the wire and was shouting into the mouthpiece, "Hurry up, Joe, I want my blinking tea." The tanks stopped and turned back into the battle and we set off to Headquarters again and the signaller went for his tea. It was astounding how, in these hot days when the sweat rolled down your back even if you just sat still in the shade, the British soldier would still drink nothing but hot, strong, sweet tea.

By some centrifugal process, news of what was happening flowed constantly out to the edges of the battle, and I used to drive round picking up all I could. Already hundreds of men had been captured by the Germans and got away again. Some had escaped by their own efforts. Others, after ostentatiously good treatment, had been deliberately freed by the Germans who had no facilities for dealing with prisoners anyway and thought they might as well do a bit of anti-atrocity propaganda. The Germans, it seemed, had started off this campaign with even greater confidence than the British. Rommel had referred to it in his order of the day as "the decisive attack against the British forces in Libya." They were talking about taking Tobruk in one day and Cairo in five. They had come only with skeleton rations of food and water, assuming they would capture plenty of both. And German prisoners to whom I talked were self-assured and almost pitying in their condescension. They hardly regarded the campaign as serious at all, and they thought of their capture as a merely temporary inconvenience.

There was the usual wealth of dramatic personal incident in those first days. General Gott had once again fought his way through the enemy at night, though this time he had been slightly wounded in the knee. General Messervy, who commanded the Seventh Armoured Division, had been captured and got away again. The South Africans at Gazala had had seventeen Stuka raids in five hours. And then they had shot down General Cruewell, Commander of the Afrikakorps (Rommel was now Commander-in-Chief), who came flying over their lines in a little monoplane. The Germans had unsuccessfully tried a landing on the coast west of Tobruk. And equally unsuccessfully they had landed their planes beside the railway and tried to blow it up.

It was not till the third day, when the tank battle was still spluttering indecisively up and down inside the Gazala Line, that I finally got into Knightsbridge, which was the focal point of the whole thing. As a fortress Knightsbridge was ridiculously unimpressive. In fact, it was practically invisible. It looked like a huge empty rectangle of desert enclosed by a slender barbed-wire fence. But its real defences, the mine fields, could not be seen. Nor could its defenders, for they had simply dug themselves underground. Everything, guns and tents and trucks and dumps, was buried out of sight. As I drove in the twenty-five-pounders were firing rhythmically at some enemy transport which was hurrying past on the other side of the compound, but only the red-yellow flashes from their muzzles were visible. I had the curious feeling of anticlimax that I had sometimes experienced before on battle-fields. On the map it had looked as though Knightsbridge must be the centre of a flaming, screaming, deafening, hellish inferno. But in real life the inferno was so diluted by time and space that it seemed almost tame.

I went to talk to the men fighting here—Coldstream and Scots Guards—and I noticed a curious thing. They all staggered a little as they walked like men slightly drunk. And they talked very slowly and carefully. They were all so desperately tired. I realized that a diluted inferno spread over three days is nevertheless an inferno.

Suddenly a flock of Stukas snarled down from behind us and I ran headlong across country until I found a trench to fall into. There was a gunner already there, a man whose voice told me in his first two words that he was a Londoner. Across the high-pitched metallic crack of the bombs and ack-ack he gave me a sort of contrapuntal monologue compounded of two interwoven themes—a running commentary on what was going on overhead, and an account of what had been happening at Knightsbridge for the past three days. The Germans, I heard, had appeared on the edge of the mine field just after breakfast on Wednesday. All that day the shells fell into Knightsbridge and the guns of Knightsbridge shelled back. Sometimes the fighting was on one side of the box, sometimes on another. Once a party of Germans got tangled in the mine field and in three minutes two tanks, three staff cars and ten lorries had been hit. Once the Germans had all but forced their way into the box. Once the box had very nearly run out of ammunition and a convoy had got through just in time. It seemed to the gunners that the only respite they had had from firing was when the Stukas came over. "If it was safe to look out of this trench," said my cockney, "I'd show you what we done. The mine field's filled with what we hit until it looks like a car park . . . Blimey, look at that one smoking, he's down all right."

iii

Knightsbridge was something new in the development of desert war technique. It was an adaptation of the fortress-area theory. It was not a place in which men were supposed to fight until the last drop of their blood. It was designed as a fixed inviolable island, a sort of sanctuary in the midst of the fluid tank fighting, where field guns and anti-tank guns and infantry could remain and operate without having to pack up and flee away every time enemy tanks came near them. So far, in this first phase of the fighting, it had abundantly proved its worth. Again and again the Germans were held back because they could not blot out this island of resistance, from which guns shelled their transport as it went by, and where tanks and infantry could always flee for safe refuge.

This day when I first visited Knightsbridge was the critical day, the end of the first phase. Three days were up. The German *Panzer-divisions* had finished the emergency rations they brought with them. Bir Hacheim had not fallen, and no safe lane had been made through the mine field north of it. German supply columns were obliged to make the long dangerous trip round to the south, and British fighter bombers were attacking them all the time. The British tank forces were not decisively beaten. The Gazala Line was still inviolate. The Germans had captured no important dumps. Rommel's blitz tactics had failed.

With rapidly mounting alarm Rommel realized how bad was his failure. He must at all cost get his tanks and transport back on to his own side of the Gazala Line — it seemed his only hope. He began to bunch everything he had between the Free French and Fifty Div. while his sappers frantically picked a hole in the great mine field. Whole battalions of Italian infantry were set to work stabbing the ground with bayonets to locate mines. It looked like headlong retreat, and it was retreat.

Both we and he knew that Rommel was beaten then. We were optimistic — very optimistic. Afterwards we looked back with shame on the things we had written and said at that time, but on the whole I do not think we were unduly optimistic. The situation was very good. The Germans took it for granted — a captured staff officer confirmed this to me — that we would exploit our advantage. They expected that our infantry would smash down into their flanks. They half expected that a British tank force would be rushed round Bir Hacheim to close the western entrance to the gap through the mine field. And meantime Rommel's one thought was to get everything away to safety that he could.

But nothing happened. The British infantry never moved. The British tank forces simply yapped at the Germans' heels. Scarcely believing his luck Rommel saw he might have a second chance. The westward flow of his material through the mine-field gap slackened and halted and finally turned east again. He established a firm bridgehead on the eastern side of the gap and ringed it with tanks and powerful anti-tank guns. He jabbed out in counterattacks until he held about a hundred square miles. Almost at once this bridgehead was nicknamed "the Cauldron."

A magnificent chance had been lost — as good a chance as Rommel himself had had at the time of Wavell's last Middle East campaign. And very soon it was too late. Soon the Germans had made a second gap through the mine field and then they sent in their full tank force and overran the British 150th Brigade, which lay between the two gaps. Soon the German anti-tank guns were thoroughly dug in. The Cauldron was firmly established and fortified. Rommel had been on the very brink of disaster, but he had obtained a miraculous reprieve.

It was in those days that the Eighth Army's shortcomings began to appear. It had looked such a good army, so professionally equipped, so well prepared — easily Britain's best army this war. But it creaked badly at the joints through very newness. It was slow, inelastic, and unimaginative. Once again it was Rommel who was dictating the moves. It was so obvious at one point that a determined British thrust was called for that the censor allowed me to write "The next phase should logically be a British counterattack." But in the whole of the first three weeks we only once took the initiative. One morning we sent in infantry to take three small positions south-west of Knightsbridge. And few people were surprised when the same evening German tanks overran the infantry and pushed it back farther than it had come. Because in this desert infantry alone cannot fight tanks.

The British tank fighting had enormously improved, but there were still bad gaps. The new six-pounder anti-tank gun was used with very little imagination, exclusively as a defence weapon instead of being given an honoured place in the offensive ensemble. The Germans invariably used anti-tank guns in close co-operation with tanks, aiming to lure our tanks on to the guns. And too often a brave, impulsive, too literal interpretation of the "Attack and Pursue" slogan sent the British tanks straight into the trap.

The Germans were still ahead, too, in one of the most obvious essentials of this mobile warfare—the element of speed. Many officers in the British Armoured Divisions commented to me on the swiftness with which the enemy got packed up and into position. He always seemed to be one jump ahead of us and it always gave him the chance of picking the best spot on the battle-field and getting his guns ready and dug in. It seemed to me there were two reasons for this.

The first was that the young *Panzer* soldiers had been not so much trained as conditioned to war. They were cogs in a machine of which every part was designed functionally for speed and efficiency. They had been subjected to semi-military training ever since they could remember. They had been taught camping lore and implicit obedience and stern discipline and map reading and direction finding until these had become instinct with them. They had been accustomed to the noise of explosives in tough realistic manœuvres and they had been taught—as far as it can be taught—to use their imagination and initiative at all times. For the sake of speed the Germans ruthlessly sacrificed a number of things that are usually considered essential. They would race across the desert at night with headlights full on if necessary, only switching them off when the shells began to fall. They took no great trouble about camouflage or blackouts. They freely gave away their position at night by shooting up Very lights to communicate with one another. In moments of emergency they dispensed not only with wireless silence, but even with code.

And that leads to the second reason for the Germans' superior speed. Their methods of communicating information were swifter. Rommel could swing his forces round the desert at a moment's notice because he was usually commanding them directly himself. He had realized that, just as an admiral goes to sea with his fleet and directs the battle from the midst of it, so in these desert tank battles the commander must be on the spot himself. All relevant information came straight to him without any intermediary. His decision could be taken in a matter of seconds and his orders given in a matter of minutes. He could alter the whole course of the battle before the British information had even started on its way back to Headquarters. Our communications were slowed down first by the necessity of maintaining wireless silence, second by time lost in coding and decoding, third by being filtered through a whole series of subsidiary Headquarters. Often enough I came back from the front at the end of the day and found I knew more about what was going on than did Army Headquarters.

There was one other point about the British tank forces. When the battle began, there was in our armoured brigades in Libya only one Brigadier and no one of higher rank who was a genuine tank man. One armoured division was commanded by a former Indian Cavalry officer — General Messervy. General Gott, who had commanded the Seventh Armoured Division in the middle winter and was possibly the most experienced desert fighter we had, was given the infantry corps. And the Brigadier who had done most brilliantly of all in the winter — Brigadier Alec Gatehouse — was not in the battle at all. During the third week of the battle General Auchinleck flew up to the desert and reshuffled all the commanders, but by that time most of the damage had been done.

iv

This second phase of the campaign — when Rommel turned and re-established himself in the Cauldron — was long and confused and sanguinary. Time and again the Germans thrust this way and that, trying to take the vital strong-points in which the British were maintaining themselves on the Cauldron's edge. Incessantly they tried to reduce Bir Hacheim, sending alternately tremendous flocks of Stukas and officers with white flags to invite surrender. But the French, their pride deeply touched, held magnificently on. The processes of the fighting were too intricate to describe. But the dominating feature of the whole phase was the British failure to take the initiative.

Day after day I scouted round the edges of the battle, trying to get into it and see what was going on. One day I made my way into Knightsbridge when the summer's thickest, hottest, cruellest sand-storm closed down on the battle-field and the fighting was stifled as though a deadening beige blanket had been flung down on top of it. It started only as a honey-coloured mist. But when we reached Knightsbridge we were groping our way foot by foot through a brown fog. More by luck than anything else we found the crude dug-out where the Brigadier and his staff were living and he invited us in to get the front-line picture. We squatted round in an atmosphere like clear soup which someone was constantly stirring. In one corner a grapefruit was rapidly silting up and would soon disappear from view. If there were any other furnishings they had disappeared already. The Brigadier's map was like a blank sheet of cardboard until he rubbed away the dust to show us the coloured-pencil markings beneath. The Germans, it seemed, were going both ways through the gap which was now ten miles wide. They had made an unsuccessful attack on an important stronghold called Thamar. The Italians had sent an insulting demand for surrender to Bir Hacheim. It was all much as usual.

It took just about three minutes for the Brigadier's map to become invisible again beneath the dust, and with impatient regularity he cleaned it up. The air was thickening all the time. The grapefruit was entirely buried. Every few minutes someone would dust himself off and additional eddies would swirl in the air. You could no longer tell what was the natural colour of anybody's hair.

The Brigade-Major was telephoning about some position. "Dust your map," he was saying, "and see whether there's any enemy at point Two O Four." He listened to the reply, then told the Brigadier, "There's an O Pip six hundred yards away who gets machine-gunned every time he raises his head but of course no one can see that far now." A shattering explosion a hundred yards away interrupted him. We looked nervously at one another, unable to diagnose it. The Brigade-Major sent someone to see and it turned out to be some explosives buried in the ground which had been set off by the storm. "This *khamseen* wind has electrical properties," the Major said, holding up the telephone so that we could hear the brittle crackling in the earpiece.

We said good-bye and climbed out of the dug-out again. It was thicker still now, and the wind was driving the dust so fast that you had to lean against it to stand up. The sun was entirely blotted out, but the heat had a sharp, fiery edge on it. We groped our way gingerly through the mine field outside Knightsbridge and then stopped for lunch in the hope that it would clear. Everything we ate was brown and gritty and tasted of dust. The water in our water bottles was as hot as tea. It was disgusting to drink, but we had to drink something for our mouths and tongues were parched to a raw dryness. Tins and bottles which had been in the shade all day felt as though they had been in an oven. Every minute the air grew more difficult to breathe.

We tried to continue on a compass course, but we should have known it was hopeless. It grew so thick that we literally could not see twelve inches ahead and we just had to sit and wait. The desert top-soil blew past us still in its original geological strata. Sometimes the whole world would be grey, then it would change colours through white, lemon, honey, and salmon-pink to orange.

We tried to crawl on and ran straight into a derelict Mark Four tank whose harsh outlines had become softened under the pall of dust. We met sentries whose clothes, faces, hair and rifles were all the same colour so that they looked like statues except where their eyes were red-rimmed from constant rubbing. Truck-drivers kept their windscreen wipers going to clear the caking dust. Runnels of sweat carved little riverbeds along men's limbs. The only possible comfort in this misery was the thought that at least you were safe from Stukas.

It cleared a little towards evening and a smoky-blue sun pierced the fog. It seemed as though all the dust there was down south of us had already been blown past us. And then the wind swivelled round and it all started blowing back again. For sheer physical discomfort I shall always remember that day as the worst I lived through in the desert. For the last hour I sat dumbly, my thoughts playing without ceasing round baths and taps and long cold drinks. No pleasures exceeding those were imaginable.

Another evening during the Cauldron period, we were swept up in what was now almost officially known as a "flap." A flap is a phenomenon of desert war which looks like a panic-stricken retreat, and occurs when enemy tanks cut loose among soft-skinned, undefended transport.

That night I was with Alan Moorehead and three American correspondents. We had decided to camp with Corps Headquarters a little south-east of Knightsbridge, and while Kim — once more my Conducting Officer — was brewing up one of his famous curries, we walked across to see the Intelligence Officer. It was the day on which we had taken the initiative and sent infantry forward to capture some positions in the Cauldron. We learned that the Germans would probably try and recapture them during the night.

When we went back the curry was not ready, so we lay on our beds and discussed the stiffness of Rommel's rally. The battle still throbbed noisily in the background. We thought it was just our fancy that the sounds seemed to be growing louder. The stillness of the evening might account for it. Then we saw vehicles streaming back over the skyline, going fast in little flocks. They would hurry over the horizon and then check suddenly like insects and then change their direction. The scene bore unmistakable symptoms of "soft" transport making way before a battle.

Now the whole camp began to betray signs of effervescence. Men were throwing things into trucks and cars were dashing across to consult with other cars. We too gulped our curry and packed with the deftness of experience. We knew a flap when we saw one.

Suddenly, like three dark poplars, three shell bursts flowered on the horizon. So they were as close as that. The wreathing dust behind the vehicles thickened and flattened as they increased speed.

Off we drove bumpily in the estimated direction of sunrise. An Indian army recovery vehicle careered past us, festooned with dusky soldiers, their white teeth gleaming in half-moon–like grins. To the right and left other trucks bucketed along. It was growing dark now and fires began to gleam steadily as though holes had been punched through the black landscape to a light behind. They were tanks that had been hit or vehicles which had blundered into a mine field. The shelling boomed louder at our backs and quick stabs of flame showed where the guns were. It was alarming and curiously exciting to realize that some violent process was stirring up all this behind you and you could not tell what it was. One single tank could cause a flap of these dimensions. Or it might be the entire German armoured forces.

We came to another Headquarters, and found that they too were on the move. Then we reached the box at El Adem and they were just about to close the entrance-gap through their defences and shut themselves in behind a mine field. After a moment's indecision we determined to stay outside. We drove on while the fires grew bright and Very lights began to curve across the sky. Once something splintered under our wheels and I looked out to see regular ranks of crosses. We had blundered into a war cemetery. We re-erected the cross we had knocked down and backed out again.

Gradually things began to get sorted out. Military police were controlling the traffic, explaining that the flap was only a small one. Somewhere near Tobruk we unrolled our bedding and slept fully clothed, taking a watch of one hour each.

In the chill of next morning we heard that it had been a relatively serious affair after all. Twenty-five German tanks had run amok into the British lines. But no military damage of any sort had been done by the scare. It was just one of the normal features of desert warfare.

So the Cauldron boiled and seethed and simmered with little lulls and climaxes but nothing decisive. It looked like a phase of attrition — the battle of the last tank. Until one side or the other could get an effective superiority in armour the first invariable phase of any desert campaign — the body of the tadpole or comet — would not be over, and the swift pursuit could not begin.

CHAPTER 23

Black Saturday

IT WAS not only the ordinary material processes of desert warfare that were holding the battle in suspense during those first fiery days of June. There were other more intangible influences at work: the sustained inertia of the British; Rommel's still incomplete assessment of the quality of this new British army, of the extent to which he could gamble against it; and — very important — Rommel's temperamental horror of any threat to his flank, in this case Bir Hacheim. And towards June 8, after he had recovered his breath and his confidence, he roused himself to do something about Bir Hacheim.

The Frenchmen down there were not entirely isolated. They sent jaunty messages back to Headquarters. They thanked the R.A.F. regularly and breezily whenever British fighters intercepted a Stuka raid over them. Always when they were asked, they replied that the situation was in hand. Periodically they undertook counterattacks. They sent indignant, high-spirited replies to the incessant demands for their surrender. General Larminat himself visited them and came back safe. And at night convoys with stores for them bumped off into the darkness, tearing the silence of the desert apart with their din, fighting off enemy patrols, finally answering the quick nervous challenge of the outermost sentry, and then unloading food and ammunition there in the blackness while the unseen French voices rose and fell about them.

But their well was long since dry. They only had one "quart" — and a French "quart" means just one mugful — of water a day. The desert's biggest guns — 155- and 210-millimetres — were shelling them. The Stukas came over in layers, and they were not always intercepted. The enemy managed here and there to filter in through their mine fields and occupy their outposts. They dug their trenches deeper and their casualties were not bad. The Stuka raids were for most of them just a noise — but a noise so stupendous that no human language has words to describe it and it is a wonder that any human ear could endure it.

Hacheim was not an offensive position. There were no tanks there. But Rommel inordinately feared it. And finally he sent down there what tanks he could spare and a large proportion of the Ninetieth Light Division, which was his crack infantry. So Hacheim came to resemble a shooting target: the Free French themselves formed the bull's-eye; then there was an inner ring of attacking Axis troops; and an outer ring of British mobile units who sought to attack the Axis troops in the rear.

Gradually the pitch of the fighting rose in a crescendo. Each time the Stuka raids seemed to grow a little bigger. Behind a screen of grey-black smoke from incessant shell-fire the Axis infantry began to nibble into the French positions. R.A.F. fighters patrolled constantly over Hacheim, seeing it as an ugly, smoking, blackened scar sprawled across the desert. The French slit trenches and the symmetrical craters of the bombs looked like meaningless dots and dashes which someone had scrawled with a pencil on a dirty sheet of paper. The very sand was charred and the tinder-dry scrub was burned away.

Twice I tried to drive down there and see this great thing if only from the outside. Each time I was headed off in the perilous, empty-looking no-man's-land which surrounded Hacheim. Every pillar of dust was a potential enemy and unless you were strongly armed, it was not worth while to try and find out. The only thing to do was to get away as quickly as possible. All over the area there were units belonging to both sides deliberately looking for trouble. Every few miles or so we stumbled on little clotted battlefields, with a handful of charred trucks and perhaps a tank or two and the earth ploughed and scarred where swiftly churning tank treads had ripped it up. Sometimes a few bodies sprawled among rags and letters and spilled tools and food and aluminum eating utensils. Perhaps there would be a rough wooden cross made of packing cases with yesterday's date on it. And occasionally a little heap of empty tins told whether British or Germans had had lunch there. All we could see was a slow-rising pillar of grey smoke, and all we could hear was a muttering throb. But hour by hour the pitch of the fighting was rising. Rommel was determined to take the place. And the Eighth Army was unable to send any more help than was already being sent, for there were even more important sectors elsewhere which could not be weakened.

Finally on June 10 Brigadier-General Koenig, who was in command down there, considered that militarily the position was no longer tenable. Morally and spiritually the individual Frenchmen there were prepared to go on holding it, if that were necessary. The issue was clouded by the Germans, who began to send out phony wireless signals in Koenig's name asking permission to surrender. But finally Ritchie agreed with Koenig. The place could not be held. It was decided to evacuate it that night.

Up till the last the French were counterattacking parties of the enemy who were trying to infiltrate the mine fields. It was not till after their meagre evening meal that they all knew they were going to evacuate. Swiftly and silently they set to work, slitting the bottoms of the petrol tins to let the petrol soak away in the desert, removing the breech-locks from any guns they could not take with them, silently destroying everything they did not pack. Then Koenig formed up his vehicles into a huge oblong with guns and prisoners in the middle and an hour before midnight they marched out. The Axis troops round about knew or guessed what was happening and they shelled the French blindly as they went. Some trucks ran into a spot where a murderous cross-fire from four directions caught them, and there were many unbelievable escapes. In the darkness they steered on southwards and then eastwards, and in the morning they were safe. British armoured units met them and escorted them through the most perilous stage of their journey. About three quarters of the original four thousand defenders got away.

I went and met the men of Bir Hacheim when they rejoined the Eighth Army. They did not regard themselves as having been defeated; I nearly got knifed for my pains when I hinted at it. Personally they were not defeated—only militarily. There were burly Gascons and dark lithe Parisians and slow-spoken Bretons, but all of them had this feeling that they were not defeated, that in some small personal measure they had contributed towards wiping out the shame of the defeat of France. They wore great sprouting shapeless beards, for there had not been enough water in Hacheim to permit shaving. And their eyes still shone with excitement as they thought back to those first days when their seventy-fives had played havoc among the Italian tanks and they had shelled Axis transport passing through the mine-field gap until the barrels of their guns were literally red-hot.

An Alsatian with a red beard and a complete set of gold teeth bent down and drew me a diagram in the dust to show me how the first infantry attacks had been made. He said, "It was butchery. Their corpses were draped over the barbed wire like pigs at a market. They were heaped on the ground until the Boches were hiding behind their own dead comrades. First they tried to come against the Foreign Legion. Then they tried again from another direction, against the pacifique units. That, too, was formidable. My God, how we fought those days."

The bombings, they admitted, had been bad. They raised their voices and made sweeping motions with their hands as they explained how the Stukas had swung in, now from one side, now from the other. But they had borne it, and they said they could have borne more. They would not think of themselves as having been bombed out. They regarded it as a matter of military expediency. But they conceded that the evacuation had been a tricky affair. They fetched their greatcoats and showed me where the bullets had gone through. "It was a miracle," protested a crow-headed Paris fishmonger, placing his hand on a large crucifix tattooed on his chest.

I wandered on among them, talking to them as they painfully scraped off their great ungainly beards. I had started by approaching them respectfully almost as men from another world, men who had been down into the Valley of Death and had a glimpse of the other side. But few of them gave any sign of having been through a great ordeal. Already a large part of their experiences seemed to have slipped painlessly away from them. The tremendous physical impact of what they had endured had hardly left a scar on their minds.

ii

But to Rommel Bir Hacheim meant everything. For him its removal was the key to the door. He felt like someone who has been cured of a disease. Now he could become active and get about again. Instantly he sprang into action. Almost before Bir Hacheim's defenders had reached safety, the German tank forces were on the warpath. They swung down into the desert in a wide arc, went through the formality of occupying empty Hacheim, and curved up again to engage the British tank forces. Dive bombers and artillery fell upon Knightsbridge in the late afternoon. The whole, simplified desert battlefront boiled into action again.

It was easy to tell ourselves that strategically Bir Hacheim meant nothing to the enemy, that we could equally well put barbed-wire round any patch of desert and hold it, that the French troops bottled up there were now released for offensive action. The fact soon became very clear that Rommel regarded this as the crucial moment of the campaign. He simply resumed his original plan of a drive northwards against El Adem and Tobruk.

Now the campaign entered a phase of chaos so complex, so mysterious, that no one ever seems quite to have worked out what happened. A sand-storm was raging, the British forces were being radically regrouped and their commanders reshuffled, the whole area south and west of Tobruk was in a state of fluid ferment. And in the midst of it all, on the afternoon of Saturday June 13, the British armoured forces suffered a reverse which proved decisive.

It seems to have started with the Ninetieth Light Division, which had already been fighting all Rommel's hardest infantry battles. It was operating all round the fortified box which the British were holding a little south of El Adem Air Field, and at a given moment it sent out an SOS. It claimed that it was in desperate straits, and the British armoured forces heard the appeal. It looked like a Heaven-sent chance of wiping out this very fine infantry division.

So the British armoured divisions drove south through the sandstorm, trying to reach the Ninetieth Light before the German help had arrived. And there, on the rutted, dusty track called the Trigh Capuzzo, which runs from the El Adem box to the Knightsbridge box, the crucial engagement took place.

It did not take the British long to realize that either they had been lured into a trap, or else they had arrived too late. At any rate, the bulk of the Fifteenth and Twenty-first *Panzerdivisions* were there to welcome them. The battle became general all along the Trigh, with the focal point round a little cairn-crowned hillock called Bir Belefar. It is certain that in at least some cases the British tanks were manœuvred full into the fire of the German anti-tank gun screen. For a good deal of the battle it was guns against tanks, not tanks against tanks. One British tank regiment which was supposed to be protecting the flank got scooped suddenly into the battle and forced onto a line of 88-millimetre guns until the horizon was fringed with a regularly spaced line of smoking tanks. It all happened on such a scale, in such visibility and in such confusion that no one was able to get a comprehensive view of what happened. But the simple basic statistical fact finally emerged that the British had gone into the battle stronger in tanks than the Germans and come out very considerably weaker. Mr. Churchill stated afterwards in the House of Commons that the British tank strength was that afternoon reduced from 300 to 70. Throughout the Eighth Army the day was known as Black Saturday.

That was the end. Auchinleck and Ritchie recognized it instantly. The first half of the campaign — the hard core of heavy fighting — was over and the Eighth Army had lost it. The time for headlong flight had arrived, and it would have to be flight eastward by the British. Their only hope of salvation now lay in a rapid folding back on themselves until some sort of line could be formed and some sort of counterattacking force could be gathered, a simplification of their own supply problem and a complication of the enemy's, and a desperate race to get reinforcements.

The fortified boxes scattered throughout the battle area were now no longer any use, for there was no mobile tank force to operate in conjunction with them. They would have to be used as bases for small rear-guard actions and then abandoned. But the most urgent and immediate problem was the two infantry divisions which were still sitting there marooned in the Gazala Line. Somehow they must be smuggled out before the Axis forces got right round them and did to them what the British had done to Bardia and Halfaya six months before.

The clean-up of the Tobruk-Gazala area started instantly, under constant pressure from the enemy. I tried to get into Tobruk on Sunday — the day after the fatal tank battle. But it was impossible. The road was paralyzed by one of the biggest traffic jams on record. The highway itself had long ago reached saturation point and was overflowing copiously into the desert. There were three, four and five parallel lanes of vehicles where there was hardly room for two. An accident or a break-down meant that the whole procession was immobilized maybe for an hour. Huge tank transporters were getting wedged across the road and holding things up in both directions. The military policemen were frankly helpless. It was a still day, but this immense mass of trucks had created its own local, stationary sand-storm. The confusion was not, in fact, quite so bad as it looked. If you watched the pictorial divisional symbols on the vehicles you saw there was a certain rhythm to all this movement — it included whole units on their way to predetermined destinations. It was all part of the vast reshuffle. But it nevertheless remained a traffic jam and that was the first of many afternoons when we raised our eyes to the sky and with fervent piety thanked the R.A.F. For the R.A.F. at this stage produced a miracle.

All through the campaign the Tedder-Coningham team had been making air history. Despite the almost imaginary air force he had inherited a year before, despite what he had had to send to the Far East, despite the losses of the previous campaign, Tedder had once again built up a finely balanced, pliant air force, beautifully appropriate to its purposes. There was a finish and a polish about it, an absence of ragged ends or glaring gaps or organizational loop-holes. And he and Coningham were ready with the new theory of technique — still largely in its experimental stage — which they had forged out of the data collected in the winter. These two men were doing a pioneer job of incalculable importance, for they were the only two men in the world who had ever handled British air superiority in conjunction with a land battle.

The minute battle was joined, Coningham went into action with a series of orders that were frankly revolutionary. He forbade any British plane to fly at more than six thousand feet. Dog-fights with enemy fighters were to be strictly avoided. The air force was to be subordinated without reserve to the requirements of the army. If British fighters ran into enemy planes attacking British troops, well and good: they might drive them off. But there was to be no "swanning about" in vague sweeps, waiting for someone to come along. Everyone must be doing a positive job all the time. And no pilots must be lost unnecessarily. Coningham had noticed how many pilots were bailing out of their machines and walking back to safety. So he completely reorganized their emergency rations to contain a much more thirst-quenching diet. And he forbade them to wear flying boots, because that gave them blisters when they walked.

Then Coningham, as he had planned, moved into the Army Commander's camp and lunched and dined with the Army Commander every day. Soon the results began to come in, and it was abundantly plain that the new technique worked. When all the emphasis was on Rommel's supply columns and no British artillery could reach them, fighter bombers went out and rushed their own form of artillery to the spot. When a specially heavy barrage was needed on Point 209 at three o'clock one afternoon, the Blenheims appeared at two-fifty-seven, made one circle, and dropped their bombs in one deafening cascade exactly on time. The R.A.F. had never been more popular with the army. Certainly the technique worked. And there was one other thing that helped—the inexplicable inefficiency of the Luftwaffe. An expert called General von Woldau had come out specially from the Berlin Air General Staff, and von Kesselring himself was supposed to be directing air operations. The German air fields were filled with fine aircraft. But they were simply not being used. Coningham himself could not solve the mystery. He believed that in the last resort it was quality of pilots that was the operative factor.

But now, with the British starting their retreat and these immense traffic jams on the road, there were targets that even the most feeble air force could not miss. And here it was that the R.A.F. produced their miracle. They made a supreme effort to protect the retiring army. Despite heat and dust-storms each plane began doing four, five, six operations a day. They continued to operate from Gambut long after the Germans had taken El Adem, and there were times when their targets were barely ten minutes' flying away, so that they could shuttle back and forth all day long. Record after record was broken. For several days they worked to a mathematical attack programme of twenty-minute sorties, with half the squadrons out attacking and the rest filling up with bombs and petrol. There was no rest at all for ground crews. They dug themselves holes beside their aircraft, stuffed their blankets inside, and snatched a few minutes' sleep when they could. They worked at night with enemy flares burning right above them and bombs falling round them. They lay on the wings covered with their own blankets and tinkered away by the light of a hooded torch. Every evening all squadrons used to club together for one final, tremendous blitz on the enemy's landing-grounds. And so the miracle occurred. This mad chaotic reshuffle round Tobruk, this traffic jam the very sight of which sent cold shivers down the spines of desert veterans, was never attacked. And never in the whole sequence of desert campaigns has there been a better target.

Those mighty last-light raids, when the flamboyant desert sunset was speckled with the little black shapes of British planes, were immensely, illogically, encouraging. We saw the fighters fly by in shoals as we went across to the Intelligence tent to get the latest news that Sunday evening. And somehow they seemed much more real and significant than the news we got: the news that Knightsbridge was evacuated, that the Ninetieth Light had occupied El Adem, and the Axis forces were nestling closer round Tobruk; that orders had been sent to the infantry divisions in the Gazala Line to get out as best they might; that Army Headquarters was packing up its tents at Gambut and moving back to Maktila, which is in Egypt, east of Sidi Barrani.

But even allowing for the R.A.F., it was odd how undepressed we were personally in these critical hours. Part of the explanation, I suppose, was this. The tragedy did not hit us with the sudden unexpected impact of a newspaper headline seen at the breakfast table. We were experiencing it as a gradual process, we had seen all the stages of it and we could even follow it a little way into the future. It was spread thinly over all our waking hours, not concentrated into a breakfast bombshell, and we had time to build up a certain immunity. Moreover the men in the desert were not reading about it, they were doing something about it. Each man had an immediate, personal, private view of what was going on, a view bounded by the range of his own senses and his own duties. And that absorbed so much of his attention that the larger comprehensive view—the significance of the campaign as a whole—was edged into the background. We were bitterly disappointed that what had started so well was turning out so badly. But we cared nothing for the places we were losing—no more than a boxer cares for any particular part of the ring he fights in. We speculated in a joking, exaggerated way about the future, anticipating things so bad that there was no possible chance of their happening. We told ourselves that anyway all was not yet lost — worse had happened before. And all the time we went on steadily doing the ordinary routine things and snatching at any extra little pleasure we could get. In my diary for that period I find next to nothing about the gravity of the situation. But I note that I had a particularly good bathe at Sollum, that when we camped at Maktila I went for a walk in the sand-hills and found some sweet-smelling flowers like lilies, that we had time enough that evening to cook *rissoles* for dinner.

iii

The South African Division had got away from the Gazala Line. We knew that. It had streamed back along the coast road while there was still time and it had had a little bit of Stuka trouble, but nothing serious. But where was Fifty Div.? It had turned down south into the desert, and no one had heard from it since. For the moment it was "The Lost Division." It had to maintain wireless silence for fear of giving away its position. So Richard Macmillan of the British United Press and I set off to find it.

At Buqbuq, by a mere fluke, we got a clue to the point where it was supposed to be rallying. So we turned down inland over one of those freak slices of desert where the surface is strewn with great sharp-edged boulders. My whole immediate experience that morning was compounded of heat and dust and jolts. As often before I tried fantasy as an antidote. I made my mother put a basket over her arm and walk out of her front door in England and into the green, shade-dappled lane. Then I followed her every inch of the way into the village until she stepped into the cool, dark cavern of Mr. Masters' shop with its lovely smell of coffee and bacon and sawdust. Or I stood myself on top of the Kitzbuehler Horn and skied brilliantly all the way down to St. Johann through deep new powder-snow. But the sour smell of dust in my nostrils would not be exorcised.

We passed the ramparts of Graziani's old Sofafi camps and crossed over the new railway line beyond it. And then we began to find Fifty Div. They were airing their blankets in the sun and brewing tea and crouching in the shade of their vehicles like anyone else. When we asked them they said in slow, indifferent North Country voices, "Yes, we're Fifty Div.," as though nothing unusual or exciting had happened. But gradually we drew the story from them.

It was the story of an attack, rather than of an escape. Their divisional orders had explicitly referred to it as an attack. When General Ramsden, the divisional commander, had received the orders to evacuate, he had said, "This is a case of knocking them out of the way and nothing on earth is going to stop us." In the event two Italian divisions, the Brescia and the Pavia, had tried to stop them. And Fifty Div. had attacked and broken through. They regretted very sincerely that they had not been allowed to stay behind and finish the thing off.

Fifty Div. had been holding the middle of the Gazala Line, with the South Africans on their right and Rommel's gap through the mine field on their left. There was not room enough for both them and the South Africans to evacuate along the main road. So Fifty Div. made plans to come through the desert.

They spent most of Sunday doing their demolitions. Water, petrol and food were given complete priority. All other kit was destroyed. They spoiled things with petrol and pick-axes, because they dare not give the show away by using fire. Holes were punched in canned foods and clothing was torn to shreds. Explosives were used for booby-traps and all surplus ammunition was fired off at the enemy. By eight o'clock in the evening, which was zero hour, they were ready to go.

First two battalions went forward to establish bridgeheads and hold two gaps open through the Italian lines. Their orders were to maintain the gaps until either five o'clock Monday morning, or until all Fifty Div. had got through, whichever was the earlier. The left-hand gap was punched through the Italian positions at a place called Fachri and the right-hand gap at a spot without a name.

It was known as Map Reference B13. Then between the two gaps went sixteen Valentine tanks, charging flat out in order to frighten the Italians. Behind them came the rest of Fifty Div. motoring straight into action in troop carriers as hard as they could go. And from then on it was a fantastic personal-adventure story for every man in the division.

I heard one from a little British Major who stood in the dusty sunshine with a huge sun-hat on his head and the only shirt he had in the world flapping outside his shorts. He came up and said diffidently, "I know it's a lot to ask, but you don't happen to have a handkerchief you could lend or sell me? I seem to have lost mine in last night's to-do."

I gave him a spare one I had and asked, "Did you have much trouble?"

Apologetically he said, "Oh no, not really. What happened to me was all pretty tame. In fact for the first hour I hardly saw a thing."

"What happened then?"

"Well, you see, I rather thought I might be lost. So I got out to take a compass bearing and I found myself standing in a group of five Italians."

"What did you do?"

The Major coughed in some embarrassment. He said, "Well, it was all rather silly really, I suppose I lost my head. I stuck my finger into the ribs of the nearest one and told him to put his hands up. Such an absurd thing to do. I mean, they could hardly get away with that in Hollywood nowadays, could they?"

"Then what?"

"Well, all five put up their hands. I tried to think back to the adventure books I read as a boy, but I couldn't remember what was the next thing to do. It was all so ridiculously melodramatic. In the end I made them sit down and take their boots off. I've got the boots here if you want to see them. Rather poor quality stuff."

"What came next?"

"There was nothing else specially exciting. There were about a hundred different little fights going on all round, but it was pretty easy to avoid them. We kept getting into slit trenches and bomb craters. But we found a recovery truck so we towed that along with us and pulled ourselves out whenever we got stuck. Once we ran over an Italian anti-tank–gun position. The gunners made the most curious screaming noise as they ran away."

"Did you have no more trouble?"

"Not really. I was a little nervous once when we slid down a sand-bank straight into a German tank park. We couldn't go back up the sand-hill, so we went on. It was curious," said the Major, dropping for the moment his pose of understatement, "the way I felt that I was trying to make the car tip-toe as we went through. And I was quite unnecessarily holding my breath. But no one seemed to be awake. Except at the other side of the camp, that is. A gun crew there woke up and began shooting in pretty nearly every direction. Happily that didn't include the right one."

"Was that all?"

"Yes, really. Once a German supply column came right across our bows and we had to wait till it went away. Then we found another one going parallel with us, and somehow that was more alarming. But we shook it off, we got to the turning-point, down beyond Bir Hacheim, and by morning we were going east. There wasn't anything else. I'm afraid it was a relatively dull trip."

He may have been right. For almost everyone had fantastic adventures to relate. A South African Sergeant, after steering his way through trouble for three hours, had got out to fiddle with his windscreen. Ten yards away an Italian sentry bent forward to stare at him in the darkness and then started a challenge. He had got out the one word "*Chi*" when the Sergeant plugged him in the stomach with his revolver. And so one Bren-gun carrier and five trucks — perhaps twenty-five men in all — found themselves taking on the entire Headquarters of the Brescia Division.

Italians in pyjamas and even night-shirts were diving hysterically from tents into slit trenches, while British soldiers chased them blasphemously with tommy-guns. An Italian Lieutenant jumped on the running-board of a truck and with tears in his eyes begged the bewildered British driver to take him prisoner. The British began to take each other prisoner. One of them raised his hands and joined a file of Italians who were being rounded up, asking anxiously, "We are prisoners, aren't we?"

But it could not last. The Italians were getting to their guns and it was time for the British to be going. The Sergeant yelled to his men, "That's enough, you bastards." He heard a machine-gunner yelling back, "Just one more, Sergeant, let me get one more." Then they pulled clear of the blazing tents and trucks and petrol dumps and were engulfed again in the darkness of the night. They found they had eight prisoners. In the back of one truck sat Lieutenant Vincenzo Fato—though no one remembered capturing him. He said, "If you had only gone another hundred and fifty yards you'd have caught the General."

I met the machine-gunner who had asked permission to get just one more. He was a Liverpool dock worker with a crucifix and four cherubs tattooed on his hairy chest, a Union Jack tattooed on his shoulder-blades and a strange knitted thing on his head. I asked whether he had got his one more. He said off-handedly, "Oh yes, I riveted him, all right."

The whole Division had had adventures like this. Some men had got clean through Italian camps by answering challenges in bogus German. Others had been joined by a lorry load of Italians who had politely asked whether they could come too. No one ever expected to see anything more of the sixteen tanks which had led the original charge into the Italians—it was assumed they would have to be abandoned and blown up. Yet they all reached safety after a journey that was a technical impossibility.

Very genuinely, without any after-the-event heroics, most of these men regretted that their operation had not been a purely offensive one. For they were convinced that they could have annihilated these two Italian Divisions. It seemed tragic that they had not been allowed to try it much earlier in the campaign. Even now they might have done so much damage to Rommel's supply lines that the whole course of the battle could have been changed. But they had to carry out their orders.

One might say that that night's fighting was the triumph of morale. But morale is an awkward word to apply to the British: for they are not a temperamental people and their morale varies within extremely narrow limits. It was rather the triumph of ordinary high spirits and of an unformulated superiority complex vis-à-vis the Italians. The exploits achieved that night were of the sort that appeal most strongly to the British who, if they are not temperamental, are nevertheless incurably romantic. And the story came as a very helpful tonic in a very dark hour.

CHAPTER 24

Tragedy at Tobruk

THE SENTRY shouted after us.

"Hey . . ." he said. "D'you mind telling me where you're going?"

"Tobruk."

"Oh. . . . Well, you'd better be careful."

"Why?"

"Well, the jerries have cut the road. About ten minutes ago."

"Oh. Well, in that case how are we supposed to get to Tobruk?"

The sentry pushed up his tin hat to scratch his head. "Frankly," he said, "I don't see how you can."

We peered up the empty black stretch of tarmac to where the horizon quivered like a jelly in the heat, but we could see nothing.

"Armoured cars, they was," added the sentry. "Last lot of people that come along this road come in a 'ell of a 'urry." He strolled back to a large bit of wood on which he was painting a notice about this being the front line.

So now we knew for certain. This was the answer to the question the whole desert had been debating furiously for the past three days. We were, after all, going to try and hold Tobruk. We had *got* to try and hold Tobruk now for it lay there isolated while Rommel nipped off the defended boxes which surrounded it like claws protruding from the paw of an animal. We had been arguing the matter all ways ever since it became obvious that we must retreat. There were those who said that the fortress-area theory was finally exploded, that only a very special combination of circumstances had permitted Tobruk to hold out the previous summer. There were those who said that Tobruk last summer had proved the truth of the fortress-area theory, that it had been the key to our success in Crusader. We did not know which argument Auchinleck supported. Nothing, naturally, had been announced or even hinted. At all costs the enemy must not know our intentions in this matter. Even the men who might or might not have to defend it could not know. But now they knew. Authority was on the side of the fortress area. Tobruk was going to be held.

But it is my personal conviction — though I have no proof of this — that General Auchinleck was not in favour of holding Tobruk. He was not a believer in fortress areas. It was extremely significant that five months previously he had abandoned the plan for the defence of Egypt based on Mersa Matruh, and had secretly started to fortify a line at Alamein. He knew that sentimentally and strategically it was highly *desirable* to hold Tobruk. But militarily, I believe, he did not think it *possible*.

Yet he tried to do it. Certainly circumstances did not force his hand, for there was plenty of time to evacuate the place. So, if it is true that his own judgement was opposed to defending it, then it can only have been on specific orders from the highest quarters in London that he finally acted.

For quickly and deliberately, after June 13, he amputated a portion of the Eighth Army and immured it in Tobruk. He could spare it about eighty field-guns to cover the full length of the thirty-mile perimeter, and a small quota of anti-tank guns. Rather over fifty tanks were allotted, nearly all of them British Valentines with the two-pounder gun. The two brigades of the Second South African Division were already in Tobruk, and as the rest of the army withdrew through the place, a Guards Brigade, the Eleventh Indian Brigade and another South African Brigade were detached to stay behind and defend it. There were some 28,000 men there, about 15,000 of them fighting troops. The fortress was put under the command of General Klopper, a plump, sensible Afrikaner whom I had known the previous winter as General de Villiers' chief staff officer at the attack on Bardia. That was his previous experience of fortress areas — he had had ocular demonstration that they could be taken by a couple of brigades in a couple of days. It cannot have been very encouraging.

On one thing Auchinleck was determined: never again would the navy be called on to supply Tobruk. So the greater portion of the huge food and petrol dump under the cliff at El Duda was moved there. The defenders were given enough to last them for three months. But I am convinced Auchinleck never for one moment contemplated that they would have to hold out for three months. The idea was that Tobruk should engage the attention of the enemy for, perhaps, ten days while the British armoured forces were being reorganized and refitted in Egypt. Then would come the big counterattack and Tobruk would again play its vital part. It was essentially the modified British version of the fortress-area theory — the fortress plus a mobile force operating outside.

Now it was Rommel's move. He could either move at once, or make a pause. He could either attack Tobruk, or Egypt. We discussed endlessly the possible combinations of these parallel alternatives, but there was not really very much doubt. He would attack Tobruk, and attack it quickly. It was true that he could not have a great many tanks, and that those he did have must be desperately in need of repairs; his *Panzerdivisions* and the Ninetieth Light had been in unceasing action for three weeks and their men must be very near exhaustion; it was certain that Fifty Div.'s brilliant night raid through the Brescia and Pavia Divisions must have dislocated the Axis supply lines for at least a day. But we had now fought Rommel so often in such similar circumstances that we almost instinctively appreciated his intentions and his mental processes. And most of us were sure that he would call on his troops for that last extra ounce of energy which men can get not only out of themselves, but out of their machines, when they strike a winning vein. With his fine sense of timing, he would surely try for a quick attack. And he was certain to choose Tobruk. For not only did it represent the thing he most hated — a threat to his flank — but it stood there almost as a symbolic challenge to his sense of invincibility.

So he brought up his Italian infantry and put them round the perimeter and his big guns began a barrage of rising fury. This time he knew the place, and he had a plan for its assault already in his pocket—the plan he had been about to use on his fiftieth birthday last November. Inside Tobruk the new defenders were digging out the loose sand that had sifted into the old gun sites and tank traps and slit trenches. The elaborate supply system of alternative communications and supply routes, the arrangements for mutual reinforcement in depth, had fallen in pieces. The original Australian and Polish and British defenders were a thousand miles away. The new defenders barely knew who was on their right hand and on their left hand, and they had no time to become familiar with the terrain or practice any plan of defence. All that could be produced was a rigid, evenly spaced defence ring with a counterattacking force of infantry and tanks waiting in the middle.

So for three days, in the thick brazen heat, the desert lay taut with expectancy. We did everything with a strange sense of temporariness, a knowledge that the Eighth Army had come to rest in an attitude it could not possibly sustain. In a preoccupied way we bathed at our seaside camp and rinsed our sweat-caked clothes in the salt water and dried them on the rocks. We watched the first American Liberators fly by out to sea and saw a great convoy returning after a vain attempt to reach Malta. But the waiting became intolerable. And Richard Macmillan and I went back into Libya, deep down inland, trying to find the mobile tank force which we knew must be there.

They were camped in last winter's battle-field, where myriad ruts had become half-silted up with rose-red sand and innumerable petrol tins had rusted to the colour of the desert. It was like going through some queer museum. All the debris of the previous campaign, preserved by the dryness of the climate, was lying just where it had been left. Again and again our glasses showed us the skyline punctuated with unmistakably German vehicles, but always when we got to them they were old, abandoned relics.

There was a sense of overwhelming loneliness about the little makeshift crosses at the heads of the six-months-old graves.

The British tanks were strewn across the desert — not very many of them, it is true, but not completely negligible as a force. They had come here from Tobruk, fighting a neat, compact, expert tank battle at Sidi Rezegh on the way — a mature, adult tank battle which the men who had been there appraised with an almost æsthetic pleasure, as they might have judged a work of art. Then, so tired that quite literally and honestly they could not stand on their feet, they had come down by night to this remote corner of the desert. Now the tanks had had a full day's maintenance and the men had been given rest and hot meals and a change of clothing. And with the extraordinary resilience of fit men and well-made machines they were now ready to fight again.

Macmillan and I thought we would go with them when they counterattacked towards Tobruk. But then there happened to us the worst thing that can happen in the desert. The radiator of our car began to leak. We plugged it with candle grease and chewing-gum but we could not mend it. It cost us every drop of water we had, and in the end we simply had to go. We could not ask for the water of a fighting unit. So we got someone to tow us back to the coast, and on the way we saw nothing whatever because we were travelling in a private artificial dust-storm created by the wheels of the truck which was towing us.

Next morning — Saturday June 20 — we heard that the Axis assault on Tobruk had begun. The same evening I took a walk along the shore and met a friend who told me that the German tanks were well inside the perimeter defences. After breakfast next morning it was all over.

ii

The fall of Tobruk is an abstruse subject. I do not mean that there is any great mystery about it, or any sensational secret. I believe that the known facts satisfactorily explain what happened. But exactly how or in what order those facts occurred it is hard to say. The available data are so very small. General Klopper gave a bald play-by-play account over the radio as the battle proceeded. And of the few hundred men who escaped from the place after it had been captured, none could offer an authoritative version of the fighting as a whole. Each one knew just exactly what he himself had experienced and very little more. After Tobruk fell, I went to the transit camp at Mersa Matruh and met these refugees as they arrived. And on the basis of their stories I finally pieced together my account of what happened.

The attack started before dawn on Saturday. It came against a very little sector, just a few hundred yards wide, on the south-east perimeter. It was exactly the sector where Rommel had planned to attack the previous autumn, the weakest sector, easily the most difficult to defend. Into it had been put an Indian Brigade—Mahrattas in the centre, Camerons on one side, and Ghurkas on the other. And the full, total weight of Rommel's strength was flung against the Mahrattas.

First, two groups of German lorried infantry established themselves at two points opposite the Mahrattas and began to make gaps for the tanks through the mine fields and the wire. Heavy artillery laid down a box barrage round them to protect them, and as the sun rose a smoke-screen was added. Stukas came over and bombed the mine fields to blaze a safe path and the tanks and lorries came in afterwards where the bombs had set off the mines. Probably many of the mines were faulty, for they had been buried there a good year and their contacts may have rusted.

As soon as it was light enough to read, the Germans showered down pamphlets on the Indians in their own tongue—Rommel knew exactly who was opposite him there. The pamphlets were stamped with a big circle enclosing a drawing of a spinning-wheel—the symbol of Gandhi's non-violence creed. On the back was a short text in Urdu or Hindu. And at the bottom was a legend in Italian and German saying "This paper is a safe-conduct for Indian officers and men."

With the light came a tremendous air blitz all round the perimeter and down on the harbour. Every plane Rommel could muster was there, seeking to paralyze all movement and activity in the fortress. Italian Savoias in groups of twenty ventured down lower than they had dared to fly for years and rained their bombs on the defences. They came without escort, for there could be no danger from British fighters. All the R.A.F.'s air fields were now too far away.

Under cover of this, the gaps in the perimeter were made and widened and forty tanks came through. The Mahrattas were mown down under the pounding weight of the German armour. Remember, they were one battalion. Against them came part of the Ninetieth Light Division, the Fifteenth *Panzerdivision,* the Italian Ariete Armoured Division and the Trieste Motorized Division. The enemy had complete domination of the air and everything was concentrated on this one little sector. Elsewhere the defenders of the perimeter saw the smoke and heard the noise. But they themselves were being bombed and shelled and could not move. There had been no time to organize the supple defence system of last summer. The perimeter was punctured. And at ten o'clock Klopper reported briefly that some forty or fifty enemy tanks were operating inside it.

The gaps were widened and the Mahrattas completely overrun. The Italian tanks were held up at one point and Rommel offered them the choice of an easier passage or a Stuka raid. They chose the Stuka raid and caught up with the Germans. Then the British tanks moved forward to counterattack. They advanced eastwards from the T-shaped cross-roads in the middle of Tobruk and engaged the Germans. Everyone who saw them said they fought with conspicuous gallantry. They always did. But bravery alone was not enough. It had to be disciplined and well-directed bravery, and it was sad to hear that once again British tanks had been lured forward and stood up against the 88-millimetre anti-tank guns and massacred.

It was hopeless then. Klopper, who had been forced to move his Headquarters, came on the air again at lunchtime and announced that all the British tanks, without exception, had been wiped out and the enemy were rallying round the T-shaped cross-roads, right in the heart of Tobruk. The Coldstream Guards tried to make a counterattack there, but they knew it was useless when they saw what happened to the tanks. They watched their Brigade Headquarters being overrun almost beside them. And then the Germans rushed up their mobile artillery and the Coldstreams had to retire.

At that point everything broke down. The progress of events is not describable in military terms. The Germans split into two parties at the cross-roads and rolled over Tobruk like a steam-roller. The right-hand party went down to the port and the left-hand party made for Divisional Headquarters farther west.

Down by the harbour naval ratings and dock-side workers were frantically destroying things. They had blown up most of Navy House and the jetties and the fresh-water installations. They were not very expert at it and they nearly blew themselves up when they demolished the wireless station. Then an enemy mobile gun appeared at the top of the cliff across the harbour and there was a rush for the boats. A few minutes later German tanks came winding down the road and there took place one of the most unorthodox battles on record. A tank opened fire and sank a small tug in the harbour. The men in the tug scrambled aboard a near-by minesweeper, and as they did so, they saw a Bofors light ack-ack gun swing down its barrel and start firing at the tank. And then the tank lurched suddenly from the road and toppled into the sea.

All the seaworthy ships in the harbour began to cast off. As the last one moved away, men in khaki came racing along the quayside. Someone shouted, "Wait a minute, here's some more passengers." But before he had finished speaking, the men on shore opened up with tommy-guns. They were German infantry. And as the ships sailed out with bullets rattling on their hulls, the men aboard them saw German tanks nosing through the ruins of the San Marco water tower, right beyond the town.

Meantime General Klopper's Headquarters was being chased from place to place. There was no organized defence any more.

Individual units began to retire west, fighting as they went. Spasmodically demolitions were taking place, but the man responsible for giving the order for general demolitions was captured before he gave it. Most of the petrol was destroyed and many vehicles — too many, probably, for thousands more could at least have tried to escape in their own trucks. But huge dumps of ammunition and food — pyramids of packing cases containing the best rations ever eaten in the desert — were left. Workshops and guns and spare parts went to swell the booty. It was an immensely valuable prize.

By sundown on Saturday matters were in shapeless confusion. General Klopper asked Auchinleck for permission to fight his way out of Tobruk and it was given, but there was never any means to transmit the order to the fighting units. Already infantry and armoured cars were fanning out behind the German tanks inside the perimeter, mopping up the defensive positions as they came. All through the night the place was a turmoil of gunfire and explosions and chaotic movement and mad destruction. When the sun rose next morning it was nearly all over. At seven o'clock General Klopper wirelessed that he was signing off for good. A few minutes later his Headquarters was overrun and he was taken prisoner.

There was no organized surrender. Some of the South African units seem to have received an order to lay down their arms, but for the most part no such order could have been transmitted. The confusion had been too great. All through Sunday, beneath the pall of black-grey smoke shot with flame that hung torpid above Tobruk, individual units were fighting to the death or fighting their way out. But through most of the fortress, Italian infantry from the Trieste, Brescia and Pavia Divisions were marshalling the prisoners and checking the booty. Rommel had left the Italians in charge of this prize where no German had previously set foot except as a prisoner. Already he had plucked his tanks from the smoking ruins of the place and was swinging them across towards the Egyptian frontier.

iii

I think that morning, when we learned of the fall of Tobruk, was the bitterest moment I have known in the desert. At first it was a purely sentimental bitterness — a ridiculous, unwarrantable regret for a ruined, stinking, fly-blown town which had nevertheless come to mean so much to us. But then that was overtaken by a more immediate, human bitterness — a sick misery at this futile loss of so many men and so much matériel, at this gratuitous additional catastrophe in a campaign that was already going badly.

This time Auchinleck knew quite certainly what he ought to do. The logic of the situation was clear now. He came up to the desert himself and took over command. For the second time — but this time secretly — he removed his Army Commander in the middle of a campaign. Nominally still under Ritchie, but actually directly under Auchinleck, the fragments of the Eighth Army began to fold back into Egypt. A thin rear-guard screen only was left at Halfaya and Sollum and down the frontier between the gaps in the mine fields. Its orders were to retire as fast as Rommel advanced, no faster, no slower. And the rest of the army came back towards El Alamein in another horrifying traffic jam.

Tedder and Coningham searched the Middle East for new and old planes to put into the air. Everything that could possibly fly was sent out to help protect this retreat. A new, experimental "leap-frogging" technique made it possible for squadrons to move from air field to air field without ever ceasing to operate. The fighters had continued using Gambut until the enemy were within shelling distance of their landing-grounds. The Bostons had actually gone out bombing from an air field which was captured before they returned, and they had to fly on to another one. All the way back through Egypt this was kept up, often well beyond the margin of safety. And again that hideous traffic jam resolved itself into order without a single serious attack from the Luftwaffe.

Rommel gave his *Panzers* three days' rest and then brought his army on into Egypt. It was a tired, worn army now, nearly exhausted after a month of furious fighting. But it was a winning army, and that knowledge kept it going. Its trucks were filled with the loot of Tobruk, and only a retreating, broken enemy separated it from Alexandria. Rommel always drove his men to the limits of endurance and they cursed him for it. But they respected him too, and they obeyed him wearily but willingly when he led them into Egypt, buoyed up with the promise of glittering conquest.

CHAPTER 25

The Flap

So THROUGH the sullen indifferent desert, sodden with heat and light, we retreated. The road to Alexandria was one long tunnel of dust, choked with an endless traffic jam. Back and back went the Headquarters camps and the workshops and the field-hospitals and the fighter squadrons, leap-frogging neatly over one another. Once more the Bedouins folded their patched black tents and trekked east to the edge of the Delta, where they would wait fretting and miserable until they could return to the limitless freedom of their desert. And theirs seemed the only real human tragedy in it all. For the desert with its clean cathartic emptiness and thick smothering sunshine was no fit setting for tragedy.

Desperately now Auchinleck needed time: time to unload the eighteen ships that were already sailing up the Red Sea with reinforcements, time to bring the fresh Australian and New Zealand Divisions down from Palestine, time to evolve a deeper defence plan in case the desert could not be held. Desperately he needed time, but he could not afford to pay for it. He dared not risk a major battle anywhere. So he switched the Eighth Army over to a subtle, expert technique.

At every point he softened and loosened and dissolved his forces. He left no rigid surfaces anywhere. Deliberately he created confusion and disorder. The two hard Axis columns came prodding ahead into Egypt, jabbing constantly into an amorphous mass that always gave way before them but closed back round the sides of them, worrying and nagging without ceasing. Everything was very secret and very mobile and apparently very chaotic. The whole army was reduced to the status of Jock Columns. New, vague units called "battle groups" were sent out — units whose very high fire power was their only common characteristic. Fragments of the army were split off to fight brisk little skirmishes down in stretches of virgin desert never yet scarred by battle, and were then reabsorbed in the parent body. In vain Rommel sought a decisive engagement to put a stop to this shadow-boxing.

Quite deliberately Auchinleck jettisoned Mersa Matruh. That came as a bad shock to many, for the place had for two years been known as the bastion of Egypt, the kingpin of the whole defensive system. But Tobruk had removed from Auchinleck's mind any lingering faith in the fortress-area theory. He was planning to hold, not the line farthest from the Delta, but the most holdable line. So Mersa Matruh went, and newspaper readers in England accepted with understandable but unjustified skepticism the explanation given afterwards that this was "according to plan." The evacuation of it was not, as a matter of fact, completely successful. As though by some projection into the future of the influence of the old, abandoned plan, the troops there held on too long. The Germans saw and heard the first demolition explosions and they attacked immediately. But in the end not much was lost and the Eighth Army went on oozing slowly backwards, spitting and clawing like an angry cat as it went.

So Auchinleck kept his army and stole some of the time he so urgently needed. But things were very, very desperate during those last days of June. As matters then stood, the chances were that Britain would lose Egypt. An attempt to stem the Axis army would be made at El Alamein, where the British had been secretly digging and wiring some sort of defensive line. But if that failed the South Africans were to fight a rear-guard action back through Alexandria. Cairo G.H.Q. was organizing its own move to Gaza in Palestine. A force called "Delta Force" was being formed with Headquarters in various Egyptian provincial towns and plans to hold the line of the Nile and certain canals. Auchinleck issued a "backs-to-the-wall" order of the day. Demolitions on a tremendous scale were being prepared. Apart from the actual fighting troops, the Eighth Army consisted largely of a milling traffic jam covering hundreds of square miles of desert west and south-west of Alexandria. I used to sit at my typewriter trying desperately to write something that would be neither too pessimistic nor too optimistic, and would at the same time get past the censor.

On came the Axis army, growing feebler in strength but stronger in triumph and anticipation. Mussolini arrived in Africa with uniforms, flags, bands and a white charger ready for entry into the cities of Egypt. He brought his flashiest regiments, the Novara Lancers and the Sardinian Grenadiers, with fragile parade tanks that broke down hopelessly in the desert but would probably have negotiated the streets of Cairo. The German and Italian radios began to announce high-sounding proclamations promising complete independence to the Egyptian people. Medals were struck and occupation money prepared. Experts worked on a scheme for civil administration. The German radio made dates for the Afrikakorps with the ladies of Cairo and Alexandria. At night in their messes, while they ate British food taken in Tobruk, weary German officers discussed the baths and clean sheets to come. The Italians wrote home and said they could already see the towers of Alexandria.

It looked a practical certainty for Rommel. But day by day, hour by hour, two sets of forces were at work with cumulative strength. It was hard to calculate mathematically the exact influence of these forces, but it was certain that both were working against Rommel. One set was acting as a brake on his army, holding it back, dulling its impetus, draining its strength. The other set was tending to endow the Eighth Army with fresh power and order and energy.

The influences working against Rommel were these: his men were growing more tired every hour. Already the Ninetieth Light, who had fought magnificently, were rocking on their feet with weariness. Every day a few German tanks were being lost, and no new ones were coming up. British bombers scored annihilating hits on a tank recovery workshop. Supply lines were stretching and stretching. Transport was wearing out. The wells of Egypt had been salted or oiled or blown up, and every drop of water must come by land. The Luftwaffe had lagged dangerously behind in the advance, and when it had made a supreme effort to get ahead, it had come too fast, without proper protection, and the R.A.F. had made mincemeat of its planes on the ground. The British had put every plane they could in the air, and were concentrating fiercely on the fragile, elongated Axis supply routes. British mobile columns were hitting hard at weak spots, and in particular a force which drove westwards south of the eastward-moving Germans was wreaking great havoc.

All those things were holding Rommel back. These things were renewing the British strength: the convoy of eighteen ships had reached Suez and was being frantically unloaded. Every gun and tank as it was unpacked was rushed straight across to the front. Since every man possible was needed for fighting, girl A.T.S.'s drove new trucks for fourteen hours a day from the ports to Cairo and handed them over to the army drivers. The New Zealanders, with the emblems on their trucks painted out and their distinctive hats packed away for the sake of secrecy, came racing down from Palestine and up to the desert. They first went into action near Mersa Matruh — fresh, vigorous troops without the memory of hundreds of miles of retreating immediately behind them — and when they got surrounded, Maoris went in with bayonets at night to chop a way out for them. The Australian Ninth Division, too, was on its way to the front. With every day's retreating, the base workshops and the reinforcement dumps were nearer and the army was falling back onto its own strength. The R.A.F. was retiring onto its own well-equipped air fields and it was working without ceasing. Kittyhawks went out bombing, fighting and escorting all in one operation. Tedder and Coningham made a major effort which many people believed was the decisive element in the situation.

So the balance was swinging back to level. Rommel began to realize just how seriously time was against him. He must get

Alexandria before the balance did swing back to level, or he would have to give up for the time being and prepare a whole fresh campaign.

The crisis came at the very beginning of July when the Axis forces, now moving very slowly, came butting against the Alamein Line. Alamein is another placeless name, a spot on the coast where there is a barely justifiable station on the railway. But here the desert narrows down to a forty-mile bottleneck, bounded on the north by the sea and on the south by a low-lying, marshy, impassable basin called the Qattara Depression. Auchinleck had put a defended box on the coast and another down inland and connected them with a line of dug defences and gun positions.

The momentum of Rommel's forces carried them right past the two boxes and into this line. The line was weak, but it was elastic and it was tethered at both ends by the two fixed boxes. It gave, but it did not break. And finally it snapped back into place and the German spear-head recoiled. Four times this happened, on the first four mornings of July. The elastic was growing very weak, but each time it had just enough strength to hold, and just enough resilience to straighten out again. Each morning the German thrust was perceptibly feebler. And on the fifth morning there came no thrust at all.

There was the turning of the tide. In those four mornings the crisis had come and gone. Imperceptibly, but with surprising suddenness, that double set of influences had swung the delicately poised balance back to level and then tipped it gently down on the British side. On that fifth morning of July the Eighth Army woke with an overpowering intuition that it was no longer a beaten army. There was a mood, an almost palpable atmosphere, of assurance and renewed confidence, a feeling that things were in hand. It had been touch and go, but now the worst was over.

There had been a score of little signs that may have built up this mood. The German prisoners taken were reeling with fatigue, and many of them either became hysterical or fell straight asleep. Groups of trucks and even tanks were found abandoned for lack of petrol. Six hundred men of the Ninetieth Light, a division with a superb record, surrendered under shell-fire. A South African squadron had brought men cheering from their trenches by shooting down fourteen out of fifteen Stukas—it was maliciously pleasant to picture that one lonely pilot returning to his base and going into his mess for his solitary lunch. For three days the British communiqués had made no mention of retreating. The German press had stopped talking about Egypt and had started talking about the annihilation of the Eighth Army. The Italian radio was complaining that Auchinleck had been heavily reinforced.

All these and many other things may have contributed to that sudden new atmosphere that pervaded the desert. But I think they were really parallel symptoms rather than causes. It was rather a direct sensing of the condition of things—as a dog will go out of a house and sniff to get the feeling of the day as a whole—that told the Eighth Army then that it was no longer beaten.

CHAPTER 26

Escape from the Desert

THROUGH July the Alamein Front thickened and hardened and formed a crust, and as it did so the feeling of tension and emergency died. Australians, South Africans, Indians, New Zealanders and British North Countrymen were holding the line, with the British tank forces mobile in the background. They formed something firmer, more static, more thickly populated with men and mines and guns than the desert had ever seen before. But even so it was not a continuous system of trenches with men defending every yard. You must think of it as a great spray of camps branching and subdividing out like a family tree from the parent Headquarters camp down to the frontmost platoons. The gaps in between them were covered with mine fields and artillery fire. And across a few narrow miles of no-man's-land the Axis forces were arrayed in an exactly complementary pattern.

For us it was a new sort of war reporting. We could, if we wished, spend the night in Alexandria, make a day trip to the firing line, and return to our hotel for a comfortable bed. We did not often do so, but it was possible. Mostly we lived in a little unofficial camping ground we had chosen at the eighty-sixth–kilometre stone out from Alexandria, where a belt of dazzling white dunes divided the road from the sea. From there we would set out each morning to get the information we needed. We could drive forward along the bare, stony Ruweisat Ridge which was the backbone of the Alamein Line. It pierced the front like an arrow set in a bow and the dust hung over it motionless in the heavy air all day long, for the traffic on it was ceaseless. Or we might go down to the

New Zealanders across a bare, flat, pink wilderness which was covered with myriads of white snail shells. Or we could drive a few miles farther ahead to Alamein itself.

Alamein was a little rocky rise which carried the main road on its back. Always it was shimmering in the heat and always it was shrouded in dust. There were two sets of subterranean catacombs there where various Headquarters worked, and a couple of derelict shacks. Otherwise nothing at all. But gradually, by virtue of its importance and the world renown of its lovely name, Alamein achieved the status and dignity of a place. Strangers approached it almost with awe, as holy ground where great deeds had been done. I had never even noticed it before, though I had driven along that road many times. But soon it became as definite and familiar to me as Tobruk or Mersa Matruh.

The main road was incessantly busy, for never before had the army been so telescoped. There were ack-ack guns all the way along which could put up an arch of fire over miles of traffic if low-flying enemy fighters came. Sometimes mobile canteens would open for business on the roadside. All the way along, in the narrow trough of salt marsh between the road and the sand dunes, there were Red Cross camps and workshops and prisoners' camps and here and there a few bedraggled fig trees. For an offhand attempt had once been made to cultivate this part, and even now odd Bedouins would appear and try to sell undersized eggs to the passing trucks.

However far afield we went, we always tried desperately to be back well before sunset. For then we could plunge our dust-caked limbs into the cleanness and the coolness and the heavenly freshness of the turquoise sea. The sheer physical pleasure of those baths passes all description. In utter relief and abandonment we would splash and run and leap about like naked children. Then, feeling gloriously renewed, we would stroll back to cook our supper and type our stories and sit on our beds talking through the cool evening while the dunes round us glowed whitely in the light of a mighty moon.

Behind the crust of the Alamein Line there was, in these choking days of July, a feeling of freshness and renewal and rebirth. It was very perceptibly the end of one period and the beginning of another. A new Eighth Army was rising Phoenix-like from the ashes of the old — and not only a new army, but a better one. And suddenly I saw the sense in this idiotic pendulum business, the pattern and design behind it all. For two years in this desert the British army had been going to school.

The British — and surely it is to their credit — are not natural soldiers. Before the war started, they had studied the arts of peace, as civilized men must do, and they had tried to cultivate their garden peaceably. But they failed to put a fence about it and they trusted their untrustworthy neighbours. And when the moment came for them to forge their ploughshares into swords, they did not know how to use them. So — without even realizing that they were doing so — they sent their army to school in this great North African desert where there was nothing to get spoiled and where it was relatively safe to make mistakes. Of course the whole army could not be sent, but that was not necessary. Rather Britain used the desert as Germany used Spain: to try out and perfect her war matériel and her technical services, to study tactics and methods of fighting with modern weapons, to train men. And now for two years British armies had been at school here, learning modern warfare by trial and error, by watching the enemy, by drawing conclusions and making experiments.

Wavell's army had been a puny little baby of an army. But it was pitted against a nation even less naturally warlike than the British and it won through by bluff and guts and blissful ignorance of its own feebleness. A year later Auchinleck sent an army into the field which was so much an improvement on Wavell's that we did not immediately see that it was still only an awkward, gangling boy. It went into battle against an army that had been born almost full-grown, whose men were natural soldiers already seasoned in other campaigns. By luck and by guts and by the strategical accident of Tobruk, Auchinleck's army won. But it was not good enough to

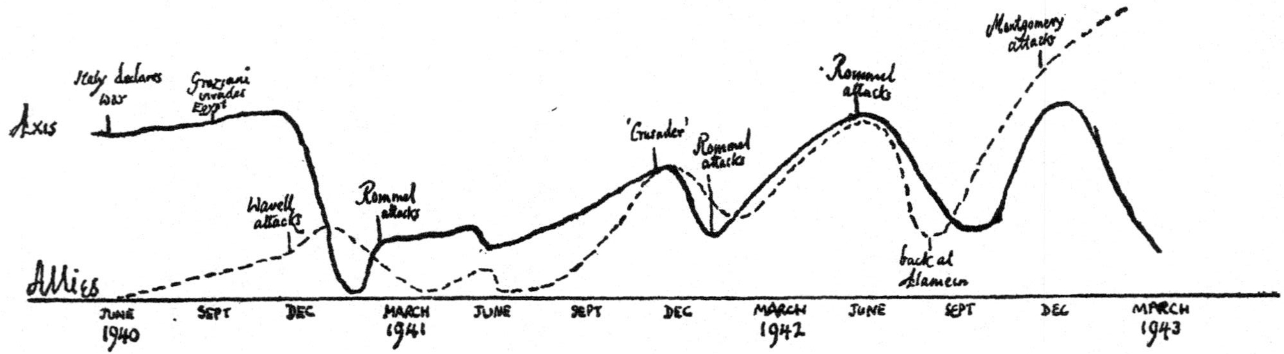

Comparative graph of Allied and Axis strengths in North Africa.

graduate right out of the desert and Rommel came back to give the next lesson. So in the summer Auchinleck had produced another army that had looked so fine and big and strong that we had been fooled into thinking it was truly adult. But then it had shown it was still only adolescent. It had almost the physical stature of an adult, but it could not yet behave like one. And once more it lost the greater part of its old equipment in defeat and was ready to start again with newer and better weapons.

This time, it seemed, the army should be really fully grown. Surely it had no more wild oats to sow. Churchill had been in Washington when Tobruk fell and there and then he had arranged for the Eighth Army to get American Sherman tanks, which were welded where the Grants were riveted and which had the great 75-millimetre gun in the turret with a traverse of 360 degrees. Bomber and fighter squadrons of the United States Army Air Force were on their way to operate in the desert. Plenty of the new six-pounder anti-tank guns were coming from England, and surely to God we had learned to use them by now. In every way weapons and equipment would be better. It looked as though it should be a good army even by German standards. It looked very much as though this time Rommel had taught us all he knew.

Seen in this light, the sequence of absurdly see-sawing campaigns in a desert which neither side wanted ceased to be such a ridiculous waste of men and machines and time. The British army had to grow up and learn its lessons somewhere, and where better than here? For here mistakes could be made and defeats accepted without affecting the main issue decisively as long as the Nile and Suez were not involved. And I am convinced that the British army could never have developed so swiftly and efficiently on the basis of pure theory. The experience gained in the desert, the anatomical lessons learned through military vivisection on this perfect operating table, were beyond all price.

The basic fibre of the army too — the men themselves — had improved incalculably in these campaigns. I realized this one day when I went to visit the Ninth Australian Division, the original

Rats of Tobruk, who were living and fighting along the coast beyond Alamein.

After the first week in July, Auchinleck had begun to take the initiative in the desert, and he had sent in the Australians to push out a five-mile salient along the coast. They had got it without very heavy fighting, and now they were defending it against savage German counterattacks. The bit of land they held was five miles long but very narrow, and it was composed of layers running east and west: first a strip of seashore, then a strip of white sand dunes, then a slice of bluey-purple salt lagoons with white sparkling crust at their edges, then the main road running along a little ridge, then the railway line. Their farthest point west was a tiny railway station called the Hill of Jesus, and the shape of the front as a whole was now like a clenched left fist with the thumb sticking out forwards.

I went along there by the coast and there seemed to be all the shelling and bombing in the world going on. The Australians were fighting off up to five attacks a day, and I felt curiously ashamed at paying just an hour's visit to them while they had to live there day and night. But for an hour I sat on the white sand-hills and talked to them and I thought I had never in my life seen men so changed.

They had come to the Middle East raw and rough — physically superb but almost totally lacking in discipline and seasoning. They had been like schoolboys with the powers and physique of men. They tended to be boastful and aggressive and quick to pick a quarrel. I think they felt they were regarded as rude, untutored colonials, and they were ready to resent the slightest innuendo. But now at Alamein I found them much quieter to talk to and much more assured in their friendliness. And as fighters they were far more deadly. Their experience had covered everything and they knew now exactly what to fear and what not to fear. They had a steadiness and a controlled ferocity in defence that they never used to have. They had become thoroughly and expertly seasoned. As for morale — well, that was a question which simply did not arise. They had something much deeper and stronger and less showy than morale: some sort of self-confidence and serenity of spirit that they would probably never lose. They still had their old buoyancy and exuberance. But they had gained immeasurably in character. And physically they were stupendous. Not more than one in five of them wore a shirt, and I should never have believed that white men's bodies could have gone that colour. It was a sort of deep, warm, glowing brown with undertones of ruddy gold, and their Italian prisoners looked inexpressibly anæmic and scruffy beside them.

So through July we watched the Alamein Front become established and strong. Rommel was flying fresh German infantry across from Crete and armoured lighters were bringing him new tanks and guns along the Egyptian Coast. Three times Auchinleck tried to pierce the German Line in the centre, on the off chance of a quick victory before the enemy grew in strength. But things never went quite right and he had to be content with only local successes.

In August there happened something that was almost melodramatic in its tragedy. General "Strafer" Gott, that grand old desert fighter, was given command of the Eighth Army and he was instructed to come back to Cairo to be, as it were, inducted into his new office. He caught the ordinary mail plane — a lumbering old Bombay transport machine which used to ply to and fro from Cairo every day. And that morning of all mornings a Messerschmitt with long-range petrol tanks flew in from the sea to attack the air field.

The German pilot saw the Bombay — a sitting target. Within a few seconds it was afire and riddled with bullets. The pilot nearly got it safely down to earth. But Gott was dead, shot through the heart.

As Jock Campbell had died, so Gott had died through a stupid, futile accident far from the front line. There were those who argued angrily that he ought to have been given a proper plane and a fighter escort. But the Bombay had always been safe before — it was a thousand-to-one chance, and the German pilot flew off home without an inkling of the blow he had struck to the Eighth Army. Gott had understood the desert so intimately, he had been so loved and so trusted by everyone. The rest of the world knew little about him, for until a few weeks ago his name had not been on the list of mentionable Generals. But in the desert he was almost worshipped. He was a man whom Britain could ill afford to lose.

ii

And then quite suddenly one morning I was utterly sick of it all. I found myself hating the desert with a neurotic, tormenting hatred. Intellectually I could work out what was behind this pendulum fighting. But immediately and emotionally I was obsessed by the waste of tears and blood and sweat that had been spent here. There had been so much anguish and labour and effort and now there was nothing, less than nothing, to show for it. Men can fight with passion when they are fighting directly for their families and their homes. But in this remote, detached desert which nobody wanted, it was impossible to keep the passion always aflame. Mine had suddenly turned sour on me. In contemporary jargon, "I had had the desert." I found I could no longer even write about it. I had lost entirely my sense of judgement, I could not tell what was interesting and what was not interesting. I had no idea how much the people of England knew or cared about it. In five years I had scarcely spent more than a week-end in England and I felt utterly remote from it. They were my people, but since I had last seen them they had passed through tremendous experiences which I had not shared, experiences so unprecedented that I could not gauge what the English reaction would be. In the past two years I had been watching the war from such close quarters that I had lost sight of what it was all about. I was stale as last week's loaf.

I found that Alan Moorehead, whose despatches to the London *Daily Express* had undoubtedly been the best war reporting from the Middle East, felt nearly the same as I did, so I knew I was not imagining things. The same mental chemistry had been at work in both of us. We had been out here longer than most other people anyway. And we could never, as others did, ignore the desert entirely, accept it as a background so negative that it was hardly experienced at all. By the nature of our work we must always remain conscious observers of it, and its impact on us had been strong and sustained. And now we had both reached saturation point.

There were other reasons, too, why I should go and my newspaper, as always, was generous and understanding. And so in the middle of August, more excited than I think I have ever been, I flew off for home.

In the weeks that followed the desert began to creep back into my system. Things kept happening out there and each time something happened I felt an urgent desire to be on the spot myself, to do something about it, at least to write or talk about it. I realized with astonishment how much I knew about it and how interested I was in it.

First of all Mr. Churchill made two visits to Cairo, sandwiching a trip to Moscow, and his return coincided with the announcement that General Auchinleck had been relieved of the Middle East Command. He was succeeded by General Sir Harold Alexander, a young and vigorous officer who had commanded the British Expeditionary Force in the last stages of the Battle of France and had been last off the beaches of Dunkirk. General Bernard Law Montgomery was appointed commander of the Eighth Army.

This would seem to have been one of the Prime Minister's snap decisions, for certainly Auchinleck knew nothing about it himself until it happened, nor had the Eighth Army expected it. The obvious, immediate inference was that this was an expression of loss of confidence in Auchinleck after the fall of Tobruk; just as Wavell's removal a year before could only be regarded as the consequence of the defeats he had suffered. And indeed these two Middle East careers were outwardly curiously parallel. Wavell had won Cyrenaica in the winter, lost it a month later, and then lost a summer battle. Auchinleck, on a very much bigger scale, had done exactly the same thing. The Middle East seemed to be turning into an annual office with a fixed programme. But under the surface the details of the two cases were widely different.

Wavell had produced a touch of genius at a moment when a touch of genius was urgently necessary. Then he had gone to India, where a touch of genius might be necessary at any minute. And Auchinleck had come to the Middle East, which was passing out of the bluff stage into the stage of serious military operations. The first tentative judgement on Auchinleck when he arrived — that he undoubtedly had talent but possibly not genius — had been largely borne out. There were an orthodoxy and straightforwardness and a curious negativeness and dullness about the whole story of his career. It had been a first-class career but in an odd way it lacked character — there was no touch of special brilliance or eccentricity or fantasy or of anything really exceptional. It was perhaps significant that there were remarkably few anecdotes about him.

As a commander-in-chief his most obvious lack of success was in choosing his commanding officers. In two separate major campaigns he had taken the almost unprecedented step of removing his army commander. In the middle of the summer campaign he had had to make a wholesale reshuffle of his corps and divisional commanders. He was reputed to have an almost uncritical admiration for Indian army officers. But against that he had, I think, saved Egypt. Whatever may have been his real views about Tobruk, he had known what to do afterwards and he had done it. Instead of appointing a successor to Ritchie he had handled the army himself in the field and done it very well. A great many of the mistakes made on the British side were nothing that Auchinleck could have helped. Technically he had to take responsibility for everything his army did, but in plain logical fact he could not be responsible for it. Wavell had bequeathed him only the remnants of an army, and England could not send him the things he knew he required because England did not have them. The blame for that lies way back in the past with the people who neglected to make England ready for war, not with Auchinleck. Some things went wrong because of the training and structure of the British army itself. Auchinleck did much to correct these faults and fill these gaps and he strove ceaselessly to compile an army equipped the way he knew it must be equipped. When he commanded in the field himself he won the confidence of his troops, and he had acquired one of the most valuable things you can have in the desert—experience. When he finally had to choose a new commander for the Eighth Army, he chose unquestionably the right man—"Strafer" Gott; and then that malicious fate which had already robbed Britain of so many of her best desert commanders stepped in and slew Gott. But to the man who succeeded him in the desert—General Bernard Law Montgomery—Auchinleck handed over an Alamein Line already formed and mature, an army better-equipped and trained and seasoned than any desert army had been before, and the rudiments of a plan for beating Rommel. The Australian-held salient along the coast was the foundation of that plan.

Then in September, when I was still in England, the Axis army in the desert made a tentative offensive. It made a pass at the Eighth Army, and the Eighth Army without any great flurry or excitement rejected its advances. The British front was L-shaped, running due south from the coast at Alamein and then turning eastwards towards the Egyptian Delta, and pretty nearly the whole enemy tank force began advancing eastwards below the base of the British L. With rare patience and self-control the British just waited. The German *Panzers* sniffed their way along, unable to turn the line and unable to find a hole in it. Theoretically they could have run on eastwards as far as they liked, but practically it was impossible. Finally they selected a sector of the British southern front and attacked. And although the attack was so concentrated that at one moment a single squadron of British tanks was apparently holding the whole enemy army, the defence this time was sound and solid and skilfully integrated. Tanks and anti-tank guns and field guns worked together as never before, and the R.A.F. gave beautifully timed co-operation. In the end the Axis forces retired, very seriously discomfited, and claimed they had only been making a "reconnaissance in force."

There had been something odd about this Axis offensive right from the beginning. And finally the truth came out: Rommel himself had not been there at all. He had been secretly in a Sanatorium in Athens, reputedly undergoing a rest-cure. A little later he appeared in Berlin, apparently in perfect health, and announced bombastically at the Sportspalast that Egypt was as good as conquered. There is every sign that he deliberately avoided being associated with the abortive "reconnaissance in force."

He had been reinforcing and re-equipping his forces as fast as he could, and once again he knew that there would come an optimum moment when he would be stronger vis-à-vis the British than at any other point in the foreseeable future. Once again he had to take a short-term view based on the greater speed with which he could be supplied from Europe. But this time that optimum moment was not going to be very good. Rommel must have had very serious doubts about it. He had proved himself a fine general, but there is little sign that he had any other admirable characteristics. He was notably unscrupulous and madly ambitious. He had no interest whatever in being associated with a defeat. And it is quite credible that he purposely avoided this battle because he did not believe it had a reasonable chance of success.

But to the British that September episode was very valuable. It proved the strength and the new quality of the Eighth Army. It did much damage to the enemy. And it established very opportunely the reputation of General Montgomery, the new army commander.

I was as certain as I could be that a British offensive was due in the late autumn or the early winter, and I knew now that, despite all my hatred of the desert, I must be there. I wanted desperately to see the whole thing through. But before I had time to hurry back to Africa the great Alamein battle had begun.

CHAPTER 27

Alamein

You cannot properly describe a battle, for it is something beyond the scope of human language, like Music or God.

You can, if you like, give the bare, dry, tactical moves and processes, and you get something about as interesting as a play-by-play account of a chess game. Or you can describe everything that one man sees or feels and you get just one hundred-thousandth of the battle. Or you can try and fit it all into the compact, familiar phrases of conventional military jargon, and there emerges only a shadowy, blurred travesty of what really happened. Few things have a smaller comparative second-hand value than a battle.

The difficulty is one of language. The facts of modern warfare are outside normal human experience, and strictly speaking only the facts of normal human experience are reproducible in words. But the words must be used; and here there is an additional handicap. For the stock phrases of communiqués and all the ordinary adjectives and even the more far-fetched descriptions quickly become so familiar that they scarcely stir the attention at all. With the passage of time they become progressively emptied of significance. The phrase "heavy shell-fire" means almost nothing now. It cannot even faintly hint at the tight, taut feeling while you are waiting for the shell to come and the whining, whimpering scream of it and the nerve-jarring crack of the explosion and the whirring and the tinkling of the fragments flying around you and the quick pang of relief that that one did not hit you and the immediate realization that the next one may. Words cannot possibly reproduce in the mind the feeling you get when you hear the high whining snarl of a Stuka going into its dive and you brace yourself for the incredible noise of the bomb. An unthinkable amount of agony and tragedy is slurred over in the suave phrase "heavy casualties." An infinite wealth of individual human experience is poured into the monotonous and undramatic jobs of a fighting army — the sappers, the men who drive ammunition trucks, the medical services, and so on.

Even the basic background of the fighting can only be feebly sketched in. The word "dust" has been used so often that now it merely flicks across the mind in a fraction of a second, scarcely rippling the surface. But in the desert it is a permanent condition of things; something that you see and feel and taste and breathe through all your waking hours, an unceasing scourge and discomfort. And so with many other things. You must imagine an existence composed of dust and flies and heat and an utterly bare stony earth and a blue sky and unbearable noise and ever-present danger and nothing else at all. And you must think of that continuing all the time as the unchanging background of every man who fought in the battle.

Even then you will not get very near it. For there is the question of quantity as well as quality. The bigger the battle the further does it escape beyond the range of description and imagination. And hence Alamein, the apotheosis of all desert battles, is the least describable of all.

As a battle, Alamein was chiefly interesting at its two extremities: as a fact, and as an aggregate of human experiences. But compared with previous desert campaigns it was oddly dull for the simple reason that from start to finish it was a success. This time, for the first time, the British had better men and weapons and more of them and they knew how to use them. There was none of the bluff and zest of the Wavell Campaign; nothing unexpected or untoward happened. It was simply a battle in which the bigger and better side won. Everything went according to plan. And in that respect, although it was a far bigger battle than had ever happened before in the desert, it was a less interesting one.

The preparations for the battle had been long and elaborate. The tanks and guns and planes and many of the men of the army had started out from Britain and America months before, when Auchinleck was still C-in-C. The front line itself — the whole *mise-en-scène* — had been bequeathed by Auchinleck to Montgomery as a going concern. The whole orchestra was waiting there with its instruments poised to begin. It was for Montgomery to tell them what to play and then to conduct them himself.

He found himself faced with a situation that was unique in the desert and very rare in this war as a whole: an old-fashioned, static, strongly held front. It could not be turned according to classical desert tactics, for it had two firm ends, one on the sea and the other in the Qattara Depression. So it would have to be broken by frontal attack. The emphasis was no longer on speed and mobility, but on strength of fire power and quality of infantry. It was a problem much more common in the last war than in this.

The Germans were at that moment under the command of Panzergeneral Georg Stumme, who had had experience on the Russian front. He knew the British were going to attack and he knew it would be a frontal attack. He could not quite tell where it would come, but he rather thought in the centre of the line. And he made the appalling blunder of spreading his troops evenly along the whole front. He ignored the Clausewitz doctrine of the counterattack which alone could have given him a chance of making a successful defence. He should have left his front line thinly held except by mine fields and guns, and concentrated his striking force miles in the rear — fifty or sixty miles if necessary, for distance was immaterial — ready to launch a very heavy counterattack.

Alexander, in constant conference with Montgomery, Tedder and Coningham, argued it out very carefully. Above all he needed to beat this army, not put it to flight. He had understood the lessons of the pendulum and he knew that the only way to get to Tripoli was to leave the enemy with no serious army at all. At some time or other he would have to meet the full weight of the Germans in battle. So he decided to do it right away. He planned to attack a little north of the centre, where the main enemy strength lay. The Australians' salient along the coast gave him an absolutely secure right flank on the sea. Probably the last place the enemy would expect an attack was just at this point where it was most difficult. Therein lay the boldness of the plan.

It was planned with extraordinary exactness. Elaborately staged schemes persuaded the enemy into a completely false appreciation of what was happening. The British and American bombers and fighters were groomed for the biggest air blitz ever seen on the African front. Supplies sufficient for a week's heavy fighting and then an immensely long pursuit were being dumped and hidden in the forward areas at the rate of four thousand tons a day. There were huge reserves of everything. This at last was the adult army which two and a half years of painful military experience had been evolving.

On the evening of October 23 the war correspondents in the desert were summoned to General Montgomery's Headquarters. They met a small slim man with a sharp thin face and a little grey moustache and bright, quick-moving eyes. He was known to be the son of a bishop and a strict non-smoker and non-drinker, and for that the army was a little suspicious of him at first. But he had the common touch as none of his predecessors had had. He was a man of exuberant, clear-sighted energy and he was very categorical in his decisions. Never was anybody less devoted to half-measures.

In his tent that evening Montgomery said, "Well, gentlemen, the campaign starts to-night. In the moonlight there will be fought a terrific battle. My object is to remove the Germans from North Africa. It may take some time, but that is what we are going to do. I think this battle may well be the turning point of the war. It has always been my policy that we shall not have any more failures."

(That was a little hard on his predecessors. They had never had the advantages he had started with. They had collected players and painfully trained them and struggled to get the instruments and now he was being privileged to conduct the finished orchestra.)

Montgomery continued, "The great thing is morale. Other things being equal, the side which has superior morale will win."

(True, but a truism. Other things being equal the side with superior guns or superior boots or anything superior will win. But other things never are equal. And the Spanish and Finnish wars showed that morale is not enough.)

"If you look down history and search for the causes of failure, I would say that basically they can be traced to faulty command and bad staff work. The soldiery — use that good old-fashioned word — will never let you down."

(That was bold, coming from a commander on the eve of a battle. And once again it was unfair to Montgomery's predecessors. He had now listed morale as the reason for success, faulty command as the reason for failure, and the soldiery as a reliable constant factor. But those generalizations were far too wide. And what about soldiery with bad morale? The Italian soldiery had certainly let their commanders down. Montgomery had omitted two of the basic factors: the training of the soldiery and the weapons they were equipped with. Therein lay the two great advantages which he had over his predecessors.)

The General concluded, "To-day every officer and man knows what is wanted. I have addressed all officers down to the level of Lieutenant Colonel. They know all about this battle and they have passed it on to the men."

(That certainly was an excellent idea. The soldier of to-day is not cannon fodder. He needs to be an intelligent man, and the more he knows about what is happening, the better he will fight.)

Air Vice-Marshal Coningham had done the same thing. "For us the battle has already started," he said. And so it had. For hours his bombers and fighters had been passing overhead, softening up the enemy lines. They had made devastating attacks on Daba and Fuqa, which were the two foremost German fighter bases. This time Tedder and Coningham were ready with a complete scheme for using air superiority. They had collected their data the previous winter. They had tried their experiments in the summer. And now they had drawn their final conclusions and were going into action with a perfected technique.

At ten o'clock that night eight hundred guns sprang into life with an almost simultaneous roar. The desert air throbbed and pulsed intolerably with wave and counter-wave of deafening clamour. The flashes rippled from end to end of the horizon as though some giant were playing crazy scales on a piano which produced flame instead of music. There had been nothing like this concentration in the desert before. There were places where eighty British guns were shelling four Axis guns. I saw a note-book in which a German despatch rider had tried to jot down his impression of this barrage. Language failed him, as it inevitably must. All he could write was silly little blabbing phrases, repeated over and over again.

For twenty minutes the guns simply fired off ammunition as hard as they could go. Then they settled down to precision shelling and the infantry, who had gone forward into no-man's-land under cover of an aerial bombardment, moved into the mine fields. Their object was to pick two lanes through the northern sector of the front for the tanks to use.

Since this was a relatively old-fashioned front, Montgomery resorted frankly to unfashionable methods. This time he determined to send the infantry through first to clear a path for the tanks instead of vice-versa. They not only had to make paths, but safe bridgeheads at the other end where the tanks could move safely and operate. That was why through the Alamein battle most of the fighting was done at night, and the day was usually spent in consolidating.

The infantry went through in very high spirits. The Fifty-first (Highland) Division marched into battle with bagpipes shrilling bravely against the clamour of the guns, one piper to each company. At first resistance was scattered and unco-ordinated, and several Italian units were seen to be fighting in their pyjamas. In sectors, where the shelling had been heavy, there were men who had passed beyond the limit of what the human system can endure, and they either wandered blindly with staring eyes, as though half-stunned, or fought with a frantic and hopeless frenzy. The first stage through the mine field was passed easily — a distance of a thousand or fifteen hundred yards. The new Sherman tanks followed on behind along six special lanes marked out with kerosene lamps showing through V's cut in one side of petrol tins. Smart, red-capped policemen directed the traffic up into the front. It was as automatic and methodical as a stage show.

Resistance stiffened a little in the early hours of the morning and bayonets were being used. But by 5 A.M. the vitally important objective, the Mitariyar or Bare Ridge, had been occupied, one of the main bridgeheads for the tanks had been thoroughly cleared, and the other only needed a little mopping up.

The attack had been general all along the line. The Australians in the north, pivoting from their salient, had advanced due west parallel with the coast but some miles inland. Below them the Highlanders and the armoured divisions had made the main thrust. In the center the Indian Division had moved forward. And away down in the south the Seventh Armoured Division and the Free Greeks and the Fighting French were attacking. The attacks in the center and the south were diversions to be exploited if they went well. And still General Stumme could not guess Montgomery's plan. He still was not persuaded that the attack in the north was the real one. His Fifteenth *Panzerdivision* and the Italian Littorio were already up there, but he kept the rest of his German and Italian tanks down south in case the real threat should be there.

The British now had a bulge which stuck so far into the German lines that there was an Axis salient pointing east along the coast. And now on the second day the Australians began to nip this off. They turned up northwards from the tip of the British bulge and started to surround the German 164th Division and a large quantity of Italian infantry. The fighting revolved round a feature called Point Twenty-nine, which was just nine metres higher than the rest of the surrounding countryside and gave commanding views in nearly every direction.

The main thrust became a chaos of wild Axis counterattacks while the British nudged gently forwards and outwards. South Africans and New Zealanders and other British infantry divisions moved into the battle area. A vital eminence called Kidney Ridge was taken and the British grasp on the very entrails of the enemy army was strengthened. The sequence of events grew too swift and confused for description, for there were no towns or roads or woods or anything at all to which the fighting could be related. The main picture is of the British bulge working its way steadily ahead and the enemy still not understanding what it was all about.

General Stumme had been frankly baffled. He took not one single constructive step to retrieve the situation. On the second day of the battle he was killed when the R.A.F. raided his Headquarters and amid a good deal of staff squabbling General von Thoma took over. But he did nothing either. And on the third day Rommel came back from Berlin furiously, almost hysterically angry, cursed his commanders for a pack of fools, and began to act. He recognized the situation at a glance, and sent for the Twenty-first *Panzerdivision* to come north with all possible speed. He gathered all his armour together and poised it for a great counterattack.

He made in all five great counterattacks. But they failed because they came too late. The British had got too firm a grip on the Axis front line. Their six-pounder anti-tank guns lay in a great thick ring round the territory that had been won. The R.A.F. and the United States Army Air Force were bombing, bombing, bombing, day and night. Too much confusion had already been caused and was still being caused in Rommel's ranks to allow him to pull his forces together.

And so it went on. The Eighth Army was attacking only by night, keeping the enemy always on the move, and itself cleaning and simplifying its own position for the next phase. Many of Rommel's counterattacks were very heavy and moments came, as we knew they must come, when the margin between victory and defeat narrowed down almost disquietingly. But in point of fact it was a safe enough margin. It had been allowed for in Montgomery's calculations. Nothing went wrong and the issue was never seriously in doubt. And Rommel helped by the incoherence of his defence.

He tended to keep his armour north and many of his counter-attacks were desperate, costly efforts to rescue his infantry units which were being cut off. The Australians now were filling in the German salient yard by yard, nipping off pockets and then mopping them up. There was bloody fighting round a place called Thompson's Post, which was the centre point of a German regiment and which was captured the first time by a single Australian soldier. Gradually Rommel became more and more preoccupied with this slim salient.

The individual human experience of the battle was the same in quality as it had been in all previous campaigns. It was the same sort of warfare in the same setting with the same personal and physical and tactical problems. But this time everything was bigger and better and heavier and tougher. On land and in the air the scale of the warfare was enormously enlarged. And this time the British were fighting with the right weapons and with a sureness and steadiness and scientific single-mindedness that they had never had before. Rommel, I think, must have known he was beaten this time. He never recovered from the bad start Stumme had given him, and for once he was lashing about wildly and indiscriminately. Very probably he was trying to lure the British into making a dangerous error — a technique that had served him well enough before. But this time no mistakes were made.

The fighting was at times costly, as Montgomery knew it must be, and there were many great individual deeds done during those days. Chief among them must come the stand of the Rifle Brigade — desert veterans who had fought out here from the very beginning — on Kidney Ridge. Under Colonel V. Turner they held out, cut off and isolated, for thirty-six hours against savage German counterattacks. When they finally had to withdraw they had knocked out a minimum of thirty-seven enemy tanks — the final figure was probably around fifty — with their six-pounders. Colonel Turner was awarded the Victoria Cross for it, and it is no diminution of what he did to say the award really went to his whole battalion.

Gradually now the balance of everything began to shift northwards. And then on November 1 Montgomery saw what he had been waiting for. Rommel, casting about to relieve his beloved Ninetieth Light Infantry Division on the coast, split his armour. He sent his Twenty-first *Panzerdivision* northwards, and that night the British armour drove due west along the Rahman track into the gap.

They did not go along the road, as the enemy had apparently anticipated, but straight west from where they were. At one o'clock in the morning three British infantry brigades, one from Scotland, one from the North Country, and one from Surrey, started picking a hole through the last mine fields. By six in the morning they were clear. Rommel managed to get a screen of anti-tank guns in place along the track and the first British tanks which came through suffered heavily. But that was cleared up, and on November 2 the first really big tank battle of the campaign began.

This was the crucial moment of the whole thing. Rommel mustered all his tanks for a battle that he knew would be decisive, and all that day and far into the night savage fighting raged round a point called Aqqaqir. It was an exceedingly expert and well-fought tank battle, and the British used their anti-tank guns with a skill and suppleness they had never shown before. Losses were high on both sides, but the British had counted on taking losses and they were not dismayed. Rommel lost a high proportion of his dwindling total of tanks and many of his 88-millimetre guns. By nightfall the surviving German *Panzers* were edging their way out of a hideous tangle of flaming, smoking wreckage, knowing they were beaten. The great break-through had begun.

That night up in the north the Axis salient was hastily evacuated. And all the way down the front began to shift forward. In the center the Indian Division drove in a wedge to split the whole remaining Axis line in half, a wedge so neat and symmetrical and precise that it had an almost artistic beauty. It had a steel tip of shells, a mighty smoking triangle into which four hundred guns were firing, one gun to every six feet of front. Bofors guns fired down its flanks, framing it with a constantly renewed balustrade of rose-red tracer shells. It sprang into being at three-thirty in the morning and for half an hour it steadied and established itself. Then it began to creep ruthlessly forward.

Behind it moved the men of an Indian brigade, manning the wedge as a crew might man a battleship. The wall of shells was so accurate that they could move forward right close up against it, and most of their first casualties were caused by the bitter fumes of the explosive. On their right a Highland brigade and on their left another Indian brigade provided firm, unshakable pillars on which the wedge could pivot.

First the wedge merely drove a safe path through the last mine fields. Then it passed over ground where men were waiting to fight. And those who survived, when the Indians reached them, were divided into men who had passed the limit of human endurance and those who had not quite reached it. The former stumbled dazed and stupid from their trenches, seeking only to surrender. The latter fought with a last furious outburst of desperation until they were killed.

As the wedge proceeded it got beyond the range of the field guns and the mediums took over with never a break, as one runner hands the baton to another in a relay race. At dawn the Indians reached a little moon-shaped contour which was their final objective. And now the remaining tanks came through behind them to begin the chase.

For at this moment the first traditional phase of the classically patterned desert campaign was finished. The initial core of hard fighting was over, and Rommel had lost it. It had been bigger and harder fighting than ever before. And now he was faced with a bigger and longer flight than ever before.

Swiftly he began to muster whatever was most valuable and worth saving. That meant the German *Panzerdivisions* with their tanks, then the German infantry, then certain irreplaceable instruments and stores — particularly petrol — and all the guns and mines he could collect to serve as a powerful sting in his tail as he ran.

But whatever could not be taken was ruthlessly jettisoned. And that meant first and foremost the Italian infantry. For they were hopelessly under-motorized. They used boots instead of wheels. Many of their trucks had broken down; many were paralyzed for lack of petrol; many more had simply been stolen by the Germans. But even allowing for all that, the Italians had never started with enough transport. And if there is one lesson which the desert has insistently rammed home, it is the need for complete and first-rate motorization in a modern army.

So in their thousands and their tens of thousands the Italians were captured. Dumps that could not be moved were blown up. And Rommel's surviving fragments took the road in an endless line of transport, setting off on the traditional familiar race across Libya, the annual Bengasi handicap.

The Eighth Army pursued, knowing that it had won a battle but not yet certain that it had finally smashed an army. The pursuit, like everything else in this campaign, was better and more expert than it had ever been before. British armoured cars were operating almost ahead of the enemy, cutting telegraph wires, mining roads, slitting petrol cans, demolishing supply dumps. The British and American air squadrons began to fill the roads with horror. And though the German engineers laid mines and booby-traps with a diabolical subtlety — until no one dared touch so much as a battered Italian sun-helmet lying on the ground — the British sappers picked the way clean for the army with dauntless persistence.

And so while the church bells rang for joy in England, the chase went on through a desert that was gradually becoming one huge rubbish heap. Daba and Fuqa Air Fields were littered with aircraft and bits of aircraft — including some untouched specimens of the new Messerschmitt 109G. At Fuqa the Germans fought a rear-guard action, and another at Mersa Matruh where Eighth Army Headquarters got so far forward that it came under shell-fire. It must have been just about then that Rommel got news that American forces, with British support, had landed in Algeria and were advancing eastwards. So he was running not only away from trouble, but also into it.

Mersa's rubble-furrowed streets looked much the same. The place had reached a saturation point of destruction where nothing more could make much difference. A wrecked Italian merchant ship lay in the harbour. At Sidi Barrani the Italians had left a large mobile refrigerator. All the way along the road were old graves and new. Many were surmounted by the typical German iron cross and often the legend recorded that the man beneath the desert dust had been the victim of a British strafing attack. Occasionally, in cold anonymous loneliness, was a broken propeller blade stuck into the sand and the scribbled words *An Unknown British Flier.*

At Sollum a four-thousand-pound bomb had destroyed the road up Halfaya Pass, and the retreating Germans were forced into a perilous bottleneck on the serpentine highway that climbs the cliff to Bardia. And now there was a certain weariness and perfunctoriness about the chase. It was all so absurdly familiar. When in history has the same army captured the same country three winters running? There was an inevitable feeling that all this was a mechanical routine, a boring but necessary phase which had to be accomplished. Only at Agheila would interest revive, for that would be the turning point between the old and the new, that alone would show whether this time the Eighth Army had really won.

Tobruk again presented that strange illusion of still having the shape of a town when seen from the distance. But inside it was quite perceptibly more destroyed, for British bombers had been over it on a hundred consecutive nights. Miraculously the church spire still stood. And outside the town was a food dump where the ground was puddled redly with wine and the Arabs were carting away their bi-annual quota of loot. They probably feel that this much is due to them from the armies that have turned their fields into battle-fields.

Derna was barely touched — it had now become fashionable for retiring and advancing armies to by-pass the place. As usual Rommel took his main forces straight across the desert and cut out Barce and Bengasi. It was all so absurdly the same as before — a mere dull bit of padding in the composition of the campaign, the routine re-statement of a theme heard twice before. And finally, as everyone foresaw, Rommel stopped at the salt-marshes of El Agheila and tipped the sand out of his old fortifications there and laid new mines in front of them. Winter rains came down and turned the marshes into a sticky paste. And the tip of the Eighth Army, thinned out and weakened in impetus by the immense distance it had come, paused to gather in its strength again for the next decisive stage.

CHAPTER 28

Pursuit into Tripolitania

THUS matters stood when I got back to Cairo — a Cairo fuller, gayer, richer and more expensive than I had ever known it. To me, fresh from the mild half-tones of the early English autumn, even its sunshine seemed brighter and warmer. Now that the tide of war had rolled back from its frontiers once more, Egypt was riding on a wave of ungovernable optimism. Never, probably, in four thousand years of history had the country been so prosperous. No other country in the world was balancing its budget from ordinary taxation and putting aside a surplus. Egypt was spending 28,000,000 dollars a year on armaments where Turkey was spending 400,000,000. It was probably the only remaining country in the world where petrol was not rationed. British and American money was pouring in, a swelling golden stream. The British army alone was spending 12,000,000 dollars a month. Anyone, it seemed, could sell anything for any price. Only one worry faintly clouded the brows of the prosperous Egyptian merchants — a fear that the war might end before all the profits had been wrung out of it.

The papers were full of a purely frivolous controversy about polygamy. The Government was making a half-hearted attempt to control the astronomical rents of furnished apartments. The tram company complained it was carrying so many passengers that it was losing money heavily: for the conductor spent his time pinned in a corner and never got around to collect the fares. The emphasis was now all on domestic affairs, and the actual war seemed infinitely remote.

But I knew that this was the crucial stage in the desert. The pendulum stood for the third time at the farthest point west it had ever reached. This was the moment of our failures the two previous winters. As fast as I could I arranged to get up there.

Flying to the desert now was a formal, organized business compared with the happy-go-lucky hitch-hiking of the old days. Now you had to fill in forms and catch a bus at a certain hour outside the Continental Hotel with just so much luggage, and then you were taken to the civilian air field and put aboard one of the big new American transport planes. I started in the chilly darkness before dawn and slept until we touched down at El Adem, just outside Tobruk. From the air field I looked across at the empty barbed-wire compound which last summer had been the El Adem Box, and I remembered a night I had slept there when the Germans had dropped flares right above us and I had crept away into a little hole waiting for the bombs to come. But now it had that air of bright, bland indifference which the desert always shows to its conquerors, the blank emptiness of a stage when the scenery has been taken down and the actors have gone home and no echo of the tragedy remains.

At Agedabia I chanced to meet Captain David Crichton, a conducting officer in search of a correspondent. He had one already—Bill Munday of the Sydney *Morning Herald*—but he needed two before he could go up forward to the front. So I attached myself to him and we went on to the little white roadhouse which the Italians had built for the convenience of touring motorists and which David was now sharing with some military policemen. It was a little dirty, but for some reason the German engineers had left it free of booby-traps and it gave us shelter from the rain storms and the bitter night winds.

Some miles ahead of us, where the road ran on causeways across treacherous, sticky salt-marshes between Mersa Brega and El Agheila, Rommel was ensconced in the gentle undulations of the sand-hills. Mines and barbed-wire and plenty of hard digging had given him a line which could not be lightly attacked, and in it he had the remnants of his Afrikakorps. Truly it could not be very much. But it was certainly enough to beat off any premature and ill-considered offensive.

Rommel at that moment had a few wild and slender hopes left to him. He had always been supremely quick and accurate at appreciating a situation, and it was likely he knew way back in August that he was going to be beaten this winter. The Russian Front was absorbing all Germany's best reinforcements and there was little left for Africa. The matériel that came to him across the Mediterranean in August, while Malta rocked beneath another blitz, was mainly Italian and he knew that would not be good enough. He still had to be content with Italian infantry divisions, and he knew that with them his army could never fight as a German army would. Many of his *Panzer* troops and German infantry had become magnificently seasoned; but conversely many of his tanks and trucks had been growing feeble under desert conditions. All the time there was the galling knowledge that several times decisive victory had just slipped through his fingers at the last second, and each time the British army had come back bigger and better and stronger to meet him again. This time, it was reasonably certain, was going to be once too many. This time the pupil was going to beat the master.

So he was beaten as he knew he was bound to be if the British made no mistakes, but inevitably he paused at El Agheila to nourish his wild and slender hopes. A quick German victory in Russia might save him, for then he could get a swift stream of the reinforcements he needed. His colleague, General von Arnim, seemed to be holding out well in Tunisia. Something or other — a break-through in the Caucasus, trouble in India, an advance by the Japanese — might conceivably draw off part of the Eighth Army. And in any case there was no point in withdrawing farther until he was forced to do so.

So Rommel sat there, waiting for a miracle. But the Eighth Army was working furiously. Wavell had failed at this point principally for political reasons. But Auchinleck's failure had been due to his inability to solve his supply problem. And I had not been back there in the desert a day before I saw that it was different this time.

For this time the problem had been faced and solved in advance. First Montgomery had seen that everyone had all the technical equipment he needed. Then he had set them tasks which seemed more than they could humanly achieve. They went away grumbling that he was unreasonable but in the end, to their surprise but not to his, they found they had done what he asked. It was a bigger problem than before, for the British Eighth Army was bigger and had come farther, and this time Montgomery demanded quick success instead of failure. But it was solved because it had been foreseen.

Somehow 2400 tons of supplies had to be got up to the army every day. It was a very highly motorized army, and whereas a World War One division could live and move on 300 tons a day, these desert divisions needed 420 tons a day each, including water. And just maintaining them was not going to be enough. They had to be given a surplus of everything so that they could be ready to launch another offensive at once.

The men handling the job started with this knowledge: that the road would be blown up, the water-pipe severed, the railway broken in many places, that every well would be salted or oiled, that every harbour would be dynamited. So immediately behind the front they collected piles of railway metals, bulldozers, well borers, new sections for the pipe-line, cranes, harbour equipment, engineers to deal with booby-traps, other engineers to repair every form of destruction the enemy could devise. They found, much as they had expected, that the railway had been blown up 40 times between Alamein and Daba, 67 more times before Matruh, and a good hundred times between there and Capuzzo. Yet in the month after the army reached Capuzzo 133,000 tons of supplies were unloaded at the railhead. The water pipe-line was actually mended while it was flooded by heavy rains. New wells were bored. The navy kept putting stuff ashore on beaches and in little harbours, despising nothing because it was too small. Four ships were being unloaded in Tobruk within a couple of days of taking the place.

Bengasi had now been five times deliberately dynamited, and bombed almost nightly for two years. It was thought that 800 tons a day would be the extreme limit of its capacity; but before the end of December 3000 tons had been handled in a single day's work.

And there was another thing — something which was nothing new to the Germans, but which no British army had ever done before. In this campaign for the first time air transport was used on a serious scale. Great fleets of American Douglases and Lockheeds and Hudsons began to fly low over Cyrenaica, bringing up aviation spirit and spare parts and personnel and any small but urgent thing that the army needed. The air-force supply lorries almost disappeared from the road. Nothing remotely resembling it had ever been seen before on our side of the front.

All this proved that Britain did at last have a competent, adult army — an army which not only looked well but fought well and worked well. It took in its stride problems which would have left Wavell's army helpless and which Auchinleck's army had only half been able to solve. This new excellence in technical and supply services was literally half the battle; for without it the victory in the actual fighting could never have been fully exploited.

ii

The Alamein battle started on October 23. Bengasi fell on November 21. Montgomery planned to attack at El Agheila in the third week in December. And as soon as Rommel realized this he knew he must abandon his wild and slender hopes. The showdown had come weeks, possibly months, sooner than he had anticipated. He took stock of his situation and knew that he could not hope to hold any large-scale attack. At Alamein he had lost in round figures 75,000 men, a thousand guns and 500 tanks and he had had no reinforcements. In conference the Italian commanders gave their vote against withdrawing, saying that the soil of Tripolitania must be defended at any cost. But Rommel overruled them. Discreetly he began to thin out his line, sending the Italian infantry away first. His artillery was a little more active than usual, in order to give the impression that this false façade was really strong. And early on the morning of December 13, just as the Eighth Army was getting poised for attack, the German *Panzerdivisions,* with the Ninetieth Light Division and the *Panzergrenadiers* as rear-guard, slipped away up the road to Tripoli.

Rather oddly Rommel gave out that he was retiring before the onslaught of powerful British armoured units. Presumably he had to give his public *some* convincing reason for embarking on a retreat that was going to continue for several hundred miles. But of course his explanation was sheer fiction. The plain fact was that he was not strong enough to fight a battle, and he knew it and now we knew it. At that moment we knew in our hearts that we had Tripoli, though we still did not dare say it out loud.

The Germans in Africa were now playing desperately for time. As long as their armies still held out, it was well-nigh impossible for the British to think of any invasion of Europe across the Mediterranean. If Rommel and von Arnim could hold on all through the summer, or even well into the summer, a whole year might be snatched from the Allied plans. Plainly now the Germans would retire as slowly and cheaply as they could. It was disappointing for Montgomery, who had hoped to make an end of Rommel there and then at El Agheila. But the Eighth Army had already been poised for attack, so it could at once be sent forward in pursuit. Montgomery let his original plans stand.

This was not one of those mad, headlong, exciting chases. It was a dull and measured affair, curiously remote. For we were always separated from the enemy by a thick carpet of mines which he laid down a little quicker than our engineers could roll it up. We never saw or heard the enemy for days on end across this constantly renewed zone of buried death. It was tedious and cold-blooded and a little eerie — a silent, scientific warfare of booby-traps.

The Germans mined anything and everything, until no man dared enter a building or touch an abandoned vehicle or pick up anything lying on the ground. The sappers were digging up the round flat German "teller" or soup-plate mines; the two-pronged square French mines; the long thin Italian N mines which looked like a swollen length of railway line with little trap-doors in it; the horrible S mines which were filled with shiny ball-bearings and which sprang from the ground and burst breast-high; the paratroops' anti-tank mines like large finger-bowls; and the sticky little Italian booby-traps which lurked among patches of camel-thorn.

Near our roadhouse where we lived, on the edge of a mine field, there was a dead Italian infantryman. He lay there stretched stiffly, his dust-coloured boots on the road and his head in the ruddy mud, pointing downhill. His greenish uniform was soaked and stained and he couldn't have shaved for some days. But you could tell he had been a handsome lad in a sturdy, peasant way. He would have looked more at home behind a plough in Lombardy than here in Mussolini's army. For nearly a day the British sappers worked round him, ridding the ground of mines. Finally someone came to take him away. And then they found he was not just a corpse. He was a booby-trap.

So the Eighth Army nudged gradually forward in the thin warmth of the winter sunshine. Each day we were able to get a little farther ahead, until David and Bill and I were forced to leave the shelter of our warm dry roadhouse and shift our camp. We left behind the squalid, dusty, treacherous ruins of Mersa Brega Village and exchanged them for the almost indistinguishable ruins of El Agheila. Our caravan was joined by Clifford Webb of the London *Daily Herald,* and the four of us settled down into the intimate coherence of a party, with our personal wants and habits carefully, sometimes rather precariously, dovetailed into one another. In point of fact we never had a serious row. But we all knew that we might do so at any moment, and sometimes we became sickeningly tactful and forebearing towards one another. Physically we were more comfortable than we had been the previous winter. In the meantime some genius had invented canvas flaps which unrolled from the top of the truck and were built into tents, one on each side. David and I shared one side harmoniously enough, despite his seven-foot-long bed, and Bill and Cliff occupied the other. After our nightly stew and tea we would all sit round an oil lamp in one of the tents and type or read or play bridge. But most often we would reminiscently and nostalgically talk shop in the way that newspapermen love to do, recalling stories we had been out on, prowling again round restaurants and cafés over half Europe, wondering what had happened to people we had known in those days, disputing the quality of the beer in pubs all over England.

Suddenly excitement came into the campaign again. Montgomery, hoping to cut off Rommel's rear-guard, sent the New Zealand Division down into the desert on a mighty forced march. They had a strict daily schedule, and at a fixed hour they were to reappear on the coast road ahead of the German *Panzerdivisions.*

No one knew anything of the country they would have to traverse. The only certain information was that the terrain was difficult and the Italian maps utterly wrong. So they took their compasses and enough food and water to live and plenty of arms and plenty of petrol and disappeared. They had to maintain wireless silence so nothing definite could be known about them. Word came at one point that they were ahead of schedule. They had rain which turned the surface of the desert into a slimy paste, and sand-storms which made them bunch together until they were travelling bumper to bumper. Their march was strangely like the great trek of the Seventh Armoured Division from Mechili to Beda Fomm two years before. And again they caught the enemy unawares.

But this time it was different. This time the enemy were Germans, not Italians. And the New Zealanders were infantry, not an armoured division. They did in fact technically cut off a very large and rich slice of Rommel's rear-guard. Theoretically they had at least one *Panzerdivision* in the bag. But in practice they had bitten off more than they could chew. They were, in fact, considerably weaker than the people they had trapped and their own position might even have become very dangerous. They tried to straddle the road, but the desert was firm and level here and they could not stop all the gaps. The first news that the New Zealanders had got right round caused an enthusiasm which mounted steadily as it rolled away from the battle front, until in the world's headlines the German *Panzers* were fighting desperately and vainly in a trap. But in the event most of them got clean away, slipping through the New Zealanders in the night.

Once again it became a dull, routine pursuit. It became, in fact, the story of the road, for the road was bound to be the main axis of advance and retreat through this bare, waterless waste. On and around the road the German engineers lavished their most expert care, and it was always the road which the British sappers treated first. They began by cleaning the actual strip of tarmac, and the traffic went gingerly along, preferring a collision to being pushed off into the perilous edges. Then men with earphones on their heads and things like great frying-pans in their hands would begin to clean the edges. They listened to a hum in their earphones and when it rose to a high whine they knew there was metal buried beneath them. The Germans buried the mines cunningly, sometimes two and three together with the soil loose on top so that several trucks could go over the place before the mines exploded; sometimes with two mines wired together so that when the engineer lifted one the other killed him. Every few miles, at the most awkward places, the road had been blown clean away by a mighty charge of dynamite and the sappers made mine-free detours, outlining them with strips of white tape.

Rommel was conducting a masterly retreat — a real text-book job. I do not suppose that ever in history has a withdrawal been so genuinely according to plan. This earth had already been so ruthlessly scorched by nature that there was little more to do. But telegraph poles were chopped down, air fields ploughed, buildings mined, bridges and culverts dynamited, wells destroyed. Nothing was left for the British as booty. Only the road was one long rubbish-heap where the German and Italian troops had cast aside what they no longer wanted. There was at one point a whole mile of empty Chianti bottles. There were useless rags of clothing and dozens of the soft Italian sun-helmets. Hundreds of leaking German petrol cans lined the route and an endless trail of torn paper and empty food tins. And all the way there were added to them the mines which the engineers dug out from among them.

iii

In the fullness of time we reached the one item of interest in all these hundreds of bare miles. The Italians called it Arae Philenorum but we, long before we had reached it, had been referring to it officially as Marble Arch.

It was indeed an archway, a monumental Fascist structure, and the road ran through it like black silk threaded through the eye of a needle. But it was totally unlike London's gracious, familiar arch. This was an excessively elongated affair, very tall and narrow, with sides sloping inwards to a top with tip-tilted corners, so that the effect was oddly Chinese. It was built of that yellowish soap-like stone beloved of modern Italian architects, and on the inside of the arch were grotesque bas-reliefs in praise of Mussolini and some bombastically meaningless extracts from his speeches. Up above were two agonized recumbent figures in bronze and inscriptions in Latin glorifying the Phileni brothers, the real genii of the place.

It seems that these youths, famous athletes of their day, were chosen to represent the fatherland in a matter of frontier demarcation. The dispute was to be decided by two teams of walkers, who would start from their respective capital cities at an identical moment, and where they met, there would be the frontier. The Phileni did surprisingly well. And in the ensuing discussion their opponents accused them roundly of cheating — of running instead of walking. The long and the short of it was that the Phileni somewhat illogically offered to be buried alive in pledge of their good faith, and their opponents took them at their word.

But the importance of Marble Arch to the British was not this architectural gem. It was the mighty air field which lay alongside it. The engineers reached it so soon after the enemy left that they could still see the freshly turned earth where the mines had been laid. They grubbed them up there and then without waiting for the detecting instruments, and by evening they had taken out six hundred and made a safe runway for planes to land. Next morning the big American Douglases were touching down there and rolling out barrels of high-octane fuel for the fighter squadron which arrived the same afternoon. Soon different Headquarters began arriving and grouping themselves round the field. In a few days Marble Arch was the nerve center of the whole army.

On we pressed through a countryside without incident, without charm or change, just so many wasted miles. Still Rommel did not make a mistake. The nearest he came to it was at a hamlet called Nufilia, where some of his tanks ran out of petrol and were forced to fight a battle. But help came before much damage had been done and most of them got away.

Nufilia was a well in a little valley, ten miles inland from the road, and the Turks had added a theatrical three-cornered castle and the Italians a white quadrangle of buildings. There were a mosque there, a school, a dispensary, a law court and a dozen little cells which the Arabs had used as shops. It was a sort of metropolis for the Bedouins scattered over hundreds of miles of country roundabout. Our party of war correspondents came on it just before Christmas Day, and we decided to camp down there under cover. The advance was slowing down now, the campaign had for the moment expended its urgency and we could sense the lull in the air. So we swept out the council chamber, a handsome apartment with green-painted beams and a gilt wooden chandelier, and set up our beds there.

As last year, we had made no preparations for the Christmas festival, but gradually the paraphernalia of celebration began to grow up round us. We had a chicken, a morose and diffident bird called Mussolini which travelled with us and always slept on the front wheel of the truck, beneath the mudguard. It had cost us a handful of tea and it had been ruthlessly fattened on a diet of raw rice. Friends sent us up parcels of dainties from Cairo. We met a unit which had some drink to sell. We kept back the best of our rations. But the surprise came when the Eighth Army produced a real Christmas dinner for everyone.

That was the measure of the army's success in solving the supply problem. For turkeys and plum pudding were luxuries that could only be justified provided all the demands for necessities had been fulfilled. I had never for one minute believed that the situation could be as good as this. But on Christmas afternoon I walked out of our council chamber to wash myself in the sunny courtyard and I smelled a smell so incongruous that it took me some minutes to diagnose it. Finally I followed my nose down to a dried riverbed near by, and there sure enough a real traditional English Christmas dinner was being cooked for a battalion of the Scots Greys, who were encamped in the neighbourhood. The turkeys were being roasted in three big German forty-gallon oil drums which had been laid sideways on a foundation of old petrol tins and packed all round with reddish desert sand to hold the heat. Old packing-cases made glowing fires underneath. And over other fires potatoes and diced vegetables were boiling and tins of plum pudding were steaming. One cook was even making a rum sauce in a four-gallon petrol tin. The only things lacking, they told me, were mince-pies.

I do not know what the official argument was for celebrating Christmas fully and laboriously in the desert. But there and then it seemed curiously right that we should do so. In the morning there had been an informal Christmas service for the Greys, and we had stood in rows on a barren hillside singing carols. A passing Bedouin stopped dead in astonishment when he heard us, then turned and hurried agitatedly away. War he could understand, but not organized singing. And yet to us it still seemed right and proper to be doing it. On this traditionally sentimental day it relieved our sense of isolation and remoteness to be taking part in a ceremony which we knew had its counterpart in our own homes. It gave us a comforting sense of community to stand round the radio after lunch and listen to the King's speech. And the talk reached nostalgically back into the past that night when men sat round their tanks under the full moon and drank the beer that had been issued to them.

The advance began to go slower and slower. All those influences which had restrained Rommel's thrust into Egypt the previous summer were this time working in his favour. The Eighth Army's communications were becoming intolerably stretched. We had reached a region poor in air fields, so the R.A.F. was working under difficulties while the Luftwaffe was more active than it had been for nearly a thousand miles. The British forces were strung out over an immense distance, and there was a risk of the armoured spearhead outrunning the defensive elements, so that the army became a sword without a shield. Very soon it would have to pause, like an advancing caterpillar, and pull in its hinder part before it could go forward again.

The campaign left the main road and became a gentle, tentative exploratory affair down inland. We went warily now, for we had no accurate maps of the country. Every mile of it had to be scoured and tested by armoured-car patrols before we dared send our main forces into it. Kebir was yielded up to us, and then Tamet. Following up behind the patrols I dipped into each of these great valleys with a queer sense of being a pioneer. They were filled with quietness and sunshine and they gave the impression of being untrodden and inviolate through countless centuries. Once we found the bones of a camel, and once a fire which someone had built but never lit. So there had been people here, but very few. The birds showed no fear of human beings for they had never seen any. The desert up above was flat and blackened as though it had been scorched by some tremendous flame. But down in the mazy windings of the *wadis* there was white sand, greenish with stunted tamarisks, and many times we had to lay down canvas or metal sand channels for our bogged vehicles.

Beyond Tàmet the army's spearhead came to a halt. The two

great *wadis* were too soft and treacherous to let a whole army through. The coast road was still blocked by mines. Not far ahead where the Wadi Zemzem ran into the coastal marshes, the Germans were busily digging in their guns. Rommel now had a stronger force than when he left Alamein, for all along the way he had been collecting men and anti-aircraft guns and his workshops had been putting tanks and trucks back into service. The British spearhead beyond Tamet was little more than a brigade and to attack at once would have been madness. Indeed, there was the possibility that Rommel himself might try an opportunist counterattack and nip this brigade off from its tenuous lines of communications. The fact that he did not attempt it was the measure of his impotence, for he was surely bold and ambitious enough to have contemplated it.

So another phase ended. The stresses and strains natural to a moving army had dragged Montgomery's forces to a standstill and we knew that once again Rommel, in his search for time, would stay where he was until the British became strong enough to attack him. It was El Agheila all over again.

CHAPTER 29

Misurata Comedy

A LITTLE west of the white-walled hamlet of Buerat the African Coast swings abruptly north, and the main road with it. And slanting inland from this angle Rommel now built his line. The first third of it consisted of easily held dunes and marshes and there he stationed his less reliable infantry divisions. The middle third lay across the main road a dozen miles inland, and here he put his best German and Italian infantry and his best guns and a huge quantity of mines. The remainder of his line was a mobile, fluid thing held by his *Panzerdivisions,* stretching down south in front of the Wadi Zemzem.

So as the cold, bright January days slid by the Germans and Italians dug and wired and fortified. And the Eighth Army simultaneously coiled itself once more for its next spring. The attenuated spearhead toughened and broadened and grew strong. The camps now lay thick along the road and the flowery desert became scarred with ten thousand ugly ruts. The tanks came up on their many wheeled transporters, mustered in a churning of dust and a roaring of engines near Sirte, and disappeared into the blue. A motorized scraper scraped the desert clean in the shape of a great cross where the Wadi Tamet flattened out by the sea, and then planes began to land there and the air was once more filled with Allied fighters.

Once again Montgomery called on his supply services for a superhuman effort. He was aiming to attack on January 15 and get through to Tripoli with the momentum of one tremendous push. Four divisions were earmarked for the job — the Highlanders, the New Zealanders, the Seventh Armoured Division, and Fifty Div. (the North Country Division). Other units were to be unceremoniously grounded in order that this striking force might have its first-line transport in a state of one hundred per cent efficiency, and its second-line transport nearly as good. Rations for seven days must be carried, and a continuous stream of food and petrol and ammunition must follow the four divisions into battle.

Then a storm sprang up. We got it as one of those wild, cold winter sand-storms — a cruel, cutting flail of flying grit that reduced the pace of convoys by three quarters and made men pray for the evening when the wind would drop. But Bengasi got it as a monstrous tide that drove the breakers obliquely across the moles and jetties and did more damage than a thousand Axis bombers. Ships heaved and tugged at their moorings and collided and dashed themselves against the stone quays. Nothing could get in or out of the harbour while the storm lasted. This time no amount of planning or hard work could avail. Montgomery was faced with the choice of either delaying his offensive, or reducing his force. He did his calculations over again and decided that he would not alter his date. But Fifty Div. would have to stay behind.

Our party too was struggling with its own little parallel problems. We had outrun our lines of communications until each despatch meant a two-hundred-mile drive along mine-imperilled roads. We were nearly out of rations and we were sixty miles or so ahead of the foremost dump. Our clothes desperately needed laundering and mending, and our vehicles must be tinkered with before we set out on the great chase to Tripoli.

So for some days we attended to these things, camping mostly in the flowery fields beyond Sirte. They were staggering, these fields. The flowers were thicker and lusher far than that miraculous blossoming on the Gazala Line a year before. I used to gather bunches of them in the evening sometimes, wondering like a child at a botany lesson how such arid soil could distil such colour and scent and richness. Then I would stick them in an empty bean can and dump them rather shamefacedly in the middle of our dinner table.

And yet in a perverse way I almost resented those flowers; they were so incongruous that they were simply not plausible in that setting. One felt that a desert should be a desert, without any mitigation.

One afternoon the sun was so warm that I heated up a mugful of water and stripped to the skin and washed myself carefully all over. Then, still naked, I sat down to think out an article. The traffic was passing half a mile away, and I thought there was a good story in the profusion of signboards that sprang up along the roadside wherever the army moved. Every unit now seemed to have its own pictorial symbol and the array of initial letters was becoming bewildering. You found you knew the meaning of about a third of the signs you saw and could guess about a third more. But the rest were completely baffling. Some, indeed, turned out to be German signs which no one had dared to take down in case they belonged to some obscure Eighth Army formation. Or I thought I might write about the improvement in the rations since last campaign. I could dwell on the badness of the British canned bacon and the excellence of the American; and conversely the superior quality of the British sausages over the American. And I could make a fervent plea for somebody, somewhere, to invent a substitute for bully beef. Or perhaps I could write a little piece about the flies which were one of the desert's most constant and disagreeable features; their uncanny way of appearing in swarms at places where no human being had set foot for decades; and the way they had multiplied and become fat on the garbage of this war, despite all that the ingenuity of man could do against them.

Still musing thus, I put a piece of paper into my typewriter. And at the same moment there came a loud, continuous rattling from down the road where there was a big Headquarters camp.

Any fool could have told what it was. But the Messerschmitts were so low that for a few seconds I could not see them. Then they lifted over a little rise, a broad double line of them coming straight towards us, machine-gunning like mad. Instinctively I ran from the truck, which was their obvious target. And then I realized that

I was minus my usual khaki camouflage. I was stark naked. The pilots must see me clearly as a conspicuous pink figure bounding across the countryside.

As I ran one of the fighters tilted his wings and swung around after me. I tried to argue out whether a pilot would deliberately chase a naked man and I came to the conclusion he almost certainly would. His hunting instincts would be irresistibly aroused. I ran faster and he tilted his wings more.

Then I saw the earth was being ripped into sudden ruts ahead of me and I knew I was coming into another plane's field of fire. So I gave up and threw myself down among the prickly thorn. Perhaps I was less visible if I stayed still. Away to the right Bill Munday, equally naked, was still galloping about and I was shocked to find myself wondering whether perhaps he might draw the fire.

In a couple of minutes they had all passed harmlessly overhead, and I walked back, cursing, to draw myself off another mugful of water and wash myself all over again. As I did so I pondered a bitter little article about the Luftwaffe. But in the end it seemed more sensible to take a spade and dig a good deep slit trench. And when that was done, the sun was setting gaudily and it was time to light the primus stove and open a few cans to make a stew for dinner. That was a fairly representative desert afternoon.

We moved from that spot next day, resolving to camp a little ahead of the cruciform air field at Tamet until the offensive should start. As usual we bickered restrainedly about the actual camping site, and we ended up in a place nobody liked, on the skyline of a little rise near the road. Just as we had got fully unpacked an officer strolled across and said, "Sorry to bother you, old boy, but I just wondered if you knew that this is an anti-tank position. As a matter of fact, you're bang in our line of fire. But don't trouble to move unless you like. We'll tell you if we're going to shoot." So we decided to stay. The anti-tank position was obviously something of an anachronism, for the front was now miles ahead, and it was sunny and pleasant on the hilltop. We lived there for three or four days, reading and writing in the sun, and popping along to Headquarters once a day to see whether there was any news. Nothing much happened. One day someone just over the hill from us shot down a Messerschmitt with a rifle. Once a near-by battalion frightened us out of our wits by holding a practice night operation without warning us. Once Cliff Webb and I found some green, hairy caterpillars that moved about in great strings, bumper to bumper, looking like a necklace, and cruelly we guided the leader until he touched the tail-end of the procession and they went round and round endlessly in a closed circle.

Then we heard what Montgomery's plan was going to be. As strategy it had a beautiful, mathematical simplicity, and psychologically it had the excitement of a race. It was, in fact, the perfect pincer movement. He proposed to split his forces into the jaws of a pincer, and the jaws would not meet until Tripoli itself. Strategically it was good because it involved a possible chance of trapping Rommel's forces, and it avoided the danger of shooting one narrow armoured spearhead into unknown country. But the idea of making it a race was excellent. It meant that, whatever we might find there, the last advance to Tripoli could not be an anticlimax.

Montgomery's plan was this: he would put the Highland Division on the coast to follow the main road north to Misurata and then west to Tripoli. And the New Zealanders and the Seventh Armoured Division would drive round the southern end of Rommel's line and make direct for Tripoli north-west across the desert. There was just a hope that Rommel might be brought to battle, but it was a very slender one. We expected a frantic double pursuit which would bring us to the gates of Tripoli in about six breathless days.

In this race the favourites were the British tanks and the New Zealanders. It was not thought that the Highlanders would meet very heavy opposition along the coast, but it was calculated that mines and demolitions on the road would hold them up, and they were certain to get away to a slower start than the others for their zero hour was later. There was nothing pre-arranged about the result. It was an honest race. Montgomery himself was planning to take a middle route and join the winning column, whichever it might happen to be, later on. And there was a possible outsider in the shape of the British First Army and the Americans in Tunisia.

We war correspondents, almost alone of the whole army, were free to choose which column we should follow, and we found the choice exceedingly difficult. If we went with the Highlanders, we should be able to send back fairly regular despatches along the road, and we ought to be able to get some good stories from the capture of Misurata, Zliten, Homs and the towns on the coast. On the other hand the southern pincer had the tanks, and if Rommel's *Panzers were* caught, the fighting would be down there. And it was, of course, vitally important that we should be with the column that reached Tripoli first. But if we accompanied the southern pincer it would be almost impossible to send any despatches back.

My party argued it every way, and in the end we let circumstances bully us into a compromise. We decided that we would at any rate see the southern pincer start out. So on January 14 we turned down into the desert again, along an abominable track which led to the untrodden wilderness between Tamet and Zemzem.

We visited an Intelligence Officer I knew. On the door of his caravan-like A.C.V. hung his white Palestinian sheepskin coat, which had been fashionable wear for Intelligence Officers for about a year. He had one of those enormous two-way moustaches which people in the desert could afford to grow experimentally, seeing that they had no social life whatever. He was on the telephone when we arrived.

"Oh, hullo, Claude, good day to you. Listen, old boy, the shufti-kites have found a whole lot of met going flat out north along the Bungem track. . . . Well, I wouldn't know that, old boy, but Peter says they're probably wops. We thought you might give the A.L.O. type a buzz and lay something on. . . . No, we haven't much 'gen' in yet. Geoffrey seems to have bumped into something down south there and there's a bit of a party on. . . . Oh, and

Claude, about the gin. Freddie hasn't turned up yet but he's got the stuff with him. I'll give you a tinkle when he's here. . . . Well, bung ho, old boy."

He was suggesting that the R.A.F. should attack some enemy transport down near Bu Ngem. Shufti-kite meant a reconnaissance plane and was derived from the Arabic word for look. Met stood for Motorized Enemy Transport. Gen, being an air-force word, was spoken sarcastically and with a falling inflexion, to indicate that it came between inverted commas. With his moustaches and his over-cultured voice he seemed a stage English aristocrat of the new generation. But I knew for certain he was no fool and that the troops with whom he came in contact liked him. He was a peculiarly English puzzle, an absurd, unhappy stylization of appearance and manner which other nations could not be expected to understand.

He confirmed that there was very little news so far. But at five million breakfast tables, people were waiting to unfold their papers and read that the advance had been renewed. We must at all costs send something. So we turned north again along that abominable track which filled the car with a fog of dust every time it bounced on its springs, back to a point where a despatch rider was waiting for us. And then when we had written our despatches we realized that we no longer had any choice about which column we should accompany. We could never catch up the tanks and the New Zealanders now. Whether we liked it or not it would have to be the Highlanders.

The Highlanders had decided to solve the problem of the mined road in a childishly simple way. They were just going to ignore it. They planned to leave all the sappers working on the tarmac while they themselves fought and advanced parallel with the road a little farther inland. But before they started they were going to fight a battle — a frontal attack at night against the very heart of Rommel's line.

Privately we all believed that there would not be very much to fight against. With the British tanks already round his right wing,

Rommel would surely be evacuating the Zemzem Line as fast as he could go. But when we visited the Highland Headquarters in the evening a very big German gun was still dropping shells about half a mile away and that showed that the line was at least occupied. The Highlanders had everything laid on down to the last detail, and they decided to go through with it, enemy or no enemy.

As the last light streamed horizontally across the bare hills, we began to make camp in a little gulley. The broad slope beside us was covered with tanks, and their crews were putting out their fires and packing up their tea things before going into battle. When we talked to them they answered in the slow speech of the North Country, utterly unhurried and undismayed. At supper we argued about the mental qualities men need to send them so unconcernedly into battle. Lack of imagination, perhaps, and a deep belief that whoever else is hurt, it won't be you. Or perhaps they did feel afraid and did not show it. Probably it was that.

The battle proved a stock example of the new desert break-through technique. First a very considerable and picturesque artillery barrage onto the mine fields and the enemy front lines. Then an infantry advance through no-man's-land with tanks. Then the forging of a gap through the mine fields while the enemy fired low and murderously on fixed lines. Then the final assault and in this case the discovery that the enemy had fled. The leading troops could hear a lorry — the "last bus for Tripoli" they nicknamed it — racing round from position to position picking up the ultimate German rear-guard.

It was a small action, but not without casualties, for no-man's-land had been half a mile of dead flat country covered by machine-guns. The Highlanders had again gone into action with their bagpipes shrilling, and when a piper fell he passed his pipes to a friend to play on for him. In some miraculous way the tank crews had kept their primus stoves going, and during a bitter-cold lull in the advance they handed out hot tea to the infantry. When they finally got through the Highlanders threw themselves into their enemy's trenches and slept. They were still sleeping when we passed by next day.

The mine field was the thickest I have ever seen. It had everything in it. While I was looking at it, two men were blown up by an S mine in a lane that was supposed to be safe and the sappers were still hard at work. At a medical dressing station near by I found men in white masks probing in a man's intestines, picking out the shiny little ball-bearings with which the S mines were filled. "Would you care to see the pudding?" the doctor asked and showed me a great stretch of intestine, riddled through and through, that the man would no longer need. Deftly the men in white masks moved round under the powerful lamp plying their forceps. You had to look down to the brown dust floor to realize you were still in the desert.

Again we had to take our stories back to our despatch rider, hoping desperately that the Highlanders would not advance too fast for us. David and Bill went off in the car, taking a bold, dangerous short-cut across country known to be mined. We spent the night in a desolate, dusty spot and when we woke in the morning there was an enormous food convoy camped all round us. So we swiftly drew some more rations from them and pressed ahead.

ii

Now it was a plain hell-for-leather pursuit. There was a mad, infectious exhilaration in the air. Now at last we were really on the move to Tripoli. Swiftly we passed through the deep-dug trenches of the enemy and out into the flat, safe country beyond. The whole Highland Division seemed to be on the move, sprawled across the countryside in what looked like a chaotic race. Men grinned through the dust and shouted from truck to truck as they jolted past. An irresistible madness seemed to have taken hold of everybody, a wild lust for the chase.

The noise from revving engines in the stillness of the desert night was like the roar of some mighty sea breaking on a stony shore. Occasionally you might catch a snatch of song or a joke shouted across in some rich Northern accent. But mostly this pulsing roar was all that could be heard. There was little to see, either. The columns showed up against the desert surface like black, articulated snakes writhing forward in unison. Occasionally a flame would spurt up — usually the sudden flare of a sheltered match which lit some tin-hatted head in a brief cameo of colour. Once away to the left a dump of petrol or ammunition went up with a roar that took a good fifteen seconds to reach us. Somewhere on ahead a burning load of tracer bullets was giving a haphazard firework display.

Sometimes, in the pauses we had to make, men would dart to the back of their trucks and fish out a packet of biscuits to eat. The night grew steadily colder and fingers became numb on the steering-wheels. The surface at first was stony and good. Then we passed through white dust which the moonlight turned into a dirty snowscape. And finally we were swishing through fields of asphodel two feet high.

By two o'clock in the morning we were skirting the silent white farmhouses of Gioda and Crispi, two of Mussolini's model colonial villages. Then, five miles from Misurata, we stopped. The moon had set and things were too obscure on ahead. Guns were unlimbered, machine-gun units were flung out on the flanks, and tanks nosed ahead to cover every exit from the town. And all the way back along the column men wrapped themselves in their blankets and lay down to sleep among the asphodel.

While dawn was still only a faint suggestion in the east, the engines of the trucks started to splutter again. It was bitterly cold now. Dogs began to bark in the colonists' houses. Somewhere a cock crew. Men folded their damp blankets and got ready to move. Slowly against the paling sky the futuristic silhouette of Crispi's buildings took shape. "Good God, have I captured a battleship?" asked the startled Brigadier.

Then the sun rose swiftly and we saw the desert shelving down before us and the dark thick welt of palms framing Misurata's white houses. The Brigadier looked long and carefully through his glasses. All was apparently dead. He decided to do a reconnaissance himself and he asked Bill and Cliff and me to go with him.

They put Bill into the leading Bren carrier and I was in the second and we cruised forward across the weed-grown fields down towards the white houses. It looked peaceful and sunny but there could be mines or ambushes anywhere. At the first group of colonists' houses, surrounded by crumbling concrete aqueducts, we met three Italian civilians. Emphatically they assured us that the town was empty of soldiers. A grinning Arab confirmed the news and handed me two new-laid eggs as a gift of welcome.

Soon we were cruising up Misurata's pleasant tree-lined main street with its green gardens and plain, modern, rectangular buildings. Children followed us laughing and shouting until it became almost a triumphal progress. And then quite suddenly the whole thing became comic opera.

The door of the police station was flung open and a young man in uniform stepped forth. He was beautifully shaved and pomaded. His riding-boots shone like mirrors. His greatcoat was superbly cut and faultlessly clean. Behind him came a troop of others scarcely less magnificent than he. Two slick youths, uniformed something like New York speed cops, fussed up and down on red motor-cycles.

When the whole ensemble was in place the police chief informed me — because I happened to be there first and showed signs of speaking Italian — that he could and would maintain order loyally. He quite understood that anyone obstructing the British would be punished. Would we care to see the Prefect? We would? A motor-cyclist was despatched noisily to find the Prefect. There was an awkward pause and the police chief angrily despatched the other cyclist to hurry up the first one.

And then the Prefect came, staging a superb entrance. Obviously he had cast himself for the star role. He was a round, tubby little man in a preposterous uniform. His jacket seemed to be a patchwork of medals. He advanced with slow solemnity down the street while the Mayor and the Town Councillors fluttered round him like a chorus. His strutting gait and his out-thrust chin were in the purest Fascist tradition. If René Clair had been directing it as a film, I do not think he would have changed a thing.

Inevitably the Prefect stole the show from the Brigadier, who had been up all night and probably had not changed his dusty clothes for three days. The gorgeous Italian looked with wondering scorn at the shabby, sunburned Scotsman. This, he clearly felt, was surely no way to receive the formal surrender of a city. But he pulled himself together and in the course of a graceful address he intimated that his Government had ordered him to stay behind and maintain order. Water, light and telephone were working. There were no booby-traps in the town. Everything was at the disposal of the British authorities. With a lordly wave of his hand he commanded wine to be brought.

The ceremony might have gone on longer. But a platoon of dirty, untidy, unshaven British troops came swinging down the street, going about their proper business. The glittering, impeccable Italians were jostled back summarily onto the sidewalk. And after the interruption the Prefect simply had not the heart to begin again.

Soon the town had slipped on its British occupation as easily as a well-fitting glove. All the public buildings had been examined and labelled. Armed guards were standing on duty here and there. Pretty Italian girls had plucked up courage to venture out into the streets. All of Misurata's European population had gathered to watch the British.

But Bill and Cliff and I were consumed with impatience. We had this story — not vitally important but very colourful — and we had it alone. Now our problem was to send it off. And it soon became obvious that there was only one way to do it. We should have to go back all the way to Wadi Tamet — 150 horrible miles — and hand our despatches ourselves to the communications plane, which would take them to Cairo. So we hitch-hiked our way back to our own vehicles and travelled all that day and well into the night, threading our way back through the whole Highland Division and eating its dust for hour after hour. It was dark when we arrived so we had to put up our tents and light our lamp and sit down and write the story. We had barely slept at all for thirty-six hours and I can never remember feeling more tired. We were all of us dabbing blindly and foolishly at the typewriter keys with weak, fumbling fingers before we had finished.

CHAPTER 30

Tripoli

NEXT day we got back as far as Misurata and spent the night in the hotel there. Then we turned west and began to chase the army along the coast.

This now was the home stretch to Tripoli. And it looked like paradise to men who had been fighting their way through desert ever since Alamein. It was a country of red, rich earth and endless groves of green palms. As we passed by the fields were still being tilled and the flocks tended. In the open country the villages and farmhouses were still occupied, and in the oases women were still going to the wells with their huge earthenware pitchers. The placid agricultural life of the land had only been momentarily jerked out of its ordinary rhythm.

Through this country the enemy had withdrawn with skill and method, still fighting his invisible rear-guard action. Every mile or so his engineers had put two charges of dynamite under the road and blown twin craters in it. At each place the British military traffic had to go down into the colonists' fields or orchards and forge a new track through the sticky mud. We went through the yards of farmhouses where women sat with their babies in their arms, watching us pass by. Automatically they would give the Fascist salute, then check themselves in embarrassment, wondering whether they were doing the right thing.

We rose next morning in darkness and dressed with special care. We were sure that it would be Tripoli to-day. I put on a special pair of whipcord trousers I had been saving and my last pair of clean socks. Then we climbed on up into the steep verdant hills, hoping we were not going to be too late.

We need not have worried. Before dawn broke we saw the sky ahead of us flushed with sudden semicircles of light and the noise of gunfire came echoing back queerly along the deep narrow valleys. We found Divisional Headquarters camped beside a deep anti-tank ditch which the Italians had dug but the Germans had disdained to use. They told us that last night's pursuit force had run into an ambush in the hills. The Ninetieth Light was holding a line, and the fighting was still going on — infantry fighting, for the valleys were too steep and mazy for tanks.

We drove ahead until the machine-gun fire was tapping away round the next corner. It sounded trivial and harmless enough and we stood impatiently, resenting more deeply than ever the thoroughness of Rommel's withdrawal. We cooked ourselves breakfast and hung about by the roadside, waiting for the position to be cleared up. Rumours were beginning to circulate about the progress of the southern pincer and we were desperately afraid we had picked a loser in the race for Tripoli.

That worry was cleared up before midday. A tank with MONTY painted on it in Gothic letters came rumbling up the road and then Montgomery arrived himself in a staff car. It could only mean that this was the winning column. The Army Commander had come up specially from the south to join the Highlanders. So the Highlanders would be first into Tripoli. Our spirits rose and our impatience doubled.

At midday the Seaforth Highlanders stormed the German line. They had to charge uphill over bare ground without cover, and I met men afterwards who had dug themselves as many as seven trenches in the course of the advance. There was a moment when it became plain that the Germans were more numerous than the Scots, and the enemy line started to fold its ends forward in a dangerous enveloping counterattack. It cost the Seaforths the whole of a battalion headquarters in hand-to-hand fighting and much more besides before they took the position. But to us in our impatience it was just a tapping of machine-guns among the hills and an intimation from Headquarters that we could go forward another few miles. They told us there was another hold-up where the Germans had destroyed a bridge across a ravine, and the engineers said they might need all night to fix it. At any rate it would not be Tripoli to-day.

It happened that we were forced to stop just where the Seaforths' battle had taken place. It was a pleasant enough spot, with fair grassy slopes and little pockets of olive trees and here and there an almond tree just bursting into miraculous blossom. It was sunny and quiet and the birds had begun to sing again. But I do not think I have ever hated war so much as I did that afternoon. For the British and German dead and dying were still lying across the countryside, waiting to be fetched in. I nearly trod on a German who was stretched on his back with a stomach wound, looking round with staring eyes and calling deliriously for water. I chased away a couple of Arabs who were trying to pick the pockets of a wounded Highlander. Just over the wall from where we parked our truck lay a dead German, his body frozen in the very act of throwing a hand-grenade. It had been such a silly, futile little battle. It had gained the Germans just a few brief hours which they could not really need. The very smallness and triviality of it all emphasized its tragedy. It was small enough and personal enough to be comprehended, where a much bigger slaughter would have overwhelmed and stunned the mind. I walked about by myself among the hills loathing bitterly the waste and necessity of it.

There was plenty of anger among the hills that afternoon. Fierce, unreasonable anger against the Germans for fighting this action and fighting it so well.

We spent the night there under some olive trees, with two dead Germans a few yards away. Towards midnight someone woke us and tipped us off that the road would be opened at dawn for a certain picked column to go through, but it would be closed again at eight o'clock in the morning. So we rose while it was still cold and dark and got through the barrier with a minute or two to spare.

There was no holding the Highland Division that day. Montgomery himself managed to get nearly to the head of the column, but the tanks got past him again at lunch and pushed eagerly on. Neither mine fields nor the most cunning road demolitions could stop these men now. Tanks and trucks were doing things that seemed to defy all scientific laws. Once when a bad traffic jam developed in the diversion round a road crater we led our truck straight through an obvious mine field. Once we got hopelessly bogged and we held up a Bren carrier and had ourselves hauled bodily out. Once a branch somehow jammed our foot-brake full on and everyone in sight came eagerly to assist us because we were blocking the whole route. There was a place where a tank stayed on duty the whole afternoon towing vehicles up a precipice. But trucks and even guns were fighting their way through. It seemed sometimes as though the vehicles were being impelled not by their own motive power so much as by the actual enthusiasm and eagerness and will-power of their drivers. It was like that first mad rush to Bengasi two years before. Nothing could have stopped the Highlanders now.

But the Germans went on demolishing and demolishing and sometimes they unlimbered their guns and shelled us and towards evening we realized that, despite all our determination, we were not going to do it that day. Disappointed, but still too excited to care what we ate or where we camped, we put up our beds beside the roadside where a milestone said TRIPOLI 20 KILOMETRES. And next morning, January 23, we again got up in darkness, knowing that this would be the last time, to-day we really should get in.

A huge full moon was turning the road into a gleaming silver ribbon ahead of us when we started out, but then dawn began to break quickly. Quietly, serenely we sailed ahead down the last stretch with nothing now to impede us. Furlong by furlong the country grew richer and fuller. A narrow-gauge railway appeared and ran alongside the road. Great avenues of eucalyptus and gum trees bordered the highway.

In the fields the almond trees were glowing with tender blossom. A woman sweeping her doorstep in a suburb looked at us apparently without astonishment or resentment. An Arab boy was pedalling his box-tricycle up the road delivering the morning milk. Arab men and women were setting out with baskets and donkeys to do their marketing. They were so indifferent that it seemed almost insulting. How did they know that they had nothing to fear from the British?

Factory chimneys appeared next, and smart villas bathed in the rosy light of the rising sun. The road took on sidewalks and houses became more frequent. Here and there were wooden notice boards referring to enemy dumps and Headquarters and three broken-down Italian army vehicles were stranded beside the road. But otherwise there was no sign of the Axis army. It was like entering a provincial town in peacetime.

Then there were real European-looking streets, the white façades of the buildings staring blindly with shuttered windows and barred doors. The gutters were cluttered with waste paper. Dust-stained British trucks were parked here and there in little squares or gardens and men were making their usual desert petrol fires to brew their breakfast tea. Now and again Italian girls would venture from their houses and start talking to the men.

Then we came to the harbour area. Here there were signs of war. Every street showed the familiar signs of bombing—heaps of rubble, blackened hollow façades, pitted walls, twisted iron shutters and dozens of signposts pointing to shelters. But no English manufacturing town would have called this damage bad. I began to wonder whether those endless British and American raids on Tripoli had really been any good at all.

Then we swept into the Piazza Roma and round to the right into the Piazza Castello, which has one side open to the sea, and we saw at once that our bombing had been superb. The famous Spanish Mole looked like a low stony ridge. It had lost almost all resemblance to masonry. Only the derelict warehouses and installations showed what it had been. The surface of the water bristled with the rigging and funnels of sunken ships. Half a wooden schooner was moored to the Piazza Castello. The other half had been cut clean away. All round there was evidence of fine, accurate bombing.

Already the skirl of bag-pipes was echoing through the square. A piper in kilts was pacing up and down playing "The Cock o' the North," the marching song of the Gordon Highlanders. All roundabout, tanks, scout cars, jeeps and trucks were parked and the Gordons were raising their mugs of tea, toasting their entry. Suddenly I found myself brimming with more excitement than I could contain. That moment then down by the harbour with the bag-pipes playing was for me the supreme moment of achievement. It was the fulfilment of two and a half years' ambitions — the final crowning of all those grim, uncomfortable, often heart-breaking campaigns. I knew that what came next must be anticlimax, but I was prepared for it. And I turned to the immediate business of finding out who had entered Tripoli first.

It had in the end been a dead-heat between the two jaws of Montgomery's pincers, and that of course was the right solution. But if you want to be meticulous to the minute, you must give the victory to the southern column, for the armoured cars of the Eleventh Hussars had come nosing through the southern suburbs as early as 4 A.M. And I was delighted when I heard it. For these Hussars were the real desert veterans, the original "Desert Rats," and on every count they had the right to lead the Eighth Army in. But they had driven straight on out again up the road to Tunisia, following the enemy, and the streets were empty again when a Sherman tank clattered in from the east with seven Gordon Highlanders and a sapper clinging to it. Perhaps it was absurd to make a fuss about this. But Tripoli was very much more to us than a mere provincial town of 150,000 inhabitants. For two and a half years it had been the Eighth Army's goal, and the entering of it was something symbolic and deeply moving. It marked the end of Italy's Colonial Empire, and it set the seal on Rommel's defeat. We had fought very hard for this city, and now we had got it we were inclined to value it not intrinsically but on the basis of what it had cost us.

I sat down on a seat in the square to write my story. Down the broad Corso Sicilia the local population were gathering now —

robed Arabs and Italians in smart Western clothes. Ornately uniformed Italian police with rifles slung over their shoulders were standing on guard, preventing the populace from invading the square. And the same thing happened as had happened in Bengasi the first time.

I think these people had half expected a triumphal entry with gala uniforms and flamboyant ceremonial. Certainly their own army would have staged something of the sort. And they were prepared to be sullen and unimpressed when we did it. But instead of a parade they saw tanks and trucks stained with the mud and dust of endless desert travel. They saw men wearing shapeless overcoats and sleeveless leather jerkins, chipped tin hats and ragged mufflers. The dust of a thousand miles of desert shook from their clothes as they walked. For days no one had had time to clean boots or buttons. You cannot remove the stains of jam or tea in the desert. No one was really clean or smart or properly shaved except the military policemen. And in spite of themselves I think the people of Tripoli were impressed simply because no attempt was made to impress them. They saw men staring almost in bewilderment at the fountains playing in the square, and they realized, perhaps, that these troops had fought their way through hundreds of miles of desert where water was as precious as champagne. They saw the cooking going on at the roadside and the blankets being shaken out. And they realized that none of it was being done for their benefit and that therefore they lost no dignity by staying to watch.

Nevertheless there was a little ceremony later in the morning — a modest, inconspicuous affair which few people saw. It happened outside the city, at the Porto Benito crossroads. There, standing in the roadway, Montgomery received the formal surrender of Tripoli.

He had with him an interpreter and the Brigadier who was going to be in charge of administering the British occupation. Opposite them stood Commendatore San Marco, Vice-Governor of Libya, the Prefect of Tripoli, and the Lord Mayor of the city. The three Italians were exotically uniformed but they looked tired and apathetic and rather bewildered. They puckered their faces to listen as Montgomery, speaking very quietly, issued his requirements. He wished the Italian police to remain in control, and the British would co-operate with them. He did not wish to interfere at all with the Italian population, but he was very firm that there must be no obstruction or treachery on the part of the Italians. On the local authorities he laid the responsibility for providing the civilian population with food, water and light.

The three Italians listened impassively as this was translated sentence by sentence. The Vice-Governor's nose twitched a little, as though he wanted to blow it but did not quite like to. At the end they all turned to one another and frowned and whispered a few words. But finally they said they perfectly understood, and had no questions to ask. They had a split second's hesitation about saluting. You could see them saying to themselves, "Oh, what the hell, let's risk it," and their arms snapped up in the regulation Fascist greeting. Then at the critical moment they hesitated, thinking they might have gone too far, and they looked at one another out of the corners of their eyes and their arms sank weakly back to their sides. At the same instant an Arab funeral came barging down the road with mourners chanting round a white-draped coffin, and all the Generals and Brigadiers and high officials were swept unceremoniously into the gutter.

So there it was. Officially, now, the Italians had surrendered Libya. With this little ceremony the Eighth Army had achieved its ambition. But as a finale to all the campaigns that had gone before it was artistically bad. It was utterly out of proportion. I was standing beside a man I had first met in those remote kindergarten days on the Egyptian Frontier when Italy had just declared war, and he turned to me and said, "God, what bathos. I feel we ought to have had Bergonzoli here in chains." I understood exactly what he meant. In that crude moment of success, I too felt that the whole uncivilized business ought to be rounded off with pomp and ostentation. I saw now why the Roman conquerors had staged triumphs after their victories.

The inevitable anticlimax had set in. We drove back into Tripoli with that faint, puzzling feeling of futility that I was beginning to know. What glory there was had faded and now we must find somewhere to live and somewhere to eat and we must type our despatches and start out on the weary struggle of sending them off. We went to the smart Waddan Hotel, which had been German G.H.Q., and got ourselves fine rooms with bathrooms. But it was soon plain that we should get nothing more. Tripoli that day was a town of broken and unfulfilled promises — baths but no water, restaurants but no food, laundries but no soap, cinemas but no films, shops but nothing to buy. In the end we moved over from the Waddan to the Grand Hotel — a gaunt grey-painted building on the sea front which was making some pretence at catering for guests. There were still German names at the top of the page in the hotel register so we drew a line across and wrote our English names underneath. Then we went up to our rooms and found that Tripoli did at least provide one thing we prized greatly — clean sheets.

Italian waiters served us lunch with an air of professional impartiality. The wine was shocking and we kept telling one another that the Germans would never have stood for it. We drank it more as a gesture than for the sake of any enjoyment. All through the meal people kept arriving — people whose job it was to arrive early in the captured city, and many of them I knew of old. Now and again friends came in with the first wild excitement still on them and I caught faint echoes of the thrill I had experienced down by the harbour a few hours before. But the Italians by their obvious lack of shame or sorrow at being beaten cleverly robbed us of half the psychological content of our triumph — for a victor is only a victor in relation to the vanquished. For years we had been saying that whoever won the war, the Italians would lose. Suddenly on this first day in Tripoli it seemed to me that you could reverse it. Whoever lost the war, the Italians would win. Italy might lose, but not the Italians, for they had no spiritual stake in the war. Fundamentally, as people, they were interested in other things.

Never, I suppose, has any army been kept on so tight a rein as was the Eighth Army in Tripoli. The usual extravagant reactions — concomitants of victory so invariable historically that they must almost be regarded as pathological necessities — were very sternly suppressed. The main reason was not a sentimental one, but the practical fact that the British urgently needed a normal, workable Tripoli. Montgomery looked on it not as a prize, but as a harbour and a supply base, and it was very important that it should function as smoothly as possible.

Already in the public places Montgomery's proclamations were being pasted up over the florid Italian notices — the most recent one was dated the day before and it told the people of Tripoli in melodramatic language that their city was about to be occupied by the enemy. The local dignitaries were paying their respects to the Brigadier in charge of the Occupied Enemy Territory Administration, and shopkeepers were asking leave to open their shops. The British Military Authority currency — in pounds and shillings — was circulating side by side with the lira, at an exchange of 480 to the pound. To the British, accustomed to reckoning in multiples of twelve, this was child's play. But the Arab and Italian merchants were going crazy trying to do perpetual sums in their heads and never being quite certain that they were not cheating themselves.

Down by the entrance of the harbour, representatives of the British navy were entranced at the beauty of the enemy's blocking techniques. One ship filled with concrete and seven other vessels of varying sizes had sunk across the mouth of the harbour in a neat design which left them immovably wedged. Never, said the navy, had such superb blocking been seen. They almost felt it was a shame to disturb it. But that first afternoon they found an Italian diving suit and set to work as best they could until the rest of their gear arrived by air from Alexandria. Soon the waters over the block-ships began gathering themselves together and heaving themselves skywards in great spurting fountains, and the people of Tripoli raced automatically to their shelters as the noise of the explosions rolled through the streets. On the second morning British merchant ships were already anchored outside the boom, discharging their cargoes by lighter onto the beaches until the harbour should be ready. On the second afternoon a native fishing craft came out from the quayside, hovered a minute indecisively, and then skimmed out to the open sea through a gap the engineers had just made. Bit by bit they chiselled the blockage away, blasting cunningly now on one side and now on the other until the concrete ship split and fell apart. In a very few days vessels of ten thousand tons' burthen were moving in and out of the harbour. The navy did a spectacular job there.

ii

Item by item through that first day in Tripoli I gathered the story of the southern prong of the pincer—that other column which had been so separated from us that at no time had we had any idea what it was doing. And I found that its story was the story of the man behind the wheel, the man whose job was to drive a truck or a jeep or an armoured car or a tank and get the army to the places where it wanted to go. The enemy was not Rommel—he was hardly dangerous any more. It was the desert itself. It was a countryside pitted against man-made machines, and everyone who made that terrible journey admitted that the desert put up a very good fight.

The oldest desert veterans had known nothing like it before. It was not just a question of getting back onto the good going. There simply was no good going. And no one knew when this heart-breaking business would stop.

And yet they got through, with guns and supplies and everything. The desert put up a great fight on behalf of the enemy, but it lost. The Eighth Army defeated it through the excellence of its vehicles—most of them American—and the superb patience and strength and co-operation of its drivers. Anyone who could move towed someone who could not. Bren carriers and tanks stood by all day to help people out of specially bad patches. Jacks and tyres and tools were given without question to anyone in trouble. Men gave up their meal times to help dig their comrades out.

Twelve miles from Tarhuna, on January 19, the enemy came to the aid of the desert. A small force commanded by Rommel himself — a glowering, short-tempered Rommel — held the pass leading into Tarhuna with 88-millimetre guns and long-range mortars, and held it for forty-eight hours. There was no possible detour. A direct assault against such powerful positions over such appalling ground would have been terribly costly.

But gradually guns and more guns arrived — twenty-five-pounders and mediums came grinding and plunging through sand and rock and went into action as soon as they could get unlimbered. The barrage grew and grew until the enemy could endure it no longer. Rommel gave the order to evacuate.

So our armoured forces drove on over the pass and looked down with astonished eyes on the fresh green land of fields and palms and fruit trees studded with square white farmhouses. And when they clattered on into the white-walled town below the inhabitants came out and pelted them with oranges.

This popularity pleased them but surprised them somewhat until they learned the reason. It was a curious reason, but the Mayor explained it with great detail and all the townspeople confirmed it. Fourteen days before, it seemed, the discipline of the German troops had suddenly cracked so that their officers could no longer restrain their looting and drunkenness.

What had happened was this: General Cavallero, Mussolini's Chief of General Staff, had flown over to Tripoli from Rome to see whether anything could be done to save Libya. Reluctantly he had decided that the case was hopeless. He had told Tarhuna's Mayor, "The people in Italy are going to feel this badly — much more than they should." Then without inspecting any troops or fortifications he had returned to Italy.

That fact alone created a bad impression. Then the Germans were told officially that they were going to evacuate the country. Instantly their discipline flagged and cracked. They still had their fighting morale, but they felt that if they were going to lose this country, there was no point in treating it well any longer. It was a very German phenomenon — the psychosis of retreat plus a fundamental lack of respect for anything not German. Looting and rowdiness broke out and since the loot included wine that led to drunkenness. The officers could not control it, probably because they themselves were infected with the mood. One night three German officers staggered into one of our ack-ack batteries, dead drunk. Finally the spoliation became official and the Germans got away with an almond-crop worth a million dollars. Then the people of Tarhuna began to hate the Germans so much that they welcomed the British with oranges.

There was a final bitter skirmish and then the way was open. Through the moonlight on the morning of January 23 the armoured cars of this southern column, cruising warily ahead like quivering, sensitive tentacles, came into Tripoli's still streets to meet the northern arm of Montgomery's pincer. It had been a very great march, and in a certain sense a fitting climax to the campaign. The man with the gun had done his stuff back at Alamein. And the man at the wheel, whose virtues are too prosaic to get much glory, came gloriously into his own on the last lap.

And then, on the second day of the capture of Tripoli, there arrived another column, an outsider in the race whose chances no one had ever considered. They came in filthy, rackety trucks tied together with wire, unkempt men incredibly sunburned with great, bushy, shapeless beards. Their own mothers could never have recognized them. But their trucks flew the tricolour of France and the cross of Lorraine.

They were all that was left of a brigade under General Leclerc which had set out from Fort Lamy, in the Lake Tchad territory, two months before. The rest of the brigade was strewn back through Southern Libya garrisoning the places it had captured. And its story outdid any Beau Geste novel ever written.

It was a mad, impossible force. Its advance from its base to Tripoli totalled more than three thousand miles, and its supply line stretched another twelve hundred miles to the West African port of Douala. It had thirteen operational aircraft, six of them out-of-date Lysanders. It started out with the full knowledge that it could never get more than one hot meal a day and never more than half a litre of water per man. It took a camel corps with it to supplement its vehicles. It decided to solve the problem of mines by never travelling on any roads. Its front line consisted always of mobile patrols skirmishing ahead and throughout the advance it was commanded from its front line.

These men had to go through four hundred miles of shifting sand where they could make no more than forty miles in a day of twelve hours' driving. They sometimes dug until they literally struck water, trying to extricate their vehicles. The Italian air force made it impossible for them to march by day, so they grew skilful at turning themselves into a dummy oasis with palm trees during the hours of light and making bogus camps with tracks and shiny petrol tins for the Italians to bomb. For weeks they moved only at night.

And all the time they were capturing oasis after oasis from superior Italian forces. It was a mad, piratical affair which had much in common with the Wavell Campaign in the Western Desert. At Uigh el Kebir they captured the Italian garrison's dinner still cooking on the stove — beans and meat and spaghetti. Gatrun, which was left to the camel corps alone, was taken by a frantic display of noise from hand-grenades and a confident demand for surrender. At Murzuk the enemy were simply scared into evacuating. A single fighter plane trailed them and shot them up. The Italians laid a white table-cloth on the ground and arranged their petrol cans to make words signifying surrender. The pilot drew a circle of machine-gun fire round them and went for help. When he got back he found some of the Italians trying to escape and he herded them angrily back into the circle like a sheepdog herding sheep.

There was a fine little comedy at Umm el Erneb. The French Colonel was resting after lunch in his deck chair when an orderly came to him. "My Colonel," he said, "the white flag has appeared."

"Bring me my boots," commanded the Colonel shortly. And having put them on he drove over to where something white was waving above the palm trees. But when he got there he found the white flag had a red cross in the middle of it and the Italian garrison met him with defiant shouts of "*Resistenza.*"

Coldly the Colonel answered them: "I merely came to say that my artillery is opening its barrage at eight minutes past four. I thought perhaps you would prefer to anticipate it by surrendering now."

The Italians renewed their defiant cries and the Colonel drove back. At 4.08 P.M. the barrage duly opened. At 4.20 P.M. the Italians ran up their biggest mess table-cloth above their tallest palm tree.

All the way northward through Libya that sort of thing was happening. The French suffered odd mishaps but never any bad losses. They only lost one vehicle through bombing and none through mechanical break-downs. They changed a few engines and innumerable springs, but they kept going. My friend Peers Carter, who was the British Liaison Officer with the force, had his turban burned off his head by an incendiary bullet. Everything that happened to Leclerc's columns seemed to be slightly out of the ordinary.

Finally, after being pursued by a British long-range patrol, the French reached Garian and found the Union Jack already floating above the castle there. They realized they had lost the Tripoli race. But they had done something fit to be set alongside Bir Hacheim, something to raise the name of France again in the world of free men and make the Eighth Army proud to fight alongside them.

iii

Ten days later Churchill and Alexander and Montgomery stood together beneath the great walls of Tripoli's Castello and paid their respects to this Eighth Army. The sunshine warmed the ancient stone and in the blue wreck-strewn harbour, framed between two mighty columns at the end of the square, British ships were already unloading. The harsh, sentimental music of the bagpipes was filling the air, for it was mainly a parade of the Highland Division. This, perhaps, was the real curtain to the campaign, the proper artistic climax.

It was a moment very highly charged with emotion and reminiscence. I looked down from a balcony and recognized unit after unit by its heads — the tow-heads of Scotland and the dark heads of the Maoris, the sun-helmets of the South African sappers and the beards of the navy, the brown berets of the Eleventh Hussars and the black berets of the tank units. But something was wrong. The Eighth Army had cleaned itself and preened itself until it was unrecognizable. Buttons were polished and equipments pipe-clayed and uniforms were stainless and beautifully pressed. The Black Watch had new red cockades in their bonnets and some of the Highland units had immaculate kilts. I had never seen them like that before and I did not know them. It was like when you want to photograph some picturesque peasant girl in her national costume and she insists on putting on her smart Sunday hat and her new sateen dress.

The twenty-five-pounders had been newly painted and I remembered how often I had seen them, with scratched and blackened barrels, firing madly from some *wadi*. Their crews, whom I had known sweaty and unshaven and stripped to the waist, were now fully and faultlessly dressed. Only the deep ruddy tan of their faces, and the way their muscles moved restlessly beneath the unaccustomed stricture of their smart uniforms, hinted at what they had done and endured. The Prime Minister should have seen the army as it was on the morning we took Tripoli. This parade was a very fine and moving thing, but it was not the curtain. It was the cast coming forward to receive congratulations after the curtain.

That afternoon Churchill reviewed the New Zealand Division out in the countryside. They too had polished and cleaned themselves. But nothing could obscure the splendour of their physique and the character and maturity in their faces. If I had been asked to write down the best division in the armies of the British Empire,

I should have put this one unhesitatingly first. Rommel had already done so — we had captured a piece of paper on which he had listed the divisions of the Eighth Army in order of merit and the New Zealanders headed it. They were quiet men, not given to boasting, and possessing a firmness of spirit that came from thoroughly digested experience. Perhaps some day someone will write this Division's history. It ought to be the best reading of the war.

CHAPTER 31

Mariage de Convenance

Our Public Relations unit took a low white villa in a little countrified village just inside Tripoli's ramparts. It lay amid thick orange and lemon groves, and there was an old well in the garden with an ancient oaken cross-beam supported by two whitewashed pillars. And I sat down one morning in the sunshine beside the well, with the oranges glowing in their green shade round me, and tried to sum the whole thing up.

For this was a conclusion. The Eighth Army had fulfilled its proper function, its ambition was achieved. The pendulum had swung at last to rest at one of its extremities. Alexander had cabled home that the Premier's order had been fulfilled and that he awaited further instructions. Churchill had brought us laurels to rest on. It was impossible not to think then that a line had been drawn, *Finis* had been written, an era was ended.

But when I looked back through the tangled history of the past thirty months I saw that a summing up was not necessary. This African war had summed itself up as it went along. Its progression had been geometrical rather than arithmetical, cumulative rather than consecutive. Even as it fought the Eighth Army had digested its experience, drawn its conclusions, learned its lessons. Bir Hacheim, Gazala, Tobruk — all those old names that seemed so remote and stale and unprofitable now — had been used. They lived on as the body of a slain animal lives on in the creature that devours it. All those mistakes of leadership and arms, all that expenditure of men and machines, the blood and the heroism and the endeavour, were drawn together in the ultimate result. And so a summing up of the whole was not a detailed analysis but an existing thing, an army — the Eighth Army as it stood. The product of all the campaigns was an army that could win the last campaign.

That was why this last campaign had very few lessons to teach. All the lessons had been learned in advance in order that the campaign might be won, that this army might advance farther and faster than any army in history. It is a campaign that will be studied and analyzed in the military textbooks of the future; but its value will lie as much in its early, experimental phases as in its final result. For the final result was merely the right answer to the problems raised by the early stages: not the finding of the answer, but simply the using of it.

One very crucial qualification must be made. The Eighth Army was not an exclusively British Army. Apart from its guns and its fastest fighter planes, its best machines came from America. Without the Grant and Sherman tanks the victory could not have been won. For even by the end of it all Britain still had not produced a suitable fighting tank. And in addition America sent fine road transport, the P40 pursuit plane, the Douglas transport plane, Mitchell, Boston and Baltimore bombers, Honey tanks, and a dozen other things. At the opposite ends of the scale the jeep and the D.C. 3 plane were the outstanding machines in that last mighty advance when all the emphasis was on transport and supplies. And the Eighth Army's men came from every corner of the British Empire, from France, Poland, Greece and Czechoslovakia. It was in every sense an Allied Army.

This army, of course, did not come into being through a few decisions by a few generals. To argue so is an easy but very misleading over-simplification of history. This Allied Army was built up through the complex interplay of a great number of stresses and strains. Its whole career was conditioned by forces and processes and influences over most of which no one in the Middle East had any control. There were huge, remote, unassessable influences like Britain's unpreparedness for war, Hitler's attack on Russia, Japan's attack on America, the comparative lengths of the British and Axis supply routes to Africa and the progress of submarine warfare. Other influences were more concentrated and local, like the speed with which the British learned their lessons, the evolution of training and technique as new material arrived in the field, the shifting of air superiority from the Axis to the Allies.

But the dominating trend through it all was one of steady improvement. The Eighth Army in its thirty months of warfare up to Tripoli provided a wonderfully clear cross-section of Britain's rise in strength. And its enemies gave an equally clear display of their own development: in the case of Germany, a superb army thought out and put together several years ago as a final complete thing, an army built to win without any further improvements, and now being overhauled by younger and more modern armies because it had not won; and in the case of Italy, a poor army which had apparently abandoned all hope of improving, of producing any new weapons or ideas.

It is a human instinct to search for heroes, to attribute events to people rather than forces, to personify armies in their commanders. And there has, perhaps, been too much vague reference to "Wavell," "Auchinleck," "Montgomery," "Rommel," when the success or failure of their armies has been under discussion. But certain outstanding figures must, through their decisions, be regarded as potent influences in the Middle East story. Nothing can dim the essential rightness of Wavell's appreciation of the situation at the beginning, and the boldness and correctness of his decision to attack in the winter of 1940—a decision which a lesser general might have refrained from taking. A year later Auchinleck's personal refusal to agree with the advice of his army commander and withdraw from Libya was decisive. A different decision might have been taken about sending an army to Greece and leaving Cyrenaica unguarded (though that was not Wavell's decision). A different decision might have been taken about holding Tobruk. It seems that some very tiny difference might have given Egypt to Rommel in the summer of 1942.

But in fact none of these were offered to the Generals concerned as clear-cut choices to which they could answer freely yes or no. The decisions were shadowed round with a multitude of influencing circumstances impossible to assess. It is for the most part idle and profitless to look back and apportion praise and blame to individuals unless the circumstances are transparently clear. And they almost never are.

But the search for heroes is irresistible. The thirty months of warfare threw up many fine soldiers, many great leaders of men like Jock Campbell, many great commanders in the field like "Strafer" Gott and in the air like Tedder and Coningham. But if the whole great drama has a single hero, I think it must be Rommel. He was the most permanent, most prominent figure on the stage. His were the most brilliant coups, the most bitter disappointments. He came with no desert experience and he never had more than four German divisions. He had to use Italian divisions which he knew he could not trust. And he fought nearly always supremely well.

It appears that his own officers and men admired him, but disliked him personally. The Eighth Army adored him. They admired him passionately when he beat them, and when they beat him they admired themselves for beating such a clever General. They talked about him in a personal way as "Old Rommel," or even more affectionately as "that bastard Rommel." At one time the British propaganda machine dimly sensed this and set to work to discredit him. But the Eighth Army would have none of it. They knew too much. And they could not be brought to hate him either. For the desert war was a clean, straight, dispassionate war with no Gestapo, no politics, no persecuted civilians, no ruined homes. There was nothing with which to work up an immediate, urgent hatred and the Eighth Army went on admiring Rommel. It did no harm.

Sometimes they admired him a little too passionately, for he did make mistakes. He lost a great chance when he annihilated the British tank forces in Wavell's last Middle East campaign in June 1941. He could probably have taken Tobruk that summer had he gone the right way about it. Many people believe he would have won at Sidi Rezegh if he had not sent away some of his tanks on that mad "dash to the wire." But he had astonishing resilience in defeat and sound military thoroughness behind his gambles. And his retreat from Alamein to Tripoli was as near perfection as any general can ever hope to get.

ii

Even as I sat there by the white well working out that a summing up was not necessary, that perfect retreat was still going on. It was hard to prize the mind loose from the past and pitch it into the future again, to realize that this was after all not the end, that there was more to come. But I jerked myself out of the complacent atmosphere of Tripoli and drove on westwards again to see what was happening.

After Tripoli the landscape, as though exhausted by its riotous spasm of fertility, sinks gradually back into desert. At first there are little belts of oasis every few miles. Then it flattens out into a sour, salty wilderness, featureless and drab. Wild storms of rain were turning its surface into slime the consistency of tooth paste or cold cream and the attenuated advance guard of the Eighth Army was squelching and slithering moodily forward. In a curious way the zest and drive had gone out of the campaign again. There was a feeling of hangover, a feeling of clearing up the cigarette ends and the bottles and the smashed glasses after a party. We were taking a few dull little towns, Zauia, Sabratha, Zuara, but I found it hard to be interested. Even the crossing of the frontier into Tunisia happened in a muddled, unexciting way.

So at Sabratha my companions and I turned aside to examine the Roman ruins which the Italians have dug up and partially restored. An Armenian monk with a black beard that was honestly spade-shaped showed us where the Germans had laid mines, and we skirted round them and made our way to the great theatre.

It is an astonishing thing—not beautiful but astonishing. So extraordinarily sophisticated, with its elaboration of ornament. But the colour of the old sun-soaked stone is lovely, and this afternoon there were half a dozen soldiers lounging in the tiered seats and gazing with mild amazement at this surprising thing they had captured. A great deal of the city has been laid bare, and you can walk for miles through the stone-paved streets. The people who had lived here were people who lived their lives in public. Their shops and homes were tiny. But their public buildings were immense. There are two or three public baths with fine mosaic pavements, half a dozen temples, an amphitheatre in addition to the theatre, and a public lavatory in a state of fascinating completeness. Up in the museum there are more, vast mosaic pavements, including one which looks as though it had been copied from a Persian carpet. It includes every bird imaginable, the male of the species on the one side, the female on the other.

That evening we made an interesting experiment. We stayed in a little house in the modern village of Sabratha and an Italian doctor and his wife came to call on us. And we went on arguing with them until they started thinking for themselves. At first they gave us the stock Fascist answers which their spoon-fed propaganda had been teaching them for years. It was as though you put a coin in a slot machine. You asked a question, and automatically you got the exact answer you knew you were going to get. But cunningly we led them beyond that point and finally, late in the evening, the doctor's brain began turning over under its own power. He was an intelligent man and he had studied in Paris. And gradually, jerkily, the knack of independent thought came back to him. Soon he was bubbling with the pleasure of free speech, and once he had come to it he could not let it go and I believe he would have talked till dawn. When finally his wife dragged him away he shook our hands warmly and said, "Somehow I feel as though I had become an adult again."

The day after this the main body of the Eighth Army began to move across the frontier into Tunisia. The idea of Tripoli as a final goal, a full-stop, was still strong. But now we were beginning to face the fact that there was going to be an epilogue, an appendix. We had chased our enemy right out of his own ground into someone else's battle-field, but he still remained to be fought. All the Axis armies in Africa now were concentrating in that narrow slice of Tunisia where von Arnim had been fighting for three months. They were going to form a joint front. And consequently the Allied armies in North Africa would also have to join forces and form a common front. Together they would draw a cordon across Tunisia, forming a noose with the coast. And they would draw the noose tighter and tighter until the Axis armies were squeezed out of Africa or into surrender.

It was at first a new, vague future only dimly visualized. The Eighth Army had been so deeply immersed in its own campaign that it had paid very little attention to what was happening "over on the other side." In the desert few people ever saw a newspaper or listened to the radio. Tunisian geography was confusing and no one had a relevant map. No one knew the strength of the other Allied forces or anything about the country they were fighting in. At one time we had regarded them as serious rivals in the race for Tripoli, but obviously something or other had held them up.

Just a little weary now, wishing it would all finish, the Eighth Army moved on through Ben Gardane and Medenine. And then it was halted. Rommel led his army behind the Mareth Line, the French-built southern defences of Tunisia, and turned and faced his pursuers.

So for the fourth time in sixteen hundred miles the Eighth Army began coiling itself to spring. Swiftly its strength piled up before the Mareth Line. Patrols began to "lean" against the defences, tapping in here and there to test their strength as a doctor probes with a stethoscope. Round Medenine the dumps grew up, huge stores of food and fuel and ammunition. Old air fields were cleared and new ones made and day by day the squadrons bunched nearer and nearer to the forward areas. The guns were dug in and the gunners got busy with their ranges. We were told that we were now fighting on the same front as the First Army and the Americans, but we still had not met them. A chain of huge salt lakes still lay between us. The Eighth Army still had a faint feeling that this was all something extra, something it had not originally bargained for. It went about its preparations with just a slight air of being only too happy to lend a hand, but of wishing to point out that this was not strictly its business.

Then, late in February, a marriage was arranged. A marriage of convenience, for the two parties had never met. The Eighth Army suddenly found itself amalgamated officially with the other Allied Forces. Its centre of gravity was shifted abruptly from Cairo to Algiers.

There was a bewildering re-shuffle of commanders. General Eisenhower became Commander-in-Chief of all Allied Forces in North Africa. General Alexander became deputy C-in-C. His place as head of the Middle East (for the moment little more than a supply base for the Eighth Army) was taken by General Sir Henry Maitland Wilson. Air-Marshal Tedder became head of all Allied Air Forces in the Mediterranean, and he took Coningham to Algiers with him. Malta became a separate R.A.F. command, and the Western Desert Air Force became another under Air Vice-Marshal Broadhurst, who had had operational experience as a fighter pilot and was still not yet forty years old.

It meant that the Eighth Army would have to sink its individuality in a much larger army and take its orders from Algiers. But in an odd way the Eighth Army did not greatly care. It was very sure of itself now. It feared competition from no one, and it coveted the respect of no one but itself. It had, in fact, the elements of a promising superiority complex. It still had that extraordinary intimacy and coherence which had knit it together in the desert, based on complete community of problems and experience. It had a deep loyalty to the traditions it had forged itself.

But now it had been married off to this other army. And all at once it conceived an intense curiosity about its new partner.

iii

In the very early hours of November 8, 1942, British and American shock troops lowered themselves from assault boats into the ice-cold waters of the Mediterranean on either side of Algiers.

Silently they waded ashore and groped their way through the moonless night to their predestined objectives. They were "invading" Vichy-controlled French North Africa, and they hoped the invasion would be friendly.

They had come as part of the greatest invasion armada in history — some 850 transports and warships. Other American troops were even then landing at Oran and Casablanca hundreds of miles farther west, and already the repercussions of this Allied action were spreading out like ripples to Toulon and Dakar, to Berlin and Sicily and Rommel's retreating army in Libya.

But here at Algiers there was little serious trouble. The fortress of Sidi Ferruch was surrendered by an amiable French General. Blida Air Field was handed over to a British officer and an American war correspondent. There was some desultory scrapping in the Algiers suburb of El Biar while Robert Murphy, the United States Consul General, motored back and forth between Admiral Darlan and the American General Ryder. But in sixteen hours it was all over. Algiers was in Allied hands.

The strategy of it was obvious enough. The Allies were determined to secure the whole southern coast of the Mediterranean, and so open up the soft underside of Europe. To the east Montgomery already had Rommel's army in full retreat. Now the American Expeditionary Force and the British First Army were starting from the western end. Rommel was to be caught between these two armies and squeezed out of Africa.

General "Ike" Eisenhower, who was in charge of the expedition, knew that speed was essential. Between Algeria and Libya lay Tunisia with the two fine ports of Tunis and Bizerta, and these must be occupied before the Germans had time to react. So as soon as Algiers was safe, two brigades of the British First Army under General Anderson were rushed eastwards.

Distances were great and communications bad and every nerve had to be strained. On November 12 British parachutists jumped from American planes to take Bône, Algeria's most easterly port, and almost simultaneously the British Navy steamed into its harbour and took over. That meant that some troops could be brought to the front by sea. The smaller ports of Bougie and Philippeville were likewise occupied and got into working order. Troop trains began to move eastwards along the single-track railroad, but the service was a slow one for the Allies were adopting a "velvet-glove" policy towards the French and they did not want to requisition the railway outright. The Army had some road transport, but not a great deal, for there had not been enough shipping space available to bring a completely motorized expeditionary force. Nevertheless, within a week of the original landing British troops had crossed the Algerian border and were pushing on into the hills of Tunisia.

But Hitler, like Eisenhower, had realized the vital importance of speed. And the Germans had started to improvise at a startling pace. For some time they had been using Tunis and Bizerta as part of their supply route to Rommel's army, and they had a certain amount of war material ready on the spot. General Nehring, who had once commanded the Afrikakorps under Rommel, was rushed to the scene to organize a scratch force. They sent him the Panzer Grenadiers first of all, flying them over in Junkers 52 troop carriers. And on November 18 he was strong enough to demand that General Barré, the French Commander-in-Chief in Tunisia, should hand over all military installations to the Germans. Barré refused point blank, and Nehring sent for General Kesselring, the Luftwaffe chief in the Mediterranean. But still Barré would not listen. He ordered his soldiers to do their duty, and he himself escaped to Algeria.

That left Nehring in possession of Tunis and Bizerta, and rapidly he began to exploit his advantage. These two towns possessed the only all-weather air fields in French North Africa, and November is a month when you need all-weather air fields. Squadrons were flown across from Sicily in a matter of hours, and soon the Luftwaffe was exercising a complete superiority above the roads and harbours of Algeria. Its first efforts were devoted almost exclusively to the interruption of the Allies' difficult system of communications.

In the fullness of time the Tenth *Panzerdivision,* which was being refitted in France after service in Russia, appeared in Tunisia.

General von Arnim took over the command, German and Italian infantry divisions were ferried across from Europe. The Axis army took shape.

Despite the formidable swiftness of the German reaction, it still seemed worth while making a dash for Tunis before it was definitely too late. And on November 25 General Anderson advanced through the village of Tebourba and attacked the enemy in the hills round Djedeida, which is only twelve miles from Tunis itself.

The Germans fought cunningly among the hills with their heavy mortars and their 88-millimetre guns. They made full and expert use of their air superiority. And although the British with American support made some progress, they were halted outside Djedeida and they knew they had failed to get Tunis in their first rush.

On November 30 the Germans made the inevitable counter-attack, throwing their forces round Tebourba in the two arms of a pincer movement. Fighting with great bravery — perhaps with more bravery than skill — the Allied forces withdrew twenty miles in seven days towards Medjez-el-Bab. And there a balance was struck and the front hardened and crystallized.

Now the firing line began to spread all down the mountain backbone of Tunisia like a rash. The front ran roughly north and south parallel with the sea but about sixty miles inland. It tended to clot into fierce little centres of resistance wherever there was a way through the hills and it finally ended in the great salt lakes called Chotts, which are not passable, at any rate in winter. Gradually General Giraud's French forces made their appearance, gallant little men with mule-drawn transport and hopelessly under-armed by British or American or German standards. A British armoured division arrived, still inexplicably equipped with those under-gunned British cruiser tanks whose deficiencies had been so glaringly revealed in Auchinleck's first desert campaign. Later they got Shermans, and an American armoured division arrived, also with Shermans. Air fields were made in the flat valleys, and plane by plane the German air superiority was reduced and finally neutralized. New infantry divisions came from across the seas. Gradually the gaps in the original expeditionary force were filled and a fighting army was built up.

But the Germans too were building up, and no progress could be achieved. While the Eighth Army was making its sensational advances over unopposed desert, the British and the Americans in the Tunisian hills were measuring their gains and losses by yards. The weather was atrocious. There were mud and rain and sleet and hail and bitter bone-chilling cold. It was a front of great geographical complexity, depending on valleys and ridges and mountain formations which no ordinary map could show. For two years the emphasis had been so much on desert fighting that people at home were apt to imagine the whole of North Africa as desert, and to wonder what was wrong with this much-advertised Anglo-American army.

Towards the end of January, 1943, Tunisia was still a long rectangle bounded on the north and east by the sea and on the west by the front. And now Rommel's army came backing in from Tripoli into the vacant gap at the southern end of the rectangle. He plugged the Gabes gap like a cork in a bottle. And being a Field Marshal and therefore the senior Axis General present, he presumably took command of all the Axis forces in the bottle.

It was all unified and simplified now. In this long narrow corridor, with their backs to the sea, the Germans and Italians were going to make their fight for time. Just how dearly they were willing to buy that time could not yet be clear. But by any calculation they needed it badly, on the argument that the Allies could not begin an invasion of Southern Europe while there was still an Axis army fighting in Africa. The struggle now, when on the map it seemed to be almost all over, was likely to be more bitter and intense than ever. Rommel's army had grown snowball-fashion as he led it back through Libya, for he had collected all the troops guarding his lines of communications, and all base-depot staffs, all his workshops, the ack-ack artillery from half a dozen different parts, and so on. Rommel's forces plus von Arnim's made a very considerable army. And it had strong mountain positions to fight from.

Rommel's first instinct was to make a fighting defence. He began lunging about in a manner that could not be compared with that of a rat in a trap because his lunges were shrewd and well-directed. His most successful thrust was delivered on Valentine's Day — February 14 — against American armoured forces opposite the Faid Pass, on the central front.

The Germans descended from the Pass with a hundred tanks or more to attack a line which had so far seen virtually no fighting at all. The American armoured division was too spread out to offer a concentrated resistance, and the strength and importance of the German drive do not seem to have been appreciated. The American tanks were thrown in piecemeal, by battalions, and lost. There was no powerful screen of anti-tank guns. It must have seemed to Rommel very much like those early days in Libya. A retreat started which at times took on the proportions of a rout.

Back the Allied forces moved, through Sbeitla, Kasserine, Thelepte, Feriana. It was looking very serious. There was plenty of indication that Rommel was in command, and the whole affair was characteristic of him; the deep hard thrust and the swift urgent exploitation. But his gambling spirit seized hold of him and as long as things were going well he could not bear to stop. He over-exploited his surprising advantage. He turned north to attack the British, and at the turn the Americans caught him. Most of it was due to a very accurate and opportune artillery barrage against the rear of one of his flanks. His tanks were in danger of being cut off, and his infantry of annihilation. So he turned quickly and ran back all the way he had come — something like fifty miles.

It had, on the whole, been a worth-while expedition for Rommel. He had inflicted great damage and won considerable booty. He had certainly disrupted any offensive preparations which the Americans might have been making on that front. His own losses had not been great, and he had recovered most of his enemy's damaged tanks as well as his own.

It was an auspicious beginning to his back-to-the-wall fight for time. It encouraged him to turn south and try the same thing against the Eighth Army.

CHAPTER 32

Left Hook at Mareth

ON MARCH 5 ROMMEL addressed his troops in the mountains overlooking the Mareth Line. He told them that if they did not take Medenine, capture the British dumps, and force the Eighth Army to withdraw, then the days of the Axis forces in North Africa were numbered.

Next day he attacked, a regulation attack with tanks. And just as before Alamein, the British gained a rousing defensive victory. A Major who was there and who has been in pretty nearly every tank engagement in the desert described it to me as "the first perfect battle." The advancing German tanks saw the British abandon their anti-tank gun pits and run. They did not know that the pits were dummies. So, when they gave chase, they did not expect to have six-pounder armour-piercing shells crashing into them from the real pits forty yards farther on. The British tanks were never seriously in action at all. It was all done by anti-tank guns. And afterwards the engineers went out and demolished fifty-two tanks which the Germans had left behind them on the field. The British did not lose one.

That was a very signal little victory. Rommel had spent fifty-two of his dwindling total of tanks in a fruitless attempt to disturb our coming offensive. He was doubtless quite right to make the attempt; but in the event it was a mistake, because he made it in such a way that it failed. I think he still did not appreciate quite how much the British had improved since he first met them — since he had been able to say to a captured British General, "I do not care how many tanks you have as long as you go on using them the way you do."

The front settled into quietness again, and for ten more days the Eighth Army continued with its preparations. The country now was growing softer once more. The Matmata Hills stood on the far horizon like a jagged purple cockscomb, the first mountains we had yet seen. There was a faint mist of colour over the desert surface, for the wildflowers were still blooming—delicate *Iris reticulata,* little wild cyclamen, and stock that drenched the evening air with scent. Medenine was a honeycomb of vaulted whitewashed native houses, plus a little modern square with a French post-office and a dingy hotel. Beyond it a strange, table-topped hill rose abruptly from the plain, a superb vantage point. It was called Elephant Hill and its capture was undoubtedly one of Rommel's aims when he attacked on March 6.

Then someone discovered Jerba, a big square island lying only a mile off the coast. We did not know then that it was Calypso's isle, the original home of the Lotus-eaters. So we were enthralled with its myriads of palm trees and its wealth of chickens and eggs and fruit, its clean, compact little cities and its lost tribe of Israel. Anyone who could get any time off made an excursion to Jerba and came back laden with fresh food for his mess and gaudy striped carpets to send home.

I wanted to cover this coming battle from the air-force angle. For one thing, I had not yet had an inside view of the working of this mighty air superiority. For another, my colleague Paul Bewsher was now in the desert, and no newspaper was allowed to maintain more than one correspondent with the army. So I went across to Advanced Air Headquarters to see the Public Relations Officer, Squadron-Leader Titley.

He was suffering from a very acute spell of desert melancholia, and he only wanted to be left alone. But I was in search of a status in the desert, and I forced him to invite me to stay with him in his tent. Then I set to work to talk him gently out of his melancholy. He had done a fine job of reporting in Malta all through the great blitz period, and he had come straight up to the desert without any respite. His melancholy was understandable. But I knew he would be all right as soon as the battle started, for action is always the best cure.

We began to realize that this was going to be a very important battle and possibly a very hard one. The Mareth Line was easily the most serious obstacle the Eighth Army had met since Alamein. It had been completed by the French in 1939 as a bastion against the Italians, and they had worked hard on it. Its main fortifications ran inland for twenty-five miles at right angles with the sea, following the course of a natural ravine called the Wadi Zigzaou. Then the line turned north-west for another twenty-five miles through the steep Matmata Hills. Then there was a brief switch-line to hold the open El Hamma valley. And the rest of the way inland was blocked by a line of impassable salt lakes. The French had planned to hold the line in some depth, making use of Ben Gardane, Medenine and Fum Tatahouine as strong-points and defended outposts.

But in the summer of 1940 the Italian Armistice Commission had disarmed the fortifications. The weapons had been removed, the anti-tank obstacles flattened, the wire cut, the dragon's teeth demolished, the metal taken away from the prepared defences and the armour from the pillboxes. So the line as Rommel found it consisted of a series of well-sited but empty pillboxes and emplacements. He showed right away that he did not intend to defend it on the French plan, for he surrendered the outlying villages without a struggle. But we knew well enough that he would try and defend it somehow. He *must* defend it. It was the southern gateway to Tunisia, and if he did not fight there, there was no point in fighting anywhere.

Montgomery made a double plan, balancing his chances of success between two separate thrusts. It was not complicated, but it needed very subtle and accurate timing. He put the Fiftieth Division right on the coast to make a frontal attack against the line across the Wadi Zigzaou. And he sent the New Zealand Division, the great outflanking experts, on a long trek round inland behind the Matmata Hills to attack the El Hamma Gap. In the centre of the line the Highland Division had a purely holding role down in the plain, and the Indian Division was creeping up against the Italian infantry in the Matmata Hills.

Obviously the New Zealanders were the thing. If they could get through the El Hamma Gap and cut their way across to the sea, the rest of Rommel's forces would be trapped as though in a great bag. If Fifty Division's attack succeeded, so much the better. The enemy would be the less likely to make a clean escape. And the attack might even lure additional troops down into the bag.

So once again the New Zealanders disappeared on a long, secret march. And on the night of March 20, Fifty Division attacked.

The Wadi Zigzaou, swollen by recent rains, lay like a moat facing them. And while a moonlit barrage of Alamein intensity pinned the defenders to their trenches, the engineers did prodigious feats of bridging. All the way along the Wadi they had to use scaling ladders, and in default of ladders human pyramids of men standing on one another's shoulders. They heaved in hurdles and bundles of brushwood to make a firm foundation across the flooded creek. By morning a small infantry force had struggled its way over with some transport and a few Valentine tanks, and a bridgehead was established.

It was established, but it could not be held. Swiftly Rommel summoned the crack Panzer Grenadiers to buttress the Young Fascists and the Italian Trieste Division. On March 22 he counterattacked in great force. To make assurance doubly sure he threw in the Fifteenth *Panzerdivision,* and it was more pressure than the little bridgehead could sustain. The trouble was, we had not got an adequate anti-tank force across there. And so, under cover of a beautifully accurate artillery barrage, the Wadi Zigzaou was recrossed and the bridgehead was abandoned.

The first phase of the Mareth battle, at any rate, had been a failure.

ii

The only way I was going to see this battle was from the air. So I walked across the hillside to American Headquarters to talk with Captain Al Gough, a Pittsburgh newspaperman who was doing what corresponded to the British "Public Relations" job. I told him I wanted to go out with the U.S. light bombers. "Sure," said Al, "so do I. Let's go."

Somehow everything fell miraculously into place. A Colonel from Washington was just flying back to the El Assa Air Field, where Twelfth Bomber Group was stationed, and he took us along with him. We found the B25s were operating two and three times a day. Sure I could make a trip with them. Glad to have me. No trouble at all. I could go right out to-morrow morning if I liked. I was overwhelmed with an open warmth of hospitality I had rarely met among my own countrymen.

Someone invited me to share his tent. Someone else took me off to the mess, and I ate things I had never eaten in my life before and I learned to say "mission" instead of "sortie" and "ship" instead of "plane." It was all utterly different from the quiet-toned R.A.F. mess where I had been living. The British fliers, after three years of war, had grown almost into a caste, a race of men not entirely of this world. The strangeness and incommunicability of their operational life—the most important part of their life—enclosed them in a small, esoteric circle. They could only share their experiences with one another. More than ever their talk was a clipped jargon. For emphasis they relied on understatement. They practised an agile economy in conversation, leaping from one idea to another apparently unrelated idea, and omitting the intervening stages as being too obvious to need expression; yet to an outsider those intervening stages would probably not have been explicable at all.

But these Americans were utterly different. They were far more expansive and exuberant and personal. They had none of the withdrawn separateness of the English pilots and they had developed no acrobatic conversational shorthand of their own. On the other hand, when they talked about non-air-force subjects their language was twice as quick and vivid. It was a difference of attitude that sometimes made the British feel that the Americans were frivolous about the war — wealthy, gifted amateurs; and conversely the Americans often thought the British were blasé and patronizing. But it was very much on the surface, this difference — nothing fundamental. It was always fascinating to watch a British pilot meeting an American pilot: both wary at first, like two dogs walking stiff-legged round each other; then feeling their way to a common level of understanding; then building up eagerly from there.

Next morning I went up to a yellow-painted trailer beside the dusty air field and was briefed with all the pilots. I didn't get all the details about the target, because at that moment somebody's pants split right down the seams and he said, "Gee, I'm going to be kinda embarrassed if I have to bail out like this," and somebody else said, "Maybe you rate a medal for that," and then they were talking altitudes and speeds and angles again and I hadn't heard about the target. But generally the idea was that the Germans were putting in this counterattack on the coast and it was getting to look pretty serious and we were to bomb their tanks and vehicles right slap in the front line.

Then we were driving out to number 99, which was my plane. There had been some slight doubt about 99. Yesterday she had been shot as full of holes as a pepperpot. But they had patched her up and now she was serviceable all right. So the pilot borrowed a pencil to scrawl *13* — his lucky number — alongside a lot of other thirteens on the fuselage, and we climbed in.

The cabin filled brimful with noise till everything was vibrating with it. Then the B25 nosed its way through the yellow dust to the end of the runway and we were off.

The other planes formed up round us and they hung there in the sky as though on strings, bouncing slightly up and down above and below our own level. People were making signs and waving to friends in neighbouring planes like parties in different busses all going to the same Sunday-school picnic. Our front gunner was telling some long story by signs to his opposite number in 67 on our left. The way I read it, this was his thirteenth mission and the other gunner was wishing him luck.

Down below our shadows kept pace with us, bounding up hill and down dale across the rough countryside, but always in perfect formation. The ground was greeny-brown and dry with sometimes neat rows of toy olive trees. We passed little clots of black Arab tents and huge sprawls of British camps. Herds of goats rushed into frantic huddles and a hobbled horse went bucketing painfully away. There was a white village and people were going into the Mosque. I wondered what day it was down there — certainly not Friday.

The sea was blue-green and crinkly when we came to it and our shadows moved smoothly and evenly across it. "Here they come," said the pilot into the intercomm, and my heart gave a sudden jump. But it was our Spitfire escort coming up to meet us, rising like little black finger-nail parings against the white clouds.

Now the note of our engines changed and we began climbing steeply. The leading formation was lifting steadily just ahead of us and I could see their propellers like faintly iridescent haloes round the nacelles. Down below the earth was losing its detail and turning into a map. It got colder and brighter and maybe it was the altitude that made me feel so excited.

The clouds were firm and shapely all round us, like mounds of whipped cream. It was extraordinarily clean up there. At last there were no more clouds above us at all, and the sky was a dark and brilliant blue. We were floating in liquid sunshine. The whole cabin was filled with the high singing of the engine. This now was our world. That world down there seemed fantastically remote.

But our job was to bomb it. So we swung in again towards land. Ahead of us some little black splinters were burrowing through clouds and leap-frogging about on top of them. Then suddenly they peeled off and came spiralling round towards us.

"Spitfires," said someone into the intercomm and someone else said "Spitfires hell. Those are Messerschmitts." Then our own Spitfires above us snapped out of their crisscrossing and weaving and went sailing down there to do battle. But whether they did it I couldn't tell. For they went twirling and spinning away into a white cloud that looked like Saint Paul's Cathedral and we swerved in to our target.

Away down there—an hour and a half's brisk walk away down to the earth—a battle was going on. I could pick out the little yellow sparks of British field batteries firing and there was a big oblong of ground where tiny puffs of grey smoke kept starting up and blowing all together into a spreading cloud. That must be the battle-field itself. So it was our target. Back on the landing-ground the Colonel had told us to attack tanks and trucks moving into this battle. He had said, "O.K., boys. Just knock the hell out of that track. Make them so goddam scared they won't dare use it any more."

Then the pilot leaned back and nudged me and I looked up and ahead and saw number 25's belly splitting and opening and I could see the yellow bombs up there in the bomb bay. So here we go. Number 25's bombs came tumbling and turning down slap ahead of us and it seemed crazy that we did not run right into them. Then our bomb aimer started to count out our bombs in his slow Southern drawl and I jammed my eye to the drift-meter sight and watched them go down, at first all higgledy-piggledy, then straightening out and getting smaller and smaller as they dropped until I couldn't see them any more. But I kept watching so as to see them burst.

The ground down there was blue. It must have been wildflowers. And among them were little dark rectangles and running from the rectangles were little dark shapes that were men. I had been down there often enough when this had happened and I knew pretty much the way they must be feeling. But these two points of view are so far apart you just cannot bring them together—the point of view of the bomber and the point of view of the bombee. Now I was just hoping that we had bombed well, and I shouted stupidly with excitement when I saw the bombs burst and two great fires flare up.

Then there was a noise as though the sky had cracked open and we lurched crazily sideways and upwards and something ripped in through the fuselage and went tinkling away down towards the rear gunner. I looked out and saw the whole sky peppered with sudden puffs of black smoke which hung aimlessly around as we cut through them. So the flak gunners had got our range. Rapidly I began to work out that they had a three-dimensional possibility of error. It wasn't like shelling on land. Up here they could miss you ahead and behind and both sides and above and below as well. But they didn't seem to be doing it. This was very good shooting indeed.

Suddenly there was a blinding orange flash above number 25's port engine, and a big white veil of smoke started to stream stiffly behind him and he sank down and away behind us. "The bastards," shouted our pilot. Then he added, "That's Ingram. He's the best pilot in the whole outfit, so if anyone can get that ship down safe he can." We lurched again from another near-miss, and I glimpsed Ingram away down below us heading for home across the sea. Then I remembered that Al Gough was in that plane too.

Down around Mareth the ground was still twinkling with flame from the German ack-ack guns. But we swung high and wide and away out over the blue-green crinkly sea, manœuvring deftly to reshape the formation, for Ingram was the leader of the squadron. Behind us there was a great curved trail of black flak smoke and it seemed incredible that we could have got through it safely.

Along that track we had blasted there was a sooty-grey screen of smoke shot faintly with flame. I imagined to myself the men picking themselves up and cursing and trying to get the deafness out of their eardrums and looking around to see what damage had been done. I hoped it was plenty.

So we were on our way home. The firm line of my pilot's jaw was still moving rhythmically up and down on his chewing gum, like a piston. He had been chewing like that all through everything. I found I was hungry, and I began to think of the meal I should get back at the air field; probably hash and sweetcorn and sweet potatoes and hot cakes and peanut butter—all those peculiarly American things which they somehow managed to get in the desert.

Then we saw number 25 swinging low across beneath us. Surely he would be all right now. I hoisted myself up so that I could look backwards out of the astral hatch. But I couldn't see him any more. There was a huge plume of purple smoke billowing up from the ground. Surely . . .

When we landed the Colonel was waiting on the field and I saw at once from his face that it was true. Twenty-five hadn't been able to land. It was impossible to know why. The machine had exploded and they were all dead. Including Al. I went back to my tent with all the excitement drained out of me, hating to have to write the story at all.

iii

Our bombing had been good. British Headquarters sent a message of congratulation on it. When I got back to the R.A.F. next day I found that the German counterattack across the Wadi Zigzaou had been halted and held.

But it meant a certain reorganization of Montgomery's plan. For the two attacks could not now be complementary. Fifty Div.'s half had failed before the New Zealanders' half had begun.

The New Zealanders were still on their long trek round behind the Matmata Hills towards El Hamma to deliver their "left hook." For inevitably Montgomery's strategy was being talked of in terms of a neat boxing metaphor: Fifty Div. had delivered a straight right to the jaw of the Mareth Line, and now the New Zealanders were to finish it off with a left hook. As seen on a map, it was a beautifully apposite description.

Now, even while the New Zealanders were still travelling, Montgomery converted them into the main thrust. He sent them his mobile centre of gravity, which was his First Armoured Division. They already had an armoured brigade with them, so that the addition of the division turned them into a very formidable fighting force. And dead on schedule they reached the El Hamma valley.

Waiting there to receive them was a rather motley Italian force under General Mannerini. But Rommel knew well enough what was happening and already he was sending help. The Twenty-first *Panzerdivision* was brought down through Gabes and sent west to El Hamma. In support came the 164th German Infantry Division and the Italian Spezia. The Fifteenth *Panzerdivision* was still down around the Wadi Zigzaou, but it was ready to come north should it be needed. The remaining *Panzerdivision* in Tunisia, the Tenth, was being pinned down by General Patton's Second American Corps round Gafsa.

El Hamma was a beautiful little battle, extremely simple in conception, but depending on complete integration of the forces involved and very accurate timing. It took place in a valley about two miles broad with little side valleys where the German tanks and anti-tank guns had dug themselves into hidden pits. They were grey-brown stony hills and there was an old Roman wall running across the valley.

For the first time in its history the Eighth Army was fighting from west to east instead of from east to west. Therefore it could attack in the afternoon with the late sun slanting into the eyes of its enemies and turning its dust into a golden opaque haze. Zero hour was 3 P.M. on March 26. And at 3 P.M. something started to happen which was unprecedented in this war. Montgomery used that word about it in a message he sent to Air Vice-Marshal Broadhurst the same evening. It was an example of concentrated air support such as the Luftwaffe had never given the German army in its palmiest days.

It was a programme covering very nearly three hours and it was composed on strict contrapuntal lines. You could even work out the musical analogy to prove that this blitz was in sonata form. It opened with a mighty flourish of bombs from light bombers — British, American and South African squadrons — in waves of eighteen. Then came the real theme of the afternoon — low-flying fighters and fighter bombers. Throughout those three hours there were at no time less than two squadrons working on the two-mile front. They flashed from side to side of the valley in long low swoops, attacking any movement they saw. Anti-tank gunners were kept from their guns at critical moments. Crews were kept away from their tanks, and tanks from the battle. If men ran or fired or did anything at all they were machine-gunned. Low-flying Hurricanes with heavy cannons wove themselves into the scene and attacked tanks with armour-piercing shells. At stated intervals the bombers reappeared and the stage was cleared while they dumped their contribution. There was a constant overtone of Spitfires, floating high overhead ready to deal with anything the Luftwaffe might do.

All this time tanks, Bren carriers and infantry were advancing up the valley with a line of shell-fire moving before them like a metal screen. This line of bursting shells was the bomb line — it told the pilots exactly how far west they could operate. It was all exquisitely synchronized and dovetailed. And it worked.

This completely non-stop air support meant that the Germans on the ground were fighting in three dimensions while the British were fighting in two. Air superiority can be a negative thing if it is not properly applied, but here it was positive and constructive to the last degree. The actual destruction the planes did may or may not have been great. That was beside the point. For the point was to keep men out of the battle, to prevent them from fighting, to disturb their aim and drive them into trenches and deafen their ears and absorb their minds. The paradoxical advantage of planes over artillery in this is that men can *see planes coming*. They may go on fighting through shell-fire, because they cannot possibly tell where the next shell will land. But they can see where a fighter is going to attack and they can take cover. And they will do so. And as long as they are doing so, they are out of the battle.

That evening was gusty with local sand-storms and pilots were coming down wherever they could see an air field clear. For a few hours squadrons were hopelessly scrambled up all over the desert, sorting themselves out by telephone. I was dining in an American fighter squadron's mess and airmen who belonged miles away were touching down and coming in and being made to stay for a meal. They were all wildly excited. They had been taking part in a constructive scheme and they had loved it. They had a sense of being intimately involved in the army's advance and of materially winning the battle.

For the battle had been won. The El Hamma Pass was forced that evening under cover of this history-making blitz. But the Twenty-first *Panzerdivision* still remained to be fought before the Gabes gap could be closed and the Mareth bag stoppered and sealed. And the final stage was a really bizarre tactical masterstroke.

By the light of the moon the New Zealand Division opened its ranks for the First Armoured Division to pass through. And by astute navigation the First drove ahead *beyond* where the Twenty-first *Panzerdivision* was camped for the night. Astounding things happened. A British armoured regiment leaguered only two hundred yards from a German tank park. An Italian truck drove innocently into the British lines and delivered rations for a thousand men. All night long the two sides exchanged fire. And in the morning the Twenty-first *Panzerdivision* woke up to find itself *between* the New Zealanders and the First Armoured Division.

The First might then have driven on to Gabes. But the enemy were across their supply lines and it was better to clean the position up. So a ragged tank engagement was fought all that day, and the break-through was finally consolidated when what remained of the Twenty-first *Panzerdivision* battled its way clear and extricated itself through the Gabes gap.

Now the whole Mareth Line began to crumble. On the right of the New Zealanders the Indians had been edging their way up through the Matmata Hills. Gurkhas with their little knives had been doing things of devilish subtlety. Again and again they accomplished their tasks "without expenditure of ammunition." Once they found three Germans lying asleep side by side and they slit the throats of the two outside ones and left the middle one still sleeping. Now they were mopping up the fleeing Pistoia Division. Along the main part of the Mareth Line only the Ninetieth Light now remained, as usual fighting the rear-guard action. The Fifteenth *Panzerdivision* had rushed back to hold the gap open until the last moment. And during the night of March 27 Rommel whipped out all his remaining troops and left the line clean and empty.

It was a beautiful battle. It was the first real fighting since Alamein and it showed that the Eighth Army's hand had not lost its cunning. There was a cleanness and artistry about the way the centre of gravity was switched from the coast to El Hamma when the coastal thrust failed. There was something epoch-making about those three hours of incessant air support. There was a fullness of co-operation which extended right up to the Americans at Gafsa, for they kept the Tenth *Panzerdivision* out of the battle. And there was that fine defensive victory of March 6. That was when the Mareth success really took shape. For on that date Rommel expended the tank reserves he was going to need at El Hamma.

CHAPTER 33

The Junction of the Armies

North of Gabes the land narrows down to a fifteen-mile neck between the sea and the salt lakes. And here once more the retreating Axis forces turned and fought. They took for their line a watercourse that was sometimes almost a canyon and they fortified it with the usual means — wire and mines and plenty of spade-work. It was called the Wadi Akarit.

Montgomery sent his army through it on the straightforward head-on break-through plan. In a moonlight attack that was very savagely disputed six gaps were made in the enemy line in groups of two. The Highland Division, the Indian Division and the Fiftieth Division each made two, and the First Armoured Division and the New Zealanders went through. Then they fanned out into the broad plain, pursuing such of the enemy as had not already surrendered, and the Western Desert Air Force turned on its special "pursuit blitz," a type of attack designed to keep fleeing columns paralyzed and disorganized.

The inevitable counterattacks were made, but there had been plenty of time to bring up the anti-tank guns this time. The enemy commander had badly mistimed the movements of his Armoured Divisions. He failed to assess correctly the relative menaces of the British Eighth Army and the American Second Corps at Gafsa. And the Akarit break-through caught him with his tanks in the wrong place — so much in the wrong place that he missed the decisive moment for a counterattack.

The British had not expected to get through Akarit so quickly. They had not expected to capture so many thousands of prisoners.

At last a flaw had appeared in Rommel's perfect retreat, a miscalculation had been made. One hard bang had opened the south doorway to Tunisia. There was no other line which the enemy could attempt to hold for at least 150 miles. We had another wild, hectic advance before us.

The Eighth Army went up Tunisia like a plunger being pushed into a tube. On the right hand lay the sea, and on the left the First Army and the Americans stood in their hills and watched us go by. Out on the left wing armoured cars of the Eleventh Hussars were cruising into unknown country rounding up prisoners. Somewhere near the Gafsa road they trained their glasses on some troops who might have been Germans but somehow looked subtly different. Finally someone recognized American steel helmets and American vehicles with stars on them. And so, informally and accidentally, the two armies which had started out at opposite ends of Africa at last shook hands. It was an unemotional, business-like meeting, but curiously suggestive of the difference between them. The Eighth Army soldiers were reddened with the sun and dusty with the sand, already dressed in dirty shirts and ragged shorts — a desert, summer army: the Americans had Mackintosh wind-jackets and baggy trousers and gaiters and boots and iron-grey vehicles — a winter, mountain army. But now they were one united fighting force and gradually the differences would become blurred and smoothed over until they were no longer perceptible save to the expert eye.

At this point I went back from the air force to the army, and drove ahead with advancing troops. Swiftly now the desert was softening and relenting, blossoming suddenly into little clumps of palms and patches of cultivation. And then at Sfax we came into the country the Eighth Army had been dreaming of for a thousand miles. It was a country of fragrant orchards and tender fields of barley and trees and grass and a florid abundance of wildflowers. The olive groves quilted the land with silver-green spots against a red-brown earth and great cactus hedges lined the mud walls alongside the roads. For a thousand miles we had been capturing names without places. Now we took villages of which we did not even bother to learn the names. In urgent pursuit the sandy trucks of the army streamed through the little huddles of whitewashed squalor while the inhabitants sat in their doorways and gazed at us with languid indifference; as though we were just interesting enough to be worth looking at, but only just. The more energetic stood holding up new-laid eggs in the hope of bartering them for tea or sugar. But most just sat.

There was no fight for Sfax. We found it an empty city, utterly ruined as far as its European quarter was concerned. It is a town built round a harbour, and in attacking the harbour the British and American air forces had inevitably destroyed the town. But the native quarter was miraculously untouched. It was absurdly picturesque — a maze of quiet, wandering little alleys with glimpses of cool sunny courtyards through old ornate gateways and delicate iron grilles shielding all the windows. A high battlemented wall ran round the whole thing, with the square white towers of mosques rising above it. But where the inhabitants were I do not know. Furtive, bony cats were its only population.

The pursuit sped on northwards, past the great Roman amphitheatre of El Djem, through a landscape extravagantly painted with flowers. On April 13, two days after Sfax, the New Zealanders came into Sousse and found another empty, bomb-shattered seaport. It was melancholy to drive through the streets and know that this had been a friendly town, a French town, and it had been necessary to turn it into a chaos of twisted blackened girders and unrelated chunks of masonry and mounds of splintered furniture. The port was untidy with sunken ships and uprooted cranes that had toppled into the water. While I was looking at it a man — a Frenchman — rode up on his bicycle and said good day. Stupidly I asked him whether there was a restaurant open where we could get some food. "No — there is nothing," he said. "But if you care to lunch at my house, I shall be honoured."

His home was a poor little house on the edge of the badly bombed area. He only had some brown bread and a tin of tunny fish and some wine. But he and his wife and his family welcomed us with a hospitality that was almost pathetic. We hated to take their food, for they had very little, but it was going to hurt them much more if we refused. They were really genuine French people and nothing had been able to shake them. "I never thought I should be so pleased to see you after all the bombing you have done," the old grandmother said to me. All the women wore little paste Crosses of Lorraine which they had kept hidden for months. They had a radio to which they secretly listened. They had been living, in this stuffy little room of theirs, the life that millions of men and women were still living in Europe — a secretive underground life built on hope and determination. And this morning it had ended for them — ended when a New Zealand jeep flashed past their house flying a Union Jack. I kissed them all and shook hands again and went outside to write my despatch in the car. And then down the street came Alan Moorehead, Ward Price of the *Daily Mail,* and Christopher Buckley of the *Daily Telegraph.* I knew them all well and at first I did not realize the significance of seeing them here. Then abruptly I remembered that they were all First Army correspondents.

So that had happened too — the First and the Eighth Armies had joined. They had made contact the day before in the holy city of Kairouan, twenty-five miles inland from Sousse. It had been another casual, accidental meeting between patrols, and since no one could be sure that his was the first encounter no one had made any ceremony of it. But Alan and the others had taken their car and driven warily along the road to the sea, and they were the first representatives of the First Army to get through.

Then Geoffrey Keating arrived and Russell Hill and other friends and it became a party. Now it really seemed that the end of the campaign was near. The excitement of this last swift advance was still strong in us. Alan and I had not met since the previous summer, for he had been to America, and we had unnumbered things to tell one another. There was wine to be had in Sousse, and we found a clean, undamaged villa by the sea. It was as pleasant an evening as I have ever spent.

Next day Geoffrey and I drove up north to the front in his jeep. The advance had stopped. It had swept on like a tide until it came to the barrier of hills north of Enfidaville and there it had been halted. It was lapping among the foothills, finding its own level, but the barrier was firm and strong. Once more the Germans had dug in their artillery and placed their anti-tank guns and were ready to resist. Their shells were dropping with a steady, lazy rhythm into the flowery plain that led up to Enfidaville. The whole tempo of the campaign had abruptly slackened again. A group of brigadiers was picnicking in a hollow by the roadside for all the world as though they were on holiday. In huge fields of poppies the men of the Eighth Army were sprawled luxuriously, dozing in the spring sunshine and tasting with conscious delight the pleasure of lying in cool green grass.

A shell fell thirty yards from our jeep and we started telling one another how ridiculous it would be to get hurt by a stray shell on a quiet sunny day at the front. So we went back to Sousse.

ii

For a week there was a lull—the last calm before the last storm. The Eighth Army had time to look around and discover a great many things. It found itself operating in a geography of bewildering complication. The divine simplicity of the desert, with its single coast road and nothing else, was left behind. This country was a maze of hills and valleys and roads, and at first the desert veterans felt a very real sense of frustration at being unable to go direct from one place to another on a compass bearing. After the flatness and emptiness of the last fifteen hundred miles the hills produced a faint feeling of claustrophobia. It seemed almost as though a new dimension had been introduced into the fighting. At last the Eighth Army began to understand what had been holding the First Army up all this time.

But for all its geographical intricacy this common Allied Front could be reduced to a relatively simple formula. Close your left fist with the back upwards and stick out your thumb and you will have an almost perfect model of it. The thumb is the Cap Bon Peninsula, jutting out towards Sicily. The knuckles are the last ring of mountains spread like a fan round Tunis, the enemy's ultimate line of resistance. The hollows between the knuckles are the four ways through the mountains. Reading from left to right they are as follows: first the Sedjenane Valley, the key to which is the town of Mateur; second, the Medjerda Valley, dominated by Medjez-el-Bab; third, the pass of Pont du Fahs; and fourth, the eastern coastal road through Enfidaville. The American Second Corps under General Patton was headed down number one; the British First Army down number two; the French Nineteenth Corps down number three; and the Eighth Army down number four.

The Eighth Army, with its fantastically long communications lines stretching interminably behind it, had another tough supply problem to solve before it could attack again, so a pause was inevitable. I was now working with Chester Morrison of the *Chicago Sun* and Ned Russell of the United Press, and we camped down in a little olive grove beside a gloomy group of people called the "Graves Registration Unit." The commanding officer, inevitably known as "The First Gravedigger," kept a large stack of *New Yorkers* always beside him to lighten the depressing nature of his work.

The lull crept into our despatches, but in the outside world interest in Tunisia was still intense and a lull was not welcome. Our offices began to prompt us with suggestions for stories. At one and the same moment Chester was asked to hunt up some heroes, preferably born in Chicago, Ned was told to "Keep it coarse — Hell, this is war!" and I was instructed to probe into the secrets of Montgomery's boudoir. They may have looked like good suggestions in Chicago, New York and London, but to us in our olive grove they seemed just silly. Instead we decided to pay a visit to the First Army.

All the way over there we argued — as men were doing along the whole front — about the enemy's plans. There seemed to be three possibilities: a wholesale evacuation by sea; a fight to the bitter end; an organized surrender.

The evacuation theory had certain things to recommend it. The Germans had been building little wooden jetties out into the sea at half a dozen places along the coast of Cap Bon. The peninsula itself was thought to be defensible and it was only twelve hours' journey from Sicily. Captured Germans had started asking their captors: "Were you at Dunkirk—what was it like there?" The Germans were massing great numbers of Junkers 52 transport planes and some of their vast new six-engined Messerschmitts. It seemed unlikely that Hitler would cold-bloodedly sacrifice crack German units like the three *Panzerdivisions* and the Hermann Goering Regiments without making some attempt to rescue them.

The fight-to-the-finish theory was recommended by the argument that thus would the Germans gain their objective. By fighting on as long as possible they would gain time, and that was what they were fighting for. The German High Command would certainly have worked out the evacuation chances down to the last detail, and they might well have decided that the thing was impossible. Britain had three great air forces poised to attack—the Western Mediterranean, the Western Desert, and the one stationed in Malta. The British Navy would certainly have every offensive plan for frustrating a Dunkirk. Hitler and his Generals would have very good reasons for deciding to turn Tunisia into a Stalingrad rather than a Dunkirk.

The third theory—an organized surrender—was possible but very improbable. The Germans would have nothing to gain by it. But there was one curious point. Just about this time we received definite confirmation that Rommel had left Africa. That looked as though no further active operations were intended by the Axis armies. It was a clear enough admission that the end was not far off. Rommel must have made a final set of plans and left them to be carried out. He must have seen clearly enough that the situation held no more possible opportunities for him, and he never liked being associated with defeat.

Arguing thus we drove on through the walled city of Kairouan — so holy that four visits to its great mosque equal one visit to Mecca — and came into the First Army's country. And for the first time we became conscious of the inevitable rivalry between the two armies.

The difference in appearance was striking enough. All their transport was dark-grey, while ours was beige. Their faces were paler and their clothes thicker, for they had not long been out from England and they had been fighting in cold, wet hills. They looked like a home army, a European army, and by contrast the Eighth Army looked every inch an overseas army. I had not realized until then how changed the men of the desert army had become. Only now, by this contrast, could one measure the permanent depth of sunburn they had attained, the hardness and leanness resulting from living night and day in the open, the slightly strained look about the eyes that comes from the glare of the sun and the distant horizons of the desert. And the Eighth Army had become a little shabby, too, in the course of its great march from Alamein. You cannot maintain strict discipline about dress in the desert. You cannot complain if people start wearing plum-coloured corduroy trousers or whatever they happen to have. You can try and remedy it as soon as possible, but a certain amount of licence must be allowed if the army is to remain clothed at all. And so the dusty, torn, bleached garments of the Eighth Army compared unfavourably with the uniform neatness of the First. The desert vehicles were of an earlier vintage anyway, and their tremendous treks across uncharted country had not improved their appearance. But in the presence of this contrast the Eighth Army refused to feel any humility. It knew its scars had been honourably come by and it knew it was a functioning army. It looked at the First Army with interest and sometimes, perhaps, with a touch of condescension: the condescension of a ripe, experienced man towards an extremely promising junior.

Of course to the First Army it was very galling. The First was a very self-critical army, deeply conscious of its mistakes and shortcomings — just as the Eighth had been a year before. It felt that its problems had never been understood. For nearly three years all emphasis in Africa had been on desert fighting and immensely long and swift advances. It had never been fully realized that this Tunisian fighting was utterly different. So the First Army welcomed the Eighth warily, keenly on the look-out for a hint of patronage or criticism. And it looked forward very eagerly to seeing the Eighth in action among these mountains.

Of course as soon as the shock of the first impact was over this implied jealousy and animosity began to fade. Cunningly General Alexander borrowed an armoured division from the Eighth and put it right in among the First — a sort of good-will ambassador. The two armies began to compare experiences and equipment and rations with real friendliness. They discovered they had totally distinct sets of slang terms. When I met an old friend in the First Army he said: "What about a spot of sprog to celebrate this?" "Well," I said, not understanding, "I thought we might brew up." He did not understand either. But what we both meant was "Let's have a cup of tea." In dozens of the minor matters of everyday life the two armies were mutually incomprehensible. The Eighth talked a good deal in a sort of bastard Arabic sprinkled with technical desert terms. In this long tunnel of separate experience through which it had passed it had acquired a set of habits and conventions and compromises which were peculiarly its own. The First was a far more civilized army and the Eighth began to learn its manners again.

The impact of the Eighth Army on the American troops was totally different. The Americans showed a genuine, open-hearted admiration which the British found embarrassing. And in return the British did not pass judgement on the Americans for they simply knew nothing about them. Privately they considered the Americans were perhaps a little over-equipped. They believed there was a time to wear a steel helmet and a time not to wear a steel helmet and the Americans seemed to wear them all the time. The Americans even in the back areas looked three times as tough and warlike as the Eighth Army in the front line. But the Eighth had arrived at their appearance of shabby boy scouts by usage and experience, not by theory; and clearly enough the Americans were still in a somewhat theoretical, experimental stage.

iii

I drove back to the Eighth Army feeling as though I were going home after visiting a rich relation, and I got there just in time to see the new offensive launched.

On the night of April 19, while the rest of the Allied Front remained quiet, the Eighth Army stormed up into the Enfidaville hills. This was not intended in any way as the main attack. It was at best a diversion, designed to look like the main attack and thus to draw enemy troops off from other sectors of the front. The main thrust was to go in three days later in the centre of the front, and thus for three days the Eighth Army had the limelight all to itself. And it was very eager to acquit itself well.

An hour before midnight massed artillery burst forth in a mighty barrage. From my bed I could see the vast semicircles of radiance shooting suddenly into the northern sky and the noise was a thick heavy grumble without any intermission. Under cover of it New Zealanders and men of the Indian Division went forward on foot to clamber up the first steep slopes and fight the enemy with hand-grenades or bayonets or even knives. A few hours later when we groped our way through the dark, dew-wet fields to New Zealand Headquarters, we heard that the first objectives had been taken. But when morning came details of the fighting began to trickle back, and we realized the full implications of the task the Eighth Army had been given.

These hills rose straight from sea-level, very lovely in their blue and chocolate coloring dappled with the purple shadows of the puffy white clouds. But the grain of them ran east and west in parallel streaks of mountain and valley; and that meant that each time the enemy were prized loose from one range, they could retire back across a valley to the next. It was superb defensive country. The Germans and Italians dug and blasted themselves trenches in high positions so that they had a clear field of fire below them across steep, empty slopes. Constant shelling might worry them, but unless a shell fell clean into one of these trenches it could not do much harm. Accurate bombing was difficult in these tumbled hills, and the opportunities for camouflage were superb. The enemy themselves were tired men, but they were very fine troops with plenty of experience. The situation was not impregnable — almost no situation is impregnable in modern war if you are prepared to lose enough men to get it. The Eighth Army, I suppose, could have fought its way through. But it would have come out the other end a crippled, almost ruined army.

There seemed one possible way of handling these hills. On the left flank there was a massif called Garci which extended back right across the grain. If you think of the hills as a piece of wood with the grain running right and left, then Garci was a knot. Whoever held Garci could command the valleys stretching away laterally to the east. And the main objective of the Indian Division's attack was the capture of Garci.

But they came up against something which their maps had never even suggested. They found themselves faced with a sheer precipice that was simply not climbable. Many of these were men of the hills, men to whose feet the feel of mountains was as familiar as your sitting-room carpet is to you. And they doubted whether they could have got up this cliff in any circumstances at all. Certainly it was not possible with the enemy leaning over the top and dropping down grenades — not throwing, simply dropping.

Farther to the east the New Zealanders had found something nearly as bad. It was a flat-topped pinnacle of rock very like the Acropolis of Athens. From it the enemy rained down mortar fire onto them and the machine-gun bullets sprayed out all round it like water from a fountain. A battalion of New Zealanders crouched below it in their hastily scraped trenches and debated how they could possibly tackle it. One by one through the night the officers were killed or wounded. Towards morning a Maori sergeant said to four of his men, "Come, let us go up there."

They started up the slope with their Bren guns held high above their heads, firing straight up into the air. Halfway up men of the Italian Folgore regiment — crack parachutists — came out of caves and fought like demons. But the Italians were short of ammunition and the Maoris went from cave to cave tossing a hand-grenade into each. Then they sent the disarmed Folgore down the hill and went on climbing.

They breasted the slope and managed to run to a safe position without being hit. All day they maintained themselves up there, and man by man the New Zealanders down below crept up as reinforcements. And in the evening the final scene was played out in a savage burst of close-quarters fighting, with bayonets and grenades and rocks and knives. Men even wrestled together bodily on the edges of precipices, trying to hurl one another over.

I think we realized then and there that the Eighth Army could only get through at the cost of appalling sacrifices. The battle flowed on slowly and painfully into the hills. There were wild, bloody engagements for possession of some slight slope whose value depended on a subtle calculation of fields of fire and vision. Step by step the first ridge of hills was won and the enemy retired to the second. The second ridge pivoted on a razor-backed summit which looked even worse than anything in the first ridge. The Indians could not get Garci, so the plan of securing lateral command of the valleys collapsed. The fighting sank down to a weary skirmishing.

On April 22 the main thrust started. The Sixth Armoured Division belonging to the First Army and the First Armoured Division belonging to the Eighth Army attacked the very middle of the front, halfway between the Medjez Pass and the Pont du Fahs Pass. They drove forward into a flat space called the Goubellat Plain and they made some headway. But the Germans suddenly produced, with considerable success, a new tank-buster aeroplane. It was a weapon which the Russians had first used, and then the British. Now the Germans came into the field with it and they destroyed a lot of tanks. Their 88-millimetre anti-tank guns were dug in cunningly round the hills and they barred the way out of the plain. The British armoured divisions could make no further headway, and that plan had to be abandoned.

So the centre of gravity was swiftly shifted again. The British

First Army began to push down the Medjerda Valley, and the American Second Corps down the Sedjenane Valley. In each case the valley possessed a key in the shape of a vital hill whose possession was decisive. In the Medjerda Valley — not at the side of it but right in it — lay Longstop Hill, an isolated black massif like the back of a rhinoceros. No one could move either up or down the valley while his enemy still held Longstop. And in the Sedjenane Valley the Green and Bald Hills occupied a precisely similar position.

The British got Longstop on April 26, and it cost many lives to get it but it was worth it. And some days later the Americans got their two hills and early in May they marched into Mateur, the stronghold of the valley. Something had happened to the Americans. Now they were fighting like veterans, with a magnificent poise and drive and sense of timing. Their early experiences had suddenly crystallized inside them and almost overnight they had changed from a textbook training-school army into a mature, adult army. They did the right thing now as though by instinct, and they had complete control of their own bravery. They met very fierce resistance indeed, for the Germans were putting their last ounce into this final stand. Von Arnim had issued a backs-to-the-wall, fight-to-the-finish order to his troops, and they were holding desperately to their excellent hill positions. But the Americans drove magnificently through.

So, at the beginning of May, you had this position. In the north, in the Sedjenane Valley, the Americans had captured the necessary key point. In the Medjerda Valley the British First Army had Longstop Hill. At Pont du Fahs the French Nineteenth Corps was holding considerable enemy forces. On the east coast the Eighth Army was stuck into the Enfidaville Hills, only able to get forward at the cost of great losses. Hitler had ordered the Axis armies to continue resistance. The summer was coming on and valuable time was being lost. The stage was now fully set for the grand finale.

CHAPTER 34

Hitch-Hike into Tunis

Now the Allied commanders met in conference. They said, in effect, "Let us put a stop to all this nonsense. We have plenty of divisions here. Let us use them." They decided to abandon the strategy of even pressure all the way along the mountain front. They determined to treat the position like those old fortress areas in the desert — that is to say, concentrate their fire power, forge their best forces into a single spearhead of tremendous power, and thrust it irresistibly through on one narrow front.

Of the four possible ways through the mountains the Medjerda Valley offered the best hopes. The key to it, Longstop Hill, had been taken in the fighting of the previous ten days. Tunis lay straight ahead, barely thirty miles away. A fast and successful thrust was calculated to split the Axis armies clean in two. It was one of those sublimely simple plans which always had most success in this African war.

The basis of the spearhead was the British First Army. And the Eighth Army contributed two of its very best divisions — the Seventh Armoured and the Fourth Indian. They were the team which had inaugurated this whole series of campaigns with the Wavell offensive of December 1940. It was beautifully fitting that they should be given star roles in this final climax.

The Eighth Army was ordered to cease all offensive operations at once. If the new plan succeeded, there would be no need to waste any more lives in the Enfidaville Hills. The Seventh Armoured and the Fourth Indian received instructions at extremely short notice to pack up and get on the road. Few of them knew where they were going or why. There was no time to change their camouflage, and they found themselves travelling south, then west, then north again over winding, soaring mountain roads until their sandy vehicles were mingling with the iron-grey trucks of the First Army. In just about three days they were in position.

The Eighth Army was now weak to the point of impotence. At that moment, in fact, it ceased to exist as a coherent fighting force. It was nothing more than two or three infantry divisions thinly spread across the plain below the Enfidaville Hills. There was a possibility that the enemy might find this out and attack. It was even conceivable that Sousse might be lost. Had Rommel been there, I am sure he would have considered the plan very seriously. It was precisely the sort of coup that always appealed to him. But the German and Italian commanders left in Africa now were not gamblers, prone to lightning decisions. It was a risk the British commanders could fairly safely take.

But whatever happened, the remains of the Eighth Army could not in any circumstances attack. They were out of the news altogether now, and I was fiercely determined to see the end of this whole thing, to be in at the kill. Almost instinctively we began to drift westwards, across to where the real fighting was to be.

We drove over the dusty hill roads, sweet with the scent of pines and gay with flowers, and passed through the rear of the French Nineteenth Corps's positions at Pont du Fahs. The French were playing the opening gambit of this last great Allied thrust — a diversionary attack towards the mighty peak of Zaghouan, and I turned aside to see them.

The French were nearly three divisions under General Koeltz, mostly colonial troops with white officers and N.C.O.'s. They were pitifully under-equipped. They had never been a very modern army and the few things of value they had possessed had been stripped from them by the Italian Armistice Commission. Their transport was mainly mule-drawn — creaking old wagons pulled by tired mules. Their beautiful 70-millimetre guns were nearly worn out. They had no planes at all. Their technical equipment was hopelessly out of date. The British and Americans had done their best to make good these deficiencies but it was still a sketchy, under-armed, very gallant little force, the poor relation of the finely equipped Allied armies fighting on either side of it.

I clambered to the stony ridge which the Foreign Legion had captured by storm with the object of stimulating the enemy's interest in this particular front. There was a zigzag of trenches along the crest and a series of observation posts looking straight down over the woods and fields and farms where the enemy were encamped. I sat most of the morning in one of these observation posts with the Colonel commanding the regiment. We seemed infinitely remote from the super-mechanized front lines of the British and Americans. There was a strong and oddly attractive last-war flavour about this, the exact atmosphere of "Journey's End" and all the other books and plays and films about it. The Colonel gave me wine from his water-bottle and sheep's milk cheese and French bread and talked with brilliance and nostalgia about his home in Nice. Unshaven little men wearing the dramatic steel helmet of France came bringing him messages, and he conducted his sector of the war with a very Gallic verve and flourish and temperament. But the point that emerged from his talk was that these French were sure of themselves and proud of themselves. Like the French of Bir Hacheim, like the French of General Leclerc's force, they were working their way out of France's nervous breakdown. They had regained their own self-respect as the first step towards gaining the respect of others. Of French politics they would not or could not talk. They were for the moment absorbed in this war, and they were happy about it. "After all," said the Colonel, "for France the Boche is always the enemy."

Next day — May 6 — the main thrust burst like a thunderclap down the Medjerda Valley, away on the left wing of the French. It started at four o'clock in the morning with a field gun firing on every seven yards of a 3500-yard front. In groups of twelve or eighteen the light bombers swung in across the hillsides from every direction, ploughing the Axis lines with neat rectangular patterns of bombs. Before dawn lit the crests a terrible volume of explosive and metal had been funnelled into the narrowness of the valley. Brutally the minds of the defenders were wrenched off balance by the noise and the fear and the danger. And then the British infantry came to make a path for the armour.

On the left of the main road came the Fourth Indian Division and on the right came the Fourth British Division. As usual the sappers did their fine steel-nerved job with the mine fields and the wire, and the infantry stormed the mortar positions and machine-gun nests. Mines, mortars and machine-guns — the backbone of German defensive techniques — were neutralized and made harmless. Then storming down the valley came the tanks.

On the left came the Seventh Armoured Division, its emblem still showing on its yellow, sandy camouflage. The tanks ground down the tender vines and squelched through the pulpy moistness of the cactus hedges. They ribbed the red earth among evenly placed haystacks and scattered the goats on the upland pastures. It was such a narrow front — just two miles — that the men in the turrets could look across the road to the right and see the dark tanks of the Sixth Armoured Division driving along parallel with them.

There was resistance, but it was unorganized and unsystematic. The very strength of the British sword was also its shield, and casualties were just about one fifth of what had been expected.

The speed and the hardness of the initial blow crippled the German defences. They had not properly foreseen the size and importance of this armoured spearhead. They had half thought — as we hoped they would — that the main thrust would come through Pont du Fahs. As before Alamein, as before Mareth, they had made an abortive attempt to anticipate our offensive and throw it off balance, and as before they dissipated their reserves without gaining anything. Now, when it was too late, they rushed heavy A.A. guns out from Tunis and tried to use them as artillery in the field to stem the tide of tanks. But everything they did was timed a little too slow. The A.A. batteries were captured before they had got into action. The flanking positions up in the hills were swept aside before they had received their new orders. The village of Massicault fell and in the evening there were British troops round Saint Cyprien, only twelve miles from Tunis itself.

When I read the reports that night at French Headquarters I knew that I should miss the fall of Tunis if I delayed any longer. And next morning I set out on a desperate hitch-hike to try and catch up.

I fell in with a Signals vehicle which took me eighty miles to Thibar, whose little hotel was the Headquarters of the First Army Correspondents. All the way through the rear areas the normal life of the army was going steadily on, and no one had any news. But at Thibar they said Tunis was about to fall, had probably already fallen. Terry Ashwood, the Paramount photographer, and Frank Gillard of the B.B.C. were just starting for the front in a truck, and I abandoned everything but my typewriter and climbed up behind onto their spare wheel.

The roads had been writhing all night with urgent supply columns, but now they were empty. We dropped down through castled Beja and on through the narrow green furrow of the valley to Medjez. Great clouds were boiling up above the bare crouching hills and sometimes a sharp squall of rain stung my face. The traffic thickened a little after Medjez, but it was all moving fast and all going towards Tunis. Excitement began to simmer up inside us.

We came to the battle-field, and the debris of the fighting lay trailed loosely along the valley. Bombs had dug blackened pits among the vines. Every half mile the smouldering skeleton of a German truck was being hauled off the road. A little white church stood like a broken toy on a knoll. There was a stretch where the sappers had not yet had time to clean the mines from the sides of the road.

Sometimes the road would become uncannily empty and we drove on leaning tensely forward in our seats, peering from side to side for something to show whether we had passed the front line or not. Then a despatch rider would swing round the corner ahead of us and we would relax, knowing there was still someone in front. We hummed through the row of little white cottages which formed the village of Massicault, and on beyond. There were tanks on the edges of the hills away to the right and left of us. Sometimes for no explained reason the traffic had left the road and made a detour through the fields, and we followed the churned tracks just in case there should be mines.

The bombers were going overhead in their stately formations but we could not see where they were dropping their bombs. From the direction of Tunis great twists of black smoke were curling slowly up to meet the low clouds. Beyond Saint Cyprien a battery of British mediums was firing from the shelter of a little gulley. From time to time a single German gun replied. We stopped beside a big German war cemetery where a Mark Three tank was blazing spasmodically. To judge by the smell the crew was still inside. We moved a little farther on in case there should be ammunition in it, and stopped to get out some biscuits and cheese and pickles for lunch. I sat down on a milestone which said TUNIS 14 KILOMETRES.

Some other war correspondents drove up, but they knew nothing. The hills stretched round before us in a shallow amphitheatre and Tunis was straight ahead beyond them. Someone said these hills were the city's last line of defence. The Germans were certain to stand in them. I sat eating my cheese and watching some dark tanks moving slowly through a field on the right wing.

Suddenly a little wisp of white smoke stood before each tank. They were firing at something. The reply came from a fringe of trees on the skyline immediately between us and Tunis, and balls of flame seemed to roll through the field where the tanks lay. Like ants disturbed the tanks scuttled this way and that, then ran ahead until they were sheltered behind a hill.

It was the last battle for Tunis and it developed round the curve of hills ahead of us as we sat there lunching. It was completely simple. On the right were perhaps a dozen British tanks; on the left were four German 88-millimetre guns; and it was a duel between them.

The tanks wove circuitously among the folds of the hills, edging nearer the guns, but keeping always under cover. Then they came to a place where they must charge in the open up a brown ploughed field, and again the balls of flame rolled among them. One stopped with a lurch but the rest ran safely on to hull-down positions just under cover again.

Now the duel started in earnest at much closer quarters. Once beside the guns there rose that slow, pulsing crimson bank of flame which means a direct hit on an ammunition dump. Once through my glasses I saw men running wildly round their gun-pit — perhaps succouring wounded. The British mediums began to shell the German positions.

The flashes of the 88-millimetres ceased and for five minutes nothing happened. Then one of the tanks scouted warily forward over the rise. Still nothing happened. The mediums fell silent, and it was so quiet that you could hear the thin rain falling with a soft hiss on the tarmac road.

We drove on to the next village and French men and women came out of their houses with umbrellas to shake our hands and welcome us. But we were concerned with Tunis and the old villagers kept disturbing us with their enthusiasm as we discussed what to do. Terry said, "It won't be to-day now. We never take a town in the evening. The Germans will evacuate during the night and we shall go in in the morning." That was how it had always happened before.

The commander of the corps which was fighting the battle was standing there beside the road. We knew him well. We asked him for advice. And he told us that even while we had been watching this tank battle, Tunis had been entered.

With a superb sense of showmanship the Eleventh Hussars and the Derbyshire Yeomanry had gone in simultaneously. The Eleventh were the armoured-car unit of the Seventh Armoured Division, and they were the *doyens* of the desert, the real veterans.

They were almost the mascots of the Eighth Army and we liked to think that they were first into everywhere. But the Derbys were the armoured cars of the Sixth Armoured Division, and they were to the First Army exactly what the Hussars were to the Eighth.

They had driven through the suburbs into the streets of Tunis soon after two o'clock that afternoon. And they had seen things which they could scarcely believe. German soldiers were sitting there in barbers' chairs having their hair cut. German officers put down their glasses on the bars of hotels and came out to see what was happening. A whole beer-hall full of German infantry surrendered in blank amazement to a British officer who pushed open the door with a gun in his hand. A delirious mob of Frenchwomen cheered on an armoured car as it edged round a corner to duel with an enemy anti-tank gun position.

The Axis troops had been utterly and completely surprised. Everything must have broken down. The British armoured cars edged hastily back to consolidate their positions before the Germans got their wits back.

That had been two hours ago. We scrambled for our cars and drove urgently ahead, up the road that was marked TUNIS 8. The rain was falling gently but steadily now, and I sat on the roof of the truck not noticing it at all. Halfway up the hill we met a wet, sullen file of Germans—the crews of the 88-millimetre guns we had been watching. A little farther was the scorched shell of the ammunition lorry which had been hit. And at the top we looked down on Tunis itself.

It looked grey and dead under the rain. The smoke rising from half a dozen fires was forming a low black canopy beneath the clouds. A mass of trees obscured many of the houses and it did not look large or impressive. We drove on swiftly down.

In the outskirts dark-green Sherman tanks were jostling their way among the sand-coloured vehicles of the Seventh Armoured Division. It was fine to see them there, to know that the Desert Rats were in at the kill. We threaded through them, on across a square with a tram stop and down a shady road where there was a big signboard saying TUNIS.

Suddenly the street was full of people. They surged into the road, pressed back as each truck went by, and then surged forward again. There were pretty girls in gay frocks, bearded old men wiping their glasses, women pushing prams, little children with British and American flags that must have been made in the last half hour. They shouted and cheered and gave the V sign with their fingers and threw flowers and offered wine. There was so much laughter and cheering that you could not trust yourself to speak.

We drove between the arches of some ancient aqueduct and then stopped, for there was a block ahead. When we climbed down onto the pavement people ran to kiss us, to finger our uniforms, to touch our trucks. They bubbled with questions that could not be answered: "Why have you been so long?"—"When will our French troops be here?"—"How soon will you liberate France?" Anyone who could speak two words of French was mobbed.

A man in a French steel helmet nudged me and said something about the Germans being two hundred yards away. Of course they were. There they came, marching in file as prisoners, with the French shouting at them. There was a brittle trill of machine-gun fire from down the street. The crowds went on laughing and cheering wildly. There was another burst of fire. On the pavement someone crumpled and fell—a little girl. The crowd gave a long-drawn gasp and melted suddenly away.

The worst thing about street fighting is that you don't know where the bullets are coming from or where they are going. I edged along the street jerkily, wondering where to go for cover. Just across the way hand-grenades started to explode. I drew in my breath sharply as a burst of fire whined straight across beside me above my shoulder, and I stared bewildered when I saw that a British soldier had fired it. Then I looked behind me and a German was squirming in his own blood in the garden of a villa.

One of those baby Fiat cars shot out of a side lane and tried to cross the main road. It was stopped and two Italian officers looked up at me out of it with eyes of desperate anxiety. They pointed to the big Red Cross brassards on their arm and asked, "Can we go?" "No, get out," they were ordered, and when they got out I saw that each had been sitting with a tommy-gun beneath his knees and the back of the car was stuffed with rifles and ammunition.

A door opened just beside me and two Italian snipers came out with raised hands. They had finished their ammunition. The British troops were growing very angry now. They stopped civilian cars with savage shouts and as often as not the occupants were enemy soldiers. They began to creep down sidestreets and into buildings and the patter of machine-guns ran round the city like thunder round the sky. Down the road Terry Ashwood was filming away frenziedly, too absorbed in his job to feel afraid.

I began to think it was time to be going, and I got into the little Fiat car which was still ticking over beside me, wondering whether it would take me all the way back to Thibar. Then Alan Moorehead drove up and offered me a lift. He had penetrated still farther into the town and he had come from lying in a ditch with the bullets chipping away the plaster of the wall above his head.

We drove back through a rainy dusk to Thibar to write our stories, and when a Spitfire belly-landed beside us on the way and burst into flames we scarcely turned to watch. We were still utterly absorbed with the greatness of this day. The capture had been perfect in swiftness and timing and balance. There had been no loose ends to it, no silly delays as before Tripoli. The place had not been tamely yielded to us. We had fought our way into it as conquerors and the people had given us the welcome we had hoped for.

CHAPTER 35

Grand Finale

For a few days then Northern Tunisia was a madhouse. The picture was one of absolute bewilderment. The total of prisoners began mounting to an astonishing number of thousands and we realized that it was true — the Germans had been taken unawares, their plans had been utterly dislocated by the speed of that great thirty-six-hour thrust. Militarily they had fallen into such chaos that it was impossible to trace even the bare lineaments of their defensive strategy.

It was not, of course, the end. There was still the Cap Bon Peninsula, still the outside chance of a Dunkirk. We had thrown their main fighting forces into such confusion that they would probably not be able to pull themselves together at all. But on the Enfidaville Front opposite the depleted Eighth Army, the enemy had not moved. Somewhere there might still be a line that could be held, and von Arnim still had troops to hold one. It was a period when one had to suspend judgement and wait for the front line to get sorted out.

But Bizerta, the great French naval base, was of immediate interest, and I went up there the day after Tunis fell. Troops of the American Second Corps under General Patton had entered it the afternoon of May 7, almost at the exact moment when the British were entering Tunis. It was a coincidence almost too beautiful to be true, but it was nevertheless a fact. The Americans had advanced from Mateur and then split their forces into two; one prong turned north up to Bizerta, while the other drove on towards Tunis, with orders to capture certain high ground which might have threatened the First Army's flank.

They had fought their way against a desperate, nervous enemy — an enemy who resisted with redoubled venom because he realized that his retreat was being cut off. And on the left of the Americans, along the coast itself, crept the grim, mysterious Goums. These were the most irregular of any irregulars ever employed. They were mostly Moroccans and I suppose their best friends would have admitted they were fundamentally bandits. They were practical jokers on a fearful, fatal scale. They went on leave when they liked and no one ever forbade them for they always returned with several friends to join the band.

The Goums appeared to dress in old striped dressing-gowns, and the Americans did not often see them. It was difficult to include them in any constructive strategy. For one thing they could not read maps and for another they could not always tell the time. But in friendliness they were charming and childlike and the Americans round Bizerta were full of unbelievable tales about them.

When we got to the outskirts of Bizerta that day after Tunis fell there was something familiar and inappropriate in the atmosphere. There was, for one thing, too much noise. There was a tendency to strict dispersal and to keeping under cover. There was an almost palpable tension in the air. Quite obviously there was still a front line here.

We pulled off into an orchard near the great naval air field and an American Sergeant, attracted by our yellow camouflage, strolled over to us. His Southern accent was so intense that we could barely understand him. He had never met an Eighth Army vehicle before and he stormed us with compliments and questions. He had no compunction whatever about telling us we were a wonderful army, and we squirmed with embarrassment and said we thought the Americans were pretty good too. Then he gave us a huge basin of canned peaches. At last we persuaded him to tell us about Bizerta.

It was true enough that the town had been entered the afternoon before. The operative word was "entered." Whether you could say the place was taken was another matter. This Sergeant thought definitely not. It was still very easy to die in Bizerta's streets. He advised us to go forward and see — but to go carefully.

At the last bend before the town itself men were lying on the upslope of a grassy bank, peering warily over the top. There were several trucks parked near by, carefully under cover. A battery of American field-guns was firing from an orchard just beside us. We crawled to the top of the grassy bank and again made inquiries.

Bizerta is built on the western edge of a short, narrow strait of water, something like the Dardanelles, leading in from the sea to a blue-green lagoon. We were now on the western side, just beside the city. But the Germans were across the eastern side in some force. For instance there was a man there with an 88-millimetre gun trained exactly on this stretch of road where we lay, and he fired at each vehicle that passed. We should probably be able to get past that all right if we went fast enough, they told us, but then we must watch out for the man in the water-tower who appeared to be very accurate with a 40-millimetre anti-tank gun. And we must be specially careful at street corners.

They had not exaggerated. Bizerta's ruins that afternoon were very perilous. It had been a neat modern town on the American plan with streets crossing at right angles, and some of these streets led straight up from the waterfront. It was childishly easy for the Germans to sit across the other side of the water with a heavy machine-gun trained up each street. Each crossing was an ambush and trucks were making wild, jerky dashes through the town with bullets singing past them every block.

The town was utterly destroyed — it was Sfax and Sousse over again on a major scale. There was no special feature about its destruction — bombs make all towns look curiously alike. It was simply a ruin, with the crackle of glass and masonry in the streets and the smell of burning and plaster in the air and hideous wallpapers gaping from the upper stories of split houses. Again the comment which sprang to the minds of all of us was: "If this is what happens to a town whose harbour gets a number of quite ordinary bombings, what can a thousand-bomber raid be like?"

As we came out again a Frenchman was hovering indecisively behind the grassy bank, wondering whether it was safe enough for him to inspect the ruins of his home. We asked him where the inhabitants of Bizerta had gone and he said mostly to Ferryville, a naval arsenal a dozen miles away on the shores of the lagoon. So we went to Ferryville.

This was quite different. The shady main street with its *cafés* and arcades and advertisements and petrol pumps was quite undamaged. And it was filled to overflowing with laughing, shouting people, all dressed in their best, all fighting to welcome the British and Americans. Again one found oneself a hero merely because of the uniform one wore. Again there were the wild, urgent questioning, the wine and flowers, the laughter and the tears. There were fights too, absurd incidents with an undercurrent of seriousness like the one that happened to us.

A man stopped us in the streets of Ferryville and said, "Have you any chewing gum?"

Another man pushed forward and said, "At a time like this one does not ask officers for chewing gum."

The first said, "Nevertheless my wife is pregnant and she has a craving for chewing gum."

The second said, "Nevertheless one does not ask for chewing gum — especially English officers."

"It is a fine thing to hear that," answered the first, "from one who has for two years been the servant of Vichy."

"Liar . . . toad . . ."

"*Collaborationiste* . . ."

One man kicked the other, one wife burst into tears and the other smacked her husband's face, and the police broke up a showy but perfectly harmless fight. The crowd looked at us sideways to see what line we would take. But we merely regretted that we had no chewing gum and hurried off to see the arsenal.

This was the most beautiful bombing I have ever seen. It had been American daylight precision bombing and only one bomb had ever fallen outside the target area. No single inhabitant of Ferryville had been killed. Yet the workshops, the warehouses, the power-houses, the engine shops, the torpedo sheds, the cranes, the assembly plants had been blasted until nothing usable remained. It was a square mile of the most incredible destruction. Three bombs had hit a ship laden with thirteen hundred tons of explosive and that alone had flattened everything for a quarter of a mile around. It had pulled a 100-ton crane out of its stone foundations and tossed it across three dry docks. It had sunk the French destroyer *Audacieux*. It had completely levelled a huge electrical installation. But quite apart from what this munitions ship had done, the bomb damage was nearly one hundred per cent. It did not seem possible that anything could even be repaired. It looked as though they would have to start again from scratch.

The guns were still firing in the hills as we drove back through Mateur and then wound among the sunset valleys to Thibar. But there was no front left here, no organized resistance. It was nothing but a very big-scale job of mopping up. Bizerta would be made safe to-night as Tunis had been last night. For Tunis was now a town of mad delirium. When I went back there next day it was still in a permanent state of carnival. Every scrap of red, white and blue bunting the place possessed was hung out. The streets were so full of crowds and celebrations that traffic could barely move. It was the very antithesis of Tripoli. This was a vivid, genuine, alive town with smart shops and good buildings and clean streets and a fine broad central avenue where the people strolled in the evening beneath thick trees. There was nothing of Tripoli's pretentious façade with the tawdriness behind. This was no anticlimax at all. It was a climax that was being maintained for days. The London Irish played their bagpipes in the avenue in the afternoon. The Americans gave people rides in their jeeps. The compositor of the local paper piled up all the blocks the German printers had been using and swept them off his table into the corner with one superb gesture. A wildly pro-Allies paper was being sold on the streets almost at once and the Allies put a notice in it increasing the bread ration and announcing a distribution of coffee. Political refugees crept out of hiding. The first member of General Giraud's forces who reached the city was nearly suffocated with kisses — literally nearly suffocated. It was sunny and gay and lastingly exciting.

Some French families threw open their homes and gave parties that never seemed to stop. They took you round to little hidden restaurants where the food — after months of desert-cooked rations — was exquisite. There seemed endless things to do, endless stories to dig up, endless people to meet. But on May 9, two days after Tunis fell, the military situation suddenly became clear again.

North-west of Tunis the Fifteenth *Panzerdivision,* hard-bitten veterans of the desert, surrendered en masse to the Seventh Armoured Division. They got themselves cornered in Porto Farina, between Tunis and Bizerta, and they made a half-hearted attempt to start evacuating by sea. But the air force quickly stopped that and this whole *Panzerdivision* made formal surrender. It sent out envoys with a white flag to negotiate, and it capitulated with its Generals and its vehicles and its men.

That was one of the significant things that happened on this day. The other was that the Germans retiring from Tunis were showing signs of resistance at Hammam Lif, a few miles farther east along the coast. Hammam Lif was a sort of Thermopylæ position — a little town on a narrow coastal shelf with cliffs towering above it. The mountains ran down from there to Zaghouan and round to Enfidaville and there was no easy way through. It might be a very strong line indeed.

These two facts together made the situation suddenly clear. The speed and strength of the great armoured drive down the Medjerda Valley had indeed split the Axis armies in half and dislocated their main defensive positions. The surrender in toto of the Fifteenth *Panzerdivision* proved that the dislocation was complete and irretrievable. But the enemy still had some good troops and the secondary defensive position might conceivably be held. Already at Hammam Lif they were making ready to hold it. Given time to pull themselves together and reorganize, the Germans might still be able to buy a few more weeks of time.

That was the essence of the thing — time. The General who had steered that swift sword thrust down the Medjerda Valley and rammed it home even though his flanks were not absolutely safe saw the full implications of it. Once already he had dislocated the enemy by speed. Perhaps it could be done again. He must strike hard and quickly at Hamman Lif, and get through it before the enemy were properly installed there.

He said to the Sixth Armoured Division, "You will get in your tanks and you will travel night and day eastwards." Someone objected, "You cannot travel with tanks by night." Said the General, "You will travel by night and you will reach Hammamet, on the other side of Cap Bon Peninsula, by five o'clock to-morrow morning."

So in the evening they moved up against this Thermopylæ position. Hammam Lif was a town of six parallel streets, and there seemed to be a sniper in every house. There was one five-story building, and there was a sniper in every window. There were at least twenty 88-millimetre guns ranged at the far ends of these six streets.

They waited till night fell. The moon was very young, but it was bright enough to show the way. And by its faint radiance men with fixed bayonets climbed onto the Sherman tanks and they charged together down the six streets. At each corner the infantrymen leaped down and scattered right and left, routing out the snipers house by house and room by room. The tanks charged down on the 88-millimetres duelling at point-blank range. Hand-to-hand fighting surged up and down the staircase of the five-story building and through the gardens of the villas beyond the town. But the battle was won and in the darkness the Sixth pressed on. The sea was milky-grey with dawn when they reached it at Hammamet. It was just light enough for them to see by their watches that the time was 5 A.M.

So it had been done again. A second time the British had beaten this Axis army by speed, had split it in two and thrown it into utter confusion. Now the remnants of the Afrikakorps in the Enfidaville Hills were cut off from their comrades in the Cap Bon Peninsula. And the whole structure of the enemy forces crumbled and collapsed.

The thing was so big that the process of collapse took three more days. Inevitably there were knots of brave men who fought on because they did not know of the collapse, or because they preferred to fight. It was not until eight minutes to eight on the evening of May 12 that G.H.Q. announced the end of organized resistance. And even then a large part of the Afrikakorps still had not surrendered.

At first we did not know what was happening. Geoffrey Keating and I drove out of Tunis eastwards, along the road that led to the peninsula. There was no firing anywhere, but the sound of explosions rolled across the sea from the direction of Cap Bon and half a dozen big fires were burning there. No one could tell us anything about any front line so we simply drove straight ahead. Gradually we noticed that almost the only traffic on the road was lorry-loads of prisoners. In the village of Soliman four huge fields were being hastily ringed round with barbed wire to form a temporary cage. In the next village the streets were choked with enemy staff cars. A sweating Sergeant said, "Take your pick—have any one you want. I shall be glad to get rid of them."

We drove on east and north. Every fifty yards a ten-ton Italian Diesel truck, often with a trailer, was spluttering along festooned with men. Then the traffic changed to German, then back to Italian. Not more than one truck in every five had a British guard on it. It was impossible to say whether this was our territory or the enemy's. Certainly we were enormously outnumbered.

The situation was barely under control. It was only under control at all because the prisoners were curiously docile. British fighting troops who thought they were going into battle had suddenly found themselves turned into gaolers, and they had sent urgently for reinforcements who knew how to deal with this sort of thing. Fine Mercedes staff cars, little Fiat saloons, tinny German *Volkswagen* (which correspond to the American jeep) were strewn along the roadside. High Italian officers with mountains of baggage were trying to thumb a ride into captivity. Mounds of rifles the size of haystacks were being built up every mile or so.

Geoffrey and I looked at the map, and when we did so we gasped. We were within ten miles of Cap Bon itself. We were right in the heart of the peninsula—the fortress which the enemy had been going to turn into a Stalingrad or a Tobruk. Not till that moment did we realize that the collapse was complete, this was the end.

We kept meeting these overflowing truckloads of men and I began to shout to them as we passed, asking them whether they had surrendered yet or not. Often the answer was no. They were simply driving themselves down into the prison cages. I have no idea how many prisoners I took that morning. It was a day of sheer madness.

When I had to return to Tunis to write my story, Geoffrey wanted to go on ahead. So I simply picked the best car I could find, drove it back, and turned it in to the authorities. Once someone stopped me and tried to put me in a prison camp, but I was able to explain myself. For the most part no one took any notice at all. German and Italian cars were far more frequent on the roads than British and American that afternoon.

The quality of those three days of surrender was one of prolonged urgency and amazement. Traffic everywhere seemed to be moving with furious haste. There were so many incredible things to do or see. So many astonishing things were happening at once, and one wanted to see them all. The common things of life were ignored. Without the least hesitation one abandoned one's bedding, not really caring where one slept. We took no thought for our meals, relying vaguely on being invited to a mess or borrowing a packet of biscuits or simply finding some German rations. Transport was no difficulty at all — we had enough for two armies. The sheer size of what was happening, this concentration of history into a few hours, sustained the sense of climax for day after day.

This was the ending no one had foreseen. There was no Dunkirk. There was no fight to the finish. There was not even an organized surrender. It was a complete, muddled collapse — a collapse as swift and as wholesale as had been Graziani's collapse against Wavell.

Through those three mad days I tried hard to work out why. I studied the truckloads of German faces as they passed us in the road, striving to read some common emotion. They were not sullen or exhausted or shell-shocked or bitter or truculent or humiliated or anything that you might have expected. They were sunburned and healthy and on the whole good-looking and they seemed just ordinarily interested and neither especially pleased nor sorry. Again and again I asked them why they had given in. Some said shortly, "*Uebermacht* — we were overwhelmed; we had rifles against tanks." But that was not true. The fields and woods where they had surrendered were littered with good guns. They had petrol and food and water and ammunition. They were tired, but not completely exhausted. They could have fought and they knew it well enough.

Many of them smiled ruefully and shrugged their shoulders. Who were they to question the decisions of their High Command? Doubtless this was the solution which the Axis judged most economic in the long run. But that was obviously not true either. It was the worst possible solution. They gained no time by it, they lost their weapons and their prestige and their honour.

Bit by bit the true answer came out. I think I understood it first one afternoon when I had to race back from Cap Bon to First Army Headquarters to attend a conference summoned by General Anderson. I started out in a *Volkswagen,* but in Tunis a tire blew out and I left the car in the tram depot where Tunis's trams were waiting until the electric current should come on again. Then I had to hitch-hike and the only traffic on the road was truckloads of prisoners. So I climbed aboard among about thirty Germans and as we drove back I tried to make them talk.

They still had not evolved an explanation of their own, or if they had it was not one that could be produced in public. But from what they said the true explanation was clear. It was a matter of muddle in high places, the complete breakdown of German staff work. The trouble came from the top, not from the bottom. The troops could still fight — they still had the positions and the weapons. But no one told them what to do. Communications broke down. No orders arrived. All pattern and design fell out of the picture. Even improvisation was impossible, because nobody knew what sort of improvisation was needed. The brain and nerve-centre of the army was paralyzed, and nothing could function coherently any more.

The unexpected force and speed of the Allied thrusts — the first down the Medjerda Valley, the second through Hammam Lif — had caused this paralysis. But that was no excuse. There was nothing miraculous about what the Allies did. It was done supremely well, and perhaps the Germans still have not got used to the idea that the Allies can do anything supremely well. But it was straight, honest warfare without trickery or secret weapons, and it threw the German staff work completely out of gear. That is the important thing — the revelation of this vulnerable spot in the German machine. If it can happen in Africa it can happen in Europe or anywhere else. This was emphatically not a rout, a collapse of the fighting troops. They were beaten as an army, but not nearly so utterly and abjectly as this surrender suggested. It was muddle and lack of foresight and inadequate planning and very possibly administrative panic at Headquarters.

There were so many stories in those days that no one could collect them all. Von Arnim himself surrendered near Sainte Marie du Zit Air Field to a tired, unshaven Indian Army Colonel. Lesser German and Italian Generals were surrendering or being captured all over the place. A few devoted Germans laid themselves on an ammunition dump and blew themselves up. But the vast majority did not even attempt to destroy their weapons and equipment. Some few tried an amateur Dunkirk, and the navy reported that it had sunk thirty-seven small ships in one day and apologized for letting three others go. Tanks stood on headlands and sunk ships out at sea. Arab villagers charged German soldiers fifty francs a head for ferrying them across a river to surrender to the Eleventh Hussars. The Bey of Tunis sat in his palace and let the hostilities flow past him, then sent a friendly message to Giraud. The last air field to be taken on the peninsula was crowded with highly trained German tank technicians waiting for planes that never came to take them away.

You can measure the completeness of the German collapse by this failure of anyone — even the Commander-in-Chief himself — to get away at the last minute. One Junkers 52 could have saved all those Generals for Germany. Sicily was only an hour's flight away, and there were still air fields in Axis hands in Tunisia. But the whole army, from General von Arnim down to Private Hans Schmidt, was jettisoned.

Yet there were some people who did get away — the Luftwaffe. And that is a very strange story. Throughout that whole last phase of the fighting hardly one Luftwaffe plane flew over Tunisia. The Axis Army fought with less air protection even than we had had in Greece. The air fields of Sicily and Sardinia were crammed with aircraft, but they never left the ground. Had the German High Command abandoned this army so completely that it would not risk aircraft to protect it? Were the aircraft being hoarded for some even more important occasion in the immediate future? There is one other possible explanation, so absurd that it is only worth mentioning at all because so many German soldiers believed it.

That is, that the army and the Luftwaffe had quarreled, and the Luftwaffe refused to help the army. It is ludicrous on the face of it — that sort of thing cannot happen in a modern army. But even quite senior officers believed it. And it is a fact that minor Luftwaffe personnel got away when major army personnel did not.

One evening, exhausted after a heavy day on Cap Bon, Alan and I drove ten miles out of Tunis to spend the night with Randolph

Churchill in a villa he had secured at Sidi Bou Said. This is an artists' village, scrambled up the slopes of a hill beside the ancient Carthage, and its main street is as impossibly picturesque as a stage set. Its lovely villas look down over the sea, onto a view which is said to rival that of Rio de Janeiro. In the cool of the evening we called on the Baroness d'Erlanger whose villa is the loveliest of all. She was living in one tiny boudoir with her English books and her family photographs and she told us how the Germans had drunk her wine cellars dry and the Italian Sergeants' mess had roasted her marvellous white peacocks one by one and eaten them. Then she told us about the Luftwaffe personnel who had been quartered in the cool tracery-filled Moorish halls of her villa. Exactly twelve hours before Tunis fell — that is to say at three o'clock in the morning — they had risen and packed and driven quietly away to El Aouina Air Field. By dawn their planes were gone. They had had excellent warning. But the army commanders in Tunis itself had apparently had none.

That evening we sank deeply into the peace of Sidi Bou Said. Here, you felt, you could end your days in happiness, surrounded by the simple things that are the best things in life — reading and writing and good conversation, good food and wine, sitting in the sun, swimming in the sea, making love. Especially making love — the setting was perfect. But next morning the fever had taken hold of us again and we were off back to Cap Bon to watch this fantastic climax once more.

Rommel's old army in the Enfidaville Hills was the last to surrender. Its commander was an Italian named Messe who just at this very last moment was made a Marshal, and as such the highest-ranking Axis officer in Africa. On the evening of May 12 he tuned in to the British wave length and radioed an offer of surrender. His Headquarters were unfortunately bombed just at that minute, but he made his offer again and said he had no hard feelings. He made just one stipulation: that he should be allowed to surrender to the Eighth Army, not to the First. And we realized that that strong desert solidarity which had welded the Eighth Army into an intimate confraternity had extended even to the enemy. The

Eighth Army was very pleased with Marshal Messe for this gesture.

The Ninetieth Light Division's Commander, General Graf von Sponeck, surrendered very fittingly to General Freyberg, the great New Zealand Divisional Commander who had fought against him so often. There was a hitch in these negotiations when an escaping British prisoner smartly captured the German Corporal who was acting as go-between. But that was straightened out, and Generals and Colonels in brilliant uniforms began to roll down from the Enfidaville Hills in their staff cars. General Freyberg stood on a bank by the roadside to receive them.

Last of all — this was about midday on May 15 — the rest of the Spezia and Pistoia Divisions and the Young Fascists and the Trieste came in. Some arrived asking indignantly why the Germans had surrendered so easily. They had been in the remotest positions of all, up between Garci and Zaghouan, and the great German muddle had passed them by. They had stayed in their trenches, still prepared to fight, and they did not know why they were surrendering. It is an odd twist that the Italians, after their long record of incompetence in this African war, should be the last to surrender in it.

So it ended — an end that could bring no comfort to the Axis at all. It was pure, unmitigated loss. On balance of casualties, destruction, prisoners, territory, strategy — everything — we had won. We had gained our objectives and a very fine net profit into the bargain. Twice — in the first campaign and the last campaign — we had captured an entire enemy army. This final drive to Tunis alone had yielded 224,000 Axis prisoners and something like two thirds of them were German. In all the campaigns together the Axis must have lost at least a million men, and thousands of tanks and aircraft. And for what they had paid they had got precisely nothing. Not even time. Not even glory.

Tunis, as I write this, is still *en fête*. And the exhilaration of this finale is the right note on which to end the story — an ending beautifully clean and complete and thorough, without any false notes or untidy aftermaths. It was a very great victory.

CPSIA information can be obtained
at www.ICGtesting.com
Printed in the USA
LVOW13s2234150118
563006LV00037BA/1839/P

9 781162 806761